BEST

SHORT STORIES

Advanced Level

*Short Stories for Teaching Literature
and Developing Comprehension*

Raymond Harris

JAMESTOWN PUBLISHERS

a division of NTC/Contemporary Publishing Group
Lincolnwood, Illinois USA

Cover Design: Steve Straus
Cover Illustration: Dennis Lyall
Interior Design: Deborah Hulsey Christie
Interior Illustrations: Jan Naimo Jones

ISBN: 0-89061-672-8 (hardbound)
ISBN: 0-89061-666-3 (softbound)

Published by Jamestown Publishers,
a division of NTC/Contemporary Publishing Group, Inc.
4255 West Touhy Avenue,
Lincolnwood (Chicago), Illinois 60646-1975, U.S.A.
© 1998 NTC/Contemporary Publishing Group, Inc.

7 8 9 10 11 12 13 14 044 / 055 09 08 07

400002597

Acknowledgments

Acknowledgment is gratefully made to the following publishers and authors for permission to reprint the stories in this book:

"The Garden Party" by Katherine Mansfield. © 1922 by Alfred A. Knopf, Inc. and renewed 1950 by John Middleton Murry. Reprinted from *The Short Stories of Katherine Mansfield,* by permission of the publisher.

"A Worn Path" by Eudora Welty. From *A Curtain of Green and Other Stories,* © 1941 and renewed 1969 by Eudora Welty, reprinted by permission of Harcourt Brace Jovanovich, Inc.

"A Summer's Reading" from *The Magic Barrel* by Bernard Malamud. © 1956, renewed 1984 by Bernard Malamud. Originally appeared in *The New Yorker.* Reprinted by permission of Farrar, Straus and Giroux, Inc.

"My Oedipus Complex" by Frank O'Connor. © 1950 by Frank O'Connor. Reprinted from *Collected Stories* by Frank O'Connor, by permission of Alfred A. Knopf.

"Everyday Use" by Alice Walker. © 1973 by Alice Walker. Reprinted from her volume *In Love and Trouble* by permission of Harcourt Brace Jovanovich, Inc.

"The Guest" from *Exile and the Kingdom* by Albert Camus, translated by Justin O'Brien. © 1957, 1958 by Alfred A. Knopf, Inc. Reprinted by permission of the publisher.

"A Christmas Memory" by Truman Capote. © 1956 by Truman Capote. Reprinted from *Selected Writings of Truman Capote,* by permission of Random House, Inc.

"A Rose for Emily" by William Faulkner. © 1930 and renewed 1958 by William Faulkner. Reprinted from *The Faulkner Reader* by William Faulkner, by permission of Random House, Inc.

"The Kugelmass Episode" by Woody Allen. © 1977 by Woody Allen. Reprinted from *Side Effects* by Woody Allen, by permission of Random House, Inc.

"Sonny's Blues" from *Going to Meet the Man* by James Baldwin. © 1948, 1951, 1957, 1958, 1960, 1965 by James Baldwin. Reprinted by permission of Doubleday & Company, Inc.

"Revelation" from *The Complete Stories* by Flannery O'Connor. © 1964, 1965 by the Estate of Mary Flannery O'Connor. Reprinted by permission of Farrar, Straus and Giroux, Inc.

Contents

To the Teacher

Introduction

In addition to being good and interesting fiction, each story in *Best Short Stories* was carefully chosen to illustrate a basic element of fiction to students. For example, the book begins with a story by Katherine Mansfield. Her classic story, "The Garden Party," is an example of a *perfect* short story because it demonstrates how authors weave the various elements of fiction into their works.

Edgar Allan Poe must be included in any teaching collection because of his ability to create tone and mood. Poe is also included because his work inspired so many American and European writers. "The Black Cat" was chosen from a collection of Poe's stories to teach about tone and mood in a short story.

There are two Nobel laureates among the authors in this collection—William Faulkner, whose story "A Rose for Emily" is used to teach the meaning of symbolism, and Albert Camus whose famous story "The Guest" is used to teach plot development. Joseph Conrad's story "The Lagoon" is used to show how conflict moves along the plot of a story.

Alice Walker's story "Everyday Use" shows how authors create characters, and James Baldwin's story "Sonny's Blues" demonstrates how authors present ideas, or themes, to their readers. Both authors, of course, also provide insights into the lives of black Americans.

Bernard Malamud's "A Summer's Reading," which draws on the author's Brooklyn-Jewish background, and Frank O'Connor's "My Oedipus Complex," which is a whimsical view of growing up, are used for a lesson on how authors use different points of view in their writing.

A prizewinning story by Woody Allen, "The Kugelmass Episode," is used to teach humor and satire. You and your students may find it one of the funniest stories you have ever read. Eudora Welty's story "A Worn Path," about an older black woman on an errand of love, is used to teach about setting in a story. Truman Capote's delightful prose in "A Christmas Memory" demonstrates how authors use words to create powerful images and feelings. The last story in this collection, Flannery O'Connor's very troubling story "Revelation," is presented to students for analysis and discussion.

The Contents of a Unit

The book is divided into twelve units. The following teaching elements accompany each short story and lesson.

I. **Introduction to the Story.** The introduction that begins each unit prepares students to read with greater understanding by resolving in advance any problems that may exist with the plot, characters, or language in the story. The information provided about the author's life and writing style helps students appreciate and understand each writer. It is important that students read the introductions because they will enhance students' understanding of both the stories and the lessons.

The second part of the introduction defines the literary concept that will be studied in the lesson.

The third part of the introduction consists of four questions intended to call the students' attention to particular literary elements in the story that are used to illustrate the major points discussed in the lesson. The students should keep these questions in mind and look for the answers to them as they read.

2. **The Short Story.** Each of the twelve stories in this book is complete and unabridged. These stories were chosen both for their literary excellence and for their proven appeal to readers. Each story is particularly suited to illustrate the literary concept taught in the accompanying lesson.

3. **The Literary Lesson.** The literary lesson in each unit provides basic information about one element of literature. The first lesson introduces the short story as a literary genre and prepares students for the literary elements they will study in subsequent units—setting, point of view, characterization, plot, and so on. Together these lessons form a good foundation for understanding literary forms, elements, and content.

It is best, although not necessary, to teach the stories and lessons in the order in which they appear in the book. The lessons build on one another—each lesson unit encourages students to compare the story and literary elements they are working with to those elements they have studied in previous units.

The lesson units are divided into four parts, and each lesson part contains sample passages from the story that illustrate a literary element. Following each lesson part, students are presented with another sample passage from the story that demonstrates the same element. That passage is followed by two questions that allow students to practice what they have just learned.

4. **Skill-Oriented Comprehension Questions.** Twenty-five comprehension questions relating to the story are included in each lesson unit. These questions are keyed to ten specific reading and reasoning skills. All twenty-five questions are labeled by skill. The ten skills are recalling specific facts, organizing facts, knowledge of word meanings, drawing a conclusion, making a judgment, making an inference, understanding characters, understanding main ideas, recognizing tone, and appreciation of literary forms.

These ten question types reflect those aspects of comprehension that can be adequately sampled. Because more than one skill is used in answering any one question, true comprehension cannot be conveniently separated into ten independent activities. Therefore, the labels on the questions represent the major or dominant skill used to arrive at a correct answer.

A Comprehension Skills Profile is provided at the back of the book so that you can keep track of the kinds of questions each student misses most often. There is also a Comprehension Scores Graph that can help you keep track of the overall progress in reading comprehension.

5. **Discussion Guide.** Each unit contains nine discussion questions that deal with three aspects of literary criticism: analysis of the literary element discussed in the lesson, interpretation of meanings and implications inherent in the selection, and analysis of the author's technique.

6. **The Writing Exercise.** The writing assignment is designed to give the student firsthand experience with the literary element discussed in the lesson. The reading selections broaden students' knowledge of writing techniques, and the writing exercises deepen the students' understanding and appreciation of the writing styles found in their reading.

How to Use This Book

This book has four major objectives:
• To help readers understand the basic structure and the elements of the short-story form
• To sharpen reading comprehension skills
• To encourage critical reading
• To give readers an opportunity to introduce elements of literary style into their own writing
The following list suggests ways to use the various parts of each unit:

1. **Have the students read the introduction to the story.** You may wish to give additional information from your own experience with the story or the author. Point out that the author has written other works that students may want to read. Some of the works are mentioned in the introduction.

2. **Have the students read the story.** Tell the students that you want them to enjoy the story for its own sake, but point out that you also want them to read carefully. You may want to use the word *critically* and explain what critical reading is.

To keep the students' attention focused on the literary concept they will study in the lesson, you may want to have them keep a copy of the questions from the introduction beside them as they read. If the students are reading the story in class, write the questions on the chalkboard. Remind the students that they will have to answer comprehension questions about the story—another reason for reading carefully.

3. **Explain the lesson.** Each lesson is divided into five parts. It begins with a general introduction to the literary concept that will be studied. After the students have read the introduction, discuss the lesson to assure that they have a general understanding of the concept. Then have students read and study the other four sections of the lesson. Each section explains a different element of the major literary concept on which the lesson focuses. The students should also complete the exercises at the end of each section. After they have finished each section, pause for a discussion of the lesson so that the students can find out why their answers are right or wrong.

4. **Have students answer the comprehension questions.** In classes in which reading comprehension is the primary concern, you may want to have the students answer these questions immediately after reading the story. The comprehension questions focus on ten important reading skills:
   • Recalling Specific Facts
   • Organizing Facts
   • Knowledge of Word Meanings
   • Drawing a Conclusion
   • Making a Judgment
   • Making an Inference
   • Understanding Characters
   • Understanding Main Ideas
   • Recognizing Tone
   • Appreciation of Literary Forms

5. **Have students correct their answers.** Students can check their answers to the comprehension questions by using the Answer Key at the back of the book. Students should be encouraged to correct wrong answers and to consider why one answer is wrong and another right. Have students count the number of *each kind* of question they get wrong and record these numbers in the spaces provided at the end of the comprehension questions.

6. **Have students record their progress.** Students should plot the number of *correct* answers they got for each story on the Comprehension Scores Graph at the back of the book. Instructions are given on the page with the graph. When students use the graph, a visual record of their progress quickly emerges.
   Students should plot *wrong* answers on the Comprehension Skills Profile

at the end of the book. The Profile will show at a glance which skills a student needs to work on. Students usually enjoy keeping track of their progress, especially when they are allowed to manage this task themselves. You should also monitor the students' progress so that you can recognize and deal with any problems the students may have.

7. **Spend time on discussion.** There are three kinds of discussion questions for each story—nine questions in all. The first three questions focus on the literary concept studied in the lesson. Those questions give students a chance to demonstrate their new skills and allow you to expand upon the lesson if you wish. Questions four through six are more general and allow students to use their imaginations and to apply themes in the story to their own experiences. Finally, the last three questions deal with the author's experience and technique, and focus on the subjective aspects of literature.

8. **Have the students do the writing exercise.** The writing exercises at the end of each unit are designed to allow students to improve their writing through imitation. Each writing exercise asks students to apply what they have learned about the literary element discussed in the lesson. Encourage students to imitate the authors of the stories, if they wish. You may want to encourage an individual style among the better writers in a class.

To the Student

The stories you are about to read are among the finest in the world, written by some of the world's best short-story writers. In addition to enjoying the stories, you will be asked to think of storytelling as an art.

Like other arts, such as music, painting, sculpture, and architecture, storytelling has definable forms and content that you can see, feel, think about, and discuss. In music, for example, you can identify the beat or tempo that distinguishes a waltz from a march, rock from jazz, and blues from swing, even though the various forms of music are similar in some ways. Horns, strings, and drums give music different characteristics that, in turn, inspire different moods and feelings in you. You can discuss what the composer and the arranger have done to make the piece of music better, worse, or just different from others you have heard. You can say why you enjoyed the music or why you did not.

When you read a story, you know almost at once whether it is a mystery, science fiction, adventure, romance, or another type. Each story can be identified by its content and given a label. Each story has a form because of its own characteristics—plot, characters, tone and mood, setting, or point of view. As you read, think about how an author combines all the elements to create a story and how the story makes you feel.

In addition to a story each unit in the text contains a lesson that discusses one special aspect of the art of storytelling. By the time you have finished the book, you will have a good basic knowledge of all the major elements that make up a well-written and enjoyable short story. Each unit is followed by exercises that will help you realize how much you have learned about the elements of fiction and how well you have understood how authors use those elements in their stories.

UNIT
One

Unit One

INTRODUCTION	What the Story Is About
	What the Lesson Is About
STORY	*The Garden Party*
	by Katherine Mansfield
LESSON	*The Short Story*
ACTIVITIES	Comprehension Questions
	Discussion Guide
	Writing Exercise

Introduction

What the Story Is About

We have chosen a story by Katherine Mansfield to begin our book of short stories because she was an expert at her craft. When she describes a character, you can see the person at once. When she describes a setting, you are instantly there. When she tells you how someone feels, you recognize the feeling immediately, understand it, and make it your own. A great deal is done to perfection in "The Garden Party," which is one of Mansfield's best stories and is often considered a perfect example of the technique of short-story writing.

Laura Sheridan is the young teenage daughter of a successful upper-middle-class family living in New Zealand (where the author was born and spent her early years). In the course of one day Laura is destined to learn a great deal about the meaning of social differences and class distinctions in British society early in the twentieth century. She will also learn a great deal about herself and her own feelings.

"The Garden Party" is a story about human feelings, human nature, and the barriers that exist between people who are rich and those who are poor. Laura knows only people from her own limited world, which in this case is a rich, privileged, and comfortable one. When Laura's mother gives her an opportunity to direct a group of workmen on a small project, Laura is struck by how nice and how entirely human working-class people can be. It's difficult to know what she thought about workmen before, though you are told, later in the story, that as a child she had been warned about walking through their neighborhood.

The day of the party is a very happy one for Laura—an absolutely perfect day, in fact—until it is marred by news that a young carter (wagon driver) from the neighborhood has been killed in an accident. Drawing on her newfound social consciousness, Laura reacts dramatically. The garden party must be stopped! How can they all be happy when a poor man from the neighborhood is lying dead and his wife can hear the band playing and the guests having a good time? But cooler heads prevail. "People like that don't expect sacrifices from us," her mother tells her.

A new hat and a successful afternoon make things considerably better for Laura. Later she is sent to the dead man's home with a basket of party leftovers. Now she must truly evaluate her feelings about rich people and poor people, her world and the shabby world she will become involved in. There is a lot to think about, not just for Laura but for you as well. After all, you have your social and class differences, too. Many people are sheltered, like Laura, and rarely get to know people from outside their own world. How well do you mix with others who are different from you? How do times of great emotion change your feelings toward others?

Katherine Mansfield was especially effective when dealing with feelings and emotions. Unfortunately, her brilliant writing career was cut short by her declining health. She died of tuberculosis in 1923 when she was only thirty-four and just beginning to receive the recognition she deserved. She was born Kathleen Mansfield Beauchamp in Wellington, New Zealand, in 1888, the daughter of a wealthy banker-industrialist. She spent her childhood in the village of Karori, near Wellington, where many of her best stories, including "The Garden Party," are set.

She was a brilliant and sensitive woman and an unusually keen observer of the world around her. Mansfield characters have been called uncannily real, and her stories often have a poetic quality about them—carefully worked out in every detail and filled with intense feeling.

After reading "The Garden Party" you will want to read Mansfield's stories "Prelude" and "At the Bay." They are somewhat longer works that tell of the dreams and feelings of all the members of the Burnell family, from the grandmother to the smallest children. The stories are set in the Burnells' country home and then at their beach house, once again in the New Zealand Mansfield knew as a child.

What the Lesson Is About

The lesson that follows "The Garden Party" focuses on the short story as a form of literature. Like all literature, a short story provides you with "a slice of life," an impression of a character's daily life. A slice of life is compressed into only twenty, thirty, ten, or sometimes one or two pages of storytelling.

When you compare a short story to a novel that has hundreds of pages, you can see at once that a short-story author has a special task. In order to be a *complete* story, a short story has to include nearly all of the features you find in a novel in much less space, using very few words. You will discover how Katherine Mansfield manages to compress the features found in a novel into "The Garden Party."

You will be reading the story before you read the lesson about it, but you can prepare yourself to analyze the technique of short-story writing by thinking about the following questions as you read:

1. How does the author set the scene and establish the situation?

2. How does the author introduce the characters?

3. What is the conflict or problem that the author creates for the main character?

4. What is the most dramatic point in the story for the main character, and how does the author bring the story to a close?

The Garden Party

by Katherine Mansfield

*A*nd after all the weather was ideal. They could not have had a more perfect day for a garden party if they had ordered it. Windless, warm, the sky without a cloud. Only the blue was veiled with a haze of light gold, as it is sometimes in early summer. The gardener had been up since dawn, mowing the lawns and sweeping them, until the grass and the dark flat rosettes where the daisy plants had been seemed to shine. As for the roses, you could not help feeling they understood that roses are the only flowers that impress people at garden parties; the only flowers that everybody is certain of knowing. Hundreds, yes, literally hundreds, had come out in a single night; the green bushes bowed down as though they had been visited by archangels.

Breakfast was not yet over before the men came to put up the marquee.

"Where do you want the marquee put, mother?"

"My dear child, it's no use asking me. I'm determined to leave everything to you children this year. Forget I am your mother. Treat me as an honored guest."

But Meg could not possibly go and supervise the men. She had washed her hair before breakfast, and she sat drinking her coffee in a green turban, with a dark wet curl stamped on each cheek. Jose, the butterfly, always came down in a silk petticoat and a kimono jacket.

"You'll have to go, Laura; you're the artistic one."

Away Laura flew, still holding her piece of bread and butter. It's so delicious to have an excuse for eating out of doors, and besides, she loved having to arrange things; she always felt she could do it so much better than anybody else.

Four men in their shirt-sleeves stood grouped together on the garden path. They carried staves covered with rolls of canvas, and they had big tool bags slung on their backs. They looked impressive. Laura wished now that she had not got the bread and butter, but there was nowhere to put it, and she couldn't possibly throw it away. She blushed and tried to look severe and even a little bit shortsighted as she came up to them.

"Good morning," she said, copying her mother's voice. But that sounded so fearfully affected that she was ashamed, and stammered like a little girl, "Oh—er—have you come—is it about the marquee?"

"That's right, miss," said the tallest of the men, a lanky, freckled fellow, and he shifted his tool bag, knocked back his straw hat and smiled down at her. "That's about it."

His smile was so easy, so friendly that Laura recovered. What nice eyes he had, small, but such a dark blue! And now she looked at the others, they were smiling too. "Cheer up, we won't bite," their smile seemed to say. How very nice workmen were! And what a beautiful morning! She mustn't mention the morning; she must be businesslike. The marquee.

"Well, what about the lily lawn? Would that do?"

And she pointed to the lily lawn with the hand that didn't hold the bread and butter. They turned, they stared in the direction. A little fat chap thrust out his underlip, and the tall fellow frowned.

"I don't fancy it," said he. "Not conspicuous enough. You see, with a thing like a marquee," and he turned to Laura in his easy way, "you want to put it somewhere where it'll give you a bang slap in the eye, if you follow me."

Laura's upbringing made her wonder for a moment whether it was quite respectful of a workman to talk to her of bangs slap in the eye. But she did quite follow him.

"A corner of the tennis court," she suggested. "But the band's going to be in one corner."

"H'm, going to have a band, are you?" said another of the workmen. He was pale. He had a haggard look as his dark eyes scanned the tennis court. What was he thinking?

"Only a very small band," said Laura gently. Perhaps he wouldn't mind so much if the band was quite small. But the tall fellow interrupted.

"Look here, miss, that's the place. Against those trees. Over there. That'll do fine."

Against the karakas. Then the karaka trees would be hidden.

And they were so lovely, with their broad, gleaming leaves, and their clusters of yellow fruit. They were like trees you imagined growing on a desert island, proud, solitary, lifting their leaves and fruits to the sun in a kind of silent splendor. Must they be hidden by a marquee?

They must. Already the men had shouldered their staves and were making for the place. Only the tall fellow was left. He bent down, pinched a sprig of lavender, put his thumb and forefinger to his nose and snuffed up the smell. When Laura saw that gesture she forgot all about the karakas in her wonder at him caring for things like that— caring for the smell of lavender. How many men that she knew would have done such a thing? Oh, how extraordinarily nice workmen were, she thought. Why couldn't she have workmen for friends rather than the silly boys she danced with and who came to Sunday night supper? She would get on much better with men like these.

It's all the fault, she decided, as the tall fellow drew something on the back of an envelope, something that was to be looped up or left to hang, of these absurd class distinctions. Well, for her part, she didn't feel them. Not a bit, not an atom. . . . And now there came the chock-chock of wooden hammers. Someone whistled, someone sang out, "Are you right there, matey?" "Matey!" The friendliness of it, the—the— Just to prove how happy she was, just to show the tall fellow how at home she felt, and how she despised stupid conventions, Laura took a big bite of her bread and butter as she stared at the little drawing. She felt just like a workgirl.

"Laura, Laura, where are you? Telephone, Laura!" a voice cried from the house.

"Coming!" Away she skimmed, over the lawn, up the path, up the steps, across the veranda, and into the porch. In the hall her father and Laurie were brushing their hats ready to go to the office.

"I say, Laura," said Laurie very fast, "you might just give a squiz at my coat before this afternoon. See if it wants pressing."

"I will," said she. Suddenly she couldn't stop herself. She ran at Laurie and gave him a small, quick squeeze. "Oh, I do love parties, don't you?" gasped Laura.

"Rather," said Laurie's warm, boyish voice, and he squeezed his sister too, and gave her a gentle push. "Dash off to the telephone, old girl."

The telephone. "Yes, yes; oh yes. Kitty? Good morning, dear.

Come to lunch? Do, dear. Delighted of course. It will only be a very scratch meal—just the sandwich crusts and broken meringue shells and what's left over. Yes, isn't it a perfect morning? Your white? Oh, I certainly should. One moment—hold the line. Mother's calling." And Laura sat back. "What, mother? Can't hear."

Mrs. Sheridan's voice floated down the stairs. "Tell her to wear that sweet hat she had on last Sunday."

"Mother says you're to wear that *sweet* hat you had on last Sunday. Good. One o'clock. Bye-bye."

Laura put back the receiver, flung her arms over her head, took a deep breath, stretched and let them fall. "Huh," she sighed, and the moment after the sigh she sat up quickly. She was still, listening. All the doors in the house seemed to be open. The house was alive with soft, quick steps and running voices. The green baize door that led to the kitchen regions swung open and shut with a muffled thud. And now there came a long, chuckling absurd sound. It was the heavy piano being moved on its stiff castors. But the air! If you stopped to notice, was the air always like this? Little faint winds were playing chase, in at the tops of the windows, out at the doors. And there were two tiny spots of sun, one on the inkpot, one on a silver photograph frame, playing too. Darling little spots. Especially the one on the inkpot lid. It was quite warm. A warm little silver star. She could have kissed it.

The front door bell pealed, and there sounded the rustle of Sadie's print skirt on the stairs. A man's voice murmured; Sadie answered, careless, "I'm sure I don't know. Wait. I'll ask Mrs. Sheridan."

"What is it, Sadie?" Laura came into the hall.

"It's the florist, Miss Laura."

It was indeed. There, just inside the door, stood a wide, shallow tray full of pots of pink lilies. No other kind. Nothing but lilies—canna lilies, big pink flowers, wide open, radiant, almost frighteningly alive on bright crimson stems.

"O-oh, Sadie!" said Laura, and the sound was like a little moan. She crouched down as if to warm herself at that blaze of lilies; she felt they were in her fingers, on her lips, growing in her breast.

"It's some mistake," she said faintly. "Nobody ever ordered so many. Sadie, go and find mother."

But at that moment Mrs. Sheridan joined them.

"It's quite right," she said calmly. "Yes, I ordered them. Aren't they lovely?" She pressed Laura's arm. "I was passing the shop yesterday, and I saw them in the window. And I suddenly thought for once in my life I shall have enough canna lilies. The garden party will be a good excuse."

"But I thought you said you didn't mean to interfere," said Laura. Sadie had gone. The florist's man was still outside at his van. She put her arm round her mother's neck and gently, very gently, she bit her mother's ear.

"My darling child, you wouldn't like a logical mother, would you? Don't do that. Here's the man."

He carried more lilies still, another whole tray.

"Bank them up, just inside the door, on both sides of the porch, please," said Mrs. Sheridan. "Don't you agree, Laura?"

"Oh, I *do* mother."

In the drawing room Meg, Jose and good little Hans had at last succeeded in moving the piano.

"Now, if we put this chesterfield against the wall and move everything out of the room except the chairs, don't you think?"

"Quite."

"Hans, move these tables into the smoking room, and bring a sweeper to take these marks off the carpet and—one moment, Hans—" Jose loved giving orders to the servants, and they loved obeying her. She always made them feel they were taking part in some drama. "Tell mother and Miss Laura to come here at once."

"Very good, Miss Jose."

She turned to Meg. "I want to hear what the piano sounds like, just in case I'm asked to sing this afternoon. Let's try over 'This life is Weary.' "

Pom! Ta-ta-ta *Tee*-ta! The piano burst out so passionately that Jose's face changed. She clasped her hands. She looked mournfully and enigmatically at her mother and Laura as they came in.

> *This Life is* Wee-*ary,*
> *A Tear—a Sigh.*
> *A Love that* Chan-*ges,*
> > *This Life is* Wee-*ary,*
> *A Tear—a Sigh.*
> *A Love that* Chan-*ges,*
> *And then . . . Good-bye!*

But at the word "Good-bye," and although the piano sounded more desperate than ever, her face broke into a brilliant, dreadfully unsympathetic smile.

"Aren't I in good voice, mummy?" she beamed.

> *This Life is* Wee-*ary,*
> *Hope comes to Die.*
> *A Dream—a* Wa-*kening.*

But now Sadie interrupted them. "What is it, Sadie?"

"If you please, m'm, cook says have you got the flags for the sandwiches?"

"The flags for the sandwiches, Sadie?" echoed Mrs. Sheridan dreamily. And the children knew by her face that she hadn't got them. "Let me see." And she said to Sadie firmly, "Tell cook I'll let her have them in ten minutes."

Sadie went.

"Now, Laura," said her mother quickly. "Come with me into the smoking room. I've got the names somewhere on the back of an envelope. You'll have to write them out for me. Meg, go upstairs this minute and take that wet thing off your head. Jose, run and finish dressing this instant. Do you hear me, children, or shall I have to tell your father when he comes home tonight? And—and, Jose, pacify cook if you do go into the kitchen, will you? I'm terrified of her this morning."

The envelope was found at last behind the dining room clock, though how it had got there Mrs. Sheridan could not imagine.

"One of you children must have stolen it out of my bag, because I remember vividly—cream cheese and lemon curd. Have you done that?"

"Yes."

"Egg and—" Mrs. Sheridan held the envelope away from her. "It looks like mice. It can't be mice, can it?"

"Olive, pet," said Laura, looking over her shoulder.

"Yes, of course, olive. What a horrible combination it sounds. Egg and olive."

They were finished at last, and Laura took them off to the kitchen. She found Jose there pacifying the cook, who did not look at all terrifying.

"I have never seen such exquisite sandwiches," said Jose's rapturous voice. "How many kinds did you say there were, cook? Fifteen?"

"Fifteen, Miss Jose."

"Well, cook, I congratulate you."

Cook swept up crusts with the long sandwich knife, and smiled broadly.

"Godber's has come," announced Sadie, issuing out of the pantry. She had seen the man pass the window.

That meant the cream puffs had come. Godber's were famous for their cream puffs. Nobody ever thought of making them at home.

"Bring them in and put them on the table, my girl," ordered cook.

Sadie brought them in and went back to the door. Of course Laura and Jose were far too grown-up to really care about such things. All the same, they couldn't help agreeing that the puffs looked very attractive. Very. Cook began arranging them, shaking off the extra icing sugar.

"Don't they carry one back to all one's parties?" said Laura.

"I suppose they do," said practical Jose, who never liked to be carried back. "They look beautifully light and feathery, I must say."

"Have one each, my dears," said cook in her comfortable voice. "Yer ma won't know."

Oh, impossible. Fancy cream puffs so soon after breakfast. The very idea made one shudder. All the same, two minutes later Jose and Laura were licking their fingers with that absorbed inward look that only comes from whipped cream.

"Let's go into the garden, out by the back way," suggested Laura. "I want to see how the men are getting on with the marquee. They're such awfully nice men."

But the back door was blocked by cook, Sadie, Godber's man and Hans.

Something had happened.

"Tuk-tuk-tuk," clucked cook like an agitated hen. Sadie had her hand clapped to her cheek as though she had toothache. Hans's face was screwed up in the effort to understand. Only Godber's man seemed to be enjoying himself; it was his story.

"What's the matter? What's happened?"

"There's been a horrible accident," said cook. "A man killed."

"A man killed! Where? How? When?"

But Godber's man wasn't going to have his story snatched from under his very nose.

"Know those little cottages just below here, miss?" Know them? Of course, she knew them. "Well, there's a young chap living there, name of Scott, a carter. His horse shied at a traction engine, corner of Hawke Street this morning, and he was thrown out on the back of his head. Killed."

"Dead!" Laura stared at Godber's man.

"Dead when they picked him up," said Godber's man with relish. "They were taking the body home as I come up here." And he said to the cook, "He's left a wife and five little ones."

"Jose, come here." Laura caught hold of her sister's sleeve and dragged her through the kitchen to the other side of the green baize door. There she paused and leaned against it. "Jose!" she said, horrified, "however are we going to stop everything?"

"Stop everything, Laura!" cried Jose in astonishment. "What do you mean?"

"Stop the garden party, of course." Why did Jose pretend?

But Jose was still more amazed. "Stop the garden party? My dear Laura, don't be so absurd. Of course we can't do anything of the kind. Nobody expects us to. Don't be so extravagant."

"But we can't possibly have a garden party with a man dead just outside the front gate."

That really was extravagant, for the little cottages were in a lane to themselves at the very bottom of a steep rise that led up to the house. A broad road ran between. True, they were far too near. They were the greatest possible eyesore, and they had no right to be in that neighborhood at all. They were little mean dwellings painted a chocolate brown. In the garden patches there was nothing but cabbage stalks, sick hens and tomato cans. The very smoke coming out of their chimneys was poverty stricken. Little rags and shreds of smoke, so unlike the great silvery plumes that uncurled from the Sheridans' chimneys. Washerwomen lived in the lane and sweeps and a cobbler, and a man whose house front was studded all over with minute bird cages. Children swarmed. When the Sheridans were little they were forbidden to set foot there because of the revolting language and of what they might catch. But since they were grown up, Laura and Laurie on their prowls sometimes walked through. It was disgusting and sordid. They came out with a shudder. But still one must go everywhere; one must see everything. So through they went.

"And just think of what the band would sound like to that poor woman," said Laura.

"Oh, Laura!" Jose began to be seriously annoyed. "If you're going to stop a band playing every time someone has an accident, you'll lead a very strenuous life. I'm every bit as sorry about it as you. I feel just as sympathetic." Her eyes hardened. She looked at her sister just as she used to when they were little and fighting together. "You won't bring a drunken workman back to life by being sentimental," she said softly.

"Drunk! Who said he was drunk?" Laura turned furiously on Jose. She said, just as they had used to say on those occasions, "I'm going straight up to tell mother."

"Do, dear," cooed Jose.

"Mother, can I come into your room?" Laura turned the big glass doorknob.

"Of course, child. Why, what's the matter? What's given you such a color?" And Mrs. Sheridan turned round from her dressing table. She was trying on a new hat.

"Mother, a man's been killed," began Laura.

"*Not* in the garden?" interrupted her mother.

"No, no!"

"Oh, what a fright you gave me!" Mrs. Sheridan sighed with relief, and took off the big hat and held it on her knees.

"But listen, mother," said Laura. Breathless, half choking, she told the dreadful story. "Of course, we can't have our party, can we?" she pleaded. "The band and everybody arriving. They'd hear us, mother; they're nearly neighbors!"

To Laura's astonishment her mother behaved just like Jose; it was harder to bear because she seemed amused. She refused to take Laura seriously.

"But, my dear child, use your common sense. It's only by accident we've heard of it. If someone had died there normally—and I can't understand how they keep alive in those poky little holes—we should still be having our party, shouldn't we?"

Laura had to say "yes" to that, but she felt it was all wrong. She sat down on her mother's sofa and pinched the cushion frill.

"Mother, isn't it really terribly heartless of us?" she asked.

"Darling!" Mrs. Sheridan got up and came over to her, carrying the hat. Before Laura could stop her she had popped it on. "My child!" said her mother, "the hat is yours. It's made for you. It's much too young for me. I have never seen you look such a picture. Look at yourself!" And she held up her hand mirror.

"But, mother," Laura began again. She couldn't look at herself; she turned aside.

This time Mrs. Sheridan lost patience just as Jose had done.

"You are being very absurd, Laura," she said coldly. "People like that don't expect sacrifices from us. And it's not very sympathetic to spoil everybody's enjoyment as you're doing now."

"I don't understand," said Laura, and she walked quickly out of the room into her own bedroom. There, quite by chance, the first thing she saw was this charming girl in the mirror, in her black hat trimmed with gold daisies, and a long black velvet ribbon. Never had she imagined she could look like that. Is mother right? she thought. And now she hoped her mother was right. Am I being extravagant? Perhaps it was extravagant. Just for a moment she had another glimpse of that poor woman and those little children, and the body being carried into the house. But it all seemed blurred, unreal, like a picture in the newspaper. I'll remember it again after the party's over, she decided. And somehow that seemed quite the best plan. . . .

Lunch was over by half past one. By half past two they were all ready for the fray. The green-coated band had arrived and was established in a corner of the tennis court.

"My dear!" trilled Kitty Maitland, "aren't they too like frogs for words? You ought to have arranged them round the pond with the conductor in the middle on a leaf."

Laurie arrived and hailed them on his way to dress. At the sight of him Laura remembered the accident again. She wanted to tell him. If Laurie agreed with the others, then it was bound to be all right. And she followed him into the hall.

"Laurie!"

"Hallo!" He was halfway upstairs, but when he turned round and saw Laura he suddenly puffed out his cheeks and goggled his eyes at her. "My word, Laura; you do look stunning," said Laurie. "What an absolutely topping hat!"

Laura said faintly "Is it?" and smiled up at Laurie, and didn't tell him after all.

Soon after that people began coming in streams. The band struck up; the hired waiters ran from the house to the marquee. Wherever you looked there were couples strolling, bending to the flowers, greeting, moving on over the lawn. They were like bright birds that had alighted in the Sheridans' garden for this one afternoon, on their way to—where? Ah, what happiness it is to be with people who all are happy, to press hands, press cheeks, smile into eyes.

"Darling Laura, how well you look!"

"What a becoming hat, child!"

"Laura, you look quite Spanish. I've never seen you look so striking."

And Laura, glowing, answered softly, "Have you had tea? Won't you have an ice? The passion-fruit ices really are rather special." She ran to her father and begged him. "Daddy darling, can't the band have something to drink?"

And the perfect afternoon slowly ripened, slowly faded, slowly its petals closed.

"Never a more delightful garden party . . ." "The greatest success . . ." "Quite the most . . ."

Laura helped her mother with the good-byes. They stood side by side in the porch till it was all over.

"All over, all over, thank heaven," said Mrs. Sheridan. "Round up the others, Laura. Let's go and have some fresh coffee. I'm exhausted. Yes, it's been very successful. But oh, these parties, these parties! Why will you children insist on giving parties!" And they all of them sat down in the deserted marquee.

"Have a sandwich, daddy dear. I wrote the flag."

"Thanks." Mr. Sheridan took a bite and the sandwich was gone. He took another. "I suppose you didn't hear of a beastly accident that happened today?" he said.

"My dear," said Mrs. Sheridan, holding up her hand, "we did. It nearly ruined the party. Laura insisted we should put it off."

"Oh, mother!" Laura didn't want to be teased about it.

"It was a horrible affair all the same," said Mr. Sheridan. "The chap was married too. Lived just below in the lane, and leaves a wife and half a dozen kiddies, so they say."

An awkward little silence fell. Mrs. Sheridan fidgeted with her cup. Really, it was very tactless of father . . .

Suddenly she looked up. There on the table were all those sandwiches, cakes, puffs, all uneaten, all going to be wasted. She had one of her brilliant ideas.

"I know," she said. "Let's make up a basket. Let's send that poor creature some of this perfectly good food. At any rate, it will be the greatest treat for the children. Don't you agree? And she's sure to have neighbors calling in and so on. What a point to have it all ready prepared. Laura!" She jumped up. "Get me the big basket out of the stairs cupboard."

"But, mother, do you really think it's a good idea?" said Laura.

Again, how curious, she seemed to be different from them all. To take scraps from their party. Would the poor woman really like that?

"Of course! What's the matter with you today? An hour or two ago you were insisting on us being sympathetic, and now—"

Oh, well! Laura ran for the basket. It was filled, it was heaped by her mother.

"Take it yourself, darling," said she. "Run down just as you are. No, wait, take the arum lilies too. People of that class are so impressed by arum lilies."

"The stems will ruin her lace frock," said practical Jose.

So they would. Just in time. "Only the basket, then. And, Laura!"—her mother followed her out of the marquee—"don't on any account—"

"What, mother?"

No, better not put such ideas into the child's head! "Nothing! Run along."

It was just growing dusky as Laura shut their garden gates. A big dog ran by like a shadow. The road gleamed white, and down below in the hollow the little cottages were in deep shade. How quiet it seemed after the afternoon. Here she was going down the hill to somewhere where a man lay dead, and she couldn't realize it. Why couldn't she? She stopped a minute. And it seemed to her that kisses, voices, tinkling spoons, laughter, the smell of crushed grass were somehow inside her. She had no room for anything else. How strange! She looked up at the pale sky, and all she thought was, "Yes, it was the most successful party."

Now the broad road was crossed. The lane began, smoky and

dark. Women in shawls and men's tweed caps hurried by. Men hung over the palings; the children played in the doorways. A low hum came from the mean little cottages. In some of them there was a flicker of light, and a shadow, crab-like, moved across the window. Laura bent her head and hurried on. She wished now she had put on a coat. How her frock shone! And the big hat with the velvet streamer—if only it was another hat! Were the people looking at her? They must be. It was a mistake to have come; she knew all along it was a mistake. Should she go back even now?

No, too late. This was the house. It must be. A dark knot of people stood outside. Beside the gate an old, old woman with a crutch sat in a chair, watching. She had her feet on a newspaper. The voices stopped as Laura drew near. The group parted. It was as though she was expected, as though they had known she was coming here.

Laura was terribly nervous. Tossing the velvet ribbon over her shoulder, she said to a woman standing by, "Is this Mrs. Scott's house?" and the woman, smiling queerly, said, "It is, my lass."

Oh, to be away from this! She actually said, "Help me, God," as she walked up the tiny path and knocked. To be away from those staring eyes, or to be covered up in anything, one of those women's shawls even. I'll just leave the basket and go, she decided. I shan't even wait for it to be emptied.

Then the door opened. A little woman in black showed in the gloom.

Laura said, "Are you Mrs. Scott?" But to her horror the woman answered, "Walk in please, miss," and she was shut in the passage.

"No," said Laura, "I don't want to come in. I only want to leave this basket. Mother sent—"

The little woman in the gloomy passage seemed not to have heard her. "Step this way, please, miss," she said in an oily voice, and Laura followed her.

She found herself in a wretched little low kitchen, lighted by a smoky lamp. There was a woman sitting before the fire.

"Em," said the little creature who had let her in. "Em! It's a young lady." She turned to Laura. She said meaningly, "I'm 'er sister, miss. You'll excuse 'er, won't you?"

"Oh, but of course!" said Laura. "Please, please don't disturb her. I—I only want to leave—"

But at that moment the woman at the fire turned round. Her

face, puffed up, red, with swollen eyes and swollen lips, looked terrible. She seemed as though she couldn't understand why Laura was there. What did it mean? Why was this stranger standing in the kitchen with a basket? What was it all about? And the poor face puckered up again.

"All right, my dear," said the other. "I'll thank the young lady."

And again she began, "You'll excuse her, miss, I'm sure," and her face, swollen too, tried an oily smile.

Laura only wanted to get out, to get away. She was back in the passage. The door opened. She walked straight through into the bedroom, where the dead man was lying.

"You'd like a look at 'im, wouldn't you?" said Em's sister, and she brushed past Laura over to the bed. "Don't be afraid, my lass,—" and now her voice sounded fond and sly, and fondly she drew down the sheet—" 'e looks a picture. There's nothing to show. Come along, my dear."

Laura came.

There lay a young man, fast asleep—sleeping so soundly, so deeply, that he was far, far away from them both. Oh, so remote, so peaceful. He was dreaming. Never wake him up again. His head was sunk in the pillow, his eyes were closed; they were blind under the closed eyelids. He was given up to his dream. What did garden parties and baskets and lace frocks matter to him? He was far from all those things. He was wonderful, beautiful. While they were laughing and while the band was playing, this marvel had come to the lane. Happy . . . happy. . . . All is well, said that sleeping face. This is just as it should be. I am content.

But all the same you had to cry, and she couldn't go out of the room without saying something to him. Laura gave a loud childish sob.

"Forgive my hat," she said.

And this time she didn't wait for Em's sister. She found her way out of the door, down the path, past all those dark people. At the corner of the lane she met Laurie.

He stepped out of the shadow. "Is that you, Laura?"

"Yes."

"Mother was getting anxious. Was it all right?"

"Yes, quite. Oh, Laurie!" She took his arm, she pressed up against him.

"I say, you're not crying, are you?" asked her brother.

Laura shook her head. She was.

Laurie put his arm round her shoulder. "Don't cry," he said in his warm, loving voice. "Was it awful?"

"No," sobbed Laura. "It was simply marvelous. But, Laurie—" She stopped, she looked at her brother. "Isn't life," she stammered, "Isn't life—" But what life was she couldn't explain. No matter. He quite understood.

"*Isn't* it, darling?" said Laurie.

The Short Story

Stories are as much a part of your life as eating and sleeping. There are stories parents tell, stories on television and in the movies, stories in newspapers and magazines, family stories, and gossipy stories among friends. Of course, there are also the stories in the books you read.

People love stories. They always have and always will. Stories are one of the most important methods of human communication. Before science and written history, stories explained the unexplainable, made people proud of their country and their origins, and taught the basics of expected conduct in society. Stories, as the old philosophers said, "are imitations of life that are meant to delight and instruct."

Stories "delight" you because they stimulate feelings—they make you sad, mad, glad, excited, chilled, thrilled, or simply thoughtful. In other words, stories are entertaining. Stories "instruct" when they give you insights into human behavior and experiences.

Stories come in a variety of sizes—short, medium, long, extra-short, and extra-long. Novels are long, ranging anywhere from 150 pages to huge thousand-page volumes, while medium-length stories, 75 to 100 pages or so, are called novelettes or novellas. The stories you will read in this book are short, some having as few as eight pages, some as many as forty pages. Most are around ten pages or so, and typically named for their size—short stories.

Short stories resemble novels in many ways, yet there are many important differences. The most obvious difference is that an author of a novel has more pages to develop characters simply because a novel is so much longer than a short story. There are usually a number of different situations presented in a novel and two or more parallel stories, or plot lines, which are related and finally brought together at the end. There are many characters who are developed at some length, and many ideas or themes are dealt with.

A short story, on the other hand, most often tells of one situation or a single experience. There is one story and one plot line. Only one or two characters are developed in depth, and the story usually encompasses a relatively short period of time. Finally, all the situations, characters, settings, and other story elements contribute to the development of only one dominant theme.

Compare, for example, "The Garden Party" with Charles Dickens's *Oliver Twist*. Both deal with young people who are exposed to two levels of society. As an orphan, Oliver was raised in a workhouse, later became involved with a gang of thieves in London's slums, and still later achieved his rightful place in life as a comfortable middle-class young gentleman. Along the way several story lines twist and turn together and you meet many unforgettable characters. Dickens examines a number of social themes—from the mistreatment of the poor to conflicts between the good and evil that exist together at all levels of society. *Oliver Twist* is more than four hundred pages long—a good week's worth of interesting insight and entertainment for an average reader.

By contrast, "The Garden Party" has only one story line—the intrusion of the death of a carter on Laura's perfect day. Laura is the only character you get to know really well, and the gulf between levels of society is the major, or dominant, theme. The story is developed in ten pages, which an average reader can finish in about the same time it takes to see an episode of a favorite television show.

In the following lesson you will study Katherine Mansfield's "The Garden Party" by examining these aspects of short-story writing:

1. The author establishes the setting and the situation.
2. The author introduces and develops characters.
3. The author develops conflicts (problems).
4. A story moves from a beginning, to a middle, to an end.

· I ·
Setting and Situation

A short-story writer must give you information at the very beginning of a story. A novelist can take an entire chapter to tell you where the characters are, when the action takes place, and what is going on, but a short-story writer must give you those facts in the first few paragraphs. Notice how much information Katherine Mansfield gives you in the first paragraph.

> And after all the weather was ideal. They could not have had a more perfect day for a garden party if they had ordered it. Windless, warm, the sky without a cloud. Only the blue was veiled with a haze of light gold, as it is sometimes in early summer. The gardener had been up since dawn, mowing the lawns and sweeping them, until the grass and the dark flat rosettes where the daisy plants had been seemed to shine. As for the roses, you could not help feeling they understood that roses are the only flowers that impress people at garden parties; the only flowers that everybody is certain of knowing. Hundreds, yes, literally hundreds, had come out in a single night; the green bushes bowed down as though they had been visited by archangels.

Mansfield gives you the setting and the situation in the first paragraph. The situation is that there is to be a garden party. The setting is a very lovely and wealthy estate on a beautiful early summer day. Some of the information is told to you, while some of it you infer from clues the author provides.

You know it is early summer because the author says so, and you know this is a wealthy parklike setting from the clues she gives. A gardener is needed to mow and sweep the lawns, and there are hundreds of roses on many bushes. It is obviously not just any backyard.

The author also establishes a feeling in this setting. It is nothing short of heavenly. ". . . the blue was veiled with a haze of light gold. . . ." The rose bushes were so bowed down with their magnificent blooms that it was "as though they had been visited by archangels." You might think that the description of a nice day is rather overdone. Yet the extravagance has a purpose. "The Garden Party" is a story of contrasts, as you have seen, and the author is preparing you for the shock of the scene that comes later:

> The lane began, smoky and dark. . . . A low hum came from the mean little cottages. In some of them there was a flicker of light, and a shadow, crab-like, moved across the window. . . . This was the house. It must be. A dark knot of people stood outside.

There are really only two settings in this short story, compared to a novel wherein there are many settings to suit many situations. Contrast the two worlds that the story is concerned with: one setting is light and heavenly; the other is dark—even the people are dark and their shadows are crab-like—as if it were the underworld. One setting conveys a feeling of absolute joy; the other projects abject misery. Two settings and two contrasting situations develop one theme— the huge gulf, both physical and psychological, between the rich and poor in society. That is the kind of economy of technique that an author must use when writing a short story.

EXERCISE A

Read the following passage from "The Garden Party" and answer the questions that follow using the information you have learned in this part of the lesson.

> It was just growing dusky as Laura shut their garden gates. A big dog ran by like a shadow. The road gleamed white, and down below in the hollow the little cottages were in deep shade. How quiet it seemed after the afternoon. Here she was going down the hill to somewhere where a man lay dead, and she couldn't realize it. Why couldn't she? She stopped a minute. And it seemed to her that

kisses, voices, tinkling spoons, laughter, the smell of crushed grass were somehow inside her. She had no room for anything else. How strange! She looked up at the pale sky, and all she thought was, "Yes, it was the most successful party."

Now the broad road was crossed. The lane began, smoky and dark. Women in shawls and men's tweed caps hurried by.

1. For Laura, this is
   ☐ a. a dangerous setting and situation.
   ☐ b. an alien setting.
   ☐ c. a peaceful situation.
   ☐ d. a setting where she can organize her thoughts.

2. The author refers to an earlier setting in the story to make the point that Laura is part of the world she was raised in. Copy the sentence or sentences that make this point.

_____

_____

_____

_____

Now check your answers using the Answer Key at the back of the book. Correct any wrong answers and review this part of the lesson if you do not understand why an answer is wrong.

·2·
Developing Characters

Many short stories have only two characters, some only one. Katherine Mansfield manages to include quite a large cast of characters into "The Garden Party," but notice that she only develops one in depth, and you gain just a bit of insight into one or two others. The only character you really get to know is Laura, and you have some acquaintance with her mother and Jose.

Early in the story you meet six of these characters: Laura, her mother, and four workmen:

Breakfast was not yet over before the men came to put up the marquee.

"Where do you want the marquee put, mother?"

"My dear child, it's no use asking me. I'm determined to leave everything to you children this year. Forget I am your mother. Treat me as an honored guest. . . . You'll have to go, Laura; you're the artistic one."

Away Laura flew, still holding her piece of bread and butter. It's so delicious to have an excuse for eating out of doors, and besides, she loved having to arrange things; she always felt she could do it so much better than anybody else.

Four men in their shirt-sleeves stood grouped together on the garden path. . . . They looked impressive. Laura wished now that she had not got the bread and butter. . . . She blushed and tried to look severe and even a little bit shortsighted as she came up to them.

"Good morning," she said, copying her mother's voice. But that sounded so fearfully affected that she was ashamed, and stammered like a little girl, "Oh—er—have you come—is it about the marquee?"

In only a few paragraphs you get to know Laura intimately. She is a young lady but has enough little girl left in her so that she is not comfortable in either role. Like many teenagers she is very sure of herself until a real-life situation presents itself and she finds how inexperienced she really is. As you read more about her encounter with the workmen you see that she has the volatile feelings of a child as well as the emerging feelings of an adult for the world and people around her, and she doesn't know how to deal with her feelings or with the people around her.

From the first glimpse of Mrs. Sheridan you are likely to get the impression that she is just a flighty and perhaps a lazy rich woman: "My dear child, it's no use asking me. I'm determined to leave everything to you children this year." As it turns out, she has arranged the whole party, ordered the food, the marquee, the flower arrangements, and has everything pretty well in hand—including her daughter Laura. She probably felt that sending Laura to look after the marquee would teach her how to deal with people.

The rest of the characters in the story are either minor or simply part of the setting. The workmen, the sisters, big brother Laurie, the servants and delivery-men, the garden party guests, the people in the cottages—all make brief appearances. They contribute to what the story is about and help set the scene, but you never get to know them as you get to know Laura.

EXERCISE B

Read the following passage from "The Garden Party" and answer the questions that follow using the information you have learned in this part of the lesson.

There lay a young man, fast asleep—sleeping so soundly, so deeply, that he was far, far away from them both. Oh, so remote, so peaceful. He was dreaming. Never wake him up again. His head was sunk in the pillow, his eyes were closed; they were blind under the closed eyelids. He was given up to his dream. What did garden parties and baskets and lace frocks matter to him? He was far from all those things. He was wonderful, beautiful. While they were laughing and while the band was playing, this marvel had come to the lane. Happy . . . happy. . . . All is well, said that sleeping face. This is just as it should be. I am content.

But all the same you had to cry, and she couldn't go out of the room without saying something to him. Laura gave a loud childish sob.

"Forgive my hat," she said.

1. Laura thinks: "While they were laughing and while the band was playing, this *marvel* had come to the lane." Later she tells her brother, "It was *marvelous.*" Laura had experienced a powerful lesson in growing up. In this context what does she mean when she says *marvel* and *marvelous?*
   □ a. It was a thrilling or marvelous experience for her.
   □ b. It was marvelous to see how the people appreciated her kindness.
   □ c. She marvelled that no one was offended by the garden party.
   □ d. She had experienced the miracle or marvel of life and death.

2. Laura shows considerable adult insight in this passage. But what sentences show Laura as a young girl once again?

   _____

   _____

Now check your answers using the Answer Key at the back of the book. Correct any wrong answers and review this part of the lesson if you do not understand why an answer is wrong.

· 3 ·
Conflict

Short stories portray small slices of life. Life is full of problems or conflicts that must be dealt with. The decisions people make as characters in the stories of their lives decide how their lives will progress. It is the same in short stories, novels, and plays. Conflict and how characters react to their conflicts determine how a story moves along from beginning to end.

Conflicts are usually divided into 5 groups: conflicts between two people, conflicts between a person and society, conflicts between a person and the forces of nature, conflicts between groups, and conflicts that take place within a person's mind. You will study each of those conflicts in more detail in a later lesson devoted to conflict in literature.

In "The Garden Party" you find some minor conflicts between people—when Laura argues with Jose and her mother, for example. Yet Laura's real conflict is within herself. Notice how Laura's conflict becomes apparent in the following passage.

> Laura bent her head and hurried on. She wished now she had put on a coat. How her frock shone! And the big hat with the velvet streamer—if only it was another hat! Were the people looking at her? They must be. It was a mistake to have come; she knew all along it was a mistake. Should she go back even now? . . .
>
> Oh, to be away from this! She actually said, "Help me, God," as she walked up the tiny path and knocked. To be away from those staring eyes, or to be covered up in anything, one of those women's shawls even. I'll just leave the basket and go, she decided. I shan't even wait for it to be emptied.

This is the same Laura who had decided earlier, "Oh, how extraordinarily nice workmen were. . . . Why couldn't she have workmen for friends . . . ?" But now that she is among poor working people and their families she is frightened and ashamed of how different she looks in her fine clothing. The conflict, however, is not with the people. It is within herself. She had been so concerned with class differences before the party, but now from the midst of her inner conflict she says, "It was a mistake to have come. . . . Should she go back even now?"

In the course of a novel many conflicts of various kinds arise. In a short story there are likely to be only one or two. In either case, it is conflict that moves the story along. "Conflict drives the plot," it is said. You will see how this works in part 4 of the lesson.

Read the following passage from "The Garden Party" and answer the questions that follow using the information you have learned in this part of the lesson.

"Jose, come here." Laura caught hold of her sister's sleeve and dragged her through the kitchen to the other side of the green baize door. There she paused and leaned against it. "Jose," she said, horrified, "however are we going to stop everything?"

"Stop everything, Laura!" cried Jose in astonishment. "What do you mean?"

"Stop the garden party, of course." Why did Jose pretend?

But Jose was still more amazed. "Stop the garden party? My dear Laura, don't be so absurd. Of course we can't do anything of the kind. Nobody expects us to. Don't be so extravagant."

"But we can't possibly have a garden party with a man dead just outside the front gate."

That really was extravagant, for the little cottages were in a lane to themselves at the very bottom of a steep rise that led up to the house. A broad road ran between. True, they were far too near. They were the greatest possible eyesore, and they had no right to be in that neighborhood at all. . . . When the Sheridans were little they were forbidden to set foot there because of the revolting language and of what they might catch.

1. Laura has problems throughout the story in deciding how to feel and how to behave in various situations. Here Laura's problem is how to behave
   ☐ a. when walking through the lane of cottages.
   ☐ b. when there has been a death.
   ☐ c. toward poor workmen.
   ☐ d. toward things that are disgusting and sordid.

2. A social conflict often turns up in modern times where people in a wealthy suburb do not want low-cost housing built in their neighborhood. "That would lower the property values," they say. Copy sentences from the passage that reflect this kind of conflict for the Sheridans.

_____

_____

_____

_____

_____

Now check your answers using the Answer Key at the back of the book. Correct any wrong answers and review this part of the lesson if you do not understand why an answer is wrong.

·4·
The Plot of a Story

If you were to keep a diary of one day in the story of your life—writing down everything that you do or think from the moment you get up in the morning until you go to bed at night—you could easily fill as many pages as Katherine Mansfield did in writing "The Garden Party." But it wouldn't necessarily be a story. For example, you might write, "I arose on a beautiful day in early summer, dressed, brushed my teeth, and went down to breakfast. Mother and Father and my brother were there, and we all had bacon and eggs."

Obviously that is not a story. A story has to be more than a recitation of thoughts and events. It has to be a *progression of related events, thoughts, and ideas that are going somewhere: from a beginning, to a middle, to an end.* Novels and short stories are the same in this respect, but the progression of thoughts and events has to go much more quickly in a short story than in a novel. There are no side trips in a short story as there can be in a novel.

In both cases—in a short story and in a novel—the author carefully selects only those events and thoughts that will take the story where it is going and that will accomplish what the author has set out to do. This means a story must be planned and structured just as a road is planned and structured before it is built. Will the road go from beginning to end in a straight line, or will it meander around mountains and cities? Will the depth of pavement accommodate heavy trucks or just light vehicles? Where will the bridges be that connect the parts of the road? There must be an intelligent plan and structure in order for the road to be built successfully.

How a story gets from its beginning, to the middle, to the end, with all the elements it contains, is its *structure.* The intelligent plan for the structure is its *plot.* The conflicts or problems created by the author for the characters of the story move the plot along.

The beginning of "The Garden Party" introduces you to the setting, the situation, and the main characters. Laura's little problem with the men who came to erect the marquee moves the story toward her next encounter with workmen—the death of the carter—which creates a new conflict for Laura.

The middle of the story progresses from the death of the carter through the garden party and its aftermath. You may have noticed that for a story titled "The Garden Party," the party itself occupies only nineteen lines, and there are just the barest hints of what went on. This is an example of the author's selection of what information is important to the structure of a story and what is not:

> Soon after that people began coming in streams. . . . [You are never told who the people are. That is not important.]

> They were like bright birds that had alighted in the Sheridans' garden for this one afternoon. . . . Ah, what happiness it is to be with people who all are happy, to press hands, press cheeks, smile into eyes. [That *is* important to the structure and plot of the story. Can you tell why?]

The story moves toward an end when Laura starts out for the dead man's cottage with the basket of food. This new situation arises because of Laura's earlier conflict—going on with the garden party while a man lay dead in the neighborhood. The new situation brings new conflicts that she must work her way through.

> "But, mother, do you really think it's a good idea?" said Laura. . . .
> "Of course! What's the matter with you today? An hour or two ago you were insisting on us being sympathetic, and now—"

New conflicts arise, and you wonder what will happen next as the events in the story build to a *climax*. The climax, a high point of interest or excitement, comes when a change of some sort occurs either in the story or in an important character. The change may happen quickly or come on slowly. In a short story, because of its brief nature, the climax almost always comes quickly. In "The Garden Party" tension starts to build when Laura leaves for the cottages with her basket of food: "Laura was terribly nervous. . . . Oh, to be away from this! . . . "Help me, God. . . ." You know something dramatic is going to happen soon. The high point, or climax, of the story comes when Laura is led to view the dead man. You notice that there is a change at this point. The author creates a sudden calm:

> There lay a young man, fast asleep—sleeping so soundly, so deeply, that he was far, far away from them both. Oh, so remote, so peaceful. . . . All is well, said that sleeping face. This is just as it should be. I am content.

Sometimes an author will end a story at the point of climax, but more often something follows to bring you down from the emotional high. What follows is usually called the *resolution* of the plot because it brings the story's conflicts to an end (resolves them), ties any other loose ends together, or leaves you with a final thought. In "The Garden Party" the story is resolved as Laura and Laurie walk home together.

> "Was it awful?"
>
> "No," sobbed Laura. "It was simply marvelous. But Laurie—" She stopped, she looked at her brother. "Isn't life," she stammered, "Isn't life—" But what life was she couldn't explain. No matter. He quite understood.

Laura has come face to face with the mystery of life and cannot explain her feelings. There is really nothing more to be said, and the story ends. Like Laurie, you quite understand.

EXERCISE D

Read the following passages from "The Garden Party" and answer the questions that follow using the information you have learned in this part of the lesson.

Jose tries the piano and her voice in case she will be asked to sing at the garden party:

> *This Life is* We-*ary,*
> *A Tear—a Sigh. . . .*
> *A Love that* Chan-*ges*
> *And then . . . Good-bye!*
> *This Life is* Wee-*ary,*
> *Hope comes to Die.*
> *A Dream—a Wa-kening.*

A little later Jose exclaims over the sandwiches:

> "I have never seen such exquisite sandwiches," said Jose's rapturous voice. "How many kinds did you say there were, cook? Fifteen? . . ."
>
> "Godber's has come," announced Sadie, issuing out of the pantry. She had seen the man pass the window.
>
> That meant the cream puffs had come. Godber's were famous for their cream puffs.

1. You read in the lesson that a plot is a progression of *related* events. You also read that an author carefully selects what events go into a story and what is left out. Why is Jose's song included?

   ☐ a. In a way, the song suggests the scene to come where Laura views the dead carter.

   ☐ b. The song is included to provide deep insight into Jose's character.

   ☐ c. The author probably thought it important to show how people act when they prepare for a garden party.

   ☐ d. In a way, the song reflects Mrs. Sheridan's real feelings for people.

2. Explain briefly how the account of the sandwiches and cream puffs is related to later events in the story.

   _____

   _____

   _____

Now check your answers using the Answer Key at the back of the book. Correct any wrong answers and review this part of the lesson if you do not understand why an answer is wrong.

Comprehension Questions

For each of the following statements or questions, select the option that best completes a statement or is the most accurate response to a question.

Organizing Facts

1. The story begins
   ☐ a. before dawn.
   ☐ b. at lunch.
   ☐ c. just before the party begins.
   ☐ d. at breakfast.

Knowledge of Word Meanings

2. Which of the following choices best defines *affected* as used in, " 'Good morning,' she said, copying her mother's voice. But that sounded so fearfully *affected* that she was ashamed. . . ."?
   ☐ a. emotional
   ☐ b. artificial
   ☐ c. cold
   ☐ d. girlish

Making an Inference

3. It would seem that Laura
   ☐ a. is very pleased with her life-style.
   ☐ b. is uncomfortable living the way she does.
   ☐ c. would change her way of living if she could.
   ☐ d. is embarrassed by all the beauty around her.

Recalling Specific Facts

4. What was Laura carrying when she went to talk to the workmen about the marquee?
   ☐ a. roses
   ☐ b. bread and butter
   ☐ c. her new hat
   ☐ d. a sprig of lavender

Drawing a Conclusion

5. When one of the workmen says, "H'm, going to have a band, are you?" Laura replies gently, "Only a very small band." You may conclude from Laura's answer that she
   ☐ a. looks down on workmen.
   ☐ b. wishes it were a bigger band.
   ☐ c. feels a bit guilty about her wealth.
   ☐ d. is amused by the workmen.

Making a Judgment

6. Laura's new ideas about the working class that she forms from her short meeting with the workmen are
   □ a. realistic.
   □ b. naive.
   □ c. prejudiced.
   □ d. cynical.

Organizing Facts

7. Who brought the news of the accident?
   □ a. Sadie
   □ b. the florist's man
   □ c. the cook
   □ d. Godber's deliveryman

Knowledge of Word Meanings

8. When Laura wanted to stop the party, Jose said, "Don't be so *extravagant.*" What does *extravagant* mean in this sense?
   □ a. careless with money
   □ b. extremely silly
   □ c. unreasonable
   □ d. profuse

Recognizing Tone

9. There is an abrupt change in the tone, or attitude, of things at the Sheridans' house when
   □ a. Jose sits down at the piano and sings.
   □ b. the florist delivers the flowers.
   □ c. Laura directs the men.
   □ d. news comes of the carter's death.

Drawing a Conclusion

10. From the way the tradesman reports the fatal accident you may conclude that some people
    □ a. enjoy telling about a shocking event.
    □ b. are shy about carrying bad news.
    □ c. are bloodthirsty.
    □ d. deliberately distort the facts of a story.

Knowledge of Word Meanings

11. Which one of the following choices best defines the word *mean* as used in, "They were little *mean* dwellings painted a chocolate brown"?
    ☐ a. scantily furnished
    ☐ b. rude and impolite
    ☐ c. crude and cheerless
    ☐ d. full of significance

Organizing Facts

12. Jose appeared unsympathetic or "hard" toward Laura's plea to stop the garden party. Laura then went to her mother. What was Mrs. Sheridan's first reaction?
    ☐ a. She seemed flustered.
    ☐ b. She was alarmed.
    ☐ c. She was immediately sympathetic.
    ☐ d. She seemed amused.

Making a Judgment

13. Judging from their reaction when walking through the cottage lane, you would have to say that Laura and Laurie found the neighborhood
    ☐ a. distasteful.
    ☐ b. interesting.
    ☐ c. dangerous.
    ☐ d. inviting.

Recognizing Tone

14. When Laura tells Jose and her mother that the party must be stopped, they express
    ☐ a. amusement and annoyance.
    ☐ b. sympathy and concern.
    ☐ c. shock and horror.
    ☐ d. respect and admiration.

Understanding Characters

15. At this point in her life, Laura might be characterized as
    ☐ a. immature and unsure of herself.
    ☐ b. completely selfish and spoiled.
    ☐ c. strong, sure, and independent.
    ☐ d. having a well-developed social conscience.

Recalling Specific Facts

16. What does Laura wear to the party that makes her look quite stunning?
    - ☐ a. a long white dress
    - ☐ b. a sash
    - ☐ c. a black hat
    - ☐ d. ribbons in her hair

Appreciation of Literary Forms

17. A *simile* is a direct comparison of unlike things that uses the word *like, as,* or *resembles* to connect them. Which one of the following expressions from the story is a simile?
    - ☐ a. "The band struck up"
    - ☐ b. "They [the guests] were like bright birds"
    - ☐ c. "Ah, what happiness it is"
    - ☐ d. "to press hands, press cheeks"

Appreciation of Literary Forms

18. "And the perfect afternoon slowly ripened, slowly faded, slowly its petals closed." A *metaphor* is an indirect comparison of unlike things. This metaphor compares
    - ☐ a. the afternoon with evening.
    - ☐ b. the afternoon of the garden party with a flower.
    - ☐ c. perfection with an ideal.
    - ☐ d. a perfect afternoon with decaying fruit.

Understanding Main Ideas

19. Four short remarks that Laura made during the story follow. Which one best expresses her inner conflict throughout the story?
    - ☐ a. "Let's go into the garden"
    - ☐ b. "But I thought you said you didn't mean to interfere."
    - ☐ c. "Stop the garden party, of course."
    - ☐ d. "I don't understand"

Making an Inference

20. You may infer from the attitude of the Sheridans that when it comes to an unpleasant situation, they
    - ☐ a. will always hasten to correct it.
    - ☐ b. delight in the suffering of others.
    - ☐ c. like to share the sorrows of the less fortunate.
    - ☐ d. try to minimize its importance.

Recalling Specific Facts

21. To Laura the dead man's face appears
    - ☐ a. pained.
    - ☐ b. peaceful.
    - ☐ c. sorrowful.
    - ☐ d. expressionless.

Drawing a Conclusion

22. The person in the Sheridan household who seems to understand Laura best and whose opinion she values most is
    - ☐ a. Mrs. Sheridan.
    - ☐ b. Jose.
    - ☐ c. Laurie.
    - ☐ d. Sadie.

Understanding Main Ideas

23. Another appropriate title for this story could be
    - ☐ a. "The Idle Rich."
    - ☐ b. "A View from the Bottom."
    - ☐ c. "Two Societies."
    - ☐ d. "A View from the Top."

Understanding Characters

24. Mrs. Sheridan can best be described as
    - ☐ a. entirely foolish and lazy.
    - ☐ b. a flighty but caring mother.
    - ☐ c. very concerned about social ills.
    - ☐ d. only interested in parties.

Understanding Main Ideas

25. When it came to dealing with people, Laura was
    - ☐ a. comfortable with everyone.
    - ☐ b. not at all class conscious.
    - ☐ c. uncomfortable outside of her class.
    - ☐ d. uncomfortable with everyone.

Now check your answers using the Answer Key at the back of the book. Make no mark for right answers. Correct any wrong answers you may have by putting a check mark (✓) in the box next to the right answer. Count the number of questions you answered correctly and plot the total on the Comprehension Scores Graph at the back of the book.

Next, look at the questions you answered incorrectly. What types of questions were they? Count the number you got wrong of each type and enter the numbers in the spaces below.

Recalling Specific Facts	_____
Organizing Facts	_____
Knowledge of Word Meanings	_____
Drawing a Conclusion	_____
Making a Judgment	_____
Making an Inference	_____
Understanding Characters	_____
Understanding Main Ideas	_____
Recognizing Tone	_____
Appreciation of Literary Forms	_____

Now use these numbers to fill in the Comprehension Skills Profile at the end of the book.

Extension Activities

Discussion Guide

Discussing Elements of a Short Story

1. If "The Garden Party" were a novel you would probably have been told more about the setting and the situation—the country, the year, how the Sheridans earned their money, and so on. Why don't you need that information in order to enjoy the story?

2. "The Garden Party" follows the short-story form in that there is only one character you get to know well. Laura experiences the gulf that exists between classes of society. How do these minor characters in the story contribute to her experience?

Mrs. Sheridan	Laurie
cook	the widow's sister
Jose	the tall workman
Sadie	the dead man

3. You read in the lesson that "conflict drives the plot." At the end of the story Laura seems to have resolved her problem regarding her place in society. She will be what she is, but perhaps with a better understanding of people in other classes.

   Suppose this were one chapter in a novel instead of a short story. What new conflict could develop at the end of the story, and where do you think that conflict would "drive" the plot?

Discussing the Story

4. You are not told the ages of any of the characters or the year in which the story takes place. How old do you think Laura is? How old is the carter who died? When did the story take place? Use clues that you find in the story to support your opinions.

5. Do differences among social classes exist today in the same way that they were reported in "The Garden Party"? If you think they do, tell how. If you think there are no differences today, tell why not.

6. Support Jose's and Mrs. Sheridan's position in not stopping the garden party. Explain why you think they were right and reasonable. Then take Laura's side. Was she right, or was she just being "extravagant"? What else might she have done if she felt really concerned about the carter's death?

Discussing the Author's Work

7. In her stories Katherine Mansfield often focuses on small things that become very important. Four such things in "The Garden Party" are light, the party

food, flowers, and Laura's hat. How is each of those small details important to the telling of the story?

8. It has been said that Katherine Mansfield's descriptions are like poetry. What is poetic about the opening paragraph of the story? Find the passage where Laura hangs up the telephone and sits listening to the sounds of the house. What is poetic about this paragraph? Rewrite either of these paragraphs in the form of a poem.

9. Katherine Mansfield has a reputation for drawing "true-to-life" characters. What makes you think of Laura as a real person? If "The Garden Party" were made into a movie and if you were casting the parts, whom would you choose to play Laura and Mrs. Sheridan? Think of performers you know from movies and television programs.

Writing Exercise

Think of a social problem in your life or in the world at large. Examples may include class differences, discrimination, ethics in business or government, selfish attitudes, lack of caring or concern for others, and so on. Prepare to write a short story by doing the following:

- Describe the problem in no more than two or three sentences.
- Think of at least two characters who will be in your story and describe each of them.
- Write a short paragraph telling what the story will be about. Be sure to tell what the conflict is that involves your main character.
- Write three more short paragraphs telling how the story will begin, what will be in the middle, and how it will end.

UNIT
Two

Unit Two

Introduction

What the Story Is About

Some of the most complicated things you encounter in life seem so plain and simple that you tend to pass them by without a second thought. An old oak tree is like that. It's just there, day after day, and year after year, doing the very predictable things that oak trees do. It's not something you are likely to write a story about.

But if you stop one day and really look at the tree, and really think about it, you are likely to realize that the oak tree is something that is wonderful, beautiful, and full of meaning. Eudora Welty found this quality one day in an old black woman who was doing nothing more than walking through the country. The result is "A Worn Path" which, like the oak tree, is deceptively simple but full of wonder, beauty, and meaning.

The story tells about the old woman's journey from the country to the city of Natchez, Mississippi, to get a bottle of medicine for a chronically ill grandchild. Her "adventures" consist of catching her dress on a thorn bush, crossing a small stream on a log, and falling in a ditch when she encounters a dog. Nothing special happens, it seems. Yet when you have finished reading the story, you have the feeling you have just read an account of an epic journey.

A good storyteller can create those powerful feelings. Eudora Welty takes a subject in which there is apparently no beauty, no adventure, very little interest, and certainly no story, and turns it into a work of literary art that you won't soon forget. Phoenix Jackson, the old lady of the story, will stay with you long after you have forgotten many more exciting heroes and heroines.

Eudora Welty is one of many writers with origins in the deep South of the United States who contributed to the great literature of the first half of the twentieth century. You may recognize other names of southern writers from this period. William Faulkner, Thomas Wolfe, Harper Lee (*To Kill a Mockingbird*), Katherine Anne Porter, and two other authors you will read later in this book—Flannery O'Connor and Truman Capote. Several of these writers found the inspiration for their stories in what Faulkner called "a curse upon the land"—slavery and its aftermath of hatred, bigotry, and repression.

While there are echoes of those problems in "A Worn Path," Eudora Welty concentrates more on Phoenix Jackson as a representation of dedication to a mission born in love. The story is set in Mississippi because that is the place the author knew best; it is where she was born, grew up, and went to school. Yet it is also a story of universal concern—how people overcome obstacles to accomplish a goal even though they face the adversities of poverty, lack of education, and the infirmities of old age.

What the Lesson Is About

The lesson that follows "A Worn Path" deals with the element of setting in a story. Setting, as you will learn, is more than the location of a story. In addition to the location, setting is the time of the story, the objects and people that make up the surroundings for the action, and the things that appeal to your senses and create the story's atmosphere.

As you read "A Worn Path," try to keep the following questions in mind. They will help you discover how the setting contributes to the enjoyment and meaning of a story.

1. What descriptions in the story help to transport you into a world that is real and believable, even though the author has made up the story?

2. How does the setting of the story contribute to the action of the story?

3. How does the setting affect your feelings and the feelings of the story's characters? How does the setting create an atmosphere for the story?

4. How does the setting help to communicate important ideas or themes in the story?

A Worn Path

by Eudora Welty

*I*t was December—a bright frozen day in the early morning. Far out in the country there was an old Negro woman with her head tied in a red rag, coming along a path through the pinewoods. Her name was Phoenix Jackson. She was very old and small and she walked slowly in the dark pine shadows, moving a little from side to side in her steps, with the balanced heaviness and lightness of a pendulum in a grandfather clock. She carried a thin, small cane made from an umbrella, and with this she kept tapping the frozen earth in front of her. This made a grave and persistent noise in the still air, that seemed meditative like the chirping of a solitary little bird.

She wore a dark striped dress reaching down to her shoe tops, and an equally long apron of bleached sugar sacks, with a full pocket: all neat and tidy, but every time she took a step she might have fallen over her shoelaces, which dragged from her unlaced shoes. She looked straight ahead. Her eyes were blue with age. Her skin had a pattern all its own of numberless branching wrinkles and as though a whole little tree stood in the middle of her forehead, but a golden color ran underneath, and the two knobs of her cheeks were illumined by a yellow burning under the dark. Under the red rag her hair came down on her neck in the frailest of ringlets, still black, and with an odor like copper.

Now and then there was a quivering in the thicket. Old Phoenix said, "Out of my way, all you foxes, owls, beetles, jack rabbits, coons and wild animals! . . . Keep out from under these feet, little bob-whites. . . . Keep the big wild hogs out of my path. Don't let none of those come running my direction. I got a long way." Under her small black-freckled hand her cane, limber as a buggy whip, would switch at the brush as if to rouse up any hiding things.

On she went. The woods were deep and still. The sun made the pine needles almost too bright to look at, up where the wind rocked. The cones dropped as light as feathers. Down in the hollow was the mourning dove—it was not too late for him.

The path ran up a hill. "Seem like there is chains about my feet, time I get this far," she said, in the voice of argument old people keep to use with themselves. "Something always take a hold of me on this hill—pleads I should stay."

After she got to the top she turned and gave a full, severe look behind her where she had come. "Up through pines," she said at length. "Now down through oaks."

Her eyes opened their widest, and she started down gently. But before she got to the bottom of the hill a bush caught her dress.

Her fingers were busy and intent, but her skirts were full and long, so that before she could pull them free in one place they were caught in another. It was not possible to allow the dress to tear. "I in the thorny bush," she said. "Thorns, you doing your appointed work. Never want to let folks pass, no sir. Old eyes thought you was a pretty little *green* bush."

Finally, trembling all over, she stood free, and after a moment dared to stoop for her cane.

"Sun so high!" she cried, leaning back and looking, while the thick tears went over her eyes. "The time getting all gone here."

At the foot of this hill was a place where a log was laid across the creek.

"Now comes the trial," said Phoenix.

Putting her right foot out, she mounted the log and shut her eyes. Lifting her skirt, leveling her cane fiercely before her, like a festival figure in some parade, she began to march across. Then she opened her eyes and she was safe on the other side.

"I wasn't as old as I thought," she said.

But she sat down to rest. She spread her skirts on the bank around her and folded her hands over her knees. Up above her was a tree in a pearly cloud of mistletoe. She did not dare to close her eyes, and when a little boy brought her a plate with a slice of marble-cake on it she spoke to him. "That would be acceptable," she said. But when she went to take it there was just her own hand in the air.

So she left that tree, and had to go through a barbed-wire fence. There she had to creep and crawl, spreading her knees and stretching her fingers like a baby trying to climb the steps. But she talked loudly to herself: she could not let her dress be torn now, so late in the day, and she could not pay for having her arm or her leg sawed off if she got caught fast where she was.

At last she was safe through the fence and risen up out in the clearing. Big dead trees, like black men with one arm, were standing in the purple stalks of the withered cotton field. There sat a buzzard.

"Who you watching?"

In the furrow she made her way along.

"Glad this not the season for bulls," she said, looking sideways, "and the good Lord made his snakes to curl up and sleep in the winter. A pleasure I don't see no two-headed snake coming around that tree, where it come once. It took a while to get by him, back in the summer."

She passed through the old cotton and went into a field of dead corn. It whispered and shook and was taller than her head. "Through the maze now," she said, for there was no path.

Then there was something tall, black, and skinny there, moving before her.

At first she took it for a man. It could have been a man dancing in the field. But she stood still and listened, and it did not make a sound. It was silent as a ghost.

"Ghost," she said sharply, "who be you the ghost of? For I have heard of nary death close by."

But there was no answer—only the ragged dancing in the wind.

She shut her eyes, reached out her hand, and touched a sleeve. She found a coat and inside that an emptiness, cold as ice.

"You scarecrow," she said. Her face lighted. "I ought to be shut up for good," she said with laughter. "My senses is gone. I too old. I the oldest people I ever know. Dance, old scarecrow," she said, "while I dancing with you."

She kicked her foot over the furrow, and with mouth drawn down, shook her head once or twice in a little strutting way. Some husks blew down and whirled in streamers about her skirts.

Then she went on, parting her way from side to side with the cane, through the whispering field. At last she came to the end, to a wagon track where the silver grass blew between the red ruts. The quail were walking around like pullets, seeming all dainty and unseen.

"Walk pretty," she said. "This the easy place. This the easy going."

She followed the track, swaying through the quiet bare fields, through the little strings of trees silver in their dead leaves, past cabins silver from weather, with the doors and windows boarded shut, all like old women under a spell sitting there. "I walking in their sleep," she said, nodding her head vigorously.

In a ravine she went where a spring was silently flowing through a hollow log. Old Phoenix bent and drank. "Sweet-gum makes the water sweet," she said, and drank more. "Nobody know who made this well, for it was here when I was born."

The track crossed a swampy part where the moss hung as white as lace from every limb. "Sleep on, alligators, and blow your bubbles." Then the track went into the road.

Deep, deep the road went down between the high green-colored banks. Overhead the live-oaks met, and it was as dark as a cave.

A black dog with a lolling tongue came up out of the weeds by the ditch. She was meditating, and not ready, and when he came at her she only hit him a little with her cane. Over she went in the ditch, like a little puff of milkweed.

Down there, her senses drifted away. A dream visited her, and she reached her hand up, but nothing reached down and gave her a pull. So she lay there and presently went to talking. "Old woman," she said to herself, "that black dog come up out of the weeds to stall you off, and now there he sitting on his fine tail, smiling at you."

A white man finally came along and found her—a hunter, a young man, with his dog on a chain.

"Well, Granny!" he laughed. "What are you doing there?"

"Lying on my back like a June-bug waiting to be turned over, mister," she said, reaching up her hand.

He lifted her up, gave her a swing in the air, and set her down. "Anything broken, Granny?"

"No sir, them old dead weeds is springy enough," said Phoenix, when she had got her breath. "I thank you for your trouble."

"Where do you live, Granny?" he asked, while the two dogs were growling at each other.

"Away back yonder, sir, behind the ridge. You can't even see it from here."

"On your way home?"

"No sir, I going to town."

"Why, that's too far! That's as far as I walk when I come out myself, and I get something for my trouble." He patted the stuffed bag he carried, and there hung down a little closed claw. It was one of the bob-whites, with its beak hooked bitterly to show it was dead. "Now you go on home, Granny!"

"I bound to go to town, mister," said Phoenix. "The time come around."

He gave another laugh, filling the whole landscape. "I know you old colored people! Wouldn't miss going to town to see Santa Claus!"

But something held old Phoenix very still. The deep lines in her face went into a fierce and different radiation. Without warning, she had seen with her own eyes a flashing nickel fall out of the man's pocket onto the ground.

"How old are you, Granny?" he was saying.

"There is no telling, mister," she said, "no telling."

Then she gave a little cry and clapped her hands and said, "Git on away from here, dog! Look! Look at that dog!" She laughed as if in admiration. "He ain't scared of nobody. He a big black dog." She whispered, "Sic him!"

"Watch me get rid of that cur," said the man. "Sic him, Pete! Sic him!"

Phoenix heard the dogs fighting, and heard the man running and throwing sticks. She even heard a gunshot. But she was slowly bending forward by that time, further and further forward, the lids stretched down over her eyes, as if she were doing this in her sleep. Her chin was lowered almost to her knees. The yellow palm of her hand came out from the fold of her apron. Her fingers slid down and along the ground under the piece of money with the grace and care they would have in lifting an egg from under a setting hen. Then she slowly straightened up, she stood erect, and the nickel was in her apron pocket. A bird flew by. Her lips moved. "God watching me the whole time. I come to stealing."

The man came back, and his own dog panted about them. "Well, I scared him off that time," he said, and then he laughed and lifted his gun and pointed it at Phoenix.

She stood straight and faced him.

"Doesn't the gun scare you?" he said, still pointing it.

"No, sir, I seen plenty go off closer by, in my day, and for less than what I done," she said, holding utterly still.

He smiled, and shouldered the gun. "Well, Granny," he said, "you must be a hundred years old, and scared of nothing. I'd give you a dime if I had any money with me. But you take my advice and stay home, and nothing will happen to you."

"I bound to go on my way, mister," said Phoenix. She inclined her head in the red rag. Then they went in different directions, but she could hear the gun shooting again and again over the hill.

She walked on. The shadows hung from the oak trees to the road like curtains. Then she smelled wood-smoke, and smelled the river, and she saw a steeple and the cabins on their steep steps. Dozens of little black children whirled around her. There ahead was Natchez shining. Bells were ringing. She walked on.

In the paved city it was Christmas time. There were red and green electric lights strung and criss-crossed everywhere, and all turned on in the daytime. Old Phoenix would have been lost if she had not distrusted her eyesight and depended on her feet to know where to take her.

She paused quietly on the sidewalk where people were passing by. A lady came along in the crowd, carrying an armful of red-, green-, and silver-wrapped presents; she gave off perfume like the red roses in hot summer, and Phoenix stopped her.

"Please, missy, will you lace up my shoe?" She held up her foot.

"What do you want, Grandma?"

"See my shoe," said Phoenix. "Do all right for out in the country, but wouldn't look right to go in a big building."

"Stand still then, Grandma," said the lady. She put her packages down on the sidewalk beside her and laced and tied both shoes tightly.

"Can't lace 'em with a cane," said Phoenix. "Thank you, missy. I doesn't mind asking a nice lady to tie up my shoe, when I gets out on the street."

Moving slowly and from side to side, she went into the big building, and into a tower of steps, where she walked up and around and around until her feet knew to stop.

She entered a door, and there she saw nailed up on the wall the document that had been stamped with the gold seal and framed in the gold frame, which matched the dream that was hung up in her head.

"Here I be," she said. There was a fixed and ceremonial stiffness over her body.

"A charity case, I suppose," said an attendant who sat at the desk before her.

But Phoenix only looked above her head. There was sweat on her face, the wrinkles in her skin shone like a bright net.

"Speak up, Grandma," the woman said. "What's your name? We must have your history, you know. Have you been here before? What seems to be the trouble with you?"

Old Phoenix only gave a twitch to her face as if a fly were bothering her.

"Are you deaf?" cried the attendant.

But then the nurse came in.

"Oh, that's just old Aunt Phoenix," she said. "She doesn't come for herself—she has a little grandson. She makes these trips just as regular as clockwork. She lives away back off the Old Natchez Trace." She bent down. "Well, Aunt Phoenix, why don't you just take a seat? We won't keep you standing after your long trip." She pointed.

The old woman sat down, bolt upright in the chair.

"Now, how is the boy?" asked the nurse.

Old Phoenix did not speak.

"I said, how is the boy?"

But Phoenix only waited and stared straight ahead, her face very solemn and withdrawn into rigidity.

"Is his throat any better?" asked the nurse. "Aunt Phoenix, don't you hear me? Is your grandson's throat any better since the last time you came for the medicine?"

With her hands on her knees, the old woman waited, silent, erect and motionless, just as if she were in armor.

"You mustn't take up our time this way, Aunt Phoenix," the nurse said. "Tell us quickly about your grandson, and get it over. He isn't dead, is he?"

At last there came a flicker and then a flame of comprehension across her face, and she spoke.

"My grandson. It was my memory had left me. There I sat and forgot why I made my long trip."

"Forgot?" The nurse frowned. "After you came so far?"

Then Phoenix was like an old woman begging a dignified

forgiveness for waking up frightened in the night. "I never did go to school, I was too old at the Surrender," she said in a soft voice. I'm an old woman without an education. It was my memory fail me. My little grandson, he is just the same, and I forgot it in the coming."

"Throat never heals, does it?" said the nurse, speaking in a loud, sure voice to old Phoenix. By now she had a card with something written on it, a little list. "Yes. Swallowed lye. When was it?—January—two-three years ago—"

Phoenix spoke unasked now. "No, missy, he not dead, he just the same. Every little while his throat begin to close up again, and he not able to swallow. He not get his breath. He not able to help himself. So the time come around, and I go on another trip for the soothing medicine."

"All right. The doctor said as long as you came to get it, you could have it," said the nurse. "But it's an obstinate case."

"My little grandson, he sit up there in the house all wrapped up, waiting by himself," Phoenix went on. "We is the only two left in the world. He suffer and it don't seem to put him back at all. He got a sweet look. He going to last. He wear a little patch quilt and peep out holding his mouth open like a little bird. I remember so plain now. I not going to forget him again, no, the whole enduring time. I could tell him from all the others in creation."

"All right." The nurse was trying to hush her now. She brought her a bottle of medicine. "Charity," she said, making a check mark in a book.

Old Phoenix held the bottle close to her eyes, and then carefully put it into her pocket.

"I thank you," she said.

"It's Christmas time, Grandma," said the attendant. "Could I give you a few pennies out of my purse?"

"Five pennies is a nickel," said Phoenix stiffly.

"Here's a nickel," said the attendant.

Phoenix rose carefully and held out her hand. She received the nickel and then fished the other nickel out of her pocket and laid it beside the new one. She stared at her palm closely, with her head on one side.

Then she gave a tap with her cane on the floor.

"This is what come to me to do," she said. "I going to the store and buy my child a little windmill they sells, made out of paper. He going to find it hard to believe there such a thing in the world. I'll march myself back where he waiting, holding it straight up in this hand."

She lifted her free hand, gave a little nod, turned around, and walked out of the doctor's office. Then her slow step began on the stairs, going down.

Setting

Some readers dismiss setting as just another word for scenery—a quaint New England village, a city, a train, a slum, or the estate of a wealthy family. That view of setting is not very accurate as you saw when you read "The Garden Party." In that story, the contrast of two settings—the Sheridan's garden and the poor cottages—played a vital role in the telling of the story *and* in its meaning. The story of Phoenix Jackson would have been very different if the author had chosen to locate it in a city in California instead of in rural Mississippi.

Of course, a story has to occur in some place and in some time. This is the setting of time and place. You have seen in the two stories you have read how time and place can affect the way you understand what is going on in a story. Other elements of setting—the scenery, people, sights, sounds, odors, sensations—all contribute to making a story real, believable, and enjoyable.

Authors do not spell out every detail of the setting. This is especially true in a short story where an author must be very economical with details that are included. You weren't given a map, for example, to follow Phoenix Jackson's journey from "away back off the Old Natchez Trace" to the doctor's office. Clearly this isn't important for the effect or the point of the story. It would simply be clutter. But any detail of setting that is important for understanding a story, or for tuning in on the feeling the author wants to convey, will certainly be included by a good storyteller.

In the following lessons you will learn how Eudora Welty uses setting in "A Worn Path." You will examine the following:

1. The elements of the setting in the story are time, places, people, and scenery.
2. The setting and the action of the story work together.
3. The settings create a feeling or atmosphere both for you and for the characters in the story.
4. The settings contribute to understanding important ideas and themes in the story.

· I ·
The Elements of Setting

When you picture the setting of "A Worn Path" in your mind, you will have to take many things into account. First, there is the time: "It was December . . ." That is straightforward, but when in December? What year?

The year is not especially important to the story, but you can probably figure it as being within a certain *period* in time.

Phoenix tells the nurse in the doctor's office, "I never did go to school, I was too old at the Surrender." The "Surrender" refers to the American Civil War, of course, so Phoenix has lived through the slave era which ended in 1865. You might guess she was born about 1850 since she says she was too old to go to school at the end of the war. If you consider her present age as 85 or 90 then you can estimate the year somewhere between 1935 or 1940. Other facts in the story fit: the condescending way the whites address Phoenix as Aunt or Granny, and the long dress which an older woman would not wear today, but which might have been worn in 1935 by a few very old country women. If you had guessed 1925 or 1945 the story would work as well.

If you think back to "The Garden Party," you had to figure out the era of that story in the same way. A carter's horse was frightened by a tractor. Laura spoke to a friend on the telephone. That means the story was set in a time when motors were just replacing horses and the telephone was in common use. If you know just a little history, you can place the story within the first two decades of the twentieth century, which helps you to understand the story.

Other elements of the setting may also be spelled out or left for you to infer from clues the author works into the story. The city of Natchez is named. If you don't know that Natchez is in Mississippi, you can still infer that the story takes place in the deep South from the mention of cotton fields, alligators, and moss and mistletoe in the branches of the trees.

Pine trees, oaks, the wind, birds and animals, a scarecrow, a ditch, a road, city streets, the "tower of steps" to the doctor's office, the all-important diploma on the wall, and many more small details all become part of the setting as the story goes along. Notice what other elements of setting are included in this short passage from the story:

> "I bound to go on my way, mister," said Phoenix. She inclined her head in the red rag. Then they went in different directions, but she could hear the gun shooting again and again over the hill.
> She walked on. The shadows hung from the oak trees to the road like curtains. Then she smelled wood-smoke, and smelled the river, and she saw a steeple and the cabins on their steep steps. Dozens of little black children whirled around her. There ahead was Natchez shining. Bells were ringing. She walked on.

Now sounds are part of the setting—the gun and the bells. The smell of wood-smoke and the smell of the river become part of the setting. The children are included not as characters but as part of the scene.

What the author is doing with these details of setting is creating a world for her story that you can believe. When the author has done her job well, as Eudora Welty has, you can imagine yourself in the setting of fifty or sixty years ago, and imagine seeing it, hearing it, smelling it, and feeling it as Phoenix Jackson did. Perhaps that is the eeriest part of storytelling, and the most remarkable. Neither Phoenix Jackson nor the setting are entirely real. But through the author's artistry and magic you are able to believe it's all true and happening as you read, or as you walk the worn path yourself.

EXERCISE A

Read the following passage from "A Worn Path" and answer the questions that follow using the information you have learned in this part of the lesson.

> In the paved city it was Christmas time. There were red and green electric lights strung and criss-crossed everywhere, and all turned on in the daytime. Old Phoenix would have been lost if she had not distrusted her eyesight and depended on her feet to know where to take her.
>
> She paused quietly on the sidewalk where people were passing by. A lady came along in the crowd, carrying an armful of red-, green-, and silver-wrapped presents; she gave off perfume like the red roses in hot summer, and Phoenix stopped her.

1. Based on clues given in elements of the setting, what part of December is this?
   - ☐ a. It's Christmas day, because the author says so.
   - ☐ b. It's the day before Christmas, because the lights are on in the daytime.
   - ☐ c. It's the Christmas season, but there are no clues to tell exactly when.
   - ☐ d. It's probably early in December because the perfume smells like roses in summer.

2. Copy the sentence that uses people not as characters in the story but as an element of the setting.

   _____

   _____

Now check your answers using the Answer Key at the back of the book. Correct any wrong answers and review this part of the lesson if you do not understand why an answer is wrong.

· 2 ·
Setting and Action

By making a few minor adjustments to the story, the events in "A Worn Path" might be believable if they occurred in almost any part of the United States. They would not be very believable, however, if the story were set at the end of the twentieth century instead of the beginning. The story would make no sense at all if it were set in France or Russia at any time. The point is, there are certain settings that *fit* the action of a particular story and many other settings that don't fit.

It is also true that some settings literally *suggest* certain kinds of actions and rule out others. For instance, rural Mississippi in 1935 or 1940 works well for the kind of adventures Phoenix encounters. The same setting would work well in a story about a southern farm family in that era. It is not a setting that suggests the kind of action you would expect to find in a spy thriller or in a science fiction story. A foggy street in East Berlin is much better for the action in a spy thriller. A rocky landscape on Alpha Centauri, 4.4 light years from Earth, suggests the action you would expect in science fiction much better than a street in Natchez, Mississippi, does.

The setting of a story often *influences* the action, or at least works together with what the characters in the story are doing. Consider the obstacles that Phoenix Jackson encounters on her journey in the following passages:

> Her eyes opened their widest, and she started down gently. But before she got to the bottom of the hill a bush caught her dress.
> Her fingers were busy and intent, but her skirts were full and long, so that before she could pull them free in one place they were caught in another. It was not possible to allow the dress to tear. . . .
> So she left that tree, and had to go through a barbed-wire fence. There she had to creep and crawl, spreading her knees and stretching her fingers like a baby trying to climb the steps. But she talked loudly to herself: she could not let her dress be torn now, so late in the day. . . .

In the discussion of conflict, in the previous lesson, you learned that "conflict drives the plot." Laura Sheridan, you recall, was beset by inner conflicts that she had to resolve. In "A Worn Path," Phoenix has no such inner conflicts. Her conflicts are with her age, her infirmity, and with obstacles that deflect her from her single-minded mission.

In the passages you have just read, elements of the setting become obstacles that Phoenix has to overcome. In other parts of the story similar obstacles present themselves. The thorn bush, barbed wire, a hill, a log over a stream, a dog, a ditch, and finally the towering stairs to the doctor's office are all parts of the setting, and all of them are obstacles to be overcome. How Phoenix overcomes these obstacles and continues on her way each time are the foundation of the story's action.

EXERCISE B

Read the following passage from "A Worn Path" and answer the questions that follow using the information you have learned in this part of the lesson.

Then she went on, parting her way from side to side with the cane, through the whispering field. At last she came to the end, to a wagon track where the silver grass blew between the red ruts. The quail were walking around like pullets, seeming all dainty and unseen.

"Walk pretty," she said. "This the easy place. This the easy going."

In a ravine she went where a spring was silently flowing through a hollow log. Old Phoenix bent and drank. "Sweet-gum makes the water sweet," she said, and drank more. "Nobody know who made this well, for it was here when I was born."

The track crossed a swampy part where the moss hung as white as lace from every limb. "Sleep on, alligators, and blow your bubbles." Then the track went into the road.

1. At that point in the story the elements in the setting reflect
   ☐ a. an expectation of worse things to come.
   ☐ b. a change in the action for the better.
   ☐ c. a drifting into a dream world.
   ☐ d. a new danger from alligators.

2. The setting continues to take Phoenix and you along the path of the journey. List at least four new locations found in this passage.

   _____

   _____

   _____

   _____

Now check your answers using the Answer Key at the back of the book. Correct any wrong answers and review this part of the lesson if you do not understand why an answer is wrong.

· 3 ·
Setting and Feelings

Where you are has a lot to do with the way you feel. For instance, you are more likely to feel peaceful strolling along a quiet beach than you would jostling your way along a crowded city street. But if you change an element or two of the story, the reverse might be true. Suppose the beach is on a desert island. Flies swarm around you and there is no water. Now the feeling turns from peacefulness to fear for your life. If it's a nice day in Los Angeles and you love crowds of people, the feeling created by the setting may be exciting or exhilarating.

Every setting in a story carries certain associations that an author uses to establish a certain atmosphere. Characters in the story respond to the setting, because the characters have feelings; and you respond to the setting, too, when you enter into the world of the story.

Read the following passage from "A Worn Path." What feelings do you associate with the setting as the story opens?

> It was December—a bright frozen day in the early morning. Far out in the country there was an old Negro woman with her head tied in a red rag, coming along a path through the pinewoods. Her name was Phoenix Jackson. She was very old and small and she walked slowly in the dark pine shadows, moving a little from side to side in her steps, with the balanced heaviness and lightness of a pendulum in a grandfather clock. She carried a thin, small cane made from an umbrella, and with this she kept tapping the frozen earth in front of her. This made a grave and persistent noise in the still air, that seemed meditative like the chirping of a solitary little bird.

Different readers are likely to have different feelings about this setting. It is certainly a bright and pleasant scene. Phoenix Jackson will become the story's main character, but at this point she is more important as part of the setting—coming along a path through the pinewoods. The way she moves and the tapping of her cane are also a part of the setting.

Some people would describe the scene as peaceful. Others would say it's quaint—American gothic, perhaps. There is a feeling of sober and dependable regularity here, too, in the way Phoenix moves "slowly in the dark pine shadows" like the pendulum of a clock. Her cane made a "grave and persistent noise in the still air, that seemed meditative."

This description puts you in tune with Phoenix and creates a feeling that will dominate the story. Throughout the story Phoenix is as regular and reliable in her mission as the pendulum of a grandfather clock. Like the tapping of her cane she is inclined to be grave, persistent, and meditative. She is just as persistent when the feeling of the setting changes, as you will see in the passages in Exercise C.

EXERCISE C

Read the following passages from "A Worn Path" and answer the questions that follow using the information you have learned in this part of the lesson.

At last she was safe through the fence and risen up out in the clearing. Big dead trees, like black men with one arm, were standing in the purple stalks of the withered cotton field. There sat a buzzard.

"Who you watching?"

In the furrow she made her way along.

She passed through the old cotton and went into a field of dead corn. It whispered and shook and was taller than her head. "Through the maze now," she said, for there was no path.

Then there was something tall, black, and skinny there, moving before her.

At first she took it for a man. It could have been a man dancing in the field. But she stood still and listened, and it did not make a sound. It was silent as a ghost.

"Ghost," she said sharply, "who be you the ghost of? For I have heard of nary death close by."

But there was no answer—only the ragged dancing in the wind.

She shut her eyes, reached out her hand, and touched a sleeve. She found a coat and inside that an emptiness, cold as ice.

"You scarecrow," she said. Her face lighted.

1. The feeling generated by these settings is one of
   □ a. stark terror.
   □ b. excitement.
   □ c. country calm.
   □ d. marginal concern.

2. There are two elements in these passages that make you (and Phoenix, too) think about death. Write down at least one of the elements.

   _____

   _____

   _____

   _____

Now check your answers using the Answer Key at the back of the book. Correct any wrong answers and review this part of the lesson if you do not understand why an answer is wrong.

·4·
Setting and Theme

The setting in a story helps to present the author's ideas. If the author is trying to make the point that nature is in continual conflict with people, he or she would set the story in the bitter cold of the arctic wilderness. Author Jack London used that setting in "To Build a Fire" and other stories where nature, as man's adversary, emerges victorious.

In the first lesson you learned that the Sheridans' garden and the poor cottages in "A Garden Party" were contrasting settings that pointed out class differences that the author was dealing with. In "A Worn Path" the entire route of the journey—the *total* setting—emphasizes the meaning or theme of the story. After each adventure in a part of this larger setting, you find short sentences and phrases like these:

> On she went.
> "Up through pines," she said at length. "Now down through oaks."
> In the furrow she made her way along.

Then she went on, parting her way from side to side. . . .
She followed the track. . . .
"I bound to go on my way, mister," said Phoenix.
. . . she walked up and around and around until her feet knew to stop.

What does all this mean in terms of themes and settings? You are not always so lucky as to have an author's own comments about the meaning of a story, but you are fortunate in this case that Eudora Welty has left you her thoughts about "A Worn Path." Writing in the *New York Times Book Review* (March 5, 1978) she said:

> What I hoped would come clear was that in the whole surround of this story, the world it threads through, the only certain thing at all is the worn path. The habit of love cuts through confusion and stumbles or contrives its way out of difficulty, it remembers the way even when it forgets, for a dumbfounded moment, its reason for being. The path is the thing that matters.

You can apply those thoughts to any determined person in a single-minded pursuit of a goal. Think of someone who is determined to finish college, for example, in spite of many obstacles—lack of money, difficult courses, modest ability, demanding teachers. The important setting, the "whole surround," as Eudora Welty put it, is the school, and the only thing that matters to the student is persevering to see a diploma on the wall as Phoenix Jackson did in the doctor's office.

EXERCISE D

Read the following passage from "A Worn Path" and answer the questions that follow using the information you have learned in this part of the lesson.

> Moving slowly and from side to side, she went into the big building, and into a tower of steps, where she walked up and around and around until her feet knew to stop.
> She entered a door, and there she saw nailed up on the wall the document that had been stamped with the gold seal and framed in the gold frame, which matched the dream that was hung up in her head.
> "Here I be," she said.

1. Phoenix "walked up and around and around until her feet knew to stop." This means that
   □ a. she was extremely weary from the journey.
   □ b. her journey controlled her mind.
   □ c. all along she had been traveling in circles.
   □ d. her spirit was like the tower of steps.

2. Copy the sentence or expression that tells you the diploma represents the goal of Phoenix's journey.

   _____

   _____

   _____

   _____

   _____

   _____

Now check your answers using the Answer Key at the back of the book. Correct any wrong answers and review this part of the lesson if you do not understand why an answer is wrong.

Comprehension Questions

For each of the following statements or questions, select the option that best completes a statement or is the most accurate response to a question.

Recalling Specific Facts

1. Where did Phoenix Jackson live?
   - ☐ a. somewhere along the Mississippi River
   - ☐ b. away back off the Old Natchez Trace
   - ☐ c. in a Natchez, Mississippi, ghetto
   - ☐ d. in the dark pine woods

Recalling Specific Facts

2. What, or who, did Phoenix Jackson see first as she entered the doctor's office?
   - ☐ a. the attendant
   - ☐ b. the nurse
   - ☐ c. a large waiting room
   - ☐ d. the doctor's diploma

Organizing Facts

3. Why did Phoenix encourage the hunter to chase the black dog?
   - ☐ a. She was frightened by the dog.
   - ☐ b. She wanted time to pick up the nickel the man had dropped.
   - ☐ c. She wanted the man and his gun as far away as possible.
   - ☐ d. It was the only way she could continue on her journey.

Organizing Facts

4. Why did Phoenix stop a lady on the street?
   - ☐ a. to ask to have her shoelaces tied
   - ☐ b. to ask directions to the doctor's office
   - ☐ c. to ask for money for a present for her grandson
   - ☐ d. to ask for help because she was tired

Knowledge of Word Meanings

5. Phoenix's cane "made a *grave* and persistent noise in the still air. . . ." Used this way, the word *grave* means
   - ☐ a. like a funeral march.
   - ☐ b. slow and solemn.
   - ☐ c. ghostly.
   - ☐ d. harsh and rasping.

Knowledge of Word Meanings

6. Phoenix's cane "made a grave and *persistent* noise in the still air. . . ."
   What does *persistent* mean?
   □ a. insistent and repetitive
   □ b. noisy and scratching
   □ c. threatening
   □ d. dragging

Drawing a Conclusion

7. You must conclude from the facts of the story and from the title of the story
   that Phoenix Jackson
   □ a. was very tired and worn.
   □ b. found the journey too difficult.
   □ c. hurried on her way.
   □ d. had made the trip many times before.

Drawing a Conclusion

8. As you read about the little boy who offered Phoenix a piece of cake, you had
   to conclude that Phoenix
   □ a. enjoyed cake.
   □ b. was daydreaming.
   □ c. liked children.
   □ d. had become discouraged.

Making a Judgment

9. From comments she made in the story, you would probably judge Phoenix
   to be
   □ a. both religious and a bit superstitious.
   □ b. superstitious about wild creatures.
   □ c. frightened of ghosts and alligators.
   □ d. knowledgeable about herb medicines.

Making a Judgment

10. Considering her dress and actions you must judge Phoenix to be
    □ a. on welfare.
    □ b. not concerned about her appearance.
    □ c. extremely poor.
    □ d. seeking charity.

Making a Judgment

11. On this December day the weather is
    - ☐ a. cold and blustery.
    - ☐ b. sunny but threatening snow.
    - ☐ c. clear and crisp.
    - ☐ d. unusually mild.

Making an Inference

12. From details provided in the story you can infer that Phoenix
    - ☐ a. has very poor vision.
    - ☐ b. has no stamina.
    - ☐ c. is a bit unbalanced.
    - ☐ d. can't make the return trip.

Making an Inference

13. Because she kept noticing the sun and the shadows, you may infer that Phoenix
    - ☐ a. preferred to be in the cool shade.
    - ☐ b. was alert for wild creatures.
    - ☐ c. continuously watched for ghosts.
    - ☐ d. was keeping track of the time this way.

Making an Inference

14. From her attitude you may infer that the attendant in the doctor's office
    - ☐ a. was sympathetic to charity cases.
    - ☐ b. felt disdain for charity cases.
    - ☐ c. was a cruel person.
    - ☐ d. had no feelings for sick people.

Understanding Characters

15. The hunter was
    - ☐ a. condescending to Phoenix but otherwise considerate and helpful.
    - ☐ b. a completely hateful fellow.
    - ☐ c. entirely kindly and thoughtful of the feelings of others.
    - ☐ d. a cruel person toward people and animals.

Understanding Characters

16. Which one of the following words best describes Phoenix?

☐ a. stubborn

☐ b. resolute

☐ c. modest

☐ d. grasping

Understanding Characters

17. How would you say Phoenix conducted herself in the doctor's office?

☐ a. She was dignified.

☐ b. She was impertinent.

☐ c. She was self-demeaning.

☐ d. She was demanding.

Understanding Main Ideas

18. Another good title for the story would be

☐ a. A Trip to the Doctor

☐ b. Natchez

☐ c. Out of Poverty

☐ d. The Goal

Understanding Main Ideas

19. What does the last sentence of the story suggest?—"Then her slow step began on the stairs, going down."

☐ a. It suggests a totally frustrating experience for Phoenix.

☐ b. It suggests a less difficult time ahead for Phoenix and her grandson.

☐ c. It suggests Phoenix is starting on the worn path again.

☐ d. It suggests that this will be a happy Christmas after all.

Recognizing Tone

20. "At last she came to the end, to a wagon track. . . .'Walk pretty,' she said. 'This the easy place.' " At the point where these lines appear in the story you get a feeling of

☐ a. relief.

☐ b. excitement.

☐ c. frustration.

☐ d. understanding.

Recognizing Tone

21. When Phoenix talks about buying her grandson a windmill, she sounds
    - ☐ a. resolute.
    - ☐ b. dissatisfied.
    - ☐ c. resigned.
    - ☐ d. happy.

Recognizing Tone

22. The overall feeling generated by the descriptions of the day, the country scenes, and the city
    - ☐ a. reflects danger and difficulty.
    - ☐ b. is bright and optimistic.
    - ☐ c. provides an atmosphere of gloom.
    - ☐ d. lies heavy on the spirit.

Appreciation of Literary Forms

23. People often use figures of speech to describe how they feel. Which one of the following expressions from the story is a descriptive figure of speech?
    - ☐ a. "Seem like there is chains about my feet, time I get this far."
    - ☐ b. "Out of my way, all you foxes, owls, beetles. . . ."
    - ☐ c. "I wasn't as old as I thought."
    - ☐ d. "Ghost," she said sharply, "who be you the ghost of?"

Appreciation of Literary Forms

24. When human characteristics or actions are given to objects, the figure of speech is called *personification*. Which one of the following expressions is an example of personification?
    - ☐ a. "The sun made the pine needles almost too bright to look at. . . ."
    - ☐ b. " 'Now comes the trial,' said Phoenix."
    - ☐ c. "Thorns, you doing your appointed work."
    - ☐ d. " 'I bound to go to town, mister,' said Phoenix."

Appreciation of Literary Forms

25. "Up above her was a tree in a pearly cloud of mistletoe." The author is describing
    - ☐ a. mistletoe berries which are like little pearls.
    - ☐ b. a dream of trees decorated for Christmas.
    - ☐ c. the clouds as pearl gray.
    - ☐ d. a vision of the pearly gates of heaven.

Now check your answers using the Answer Key at the back of the book. Make no mark for right answers. Correct any wrong answers you may have by putting a check mark (✓) in the box next to the right answer. Count the number of questions you answered correctly and plot the total on the Comprehension Scores Graph at the back of the book.

Next, look at the questions you answered incorrectly. What types of questions were they? Count the number you got wrong of each type and enter the numbers in the spaces below.

Recalling Specific Facts	_____
Organizing Facts	_____
Knowledge of Word Meanings	_____
Drawing a Conclusion	_____
Making a Judgment	_____
Making an Inference	_____
Understanding Characters	_____
Understanding Main Ideas	_____
Recognizing Tone	_____
Appreciation of Literary Forms	_____

Now use these numbers to fill in the Comprehension Skills Profile at the end of the book.

Extension Activities

Discussion Guide

Discussing Setting

1. In what important ways would the story be different if it were set in Chicago in 1973?
2. The time of the story is December at Christmastime. Why is this an appropriate setting in time for the story?
3. What evidence can you find in the elements of the setting that indicate the author had been a country girl herself?

Discussing the Story

4. After reading the story, many readers wrote to Eudora Welty and asked her if Phoenix's grandson were really dead? What do you think? Give reasons for your opinion.
5. When the nurse asks Phoenix about her grandson Phoenix seems to have forgotten him. Then she says, ". . . I forgot it in the coming." How is her remark related to the title of the story, "A Worn Path"?
6. Even a well-written and enjoyable story may have what critics would call a "flaw." For instance, you could question some of Phoenix's adventures as not quite fitting for the character portrayed. Why is it that some of the adventures do not seem quite true?

Discussing the Author's Work

7. There isn't a lot of dialogue in the story, except when Phoenix talks to herself. Why do you think the author has Phoenix talk to herself?
8. Eudora Welty was a young, middle-class, white woman writing a story about an old, poor, black woman. Do you think the author did a good job creating the character of Phoenix Jackson despite these differences? Explain your opinion.
9. Katherine Mansfield set her story "The Garden Party" in New Zealand where she grew up. Eudora Welty set her story in Mississippi where *she* grew up. Many other authors represented in this book also set their stories in the places where they spent their childhoods. Why do you think authors do this so often?

Writing Exercise

1. Reread the first two paragraphs of "A Worn Path."
2. Write at least two paragraphs of your own that could be the beginning of a story.
   - Set the story in a place you know well—preferably a scene you remember from early childhood.
   - Introduce the main character of your story somewhere within the first two paragraphs.

UNIT
Three

Unit Three

Introduction

What the Stories Are About

This unit presents two short stories: "A Summer's Reading" by Bernard Malamud and "My Oedipus Complex" by Frank O'Connor.

A Summer's Reading

George Stoyonovich is a high school dropout, now twenty years old, who is encountering all of the expected problems that go with the lack of a high school diploma—no job, no money, and worst of all no respect from his family and neighbors. In answer to the question, "What do you do all day?" George begins to answer, "Oh, I read a lot."

That was only partly true. While he did leaf through magazines and newspapers, he did not have any patience for real reading. He found, however, that talking about all the reading he did, and all the reading he was going to do, brought him the respect from family and neighbors that he yearned for. He really did intend to start reading, and he even bought a paperback novel or two, but he never read them. How George's self-esteem became wrapped up in unread books is what the story is about.

Author Bernard Malamud grew up in Brooklyn, New York, in the working-class Jewish neighborhoods that later became settings for his stories. He attended the City College of New York and Columbia University, became a high school teacher in the New York City Schools and later a professor of English and visiting lecturer at several universities.

Malamud believed that good writing is writing that has an impact on readers. "To me," he said, "writing must be true; it must have emotional depth; it must be imaginative. It must inflame, destroy, change the reader."

If you would like to read more of Bernard Malamud's work you can find a wealth of material in two of his story collections, *The Magic Barrel* and *Idiots First.*

My Oedipus Complex

Oedipus is a character from ancient Greek drama and mythology who unwittingly killed his father and married his mother. In the early part of the twentieth century, the pioneering psychiatrist Sigmund Freud used the Oedipus myth to describe a theory about the development of children. Young children, Freud believed, go through a stage when they are attracted to the parent of the opposite sex and are hostile toward the other parent. Freud called these feelings an "Oedipus complex" after the unfortunate king in the Greek legend.

Many people are shocked and horrified by the idea of young children having such feelings, but Frank O'Connor decided to turn his Irish sense of humor on the theory. The result is the charming and humorous story which he playfully titled "My Oedipus Complex." It's about a five-year-old boy who decides that three's a crowd when his father returns home from World War I and claims his share of his mother's attention. Just as Freud said, the little boy wants to be rid of his father and marry his mother. Only Frank O'Connor makes the whole thing seem less outrageous and more appealing than Freud ever intended.

Frank O'Connor (1903–1966) is best remembered for his witty and moving stories about Irish family life. He was born Michael John O'Donovan to a poor working family in County Cork, Ireland. Frank O'Connor is his pen name. He was mainly self-educated. Despite his lack of a formal education, he began writing at the age of twelve.

As a young man, O'Connor was active in the revolution for Irish independence, and spent a year in jail for activities with the Irish Republican Army. Even while in jail, however, he managed to continue both his education and his writing. About fifteen years later he became a co-director of the famous Abbey Theatre in Dublin (with William Butler Yeats) and was considered one of the writers who helped create a purely Irish literature early in the twentieth century.

O'Connor was such a prolific writer that you can find many of his story collections in almost every library. If you are interested in finding out more about this fascinating writer, read his autobiography, "My Father's Son," where, among other things, he tells about his "Oedipus Complex," which he confessed was quite real for him when he was growing up.

What the Lesson Is About

The lesson that follows the stories examines the presence of authors in the stories they write. An important part of this is the "point of view" an author uses in telling a story. For example, you have read many stories where a character seems to be talking to you, telling the story in which he or she participated in some way. That character uses first-person pronouns—*I, we, me, us*—to tell the story, and so this point of view is called the *first-person point of view*, or a first-person narration.

Another way of telling a story is for the author to act as an unseen observer and commentator. In this case the author uses third-person pronouns—*he, she, they*—to tell what happens and what people are thinking. That third-person narration is called the *third-person point of view*.

You will also examine other ways that authors participate in their stories: how the author stages and manages a story, how the author speaks for the characters, and how the author observes and interprets a story for readers.

As you read the stories, try to keep the following questions in mind. They will help you to see how authors present their characters.

1. Who is telling the story in each case? Is the narrator a part of the story or an unknown person in the background telling what is happening? (One of the stories you will read is told as a first-person narration; the other is a third-person narration.)

2. You will notice that the authors skip from place to place and from one time to another in the course of telling the stories. How do the authors manage things so that the stories come out just the way they want them to?

3. How do the authors present their characters? Who is really speaking when a character talks or thinks?

4. How do the authors help readers understand the events and characters in their stories?

A Summer's Reading

by Bernard Malamud

*G*eorge Stoyonovich was a neighborhood boy who had quit
high school on an impulse when he was sixteen, run out of
patience, and though he was ashamed everytime he went looking
for a job, when people asked him if he had finished and he had to
say no, he never went back to school. This summer was a hard time
for jobs and he had none. Having so much time on his hands,
George thought of going to summer school, but the kids in his
classes would be too young. He also considered registering in a
night high school, only he didn't like the idea of the teachers
always telling him what to do. He felt they had not respected him.
The result was he stayed off the streets and in his room most of
the day. He was close to twenty and had needs with the neighborhood girls, but no money to spend, and he couldn't get more
than an occasional few cents because his father was poor, and his
sister Sophie, who resembled George, a tall bony girl of twenty-
three, earned very little and what she had she kept for herself. Their
mother was dead, and Sophie had to take care of the house.

Very early in the morning George's father got up to go to work
in a fish market. Sophie left at about eight for her long ride in the
subway to a cafeteria in the Bronx. George had his coffee by
himself, then hung around in the house. When the house, a five-
room railroad flat above a butcher store, got on his nerves he
cleaned it up—mopped the floors with a wet mop and put things
away. But most of the time he sat in his room. In the afternoons
he listened to the ball game. Otherwise he had a couple of old copies
of the *World Almanac* he had bought long ago, and he liked to
read in them and also the magazines and newspapers that Sophie
brought home, that had been left on the tables in the cafeteria.
They were mostly picture magazines about movie stars and sports
figures, also usually the *News* and *Mirror*. Sophie herself read

whatever fell into her hands, although she sometimes read good books.

She once asked George what he did in his room all day and he said he read a lot too.

"Of what besides what I bring home? Do you ever read any worthwhile books?"

"Some," George answered, although he really didn't. He had tried to read a book or two that Sophie had in the house but found he was in no mood for them. Lately he couldn't stand made-up stories, they got on his nerves. He wished he had some hobby to work at— as a kid he was good in carpentry, but where could he work at it? Sometimes during the day he went for walks, but mostly he did his walking after the hot sun had gone down and it was cooler in the streets.

In the evening after supper George left the house and wandered in the neighborhood. During the sultry days some of the storekeepers and their wives sat in chairs on the thick, broken sidewalks in front of their shops, fanning themselves, and George walked past them and the guys hanging out on the candy store corner. A couple of them he had known his whole life, but nobody recognized each other. He had no place special to go, but generally, saving it till the last, he left the neighborhood and walked for blocks till he came to a darkly lit little park with benches and trees and an iron railing, giving it a feeling of privacy. He sat on a bench here, watching the leafy trees and the flowers blooming on the inside of the railing, thinking of a better life for himself. He thought of the jobs he had had since he had quit school—delivery boy, stock clerk, runner, lately working in a factory—and he was dissatisfied with all of them. He felt he would someday like to have a good job and live in a private house with a porch, on a street with trees. He wanted to have some dough in his pocket to buy things with, and a girl to go with, so as not to be so lonely, especially on Saturday nights. He wanted people to like and respect him. He thought about these things often but mostly when he was alone at night. Around midnight he got up and drifted back to his hot and stony neighborhood.

One time while on his walk George met Mr. Cattanzara coming home very late from work. He wondered if he was drunk but then could tell he wasn't. Mr. Cattanzara, a stocky, bald-headed man who worked in a change booth on an IRT station, lived on the next block after George's, above a shoe repair store. Nights, during the hot weather, he sat on his stoop in an undershirt, reading the *New York Times* in the light of the shoemaker's window. He read it from the first page to the last, then went up to sleep. And all the time he was reading the paper, his wife, a fat woman with a white face, leaned out of the window, gazing into the street, her thick white arms folded under her loose breast, on the window ledge.

Once in a while Mr. Cattanzara came home drunk, but it was a quiet drunk. He never made any trouble, only walked stiffly up the street and slowly climbed the stairs into the hall. Though drunk, he looked the same as always, except for his tight walk, the quietness, and that his eyes were wet. George liked Mr. Cattanzara because he remembered him giving him nickels to buy lemon ice with when he was a squirt. Mr. Cattanzara was a different type than those in the neighborhood. He asked different questions than the others when he met you, and he seemed to know what went on in all the newspapers. He read them, as his fat sick wife watched from the window.

"What are you doing with yourself this summer, George?" Mr. Cattanzara asked. "I see you walkin' around at nights."

George felt embarrassed. "I like to walk."

"What are you doin' in the day now?"

"Nothing much just right now. I'm waiting for a job." Since it shamed him to admit he wasn't working, George said, "I'm staying home—but I'm reading a lot to pick up my education."

Mr. Cattanzara looked interested. He mopped his hot face with a red handkerchief.

"What are you readin'?"

George hesitated, then said, "I got a list of books in the library once, now I'm gonna read them this summer." He felt strange and a little unhappy saying this, but he wanted Mr. Cattanzara to respect him.

"How many books are there on it?"

"I never counted them. Maybe around a hundred."

Mr. Cattanzara whistled through his teeth.

"I figure if I did that," George went on earnestly, "it would help me in my education. I don't mean the kind they give you in high school. I want to know different things than they learn there, if you know what I mean."

The change maker nodded. "Still and all, one hundred books is a pretty big load for one summer."

"It might take longer."

"After you're finished with some, maybe you and I can shoot the breeze about them?" said Mr. Cattanzara.

"When I'm finished," George answered.

Mr. Cattanzara went home and George continued on his walk. After that, though he had the urge to, George did nothing different from usual. He still took his walks at night, ending up in the little park. But one evening the shoemaker on the next block stopped George to say he was a good boy, and George figured that Mr. Cattanzara had told him all about the books he was reading. From the shoemaker it must have gone down the street, because George saw a couple of people smiling kindly at him, though nobody spoke to him personally. He felt a little better around the neighborhood and liked it more, though not so much he would want to live in it forever. He had never exactly disliked the people in it, yet he had never liked them very much either. It was the fault of the neighborhood. To his surprise, George found out that his father and Sophie knew about his reading too. His father was too shy to say anything about it—he was never much of a talker in his whole life—but Sophie was softer to George, and she showed him in other ways she was proud of him.

As the summer went on George felt in a good mood about things. He cleaned the house every day, as a favor to Sophie, and he enjoyed the ball games more. Sophie gave him a buck a week allowance, and though it still wasn't enough and he had to use it carefully, it was a helluva lot better than just having two bits now and then. What he bought with the money—cigarettes mostly, an occasional beer or movie ticket—he got a big kick out of. Life wasn't so bad if you knew how to appreciate it. Occasionally he bought a paperback book from the newsstand, but he never got around to reading it, though he was glad to have a couple of books in his room. But he read thoroughly Sophie's magazines and newspapers. And at night was the most enjoyable time, because when he passed the storekeepers sitting outside their stores, he could tell they regarded him highly. He walked erect, and though he did not say much to them, or they to him, he could feel approval on all sides. A couple of nights he felt so good that he skipped the park at the end of the evening. He just wandered in the neighborhood, where people had known him from the time he was a kid playing punchball whenever there was a game of it going; he wandered there, then came home and got undressed for bed, feeling fine.

For a few weeks he had talked only once with Mr. Cattanzara, and though the change maker had said nothing more about the books, asked no questions, his silence made George a little uneasy. For a while George didn't pass in front of Mr. Cattanzara's house anymore, until one night, forgetting himself, he approached it from a different direction than he usually did when he did. It was already past midnight. The street, except for one or two people, was deserted, and George was surprised when he saw Mr. Cattanzara still reading his newspaper by the light of the street lamp overhead. His impulse was to stop at the stoop and talk to him. He wasn't sure what he wanted to say, though he felt the words would come when he began to talk; but the more he thought about it, the more the idea scared him, and he decided he'd better not. He even considered beating it home by another street, but he was too near Mr. Cattanzara, and the change maker might see him as he ran, and get annoyed. So George unobtrusively crossed the street, trying to make it seem as if he had to look in a store window on the other side, which he did, and then went on, uncomfortable at what he was doing. He feared Mr. Cattanzara would glance up from his paper and call him a dirty rat for walking on the other side of the street, but all he did was sit there, sweating through his undershirt, his bald head shining in the dim light as he read his *Times,* and upstairs his fat wife leaned out of the window, seeming to read the paper along with him. George thought she would spy him and yell out to Mr. Cattanzara, but she never moved her eyes off her husband.

George made up his mind to stay away from the change maker until he got some of his softback books read, but when he started them and saw they were mostly story books, he lost his interest and didn't bother to finish them. He lost his interest in reading other things too. Sophie's magazines and newspapers went unread. She saw them piling up on a chair in his room and asked why he was no longer looking at them, and George told her it was because of all the other reading he had to do. Sophie said she had guessed that was it. So for most of the day, George had the radio on, turning to music when he was sick of the human voice. He kept the house fairly neat, and Sophie said nothing on the days when he neglected it. She was still kind and gave him his extra buck, though things weren't so good for him as they had been before.

But they were good enough, considering. Also his night walks invariably picked him up, no matter how bad the day was. Then one night George saw Mr. Cattanzara coming down the street toward him. George was about to turn and run but he recognized from Mr. Cattanzara's walk that he was drunk, and if so, probably he would not even bother to notice him. So George kept on walking straight ahead until he came abreast of Mr. Cattanzara and though he felt wound up enough to pop into the sky, he was not surprised when Mr. Cattanzara passed him without a word, walking slowly, his face and body stiff. George drew a breath in relief at his narrow escape, when he heard his name called, and there stood Mr. Cattanzara at his elbow, smelling like the inside of a beer barrel. His eyes were sad as he gazed at George, and George felt so intensely uncomfortable he was tempted to shove the drunk aside and continue on his walk.

But he couldn't act that way to him, and, besides, Mr. Cattanzara took a nickel out of his pants pocket and handed it to him.

"Go buy yourself a lemon ice, Georgie."

"It's not that time anymore, Mr. Cattanzara," George said, "I'm a big guy now."

"No, you ain't," said Mr. Cattanzara, to which George made no reply he could think of.

"How are all your books comin' along now?" Mr. Cattanzara asked. Though he tried to stand steady, he swayed a little.

"Fine, I guess," said George, feeling the red crawling up his face.

"You ain't sure?" The change maker smiled slyly, a way George had never seen him smile.

"Sure I'm sure. They're fine."

Though his head swayed in little arcs, Mr. Cattanzara's eyes were steady. He had small blue eyes which could hurt if you looked at them too long.

"George," he said, "name me one book on that list that you read this summer, and I will drink to your health."

"I don't want anybody drinking to me."

"Name me one so I can ask you a question on it. Who can tell, if it's a good book maybe I might wanna read it myself."

George knew he looked passable on the outside, but inside he was crumbling apart.

Unable to reply, he shut his eyes, but when—years later—he opened them, he saw that Mr. Cattanzara had, out of pity, gone away, but in his ears he still heard the words he had said when he left: "George, don't do what I did."

The next night he was afraid to leave his room, and though Sophie argued with him he wouldn't open the door.

"What are you doing in there?" she asked.

"Nothing."

"Are you reading?"

"No."

She was silent a minute, then asked, "Where do you keep the books you read? I never see any in your room outside of a few cheap trashy ones."

He wouldn't tell her.

"In that case you're not worth a buck of my hard-earned money. Why should I break my back for you? Go on out, you bum, and get a job."

He stayed in his room for almost a week, except to sneak into the kitchen when nobody was home. Sophie railed at him, then begged him to come out, and his old father wept, but George wouldn't budge, though the weather was terrible and his small room stifling. He found it very hard to breathe, each breath was like drawing a flame into his lungs.

One night, unable to stand the heat anymore, he burst into the street at one A.M., a shadow of himself. He hoped to sneak to the park without being seen, but there were people all over the block, wilted and listless, waiting for a breeze. George lowered his eyes and walked, in disgrace, away from them, but before long he discovered they were still friendly to him. He figured Mr. Cattanzara hadn't told on him. Maybe when he woke up out of his drunk the next morning, he had forgotten all about meeting George. George felt his confidence slowly come back to him.

That same night a man on the street corner asked him if it was true that he had finished reading so many books, and George admitted he had. The man said it was a wonderful thing for a boy his age to read so much.

"Yeah," George said, but he felt relieved. He hoped nobody would mention the books anymore, and when, after a couple of days, he accidentally met Mr. Cattanzara again, *he* didn't, though George had the idea he was the one who had started the rumor that he had finished all the books.

One evening in the fall, George ran out of his house to the library, where he hadn't been in years. There were books all over the place, wherever he looked, and though he was struggling to control an inward trembling, he easily counted off a hundred, then sat down at a table to read.

My Oedipus Complex

by Frank O'Connor

Father was in the Army all through the war—the first war, I mean—so, up to the age of five, I never saw much of him, and what I saw did not worry me. Sometimes I woke and there was a big figure in khaki peering down at me in the candlelight. Sometimes in the early morning I heard the slamming of the front door and the clatter of nailed boots down the cobbles of the lane. These were Father's entrances and exits. Like Santa Claus he came and went mysteriously.

In fact, I rather liked his visits, though it was an uncomfortable squeeze between Mother and him when I got into the big bed in the early morning. He smoked, which gave him a pleasant musty smell, and shaved, an operation of astounding interest. Each time he left a trail of souvenirs—model tanks and Gurkha knives with handles made of bullet cases, and German helmets and cap badges and button-sticks, and all sorts of military equipment—carefully stowed away in a long box on top of the wardrobe, in case they ever came in handy. There was a bit of the magpie about Father; he expected everything to come in handy. When his back was turned, Mother let me get a chair and rummage through his treasures. She didn't seem to think so highly of them as he did.

The war was the most peaceful period of my life. The window of my attic faced southeast. My mother had curtained it, but that had small effect. I always woke with the first light and, with all the responsibilities of the previous day melted, feeling myself rather like the sun, ready to illumine and rejoice. Life never seemed so simple and clear and full of possibilities as then. I put my feet out from under the clothes—I called them Mrs. Left and Mrs. Right—and invented dramatic situations for them in which they discussed the problems of the day. At least Mrs. Right did; she was very demonstrative, but I hadn't the same control of Mrs. Left, so she mostly contented herself with nodding agreement.

They discussed what Mother and I should do during the day, what Santa Claus should give a fellow for Christmas, and what steps should be taken to brighten the home. There was that little matter of the baby, for instance. Mother and I could never agree about that. Ours was the only house in the terrace without a new baby, and Mother said we couldn't afford one till Father came back from the war because they cost seventeen and six. That showed how simple she was. The Geneys up the road had a baby, and everyone knew they couldn't afford seventeen and six. It was probably a cheap baby, and Mother wanted something really good, but I felt she was too exclusive. The Geneys' baby would have done us fine.

Having settled my plans for the day, I got up, put a chair under the attic window, and lifted the frame high enough to stick out my head. The window overlooked the front gardens of the terrace behind ours, and beyond these it looked over a deep valley to the tall, red-brick houses terraced up the opposite hillside, which were all still in shadow, while those at our side of the valley were all lit up, though with long strange shadows that made them seem unfamiliar; rigid and painted.

After that I went into Mother's room and climbed into the big bed. She woke and I began to tell her of my schemes. By this time, though I never seem to have noticed it, I was petrified in my nightshirt, and I thawed as I talked until, the last frost melted, I fell asleep beside her and woke again only when I heard her below in the kitchen, making the breakfast.

After breakfast we went into town; heard Mass at St. Augustine's and said a prayer for Father, and did the shopping. If the afternoon was fine we either went for a walk in the country or a visit to Mother's great friend in the convent, Mother St. Dominic. Mother had them all praying for Father, and every night, going to bed, I asked God to send him back safe from the war to us. Little, indeed, did I know what I was praying for!

One morning, I got into the big bed, and there, sure enough, was Father in his usual Santa Claus manner, but later, instead of uniform, he put on his best blue suit, and Mother was as pleased as anything. I saw nothing to be pleased about, because, out of uniform, Father was altogether less interesting, but she only beamed, and explained that our prayers had been answered, and off we went to Mass to thank God for having brought Father safely home.

The irony of it! That very day when he came in to dinner he took off his boots and put on his slippers, donned the dirty old cap he wore about the house to save him from colds, crossed his legs, and began to talk gravely to Mother, who looked anxious. Naturally, I disliked her looking anxious, because it destroyed her good looks, so I interrupted him.

"Just a moment, Larry!" she said gently.

This was only what she said when we had boring visitors, so I attached no importance to it and went on talking.

"Do be quiet, Larry!" she said impatiently. "Don't you hear me talking to Daddy?"

This was the first time I had heard those ominous words, "talking to Daddy," and I couldn't help feeling that if this was how God answered prayers, he couldn't listen to them very attentively.

"Why are you talking to Daddy?" I asked with as great a show of indifference as I could muster.

"Because Daddy and I have business to discuss. Now, don't interrupt again!"

In the afternoon, at Mother's request, Father took me for a walk. This time we went into town instead of out in the country, and I thought at first, in my usual optimistic way, that it might be an improvement. It was nothing of the sort. Father and I had quite different notions of a walk in town. He had no proper interest in trams, ships, and horses, and the only thing that seemed to divert him was talking to fellows as old as himself. When I wanted to stop he simply went on, dragging me behind him by the hand; when he wanted to stop I had no alternative but to do the same. I noticed that it seemed to be a sign that he wanted to stop for a long time whenever he leaned against a wall. The second time I saw him do it I got wild. He seemed to be settling himself forever. I pulled him by the coat and trousers, but, unlike Mother who, if you were too persistent, got into a wax and said: "Larry, if you don't behave yourself, I'll give you a good slap," Father had an extraordinary capacity for amiable inattention. I sized him up and wondered would I cry, but he seemed to be too remote to be annoyed even by that. Really, it was like going for a walk with a mountain! He either ignored the wrenching and pummeling entirely, or else glanced down with a grin of amusement from his peak. I had never met anyone so absorbed in himself as he seemed.

At teatime, "talking to Daddy" began again, complicated this time by the fact that he had an evening paper, and every few minutes he put it down and told Mother something new out of it. I felt this was foul play. Man for man, I was prepared to compete with him any time for Mother's attention, but when he had it all made up for him by other people it left me no chance. Several times I tried to change the subject without success.

"You must be quiet while Daddy is reading, Larry," Mother said impatiently.

It was clear that she either genuinely liked talking to Father better than talking to me, or else that he had some terrible hold on her which made her afraid to admit the truth.

"Mummy," I said that night when she was tucking me up, "do you think if I prayed hard God would send Daddy back to war?"

She seemed to think about that for a moment.

"No, dear," she said with a smile. "I don't think He would."

"Why wouldn't He, Mummy?"

"Because there isn't a war any longer, dear."

"But, Mummy, couldn't God make another war, if He liked?"

"He wouldn't like to, dear. It's not God who makes wars, but bad people."

"Oh!" I said.

I was disappointed about that. I began to think that God wasn't quite what He was cracked up to be.

Next morning I woke at my usual hour, feeling like a bottle of champagne. I put out my feet and invented a long conversation in which Mrs. Right talked of the trouble she had with her own father till she put him in the Home. I didn't quite know what the Home was but it sounded the right place for Father. Then I got my chair and stuck my head out of the attic window. Dawn was just breaking, with a guilty air that made me feel I had caught it in the act. My head bursting with stories and schemes, I stumbled in next door, and in the half-darkness scrambled into the big bed. There was no room at Mother's side so I had to get between her and Father. For the time being I had forgotten about him, and for several minutes I sat bolt upright, racking my brains to know what

I could do with him. He was taking up more than his fair share of the bed, and I couldn't get comfortable, so I gave him several kicks that made him grunt and stretch. He made room all right, though. Mother waked and felt for me. I settled back comfortably in the warmth of the bed with my thumb in my mouth.

"Mummy!" I hummed, loudly and contentedly.

"Sssh! dear," she whispered. "Don't wake Daddy!"

This was a new development, which threatened to be even more serious than "talking to Daddy." Life without my early-morning conferences was unthinkable.

"Why?" I asked severely.

"Because poor Daddy is tired."

This seemed to me a quite inadequate reason, and I was sickened by the sentimentality of her "poor Daddy." I never liked that sort of gush; it always struck me as insincere.

"Oh!" I said lightly. Then in my most winning tone: "Do you know where I want to go with you today, Mummy?"

"No, dear," she sighed.

"I want to go down the Glen and fish for thornybacks with my new net, and then I want to go out to the Fox and Hounds, and—"

"Don't-wake-Daddy!" she hissed angrily, clapping her hand across my mouth.

But it was too late. He was awake, or nearly so. He grunted and reached for the matches. Then he stared incredulously at his watch.

"Like a cup of tea, dear?" asked Mother in a meek, hushed voice I had never heard her use before. It sounded almost as though she were afraid.

"Tea?" he exclaimed indignantly. "Do you know what the time is?"

"And after that I want to go up the Rathcooney Road," I said loudly, afraid I'd forget something in all those interruptions.

"Go to sleep at once, Larry!" she said sharply.

I began to snivel. I couldn't concentrate, the way that pair went on, and smothering my early-morning schemes was like burying a family from the cradle.

Father said nothing, but lit his pipe and sucked it, looking out into the shadows without minding Mother or me. I knew he was mad. Every time I made a remark Mother hushed me irritably. I was mortified. I felt it wasn't fair; there was even something sinister in it. Every time I had pointed out to her the waste of making two beds when we could both sleep in one, she had told me it was healthier like that, and now here was this man, this stranger, sleeping with her without the least regard for her health!

He got up early and made tea, but though he brought Mother a cup he brought none for me.

"Mummy," I shouted, "I want a cup of tea, too."

"Yes, dear," she said patiently. "You can drink from Mummy's saucer."

That settled it. Either Father or I would have to leave the house. I didn't want to drink from Mother's saucer; I wanted to be treated as an equal in my own home, so, just to spite her, I drank it all and left none for her. She took that quietly, too.

But that night when she was putting me to bed she said gently:

"Larry, I want you to promise me something."

"What is it?" I asked.

"Not to come in and disturb poor Daddy in the morning. Promise?"

"Poor Daddy" again! I was becoming suspicious of everything involving that quite impossible man.

"Why?" I asked.

"Because poor Daddy is worried and tired and he doesn't sleep well."

"Why doesn't he, Mummy?"

"Well, you know, don't you, that while he was at the war Mummy got the pennies from the Post Office?"

"From Miss MacCarthy?"

"That's right. But now, you see, Miss MacCarthy hasn't any more pennies, so Daddy must go out and find us some. You know what would happen if he couldn't?"

"No," I said, "tell us."

"Well, I think we might have to go out and beg for them like the poor old woman on Fridays. We wouldn't like that, would we?"

"No," I agreed. "We wouldn't."

"So you'll promise not to come in and wake him?"

"Promise."

Mind you, I meant that. I knew pennies were a serious matter, and I was all against having to go out and beg like the old woman on Fridays. Mother laid out all my toys in a complete ring round the bed so that, whatever way I got out, I was bound to fall over one of them.

When I woke I remembered my promise all right. I got up and sat on the floor and played—for hours, it seemed to me. Then I got my chair and looked out the attic window for more hours. I wished it was time for Father to wake; I wished someone would make me a cup of tea. I didn't feel in the least like the sun; instead, I was bored and so very, very cold! I simply longed for the warmth and depth of the big featherbed.

At last I could stand it no longer. I went into the next room. As there was still no room at Mother's side I climbed over her and she woke with a start.

"Larry," she whispered, gripping my arm very tightly, "what did you promise?"

"But I did, Mummy," I wailed, caught in the very act. "I was quiet for ever so long."

"Oh, dear, and you're perished!" she said sadly, feeling me all over. "Now, if I let you stay will you promise not to talk?"

"But I want to talk, Mummy," I wailed.

"That has nothing to do with it," she said with a firmness that was new to me. "Daddy wants to sleep. Now, do you understand that?"

I understood it only too well. I wanted to talk, he wanted to sleep—whose house was it, anyway?

"Mummy," I said with equal firmness, "I think it would be healthier for Daddy to sleep in his own bed."

That seemed to stagger her, because she said nothing for a while.

"Now, once and for all," she went on, "you're to be perfectly quiet or go back to your own bed. Which is it to be?"

The injustice of it got me down. I had convicted her out of her own mouth of inconsistency and unreasonableness, and she hadn't even attempted to reply. Full of spite, I gave Father a kick, which she didn't notice but which made him grunt and open his eyes in alarm.

"What time is it?" he asked in a panic-stricken voice, not looking at Mother but at the door, as if he saw someone there.

"It's early yet," she replied soothingly. "It's only the child. Go to sleep again. . . . Now, Larry," she added, getting out of bed, "you've wakened Daddy and you must go back."

This time, for all her quiet air, I knew she meant it, and knew that my principal rights and privileges were as good as lost unless I asserted them at once. As she lifted me, I gave a screech, enough to wake the dead, not to mind Father. He groaned.

"That damn child! Doesn't he ever sleep?"

"It's only a habit, dear," she said quietly, though I could see she was vexed.

"Well, it's time he got out of it," shouted Father, beginning to heave in the bed. He suddenly gathered all the bedclothes about him, turned to the wall, and then looked back over his shoulder with nothing showing only two small, spiteful, dark eyes. The man looked very wicked.

To open the bedroom door, Mother had to let me down, and I broke free and dashed for the farthest corner, screeching. Father sat bolt upright in bed.

"Shut up, you little puppy!" he said in a choking voice.

I was so astonished that I stopped screeching. Never, never had anyone spoken to me in that tone before. I looked at him incredulously and saw his face convulsed with rage. It was only then that I fully realized how God had codded me, listening to my prayers for the safe return of this monster.

"Shut up, you!" I bawled, beside myself.

"What's that you said?" shouted Father, making a wild leap out of the bed.

"Mick, Mick!" cried Mother. "Don't you see the child isn't used to you?"

"I see he's better fed than taught," snarled Father, waving his arms wildly. "He wants his bottom smacked."

All his previous shouting was as nothing to these obscene words referring to my person. They really made my blood boil.

"Smack your own!" I screamed hysterically. "Smack your own! Shut up! Shut up!"

At this he lost his patience and let fly at me. He did it with the lack of conviction you'd expect of a man under Mother's horrified eyes, and it ended up as a mere tap, but the sheer indignity of being struck at all by a stranger, a total stranger who had cajoled his way back from the war into our big bed as a result of my innocent intercession, made me completely dotty. I shrieked and shrieked, and danced in my bare feet, and Father, looking awkward and hairy in nothing but a short grey army shirt, glared down at me like a mountain out for murder. I think it must have been then that I realized he was jealous too. And there stood Mother in her nightdress, looking as if her heart was broken between us. I hoped she felt as she looked. It seemed to me that she deserved it all.

From that morning out my life was a hell. Father and I were enemies, open and avowed. We conducted a series of skirmishes against one another, he trying to steal my time with Mother and I his. When she was sitting on my bed, telling me a story, he took to looking for some pair of old boots which he alleged he had left behind him at the beginning of the war. While he talked to Mother I played loudly with my toys to show my total lack of concern. He created a terrible scene one evening when he came in from work and found me at his box, playing with his regimental badges, Gurkha knives and button-sticks. Mother got up and took the box from me.

"You mustn't play with Daddy's toys unless he lets you, Larry," she said severely. "Daddy doesn't play with yours."

For some reason Father looked at her as if she had struck him and then turned away with a scowl.

"Those are not toys," he growled, taking down the box again to see had I lifted anything. "Some of those curios are very rare and valuable."

But as time went on I saw more and more how he managed to alienate Mother and me. What made it worse was that I couldn't grasp his method or see what attraction he had for Mother. In every possible way he was less winning than I. He had a common accent and made noises at his tea. I thought for a while that it might be the newspapers she was interested in, so I made up bits of news of my own to read to her. Then I thought it might be the smoking, which I personally thought attractive, and took his pipes and went round the house dribbling into them till he caught me. I even made noises at my tea, but Mother only told me I was disgusting. It all seemed to hinge round that unhealthy habit of sleeping together, so I made a point of dropping into their bedroom and nosing round, talking to myself, so that they wouldn't know I was watching them, but they were never up to anything that I could see. In the end it beat me. It seemed to depend on being grown-up and giving people rings, and I realized I'd have to wait.

But at the same time I wanted him to see that I was only waiting, not giving up the fight. One evening when he was being particularly obnoxious, chattering away well above my head, I let him have it.

"Mummy," I said, "do you know what I'm going to do when I grow up?"

"No, dear," she replied. "What?"

"I'm going to marry you," I said quietly.

Father gave a great guffaw out of him, but he didn't take me in. I knew it must only be pretense. And Mother, in spite of everything, was pleased. I felt she was probably relieved to know that one day Father's hold on her would be broken.

"Won't that be nice?" she said with a smile.

"It'll be very nice," I said confidently. "Because we're going to have lots and lots of babies."

"That's right, dear," she said placidly. "I think we'll have one soon, and then you'll have plenty of company."

I was no end pleased about that because it showed that in spite of the way she gave in to Father she still considered my wishes. Besides, it would put the Geneys in their place.

It didn't turn out like that, though. To begin with, she was very preoccupied—I supposed about where she would get the seventeen and six—and though Father took to staying out late in the evenings it did me no particular good. She stopped taking me for walks, became as touchy as blazes, and smacked me for nothing at all. Sometimes I wished I'd never mentioned the confounded baby—I seemed to have a genius for bringing calamity on myself.

And calamity it was! Sonny arrived in the most appalling hullabaloo—even that much he couldn't do without a fuss—and from the first moment I disliked him. He was a difficult child—so far as I was concerned he was always difficult—and demanded far too much attention. Mother was simply silly about him, and couldn't see when he was only showing off. As company he was worse than useless. He slept all day, and I had to go round the house on tiptoe to avoid waking him. It wasn't any longer a question of not waking Father. The slogan now was "Don't-wake-Sonny!" I couldn't understand why the child wouldn't sleep at the proper time, so whenever Mother's back was turned I woke him.

Sometimes to keep him awake I pinched him as well. Mother caught me at it one day and gave me a most unmerciful flaking.

One evening, when Father was coming in from work, I was playing trains in the front garden. I let on not to notice him; instead, I pretended to be talking to myself, and said in a loud voice: "If another bloody baby comes into this house, I'm going out."

Father stopped dead and looked at me over his shoulder.

"What's that you said?" he asked sternly.

"I was only talking to myself," I replied, trying to conceal my panic. "It's private."

He turned and went in without a word. Mind you, I intended it as a solemn warning, but its effect was quite different. Father started being quite nice to me. I could understand that, of course. Mother was quite sickening about Sonny. Even at mealtimes she'd get up and gawk at him in the cradle with an idiotic smile, and tell Father to do the same. He was always polite about it, but he looked so puzzled you could see he didn't know what she was talking about. He complained of the way Sonny cried at night, but she only got cross and said that Sonny never cried except when there was something up with him—which was a flaming lie, because Sonny never had anything up with him, and only cried for attention. It was really painful to see how simple-minded she was. Father wasn't attractive, but he had a fine intelligence. He saw through Sonny, and now he knew that I saw through him as well.

One night I woke with a start. There was someone beside me in the bed. For one wild moment I felt sure it must be Mother, having come to her senses and left Father for good, but then I heard Sonny in convulsions in the next room, and Mother saying: "There! There! There!" and I knew it wasn't she. It was Father. He was lying beside me, wide awake, breathing hard and apparently as mad as hell.

After a while it came to me what he was mad about. It was his turn now. After turning me out of the big bed, he had been turned out himself. Mother had no consideration now for anyone but that poisonous pup, Sonny. I couldn't help feeling sorry for Father. I had been through it all myself, and even at that age I was magnanimous. I began to stroke him down and say: "There! There!" He wasn't exactly responsive.

"Aren't you asleep either?" he snarled.

"Ah, come on and put your arm around us, can't you?" I said, and he did, in a sort of way. Gingerly, I suppose, is how you'd describe it. He was very bony but better than nothing.

At Christmas he went out of his way to buy me a really nice model railway.

Point of View

One of the first things an author has to decide when writing a story is who will tell it and how it will be told. The author is always in charge, of course; it is always the author speaking, managing things, telling you what is happening. But once you become immersed in a story you are not interested in authors; you become interested in the characters and their actions. Authors, therefore, try to be as unobtrusive as possible when telling their tales. They try to allow you to be alone with the characters so that you can enjoy yourself without being bothered by an author's intrusions. Authors do this in several ways:

1. Authors adopt a "voice" or point of view that is suitable for the story.
2. Authors manage their stories, selecting details and actions that make the stories turn out the way they want them to.
3. Authors speak for the characters and control their actions.
4. Authors direct your understanding of their stories.

· I ·
The Author's Voice or Point of View

First-Person Narration

A first-person narration, or point of view, is easy to identify by the way the author uses first-person pronouns in telling the story—*I, me, my, we, us, our.* A character within the story narrates, or tells the tale from that character's point of view. Here is an example of first-person point of view from "My Oedipus Complex."

> [Mrs. Left foot and Mrs. Right foot] discussed what Mother and I should do during the day, what Santa Claus should give a fellow for Christmas, and what steps should be taken to brighten the home. There was that little matter of the baby, for instance. Mother and I could never agree about that. Ours was the only house in the terrace without a new baby, and Mother said we couldn't afford one till Father came back from the war. . . .

Consider for a moment who this "first person" is. Is it a little boy of five speaking? Or is it a grown man thinking back and telling about his childhood? If it's a grown man, is this man the author or a character invented by the author?

You can always assume that in a story designated as *fiction* a first-person narrator is a character invented by the author, just as all the other characters are invented. The author is writing the story, of course, and has made up the character to tell the story. The character may be an important player in the story, as Larry is, or the narrating character may be a minor player or observer remembering events that happened to other people.

Frank O'Connor explains in his autobiography that as a child he was, as a matter of fact, jealous of the affection his mother showed toward his father, who tended to be abusive and drank too much. So Larry of "My Oedipus Complex" might resemble the author. But the time is wrong, for one thing, for this to be a *true* story. The story is set about 1918, during World War I. Frank O'Connor was a teenager then, not a five-year-old child. First-person narrators in stories may grow out of authors' experiences, but they are made-up characters nevertheless. For example, Phoenix Jackson in "A Worn Path" was a character who originated from Eudora Welty's personal experience, but Phoenix was embellished by the author's imagination to become part of a made-up story.

As you read further into "My Oedipus Complex," the adult narrator speaking as "I" seems to slip further and further into the background until you imagine it is five-year-old Larry who is actually telling the story. This is especially true during dialogue:

"Mummy," I said that night when she was tucking me up, "do you think if I prayed hard God would send Daddy back to war?"

A large part of the charm and humor of this story is in the childlike simplicity or *naïveté* (nah-EEV-tay) in the telling of it. In such cases it is said that the first-person narrator is a *naive* narrator. The little boy faithfully relates what he sees and what he thinks in his little-boy mind, but obviously he does not fully understand what is happening. As the reader, you do understand, of course, and therein lies the appeal of the story.

In other stories in this book you will find first-person narrators who are adults and not so simple or naive as little Larry is. In William Faulkner's "A Rose for Emily," the first-person narrator is an unidentified townsman who has no active role in the story. In James Baldwin's "Sonny's Blues" the narrator is the adult older brother of Sonny, and he plays an important part in the story. In Edgar Allan Poe's "The Black Cat" the storyteller is the main character of the tale who tells his story while waiting to be hanged for the murder of his wife. These are all variations of the first-person point of view in storytelling.

Third-Person Narration

A third-person narration, or point of view, can be identified by the author's use of third-person pronouns—*he, she, his, her, they*—spoken by a narrator who is obviously outside the story. You get the feeling that this narrator can see and hear everything that is happening, including the thoughts inside the minds of the characters. What is more, this all-knowing narrator can tell what is going on in several places at once and at all times in the past or present. To be all-knowing is to be *omniscient*. Therefore, such a narrator is also called an *omniscient narrator*. You can see how this works in the opening paragraph of "A Summer's Reading."

> George Stoyonovich was a neighborhood boy who had quit high school on an impulse when he was sixteen, run out of patience, and though he was ashamed everytime he went looking for a job, when people asked him if he had finished and he had to say no, he never went back to school. This summer was a hard time for jobs and he had none. Having so much time on his hands, George thought of going to summer school, but the kids in his classes would be too young. He also considered registering in a night high school, only he didn't like the idea of the teachers always telling him what to do. He felt they had not respected him.

The omniscient narrator seems to know George's situation intimately—how he dropped out of high school at sixteen, and how he has trouble getting and keeping jobs. The narrator also knows how George feels and what he thinks. George is ashamed that he didn't finish school. He thinks about going back to school but has excuses for not going. He feels he is not respected.

A third-person narrator has much more leeway in telling a story than a first-person narrator does. In "My Oedipus Complex" Frank O'Connor must stay within the confines of what Larry understands about events and within Larry's thoughts and feelings. Bernard Malamud, on the other hand, can range freely among the characters, examine everyone's thoughts, and even make observations himself about what is going on.

The first-person narrator, however, has the advantage of establishing a stronger bond with you. As you read "My Oedipus Complex" you feel as if little Larry is speaking to you directly. This makes it seem that you are reading a true story about a real personal experience. The third-person narrator is more like a neighborhood gossip telling what happened to someone else. But since everyone likes good gossip, you are just as willing to enter into the spirit of a good third-person narration as you are a first-person narration. How the author tells the story depends on the mood he or she is trying to create, the tone he or she wants for the story, and the effect he or she wants to create. Each technique works well in the hands of a good writer.

EXERCISE A

Read the following passages from the stories and answer the questions that follow using the information you have learned in this part of the lesson.

Passage 1

In fact, I rather liked his visits, though it was an uncomfortable squeeze between Mother and him when I got into the big bed in the early morning. He smoked, which gave him a pleasant musty smell, and shaved, an operation of astounding interest.

Passage 2

Very early in the morning George's father got up to go to work in a fish market. Sophie left at about eight for her long ride in the subway to a cafeteria in the Bronx. George had his coffee by himself, then hung around in the house.

1. Which one of the following statements is correct?
   □ a. Both first and third-person points of view are used in Passage 1: "*I* rather liked *his* visits. . . . *I* got into the big bed. . . . *He* smoked . . ."
   □ b. Passage 2 is a first-person narration because it all relates to George.
   □ c. Passage 1 is a first-person narration told by an "I" character, while Passage 2 has a third-person point of view, told by an omniscient narrator.
   □ d. Passage 1 has a third-person point of view because there are four third-person pronouns used and only two first-person pronouns.

2. Who is the narrator in Passage 1?

   _____

   Who is the narrator in Passage 2?

   _____

   _____

Now check your answers using the Answer Key at the back of the book. Correct any wrong answers and review this part of the lesson if you do not understand why an answer is wrong.

· 2 ·

Staging and Managing a Story

Here is a romantic view of how an author writes a story: After suffering through an unhappy love affair (authors always have to suffer before they can write), the author rolls a sheet of paper into a typewriter and knocks out a best-selling story before you can say "happy ending."

As you might imagine, writing a story doesn't quite happen that way. Stories must be planned. Characters must be chosen. An appropriate place and time for the story must be selected. Facts need to be researched and verified to assure believability. The author then has to put the characters in their roles and have them play out their parts. The author must also manage and direct the action and provide you with a story that will be entertaining and thought provoking.

In some ways an author is like the dozens of people who work at the different jobs that go into creating a movie. Throughout this book a short story is often compared to a movie, a play, or a television show. That's because writers enable you to "see" their stories in your mind almost as clearly as you see them on a stage or screen. If you can't "see" a story you are reading, it's either because the author hasn't done a good job, or you have turned off your imagination.

Many movies and plays do, in fact, begin as books. If you read the credits for a play or movie there is often a line that says, "Based on the novel by. . . ." or simply, "Book by. . . ." It may be a novel or short story that has been made into a play, or a writer may have been hired especially to write a book centered on an idea a producer wants to turn into a movie. The book is the source of ideas for setting the stage, for selecting a cast, and for outlining the action of the show. Read the following passages and notice how the authors make the setting and the action unfold in these scenes from "A Summer's Reading" and "My Oedipus Complex."

A Summer's Reading

In the evening after supper George left the house and wandered in the neighborhood. During the sultry days some of the storekeepers and their wives sat in chairs on the thick, broken sidewalks in front of their shops, fanning themselves, and George walked past them and the guys hanging out on the candy store corner. . . .

One time while on his walk George met Mr. Cattanzara coming home very late from work. . . .

My Oedipus Complex

Having settled my plans for the day, I got up, put a chair under the attic window, and lifted the frame high enough to stick out my head. . . .

After that I went into Mother's room and climbed into the big bed. She woke and I began to tell her of my schemes. By this time, though I never seem to have noticed it, I was petrified in my nightshirt, and I thawed as I talked until, the last frost melted, I fell asleep beside her. . . .

In each case a scene has been set and the action has been staged. George Stoyonovich is walking the steamy city sidewalks in his working-class neighborhood. Larry pops his head out of the window to see what's going on in his neighborhood and then scampers into his mother's bed to chat. How different the sounds and the feelings are in each story! Each scene was staged with a special purpose in mind, and each was planned to fit into a total story.

George had to be put on the street in his neighborhood because this is where he will meet the neighbors and Mr. Cattanzara who play such a prominent role in the story. On the other hand, "the big bed" will play an important part in "My Oedipus Complex," and this scene establishes the comfort and sense of security that Larry loses when Father comes home and competes with him for Mother's attention.

The authors had to think through these scenes in advance and know, before they were written, how they would work with the rest of the story. Very often an author will write a scene and as the story develops he or she finds that the scene as staged does not work with parts of the story that follow. Like a movie director, the writer then has to go back and redo the scene or, like a film editor, eliminate it in favor of another scene that does fit. Situations and actions must *work* as part of a whole story. The situations have to be made visible to your mind's eye and believable in the story context.

EXERCISE B

Read the following passage from "A Summer's Reading" and answer the questions that follow using the information you have learned in this part of the lesson.

"What are you doing with yourself this summer, George?" Mr. Cattanzara asked. "I see you walkin' around at nights."

George felt embarrassed. "I like to walk."

"What are you doin' in the day now?"

"Nothing much right now. I'm waiting for a job." Since it shamed him to admit he wasn't working, George said, "I'm staying home—but I'm reading a lot to pick up my education."

Mr. Cattanzara looked interested. He mopped his hot face with a red handkerchief.

"What are you readin'?"

George hesitated, then said, "I got a list of books in the library once, now I'm gonna read them this summer." He felt strange and a little unhappy saying this, but he wanted Mr. Cattanzara to respect him.

1. Authors have to plan ahead in order to relate a scene early in a story to scenes that will come later. Which scene later in the story is this one related to?
   ☐ a. George's arguments with Sophie
   ☐ b. George neglecting his reading
   ☐ c. Mr. Cattanzara reading the *New York Times*
   ☐ d. George's later conversation with Mr. Cattanzara

2. Copy at least one sentence that the author has used to have George set an embarrassing trap for himself that will be sprung later in the story.

   _____

   _____

   _____

   _____

Now check your answers using the Answer Key at the back of the book. Correct any wrong answers and review this part of the lesson if you do not understand why an answer is wrong.

· 3 ·
The Author and the Characters

When you read a story, you often become so involved with the characters that you lose sight of the fact that every character is the author's creation. You tend to forget that the characters who are speaking or thinking are really the author's creation. You don't want to read about authors; you want to read about characters.

You have already seen how Frank O'Connor creates the character of Larry, who is the first-person narrator of "My Oedipus Complex." In "A Summer's Reading" the third-person narrator sprinkles the story with expressions you would not expect from a highly educated writer like Bernard Malamud, but that you would expect from George. Here are a few examples:

> . . . George walked past them and the guys hanging out on the candy store corner. . . .
> He wanted to have some dough in his pocket to buy things with, and a girl to go with, so as not to be so lonely. . . ."

The author, the omniscient narrator, reports what George is thinking. Yet the style of writing is such that you *feel* it is George thinking. You probably recall that Katherine Mansfield also created this feeling in "The Garden Party." At times her narration gushed like an excited teenager might gush. Other times she was shy or moody. This narration kept you in tune with Laura while Mansfield herself faded into the background.

Authors also depend on dialogue to bring their characters alive. In the following passage the author virtually disappears and you are left alone with Larry and Mother:

> "Mummy," I said that night when she was tucking me up, "do you think if I prayed hard God would send Daddy back to war?"
>
> She seemed to think about that for a moment.
>
> "No, dear," she said with a smile. "I don't think He would."
>
> "Why wouldn't He, Mummy?"
>
> "Because there isn't a war any longer, dear."
>
> "But, Mummy, couldn't God make another war, if He liked?"
>
> "He wouldn't like to, dear. It's not God who makes wars, but bad people."
>
> "Oh!" I said.

Everyone who knows a five-year-old child will recognize that dialogue as a very good representation of a conversation between a real child and his mother. O'Connor uses a childish expression—"tucking me up"—to keep Larry in your mind and himself out of sight.

Not all authors are experts at imitating their characters' speech, however. When an author is not good with dialogue you notice it instantly, because you begin to lose sight of the characters and notice the author's presence instead. Some writers, such as Joseph Conrad whom you will read later in this book, tend to intrude more on their stories, but they do it in such an artful way that you adjust your attitude and accept the technique. With those writers it becomes more like listening to a live storyteller than listening to the characters themselves, as is the case with authors O'Connor and Malamud.

EXERCISE C

Read the following passages from "My Oedipus Complex" and answer the questions that follow using the information you have learned in this part of the lesson.

Passage 1

The war was the most peaceful period of my life. The window of my attic faced southeast. My mother had curtained it, but that had small effect. I always woke with the first light and, with all the responsibilities of the previous day melted, feeling myself rather like the sun, ready to illumine and rejoice. Life never seemed so simple and clear and full of possibilities as then. I put my feet out from under the clothes—I called them Mrs. Left and Mrs. Right—and invented dramatic situations for them in which they discussed the problems of the day.

Passage 2

When I woke I remembered my promise all right. I got up and sat on the floor and played—for hours, it seemed to me. Then I got my chair and looked out the attic window for more hours. I wished it was time for Father to wake; I wished someone would make me a cup of tea. I didn't feel in the least like the sun; instead, I was bored and so very, very cold! I simply longed for the warmth and depth of the big featherbed.

1. You are more aware of the presence of the author in Larry's thoughts in Passage 1 than in Passage 2 because
   ☐ a. the first passage is longer than the second passage.
   ☐ b. the author uses more adult language in Passage 1 than in Passage 2.
   ☐ c. Passage 2 deals more with remembering than Passage 1 does.
   ☐ d. the author uses dialogue in Passage 2 but not in Passage 1.

2. What details (or sentence) in Passage 1 help put you in tune with the character of a little boy?

_____

_____

_____

_____

Now check your answers using the Answer Key at the back of the book. Correct any wrong answers and review this part of the lesson if you do not understand why an answer is wrong.

·4·

The Author As Observer and Interpreter

While you may think that you are making up your own mind about the elements of a story as you read, this is not entirely true. How you look at the setting, what you think of the characters, and how you regard the themes of a story are very much influenced by the author. Even though an author stays discreetly out of the way in a story, his or her presence is still very much there as observer and interpreter.

For example, in the beginning of "My Oedipus Complex" the author has Larry describe his father's comings and goings this way: "Like Santa Claus he came and went mysteriously." Suppose Frank O'Connor had written it this way instead: "Like an evil spirit he appeared in the night and was gone by morning." The author has told you how he wants you to see and think about the father by his choice of comparisons.

You may recall reading in the introduction to the stories that Bernard Malamud has said, "Writing. . . . must inflame, destroy, change the reader." As a writer he is not just trying to tell a story; he is deliberately trying to affect you emotionally. You can't read about Mr. Cattanzara and his wife, for instance, without being forced by the author to think about the kind of people they are and about their condition:

> Mr. Cattanzara, a stocky, baldheaded man who worked in a change booth on an IRT station, lived on the next block after George's, above a shoe repair store. Nights, during the hot weather, he sat on his stoop in an undershirt, reading the *New York Times* in the light of the shoemaker's window. He read it from the first page to the last, then went up to sleep. And all the time he was reading the paper, his wife, a fat woman with a white face, leaned out of the window, gazing into the street, her thick white arms folded under her loose breast, on the window ledge.

The author does not tell you *what* to think about Mr. Cattanzara and his wife, but the author certainly shocks you into thinking about them. He has certainly nudged your thinking in a direction he wants it to go. The Cattanzaras may be one of the most undistinguished couples you will ever meet, but they are also typical of many people that Bernard Malamud observed, firsthand, when he was growing up in just that kind of neighborhood. Mr. Cattanzara comes home from his commonplace job as a change maker in the subway to his very plain flat over a shoe repair store. His life, the way the author portrays it, consists of working at his job, reading the newspaper cover to cover, and going to bed. Once in a while, you learn later, he gets drunk. His wife is portrayed as fat and sickly.

The author forces you to take a second look at Mr. Cattanzara simply by inserting a special prop in the scene—the *New York Times.* Here is an unimpressive man who reads a large, sophisticated newspaper "from the first page to the last." Do you do that? Not many people do; but as the author points out, Mr. Cattanzara does. Mrs. Cattanzara keeps him distant company all the time he is reading. Perhaps she has nothing better to do. But perhaps she likes to be seen overseeing a man who reads the *New York Times,* never skipping a page. It is their small mark of distinction in an otherwise undistinguished life.

Each reader will view this scene differently, will feel differently about the Cattanzaras, and will understand them in different ways. But it is the author who has observed them (created them) first and reported them to you in such a way that you can't help but be influenced in your thinking by the way he describes the scene.

EXERCISE D

Read the following passage from "My Oedipus Complex" and answer the questions that follow using the information you have learned in this part of the lesson.

> In the afternoon, at Mother's request, Father took me for a walk. This time we went into town instead of out in the country. . . . Father and I had quite different notions of a walk in town. He had no proper interest in trams, ships, and horses, and the only thing that seemed to divert him was talking to fellows as old as himself. . . . I pulled him by the coat and trousers, but, unlike Mother who, if you were too persistent, got into a wax and said: "Larry, if you don't behave yourself, I'll give you a good slap," Father had an extraordinary capacity for amiable inattention. . . . Really, it was like going for a walk with a mountain! He either ignored the wrenching and pummeling entirely, or else glanced down with a grin of amusement from his peak. I had never met anyone so absorbed in himself as he seemed.

1. One of the things the author observes and points out to you in this scene is
   □ a. how different the relationship is between Larry and Mother, and between Larry and Father.
   □ b. how much Larry hates his Father for stopping to talk to men his own age.

☐ c. that it was wrong of Mother to send Larry for a walk with Father in the first place.

☐ d. that Larry is basically a difficult child to take anywhere, whether with Mother or with Father.

2. How does the author point out the huge impassive presence of Father from Larry's point of view? Copy the sentence or sentences that offers this interpretation of Father.

_____

_____

_____

_____

_____

Now check your answers using the Answer Key at the back of the book. Correct any wrong answers and review this part of the lesson if you do not understand why an answer is wrong.

Comprehension Questions

For each of the following statements or questions, select the option that best completes a statement or is the most accurate response to a question. (Questions labeled MOC are based on "My Oedipus Complex." Questions labeled ASR are based on "A Summer's Reading.")

Recalling Specific Facts (MOC)
1. Where did Larry normally sleep?
   - ☐ a. He slept in the big bed with Mother.
   - ☐ b. He slept in an attic bedroom.
   - ☐ c. He slept between Mother and Father.
   - ☐ d. He slept beneath the window overlooking the garden.

Recalling Specific Facts (ASR)
2. What sorts of things did George read?
   - ☐ a. He read newspapers, magazines, and the *World Almanac*.
   - ☐ b. He didn't read anything at all.
   - ☐ c. He occasionally read the *New York Times*.
   - ☐ d. He read a few paperback novels that he had bought.

Recalling Specific Facts (ASR)
3. What was Mr. Cattanzara's job?
   - ☐ a. He worked at the shoe repair store under his apartment.
   - ☐ b. He worked as a change maker in the subway.
   - ☐ c. He worked in a fish market.
   - ☐ d. He worked in a cafeteria in the Bronx.

Organizing Facts (MOC)
4. Which one of the following events marked the beginning of Larry's problems?
   - ☐ a. the end of the Irish rebellion of 1915
   - ☐ b. the start of World War II
   - ☐ c. the British occupation of Ireland
   - ☐ d. the end of World War I

Organizing Facts (ASR)
5. Where did George go when he left the neighborhood?
   - ☐ a. He walked past the small bar where Mr. Cattanzara drank.
   - ☐ b. He wandered through the streets.
   - ☐ c. He went to a small park.
   - ☐ d. He went to watch the kids play punch ball.

Organizing Facts (MOC)

6. What were the first words spoken by Mother that gave Larry the feeling there was trouble ahead?

☐ a. " 'talking to Daddy' "

☐ b. "a baby costs seventeen and six"

☐ c. " 'Do be quiet, Larry' "

☐ d. "The irony of it"

Knowledge of Word Meanings (MOC)

7. "There was a bit of the *magpie* about Father . . ." What does that sentence mean?

☐ a. Father was swarthy or dark-complexioned.

☐ b. Father was like a peddler—a seller of magpies.

☐ c. Father tended to be stingy.

☐ d. Like a magpie, Father collected things.

Knowledge of Word Meanings (ASR)

8. People would sit outside on *sultry* days. What does *sultry* mean?

☐ a. warm and breezy

☐ b. hot and humid

☐ c. voluptuous and alluring

☐ d. boring and unsettled

Knowledge of Word Meanings (MOC)

9. Reread the passage where Larry said that after looking out his window he was *petrified*. In that passage *petrified* means

☐ a. immobilized.

☐ b. turned to stone.

☐ c. freezing cold.

☐ d. frightened.

Drawing a Conclusion (MOC)

10. It is fair to say that

☐ a. Larry wanted a new baby in the family until he got one.

☐ b. Larry really understood the relationship between his parents.

☐ c. Larry enjoyed his walks with Father more than with Mother.

☐ d. Larry preferred to see his father out of uniform.

Drawing a Conclusion (ASR)

11. Given George's attitude toward school, you may conclude that
☐ a. he will return someday to earn a diploma.
☐ b. he will reconsider enrolling after his experience with Mr. Cattanzara.
☐ c. his attitude will change after he's done some reading.
☐ d. it is unlikely he will ever earn a diploma.

Drawing a Conclusion (ASR)

12. Mr. Cattanzara says, "George, don't do what I did." What do you think he has done that George shouldn't do?
☐ a. He has spent his evenings getting drunk instead of studying.
☐ b. He married instead of finishing high school.
☐ c. He has a dead-end job due to his lack of education.
☐ d. He has done nothing but read the *New York Times* all his life.

Making a Judgment (MOC)

13. Larry objected to Father's being in Mother's bed. How did Father feel about Larry's coming into the big bed?
☐ a. Father didn't like it but he was as tolerant as Mother about it.
☐ b. Father felt that Larry was in the way and a nuisance.
☐ c. Father was impatient at first but didn't mind after Sonny was born.
☐ d. Father was secretly amused by Larry's antics in the big bed.

Making a Judgment (ASR)

14. How did Sophie feel when she found George wasn't reading?
☐ a. She felt the boy should be given more time to mature.
☐ b. She felt that George had been taking advantage of her.
☐ c. She felt she should throw George out of the apartment.
☐ d. She felt that her hopes for advancement had been betrayed.

Making an Inference (MOC)

15. You can infer from her conduct that Mother was
☐ a. a devout fundamentalist.
☐ b. a believer in fate.
☐ c. extremely superstitious.
☐ d. a devout Catholic.

Making an Inference (ASR)

16. It is clear that George's father
    ☐ a. doesn't have much influence in the family.
    ☐ b. is the principal wage earner.
    ☐ c. wants to see his children succeed in life.
    ☐ d. would have had a better job if he had read more.

Understanding Characters (MOC)

17. Which one of the following is a fair statement about the relationship between Larry and his Father?
    ☐ a. They loved one another in the way children love Santa Claus.
    ☐ b. They understood each other's special relationship with Mother.
    ☐ c. Neither one could share Mother's faith in prayer.
    ☐ d. Neither one could understand the feelings of the other.

Understanding Characters (ASR)

18. Which one of the following is a fair statement about Mrs. Cattanzara?
    ☐ a. She probably married Mr. Cattanzara out of desperation.
    ☐ b. She was an average loving wife.
    ☐ c. There is not enough information given to know what she is like.
    ☐ d. There is a subtle hint in the story that she doesn't love her husband.

Understanding Main Ideas (ASR)

19. One of the worst results of George's situation is
    ☐ a. anger.
    ☐ b. loneliness.
    ☐ c. impatience.
    ☐ d. fear.

Understanding Main Ideas (MOC)

20. The big bed becomes a symbol in the story. One thing it seems to stand for is the
    ☐ a. comfort of Mother's presence and attention.
    ☐ b. sanctity of marriage vows.
    ☐ c. relationship between husband and wife.
    ☐ d. love of a mother for her child.

Understanding Main Ideas (ASR)

21. Which of the following feelings seem to follow George throughout the story?
    - ☐ a. dismay and anger
    - ☐ b. fear and disorientation
    - ☐ c. shame and embarrassment
    - ☐ d. bitterness and sorrow

Recognizing Tone (MOC)

22. Larry's thoughts and ideas as related in the story are
    - ☐ a. insightful and clever.
    - ☐ b. selfish and repulsive.
    - ☐ c. boring but harmless.
    - ☐ d. unsophisticated and amusing.

Recognizing Tone (ASR)

23. "A Summer's Reading" has a feeling of
    - ☐ a. hopefulness and helpfulness.
    - ☐ b. unhappiness and depression.
    - ☐ c. hope for the future.
    - ☐ d. anger and frustration.

Appreciation of Literary Forms (MOC)

24. Larry says that he would get up in the morning "feeling like a bottle of champagne." That comparison tells you he was feeling
    - ☐ a. a bit tipsy.
    - ☐ b. headstrong.
    - ☐ c. crazy and reckless.
    - ☐ d. bubbly and alive.

Appreciation of Literary Forms (ASR)

25. Author Bernard Malamud makes the story sound as if it is being told by a neighborhood gossip. He achieves this effect
    - ☐ a. by using the secretive tone usually associated with a gossip.
    - ☐ b. with an association of good things and bad things.
    - ☐ c. by using simple, direct speech like that used in the neighborhood.
    - ☐ d. by pointing out the successes and failures of ordinary people.

Now check your answers using the Answer Key at the back of the book. Make no mark for right answers. Correct any wrong answers you may have by putting a check mark (✓) in the box next to the right answer. Count the number of questions you answered correctly and plot the total on the Comprehension Scores Graph at the back of the book.

Next, look at the questions you answered incorrectly. What types of questions were they? Count the number you got wrong of each type and enter the numbers in the spaces below.

Recalling Specific Facts	_____
Organizing Facts	_____
Knowledge of Word Meanings	_____
Drawing a Conclusion	_____
Making a Judgment	_____
Making an Inference	_____
Understanding Characters	_____
Understanding Main Ideas	_____
Recognizing Tone	_____
Appreciation of Literary Forms	_____

Now use these numbers to fill in the Comprehension Skills Profile at the end of the book.

Extension Activities

Discussion Guide

Discussing Point of View

1. "My Oedipus Complex" is fiction. Why do you get the feeling as you read that it is a "true" story?
2. In "A Summer's Reading" why do you think the author chose to have Mr. Cattanzara drunk when he exposes George's lie about reading?
3. How would the stories change if
   a. "My Oedipus Complex" were written as a third-person narration?
   b. "A Summer's Reading" were written as a first-person narration from Mr. Cattanzara's point of view?

Discussing the Stories

4. Reread the first paragraph of "A Summer's Reading." How does George's attitude toward school compare with your own attitude toward school? Consider both similarities and differences.
5. You keep reading about "respect" in "A Summer's Reading."
   a. What is the importance of the idea of respect in "A Summer's Reading"?
   b. Respect also plays a role in "My Oedipus Complex." Explain how.
6. What role does Sonny (the new baby) play in resolving the conflicts in "My Oedipus Complex"?

Discussing the Author's Work

7. Compare "My Oedipus Complex" with "The Garden Party" in this way: Think about Katherine Mansfield writing "My Oedipus Complex." Think about Frank O'Connor writing "The Garden Party." How would each story be different? In what ways might the stories remain the same?
8. "The Worn Path" and "A Summer's Reading" are very different kinds of stories. But can you discover some similarities between Eudora Welty's relationship with Phoenix Jackson and Bernard Malamud's relationship with George?
9. Bernard Malamud creates a more detailed setting in "A Summer's Reading" than Frank O'Connor does in "My Oedipus Complex." Why should setting be more important in "A Summer's Reading" than it is in "My Oedipus Complex"?

Writing Exercise

1. Write a short story based on a memorable event from your childhood. Write it as a first-person narration.
2. Rewrite the story as though it happened to someone else. Use a third-person point of view.

UNIT
Four

Unit Four

Introduction

What the Story Is About

In this story you will find yourself in the rural South once again—as you did in "A Worn Path"—but this time the civil rights and black heritage movements are gathering strength, sometime in the middle 1960s. "Everyday Use" is a story of two sisters and their mother.

Sister Dee is a beautiful, sophisticated college graduate who lives a modern and successful life. Mama, who has made Dee's success possible, has stayed behind in the country with a younger daughter Maggie, who is a painfully shy, ungainly girl.

Maggie and Mama are living in the old, country way when they are favored by a whirlwind visit by Dee. She has had her consciousness raised about her African heritage and now calls herself Wangero Leewanika Kemanjo. She is wearing an African dress and has brought a friend, a short, stocky man with long hair whose name is three times as long as Wangero's, and unpronounceable as far as Maggie and Mama are concerned.

Dee (Wangero) had hated everything about her rural upbringing, but now she wants to take some of her mother's country antiques because, she says, her mother and Maggie don't understand their heritage the way she does. Who really understands and appreciates their heritage—and other important moral values—and who does not, is the intriguing question that is left for you to decide.

Alice Walker was born in 1944 to sharecropping parents in Eatonton, Georgia, the same place where the mythical plantation Tara of *Gone with the Wind* was located. Walker became nationally famous when her novel *The Color Purple* was awarded the Pulitzer Prize for literature (1983) and was later made into a movie directed by Steven Spielberg and starring Whoopi Goldberg. Walker was writing long before that, however, and had five books to her credit before she was thirty. She is now in great demand as a scholar-lecturer at colleges and writing seminars around the country and around the world. While *The Color Purple* is her most famous book, you will also want to look for other examples of her work in your library. *Meridian* is a novel that centers on events of the civil rights movement. *In Love and Trouble* is a collection of short stories dealing with problems and conflicts faced by black, American women. *Good Night Willie Lee, I'll See You In the Morning* is a collection of poems.

Here is a list of terms that you may not be familiar with:

collards. collard greens; a leafy vegetable

chitlins. chitterlings; a meat dish made from the intestines of pigs

churn. butter churn for turning milk into butter

dasher. the handle of a butter churn

clabber. soured milk

quilting frame. a large frame where a quilt is hung while the quilters stitch the top of the quilt to its backing and inner layer of cotton batting (Quilt making is intricate, artful, and laborious work. The quilts described in the story would probably be worth thousands of dollars as antiques.)

checkerberry snuff. snuff flavored with wintergreen berries (One way to use this form of tobacco is to hold it in the cheek or lower lip.)

Asalamalakim. a ceremonial Moslem (Islamic) greeting meaning, roughly, "peace be with you" (Many Africans who came to the United States as slaves were Moslems, which is one reason that some black Americans in search of their African roots have turned to the religion of Islam.)

What the Lesson Is About

You read in the lesson on point of view that one of the ways an author's presence is felt in a story is through the characters—how the characters are presented, and what the author has them say and do. Character development will be discussed in more detail in the lesson that follows "Everyday Use."

People, animals, and other creatures (robots, talking trees, ghosts, monsters, and space aliens, for example) all find their way into stories as "characters." *Characterization* describes the creation of these imaginary people and things in a way that makes them seem real within the context of their story. The ability to create real characters successfully is the most important skill of a storyteller. A story, after all, is about a character or a group of characters who act out their lives in the face of problems that the author has created for them.

The following questions will help you see how Alice Walker creates the characters in "Everyday Use." Keep these questions in mind and try to answer them as you read:

1. What do you learn about the characters, and how do you feel about them from the way the author describes them?

2. What do you learn about the characters, and how do you feel about them as a result of their actions and conversations?

3. How does the author influence your feelings about the characters?

4. What can you gain on a personal level from discussing the characters after you have read about them?

Everyday Use

by Alice Walker

I will wait for her in the yard that Maggie and I made so clean and wavy yesterday afternoon. A yard like this is more comfortable than most people know. It is not just a yard. It is like an extended living room. When the hard clay is swept clean as a floor and the fine sand around the edges lined with tiny, irregular grooves, anyone can come and sit and look up into the elm tree and wait for the breezes that never come inside the house.

Maggie will be nervous until after her sister goes: she will stand hopelessly in corners, homely and ashamed of the burn scars down her arms and legs, eyeing her sister with a mixture of envy and awe. She thinks her sister has held life always in the palm of one hand, that "no" is a word the world never learned to say to her.

You've no doubt seen those TV shows where the child who has "made it" is confronted, as a surprise, by her own mother and father, tottering in weakly from backstage. (A pleasant surprise, of course: What would they do if parent and child came on the show only to curse out and insult each other?) On TV mother and child embrace and smile into each other's faces. Sometimes the mother and father weep, the child wraps them in her arms and leans across the table to tell how she would not have made it without their help. I have seen these programs.

Sometimes I dream a dream in which Dee and I are suddenly brought together on a TV program of this sort. Out of a dark and soft-seated limousine I am ushered into a bright room filled with many people. There I meet a smiling, gray, sporty man like Johnny Carson who shakes my hand and tells me what a fine girl I have. Then we are on the stage and Dee is embracing me with tears in her eyes. She pins on my dress a large orchid, even though she has told me once that she thinks orchids are tacky flowers.

In real life I am a large, big-boned woman with rough, man-working hands. In the winter I wear flannel nightgowns to bed and overalls during the day. I can kill and clean a hog as mercilessly as a man. My fat keeps me hot in zero weather. I can work outside all day, breaking ice to get water for washing; I can eat pork liver cooked over the open fire minutes after it comes steaming from the hog. One winter I knocked a bull calf straight in the brain between the eyes with a sledge hammer and had the meat hung up to chill before nightfall. But of course all this does not show on television. I am the way my daughter would want me to be: a hundred pounds lighter, my skin like an uncooked barley pancake. My hair glistens in the hot bright lights. Johnny Carson has much to do to keep up with my quick and witty tongue.

But that is a mistake. I know even before I wake up. Who ever knew a Johnson with a quick tongue? Who can even imagine me looking a strange white man in the eye? It seems to me I have talked to them always with one foot raised in flight, with my head turned in whichever way is farthest from them. Dee, though. She would always look anyone in the eye. Hesitation was no part of her nature.

"How do I look, Mama?" Maggie says, showing just enough of her thin body enveloped in pink skirt and red blouse for me to know she's there, almost hidden by the door.

"Come out into the yard," I say.

Have you ever seen a lame animal, perhaps a dog run over by some careless person rich enough to own a car, sidle up to someone who is ignorant enough to be kind to him? That is the way my Maggie walks. She has been like this, chin on chest, eyes on ground, feet in shuffle, ever since the fire that burned the other house to the ground.

Dee is lighter than Maggie, with nicer hair and a fuller figure. She's a woman now, though sometimes I forget. How long ago was it that the other house burned? Ten, twelve years? Sometimes I can still hear the flames and feel Maggie's arms sticking to me, her hair smoking and her dress falling off her in little black papery flakes. Her eyes seemed stretched open, blazed open by the flames reflected in them. And Dee. I see her standing off under the sweet gum tree she used to dig gum out of; a look of concentration on her face as she watched the last dingy gray board of the house fall in toward the red-hot brick chimney. Why don't you do a dance around the ashes? I'd wanted to ask her. She had hated the house that much.

I used to think she hated Maggie, too. But that was before we raised the money, the church and me, to send her to Augusta to school. She used to read to us without pity; forcing words, lies, other folks' habits, whole lives upon us two, sitting trapped and ignorant underneath her voice. She washed us in a river of make-believe, burned us with a lot of knowledge we didn't necessarily need to know. Pressed us to her with the serious way she read, to shove us away at just the moment, like dimwits, we seemed about to understand.

Dee wanted nice things. A yellow organdy dress to wear to her graduation from high school; black pumps to match a green suit she'd made from an old suit somebody gave me. She was determined to stare down any disaster in her efforts. Her eyelids would not flicker for minutes at a time. Often I fought off the temptation to shake her. At sixteen she had a style of her own: and knew what style was.

I never had an education myself. After second grade the school was closed down. Don't ask me why: in 1927 colored asked fewer questions than they do now. Sometimes Maggie reads to me. She stumbles along good-naturedly but can't see well. She knows she is not bright. Like good looks and money, quickness passed her by. She will marry John Thomas (who has mossy teeth in an earnest face) and then I'll be free to sit here and I guess just sing church songs to myself. Although I never was a good singer. Never could carry a tune. I was always better at a man's job. I used to love to milk till I was hooked in the side in '49. Cows are soothing and slow and don't bother you, unless you try to milk them the wrong way.

I have deliberately turned my back on the house. It is three rooms, just like the one that burned, except the roof is tin; they don't make shingle roofs any more. There are no real windows, just some holes cut in the sides, like the portholes in a ship, but not round and not square, with rawhide holding the shutters up on the outside. This house is in a pasture, too, like the other one. No doubt when Dee sees it she will want to tear it down. She wrote me once that no matter where we "choose" to live, she will manage to come see us. But she will never bring her friends. Maggie and I thought about this and Maggie asked me, "Mama, when did Dee ever *have* any friends?"

She had a few. Furtive boys in pink shirts hanging about on washday after school. Nervous girls who never laughed. Impressed with her they worshiped the well-turned phrase, the cute shape, the scalding humor that erupted like bubbles in lye. She read to them.

When she was courting Jimmy T she didn't have much time to pay to us, but turned all her faultfinding power on him. He *flew* to marry a cheap city girl from a family of ignorant flashy people. She hardly had time to recompose herself.

When she comes I will meet—but there they are!

Maggie attempts to make a dash for the house, in her shuffling way, but I stay her with my hand. "Come back here," I say. And she stops and tries to dig a well in the sand with her toe.

It is hard to see them clearly through the strong sun. But even the first glimpse of leg out of the car tells me it is Dee. Her feet were always neat-looking, as if God himself had shaped them with a certain style. From the other side of the car comes a short, stocky man. Hair is all over his head a foot long and hanging from his chin like a kinky mule tail. I hear Maggie suck in her breath. "Uhnnnh," is what it sounds like. Like when you see the wriggling end of a snake just in front of your foot on the road. "Uhnnnh."

Dee next. A dress down to the ground, in this hot weather. A dress so loud it hurts my eyes. There are yellows and oranges enough to throw back the light of the sun. I feel my whole face warming from the heat waves it throws out. Earrings, too, gold and hanging down to her shoulders. Bracelets dangling and making noises when she moves her arm up to shake the folds of the dress out of her armpits. The dress is loose and flows, and as she walks closer, I like it. I hear Maggie go "Uhnnnh" again. It is her sister's hair. It stands straight up like the wool on a sheep. It is black as night and around the edges are two long pigtails that rope about like small lizards disappearing behind her ears.

"Wa-su-zo-Tean-o!" she says, coming on in that gliding way the dress makes her move. The short stocky fellow with the hair to his navel is all grinning and he follows up with "Asalamalakim, my mother and sister!" He moves to hug Maggie but she falls back, right up against the back of my chair. I feel her trembling there and when I look up I see the perspiration falling off her chin.

"Don't get up," says Dee. Since I am stout it takes something of a push. You can see me trying to move a second or two before I make it. She turns, showing white heels through her sandals, and goes back to the car. Out she peeks next with a Polaroid. She stoops down quickly and lines up picture after picture of me sitting there in front of the house with Maggie cowering behind me. She never takes a shot without making sure the house is included. When a cow comes nibbling around the edge of the yard she snaps it and me and Maggie *and* the house. Then she puts the Polaroid in the back seat of the car, and comes up and kisses me on the forehead.

Meanwhile Asalamalakim is going through the motions with Maggie's hand. Maggie's hand is as limp as a fish, and probably as cold, despite the sweat, and she keeps trying to pull it back. It looks like Asalamalakim wants to shake hands but wants to do it fancy. Or maybe he don't know how people shake hands. Anyhow, he soon gives up on Maggie.

"Well," I say. "Dee."

"No, Mama," she says. "Not 'Dee,' Wangero Leewanika Kemanjo!"

"What happened to 'Dee'?" I wanted to know.

"She's dead," Wangero said. "I couldn't bear it any longer, being named after the people who oppress me."

"You know as well as me you was named after your aunt Dicie," I said. Dicie is my sister. She named Dee. We called her "Big Dee" after Dee was born.

"But who was *she* named after?" asked Wangero.

"I guess after Grandma Dee," I said.

"And who was she named after?" asked Wangero.

"Her mother," I said, and saw Wangero was getting tired. "That's about as far back as I can trace it," I said. Though, in fact, I probably could have carried it back beyond the Civil War through the branches.

"Well," said Asalamalakim, "there you are."

"Uhnnnh," I heard Maggie say.

"There I was not," I said, "before 'Dicie' cropped up in our family, so why should I try to trace it that far back?"

He just stood there grinning, looking down on me like somebody inspecting a Model A car. Every once in a while he and Wangero sent eye signals over my head.

"How do you pronounce this name?" I asked.

"You don't have to call me by it if you don't want to," said Wangero.

"Why shouldn't I?" I asked. "If that's what you want us to call you, we'll call you."

"I know it might sound awkward at first," said Wangero.

"I'll get used to it," I said. "Ream it out again."

Well, soon we got the name out of the way. Asalamalakim had a name twice as long and three times as hard. After I tripped over it two or three times he told me to just call him Hakim-a-barber. I wanted to ask him was he a barber, but I didn't really think he was, so I didn't ask.

"You must belong to those beef-cattle peoples down the road," I said. They said "Asalamalakim" when they met you, too, but they didn't shake hands. Always too busy: feeding the cattle, fixing the fences, putting up salt-lick shelters, throwing down hay. When the white folks poisoned some of the herd the men stayed up all night with rifles in their hands. I walked a mile and a half just to see the sight.

Hakim-a-barber said, "I accept some of their doctrines, but farming and raising cattle is not my style." (They didn't tell me, and I didn't ask, whether Wangero [Dee] had really gone and married him.)

We sat down to eat and right away he said he didn't eat collards and pork was unclean. Wangero, though, went on through the chitlins and corn bread, the greens and everything else. She talked a blue streak over the sweet potatoes. Everything delighted her. Even the fact that we still used the benches her daddy made for the table when we couldn't afford to buy chairs.

"Oh, Mama!" she cried. Then turned to Hakim-a-barber. "I never knew how lovely these benches are. You can feel the rump prints," she said, running her hands underneath her and along the bench. Then she gave a sigh and her hand closed over Grandma Dee's butter dish. "That's it!" she said. "I knew there was something I wanted to ask you if I could have." She jumped up from the table and went over in the corner where the churn stood, the milk in it clabber by now. She looked at the churn and looked at it.

"This churn top is what I need," she said. "Didn't Uncle Buddy whittle it out of a tree you all used to have?"

"Yes," I said.

"Uh huh," she said happily. "And I want the dasher, too."

"Uncle Buddy whittle that, too?" asked the barber.

Dee (Wangero) looked up at me.

"Aunt Dee's first husband whittled the dash," said Maggie so low you almost couldn't hear her. "His name was Henry, but they called him Stash."

"Maggie's brain is like an elephant's," Wangero said, laughing. "I can use the churn top as a centerpiece for the alcove table," she said, sliding a plate over the churn, "and I'll think of something artistic to do with the dasher."

When she finished wrapping the dasher the handle stuck out. I took it for a moment in my hands. You didn't even have to look close to see where hands pushing the dasher up and down to make butter had left a kind of sink in the wood. In fact, there were a lot of small sinks; you could see where thumbs and fingers had sunk into the wood. It was beautiful light yellow wood, from a tree that grew in the yard where Big Dee and Stash had lived.

After dinner Dee (Wangero) went to the trunk at the foot of my bed and started rifling through it. Maggie hung back in the kitchen over the dishpan. Out came Wangero with two quilts. They had been pieced by Grandma Dee and then Big Dee and me had hung them on the quilt frames on the front porch and quilted them. One was in the Lone Star pattern. The other was Walk Around the Mountain. In both of them were scraps of dresses Grandma Dee had worn fifty and more years ago. Bits and pieces of Grandpa Jarrell's Paisley shirts. And one teeny faded blue piece, about the size of a penny matchbox, that was from Great Grandpa Ezra's uniform that he wore in the Civil War.

"Mama," Wangero said sweet as a bird. "Can I have these old quilts?"

I heard something fall in the kitchen, and a minute later the kitchen door slammed.

"Why don't you take one or two of the others?" I asked. "These old things was just done by me and Big Dee from some tops your grandma pieced before she died."

"No," said Wangero. "I don't want those. They are stitched around the borders by machine."

"That'll make them last better," I said.

"That's not the point," said Wangero. "These are all pieces of dresses Grandma used to wear. She did all this stitching by hand. Imagine!" She held the quilts securely in her arms, stroking them.

"Some of the pieces, like those lavender ones, come from old clothes her mother handed down to her," I said, moving up to touch the quilts. Dee (Wangero) moved back just enough so that I couldn't reach the quilts. They already belonged to her.

"Imagine!" she breathed again, clutching them closely to her bosom.

"The truth is," I said, "I promised to give them quilts to Maggie, for when she marries John Thomas."

She gasped like a bee had stung her.

"Maggie can't appreciate these quilts!" she said. "She'd probably be backward enough to put them to everyday use."

"I reckon she would," I said. "God knows I been saving 'em for long enough with nobody using 'em. I hope she will!" I didn't want to bring up how I had offered Dee (Wangero) a quilt when she went away to college. Then she had told me they were old-fashioned, out of style.

"But they're *priceless!*" she was saying now, furiously; for she has a temper. "Maggie would put them on the bed and in five years they'd be in rags. Less than that!"

"She can always make some more," I said. "Maggie knows how to quilt."

Dee (Wangero) looked at me with hatred. "You just will not understand. The point is these quilts, *these* quilts!"

"Well," I said, stumped. "What would *you* do with them?"

"Hang them," she said. As if that was the only thing you *could* do with quilts.

Maggie by now was standing in the door. I could almost hear the sound her feet made as they scraped over each other.

"She can have them, Mama," she said, like somebody used to never winning anything, or having anything reserved for her. "I can 'member Grandma Dee without the quilts."

I looked at her hard. She had filled her bottom lip with checker-berry snuff and it gave her face a kind of dopey, hangdog look. It was Grandma Dee and Big Dee who taught her how to quilt her-self. She stood there with her scarred hands hidden in the folds of her skirt. She looked at her sister with something like fear but she wasn't mad at her. This was Maggie's portion. This was the way she knew God to work.

When I looked at her like that something hit me in the top of my head and ran down to the soles of my feet. Just like when I'm in church and the spirit of God touches me and I get happy and shout. I did something I never had done before: hugged Maggie to me, then dragged her on into the room, snatched the quilts out of Miss Wangero's hands and dumped them into Maggie's lap. Maggie just sat there on my bed with her mouth open.

"Take one or two of the others," I said to Dee.

But she turned without a word and went out to Hakim-a-barber.

"You just don't understand," she said, as Maggie and I came out to the car.

"What don't I understand?" I wanted to know.

"Your heritage," she said. And then she turned to Maggie, kissed her, and said, "You ought to try to make something of yourself, too, Maggie. It's really a new day for us. But from the way you and Mama still live you'd never know it."

She put on some sunglasses that hid everything above the tip of her nose and her chin.

Maggie smiled; maybe at the sunglasses. But a real smile, not scared. After we watched the car dust settle I asked Maggie to bring me a dip of snuff. And then the two of us sat there just enjoying, until it was time to go in the house and go to bed.

Character

Some literary characters are so memorable that they are virtually historical figures, part of our heritage. The very mention of their names evokes pictures in your mind. Start by recalling some of the very first storybook characters you ever knew: Humpty Dumpty, the Three Little Pigs, the Grasshopper and the Ant. Those names not only create vivid pictures in your mind but also remind you of human strengths and failings. Humpty Dumpty suggests an irretrievable collapse or breakdown; the Three Little Pigs represent carelessness versus careful planning; and the Grasshopper and the Ant are associated with industry and frivolity.

Later in your reading you met such characters as Tom Sawyer, everyone's image of an American boy; Charlotte, the heroic spider of *Charlotte's Web;* and Superman, the epitome of physical power. Many characters in fiction have seized your imagination so strongly that they seem to have a life outside of the story in which they appear. Characters in novels by Charles Dickens—David Copperfield, Oliver Twist, Sydney Carton, Mr. Pickwick—have come alive again in dozens of plays and motion pictures. Those characters have been commemorated in prints, paintings, and fine china sculptures. An interesting sidelight to history occurred when Dickens was writing his novel *The Old Curiosity Shop.* The story first appeared in monthly installments in an English magazine. At one point a character in the story, Little Nell, lay dying. She had become so real to readers in the United States that huge crowds formed on the docks waiting for the ship that would bring the next episode of the story. Was poor Nell still alive? When the author allowed Nell to die, a storm of protest followed him for allowing the tragedy to happen.

Spellbound readers still write letters to Sherlock Holmes almost a hundred years after Sir Arthur Conan Doyle had him solve crimes in Victorian England. Every year thousands of tourists visit a replica of 221B Baker Street, the imagined London residence of Holmes and his friend Dr. Watson. The character, in fact, has surpassed the fame of his author since most people refer to "Sherlock Holmes stories" rather than stories by Sir Arthur Conan Doyle. That response is the power of great characterization.

Characterization in the hands of an accomplished writer is like a paintbrush in the hands of a talented artist. By adding a line here and there, an artist can make a person look beautiful or ugly; a subtle shading around the eyes can make a person appear mean or kind, sad or cheerful. In the same way, with a word or two describing a look or an action, an author can make you like or dislike a character. Depending on how an author draws a character, you may sympathize with one and wish the worst for another.

As you will learn in this lesson, understanding the characters in a story is not something you have to work at very hard. A good author creates characters who clearly identify and explain themselves. You will see how Alice Walker manages to develop strong characters by examining these aspects of characterization:

1. The characters are developed by the author's descriptions.
2. The characters are developed in the course of the story's action and dialogue.
3. The authors influence your feelings toward the characters.
4. You participate in analyzing and understanding story characters.

· 1 ·
Creating Characters with Descriptions

If you are going to meet someone new, it is natural to want to know something about that person. Generally you want a physical description first—tall or short? fat or thin? plain or handsome?—very basic facts that create a purely physical image. Then you want to know something about the person's nature—is the person friendly? brusque? shy? domineering? considerate? selfish? If this is an important meeting, you will be fortunate, indeed, if you know someone who can describe the person for you.

An author often introduces characters in just this way—by actually describing the character in some detail. Depending on the story and on what the author wishes to accomplish, there may be considerable descriptions of physical characteristics. That was the case in "A Worn Path." Eudora Welty described how Phoenix Jackson was dressed, how she looked, how she walked, and so on. Neither Frank O'Connor nor Bernard Malamud provided many details about their characters' physical appearances. They concentrated more on the inner natures of their people.

In "Everyday Use" the author speaks through Mama, the first-person narrator of the story. Mama describes herself, her daughter Maggie, and later Dee and her friend. Walker describes the physical appearances of her characters and also tells us something about the kinds of people they are:

> Maggie will be nervous until after her sister goes: she will stand hopelessly in corners, homely and ashamed of the burn scars down her arms and legs, eyeing her sister with a mixture of envy and awe. . . .
> In real life I am a large, big-boned woman with rough, man-working hands. In the winter I wear flannel nightgowns to bed and overalls during the day. I can kill and clean a hog as mercilessly as a man. My fat keeps me hot in zero weather. I can work outside all day, breaking ice to get water for washing.

Except for the burn scars, this first description of Maggie tells more about her shy, self-effacing nature than about her physical appearance. Later in the story, when you are given more bits of information about Maggie's physical appearance, the descriptions are still used to emphasize her retiring and ungainly nature.

On the other hand, in telling you about herself, Mama describes both her physical appearance and at least one side of her nature, because they seem to go together. She is fat, strong, and wears overalls and flannel nightgowns. She has the confidence and fortitude to do hard, dirty work without complaining. You can expect certain things from this kind of woman, just as you expect very different things from Maggie. And therein lies the purpose of the author's characterization. Walker is developing characters who will be useful in telling the story, who fit a purpose and a plan. The descriptions help you to understand the characters and the actions they are involved in as the story unfolds.

EXERCISE A

Read the following passage from the story and answer the questions that follow using the information you have learned in this part of the lesson.

"How do I look, Mama?" Maggie says, showing just enough of her thin body enveloped in pink skirt and red blouse for me to know she's there, almost hidden by the door.

"Come out into the yard," I say.

Have you ever seen a lame animal, perhaps a dog run over by some careless person rich enough to own a car, sidle up to someone who is ignorant enough to be kind to him? That is the way my Maggie walks. She has been like this, chin on chest, eyes on ground, feet in shuffle, ever since the fire that burned the other house to the ground.

1. Which one of the following quotations from later in the story best reflects the image of Maggie as described in this passage?
   □ a. I used to think she [Dee] hated Maggie, too. But that was before we raised the money . . . to send her to Augusta to school.
   □ b. When a cow comes nibbling around the edge of the yard she [Dee] snaps it and me and Maggie *and* the house.
   □ c. "She can have them, Mama," she said, like somebody used to never winning anything, or having anything reserved for her.
   □ d. Meanwhile Asalamalakim is going through the motions with Maggie's hand. Maggie's hand is as limp as a fish, and probably as cold. . . .

2. The author uses a comparison (a metaphor) to describe both Maggie's physical appearance and her inner nature. What is Maggie compared to? Copy the description here.

_____

_____

_____

Now check your answers using the Answer Key at the back of the book. Correct any wrong answers and review this part of the lesson if you do not understand why an answer is wrong.

· 2 ·
Characterization Through Action and Dialogue

After you hear what an author has to say about the characters in a story, you begin to judge them yourself by what they say and do. The characters' actions and the things they say are controlled by the author, of course, just like everything else in the story is controlled. The author uses the action and dialogue to portray each person in a particular way, to develop personalities to suit the story. This is sometimes called "the dramatic method of characterization" because it is the same way characters are developed in plays and movies. Here, for instance, is a view of Dee arriving to visit her mother and sister:

> "Wa-su-zo-Tean-o!" she says, coming on in that gliding way the dress makes her move. The short stocky fellow with the hair to his navel is all grinning and he follows up with "Asalamalakim, my mother and sister!" He moves to hug Maggie but she falls back, right up against the back of my chair. I feel her trembling there and when I look up I see the perspiration falling off her chin.
> "Don't get up," says Dee. . . . She turns, showing white heels through her sandals, and goes back to the car. Out she peeks next with a Polaroid. She stoops down quickly and lines up picture after picture of me sitting there in front of the house with Maggie cowering behind me. She never takes a shot without making sure the house is included.

Dee is obviously showing off her new-found awareness of her African heritage. Her friend is making a display of his knowledge of Islamic customs. That attitude is fine in its place, but in the present setting it is totally inappropriate. There is no concern on the part of those two for Mama and Maggie. Dee is only concerned with impressing her country relatives with how superior she is to them in her culture and learning.

You have been told earlier how Dee hates her home, but now she is flitting around taking pictures of it. That, apparently, is not a change of heart; it's part of her affectation. Dee, it will develop, still has no love or respect for her home, her mother, or her sister. To Dee, her family and the house are interesting artifacts and part of her education in her "heritage." You also learn, later in the story, that her other interest is in acquiring her mother's valuable antiques.

As you read the passage in Exercise B, try to see how Dee and her boyfriend are developed through the dialogue between Mama and Dee.

EXERCISE B

Read the following passage from the story and answer the questions that follow using the information you have learned in this part of the lesson.

"Well," I say, "Dee."

"No, Mama," she says. "Not 'Dee,' Wangero Leewanika Kemanjo!"

"What happened to 'Dee'?" I wanted to know.

"She's dead," Wangero said. "I couldn't bear it any longer being named after the people who oppress me."

"You know as well as me you was named after your aunt Dicie," I said. Dicie is my sister. She named Dee. We called her "Big Dee" after Dee was born.

"But who was *she* named after?" asked Wangero.

"I guess after Grandma Dee," I said.

"And who was she named after?" asked Wangero.

"Her mother," I said, and saw Wangero was getting tired. "That's about as far back as I can trace it," I said. Though, in fact, I probably could have carried it back beyond the Civil War through the branches.

"Well," said Asalamalakim, "there you are."

"Uhnnnh," I heard Maggie say.

"There I was not," I said, "before 'Dicie' cropped up in our family, so why should I try to trace it that far back?"

He just stood there grinning, looking down on me like somebody inspecting a Model A car. Every once in a while he and Wangero sent eye signals over my head.

1. What is the author pointing out about Dee/Wangero and Mama in that conversation?
   ☐ a. Mama sees her heritage in real people; Dee sees her heritage in a name change.
   ☐ b. Mama refuses to appreciate, as Dee has, that a new era has dawned for black people.
   ☐ c. Mama is too stubborn to benefit from Wangero's superior education.
   ☐ d. Dee feels she is helping her mother by making her mother aware of her African heritage.

2. Copy the sentences the author uses to show how smug and arrogant Wangero and her friend are.

_____

_____

_____

_____

_____

Now check your answers using the Answer Key at the back of the book. Correct any wrong answers and review this part of the lesson if you do not understand why an answer is wrong.

· 3 ·

Characters and the Readers' Feelings

As authors present and develop their characters, they decide which ones you will have strong positive feelings for, which ones you will react very negatively to, and which ones will fall somewhere in between. Most major characters in good literature fall somewhere in between. In other words, the main characters in most stories have both strengths and weaknesses, good points and bad points, just like people in real life.

As you read, even before you stop to think at length about the characters in a story, you begin to develop feelings toward them. A talented author can make you feel precisely what he or she wants you to feel about a character. It's obvious, for example, that Alice Walker wants you to admire Mama, feel sorry for poor Maggie, and to dislike Wangero and Hakim-a-barber. Walker uses language and adopts a special tone as she tells you about each one. Whenever Maggie is described she is like a lame dog, she is cowering, or she is digging a hole in the sand with her foot. With Dee/Wangero and her friend the tone becomes sarcastic, sometimes bitterly so. The author makes a point, for instance, of describing Dee's appetite despite her city airs. There's no mistaking the author's contempt in the description of Dee gushing over the old things in the house—things she used to despise—Grandma's butter dish, the old churn, and even the rump prints on the benches.

Notice how the author subtly shapes your feelings about the characters in this passage:

> This house is in a pasture, too, like the other one. No doubt when Dee sees it she will want to tear it down. She wrote me once that no matter where we "choose" to live, she will manage to come see us. But she will never bring her friends. Maggie and I thought about this and Maggie asked me, "Mama, when did Dee ever *have* any friends?"
>
> She had a few. Furtive boys in pink shirts hanging about on washday after school. Nervous girls who never laughed. Impressed with her they worshiped the well-turned phrase, the cute shape, the scalding humor that erupted like bubbles in lye. She read to them.

The author doesn't let you find any redeeming qualities in Dee for a minute. She uses words like *furtive* and *nervous* to describe Dee's friends. Dee's humor is "scalding" and "erupted like bubbles in lye." Then the author leads you to the easy inference that the "friends" only liked the "smart" and "cute" things about Dee; they didn't really like Dee as a person, and you are expected to feel the same way about her.

Even in her letters Dee is arrogant and overbearing toward her mother. But simple Maggie sees through her when she asks, "when did Dee ever *have* any friends?" That little comment by Maggie forces you to take a second look at her. The author has deliberately inserted the comment to prepare you for a reevaluation of Maggie later in the story.

EXERCISE C

Read the following passage from the story and answer the questions that using the information you have learned in this part of the lesson.

Dee is lighter than Maggie, with nicer hair and a fuller figure. She's a woman now, though sometimes I forget. How long ago was it that the other house burned? Ten, twelve years? Sometimes I can still hear the flames and feel Maggie's arms sticking to me, her hair smoking and her dress falling off her in little black papery flakes. Her eyes seemed stretched open by the flames reflected in them. And Dee. I see her standing off under the sweet gum tree she used to dig gum out of; a look of concentration on her face as she watched the last dingy gray board of the house fall in toward the red-hot brick chimney. Why don't you do a dance around the ashes? I'd wanted to ask her. She had hated the house that much.

1. What is it that makes you feel sorry for Maggie?
   - ☐ a. The author points out that Dee is much prettier than Maggie.
   - ☐ b. Dee, the narrator says, is a woman; Maggie is not.
   - ☐ c. Maggie has been badly burned and terrified by the fire.
   - ☐ d. Maggie loved the house that burned while Dee hated it.

2. Copy the sentence from the passage that is a bitter, sarcastic thought apparently designed by the author to make you dislike Dee.

   _____

   _____

   _____

Now check your answers using the Answer Key at the back of the book. Correct any wrong answers and review this part of the lesson if you do not understand why an answer is wrong.

· 4 ·
Analyzing Characters

You have met many people by reading just this far in this book, and you will meet many more before you are through. Now think back over all the reading you have done throughout your life. The characters you have met through reading must number in the hundreds or even thousands. One of the great benefits of reading is that you can meet so many more people—so many *different* kinds of people—than you ever meet in real life. What is more, you get to know these people intimately. You are told about their innermost thoughts and feelings. They are developed or *characterized* for you by an all-knowing observer.

What does that knowledge of people do for you? It's entertaining, for one thing, to be able to eavesdrop and peer into people's private lives. It is also an education in learning how to understand people and the reasons why they act the way they do. That is an important life skill and essential for surviving and getting ahead in a difficult world.

In "The Garden Party" you came to understand how a person reared in luxury has difficulty adjusting to others outside of her class. In "My Oedipus Complex" you were able to consider the confusion in a little boy's mind in working out his relationships with each of his parents. In "A Worn Path" you saw how powerful a force love and duty can be in a person's life. In "Everyday Use" you see the overbearing arrogance of a daughter who is very full of herself and looks down on her mother and sister.

Understanding people is character analysis. It is not just something you do for English or for a reading course. Analyzing characters is something you do every day in real life situations. Authors help educate you to understand people when they create interesting and complex characters for you to think about.

Characters are created for a variety of purposes. As you have seen, some characters are merely used for setting—the people sitting on the sidewalk in "A Summer's Reading" or the guests in "The Garden Party," for example. Other characters are given small parts to make a point or move the story along. You never get to know these people very well. The hunter and the receptionist in the doctor's office in "A Worn Path" are examples of that.

Certain characters are called "flat" because only one side of their natures is shown. Superman, for instance, is a "flat" character. He is always good, always powerful, always a winner. You never see him as a failure, he is never particularly worried about a problem, nor is he ever in doubt as to how to deal with a situation. Hakim-a-barber is a "flat" character. Alice Walker makes him a silly man and never develops him beyond this.

The main characters in stories are usually "round" characters: the author has developed them so that you can see several sides of their natures. A character may be basically good, for example, but is forced by circumstances into violating a code of ethics. You get a very thorough look at a character in such circumstances. You saw both the flighty side and the serious side of Laura in "The Garden Party." Both George and Mr. Cattanzara in "A Summer's Reading" are complex characters who require some thought on your part if they are to be understood.

Characters cannot be developed as thoroughly in short stories as they are in novels because the short-story author does not use as many words or descriptions. There is a great deal to be learned about people, nevertheless, as you can see in this study of Maggie in "Everyday Use."

> Maggie by now was standing in the door. I could almost hear the sound her feet made as they scraped over each other.
>
> "She can have them, Mama," she said, like somebody used to never winning anything, or having anything reserved for her. "I can 'member Grandma Dee without the quilts."
>
> I looked at her hard. She had filled her bottom lip with checker-berry snuff and it gave her face a kind of dopey, hangdog look. It was Grandma Dee and Big Dee who taught her how to quilt herself. She stood there with her scarred hands hidden in the folds of her skirt. She looked at her sister with something like fear but she wasn't mad at her. This was Maggie's portion. This was the way she knew God to work.

It was pointed out earlier in the lesson that there are times when the author deliberately makes you take a hard look at Maggie, just as Mama does in this scene. The general picture of Maggie has been hangdog, unattractive, slow, dopey. Now you see a certain nobility, even dignity in Maggie. She is creative—she can quilt, which Dee with all her knowledge of the value of quilts cannot. Maggie has a deep-rooted sense of her heritage: "I can 'member Grandma Dee without the quilts." She is pictured as saint-like in her patience: "This was Maggie's portion. This was the way she knew God to work."

When you analyze a character, you want to look for that character's multi-faceted development. It is the same in real life. Is a blustery boss all bad or is he or she really defending the company and your job? Is the politician really as good as he or she seems, or is his or her good side reserved for television appearances? It takes analysis, an examination of all sides of a person, to come up with a true picture.

EXERCISE D

Read the following passage from the story and answer the questions that follow using the information you have learned in this part of the lesson.

> When I looked at her like that something hit me in the top of my head and ran down to the soles of my feet. Just like when I'm in church and the spirit of God touches me and I get happy and shout. I did something I never had done before: hugged Maggie to me,

then dragged her on into the room, snatched the quilts out of Miss Wangero's hands and dumped them into Maggie's lap. Maggie just sat there on my bed with her mouth open.

1. Mama has been portrayed as a tough, practical woman. What side of her is shown in this passage?
   ☐ a. her weak side
   ☐ b. her softer side
   ☐ c. her sensible side
   ☐ d. her creative side

2. Copy a sentence or expression from the passage that shows Mama has experienced a sudden understanding of Maggie's character.

   _____

   _____

   _____

Now check your answers using the Answer Key at the back of the book. Correct any wrong answers and review this part of the lesson if you do not understand why an answer is wrong.

Comprehension Questions

For each of the following statements or questions, select the option that best completes a statement or is the most accurate response to a question.

Recalling Specific Facts

1. How did Mama and the church use the money that they raised?
   - ☐ a. They used it to treat Maggie's burn scars.
   - ☐ b. They used it for a civil rights cause.
   - ☐ c. They used it to foster interest in black history.
   - ☐ d. They used it to send Dee to school.

Recalling Specific Facts

2. What was it that Hakim-a-barber declared to be unclean?
   - ☐ a. the house
   - ☐ b. pork
   - ☐ c. collard greens
   - ☐ d. the yard

Organizing Facts

3. Where did Mama and Dee appear on a TV show?
   - ☐ a. at school in Augusta
   - ☐ b. on the Johnny Carson show
   - ☐ c. in Mama's dreams
   - ☐ d. on "This Is Your Life"

Organizing Facts

4. When will Maggie get the quilts that Mama is saving for her?
   - ☐ a. She will get the quilts when she marries.
   - ☐ b. She is not likely to get the quilts at all.
   - ☐ c. She will get the quilts after Dee hangs them.
   - ☐ d. She will get the quilts after they are repaired.

Knowledge of Word Meanings

5. While Dee was taking pictures, Maggie was *cowering* behind Mama. What does *cowering* mean?
   - ☐ a. hiding from embarrassment
   - ☐ b. making hand signals
   - ☐ c. shrinking away in fear
   - ☐ d. seeking shelter

Knowledge of Word Meanings

6. Speaking about Mama's neighbors Hakim-a-barber says: "I accept some of their *doctrines.*" What are *doctrines?*

☐ a. customs or habits
☐ b. rules or principles
☐ c. medical treatments
☐ d. ceremonies

Drawing a Conclusion

7. From the way Mama is described, she seems to be

☐ a. indifferent to Maggie.
☐ b. unable to make decisions.
☐ c. unhappy with her life.
☐ d. a strong and reliable person.

Drawing a Conclusion

8. What can you conclude about Dee from Mama's description of her as a teenager?

☐ a. Dee liked to be the center of attention.
☐ b. Dee was sulky and shy until she went to college.
☐ c. Dee had set fire to the house.
☐ d. Dee could have married anyone she wanted.

Making a Judgment

9. Dee is probably trying to dress

☐ a. to please her mother.
☐ b. as she feels an African woman would dress.
☐ c. in a way that will shame Maggie.
☐ d. in a way that will shock her mother.

Making a Judgment

10. Wangero and Hakim-a-barber send eye signals over Mama's head. Why?

☐ a. They think Mama is both stubborn and ignorant about using their old "slave" names.
☐ b. They don't want Mama to feel bad that they are better educated than she is.
☐ c. They are secretly conspiring to take away Mama's possessions.
☐ d. They hope to convince Mama to change Maggie's name, too.

Making a Judgment

11. Dee contends that Maggie can't appreciate the old quilts. Which one of the following statements is most accurate based on evidence in the story?

   ☐ a. Dee is right, considering Maggie's lack of education.

   ☐ b. Dee is wrong. Maggie has an artistic soul.

   ☐ c. As a quilter Maggie can appreciate the old quilts.

   ☐ d. Dee understands quilts better than Maggie.

Making an Inference

12. Why didn't Dee want the quilts that were stitched by machine?

   ☐ a. They weren't directly connected to her heritage.

   ☐ b. They lacked the African motif that she preferred.

   ☐ c. They would offend Hakim-a-barber's doctrines.

   ☐ d. They weren't as valuable as the other quilts.

Making an Inference

13. Evidence seems to suggest that the fire had

   ☐ a. left the family much the same as before.

   ☐ b. left emotional as well as physical scars on Maggie.

   ☐ c. made Mama hate Dee.

   ☐ d. set the stage for a new way of life for Dee.

Making an Inference

14. What is the most likely reason that Dee hated her house?

   ☐ a. It was a symbol of slavery and oppression.

   ☐ b. It was nothing she could show off to Hakim-a-barber.

   ☐ c. She was uncomfortable having roots in poverty.

   ☐ d. She wanted better things for her mother and sister.

Understanding Character

15. Mama's description of herself indicates that she is

   ☐ a. a confirmed dreamer of dreams.

   ☐ b. an independent woman.

   ☐ c. a typical old-fashioned mother.

   ☐ d. a chronic worrier.

Understanding Character

16. The author says that everything in the house delighted Dee. Knowing Dee as you do, this means that
    - ☐ a. Dee had recognized her true heritage at last.
    - ☐ b. Dee was a romantic at heart.
    - ☐ c. Nothing really attracted Dee. She was bluffing.
    - ☐ d. Dee looked for anything valuable that she could take with her.

Understanding Character

17. Dee had been courting Jimmy T. What was the character trait that scared him off?
    - ☐ a. her obsessive interest in black heritage
    - ☐ b. her vivacity
    - ☐ c. her faultfinding
    - ☐ d. her faith in Islam

Understanding Main Ideas

18. Why does the author include in the story Mama's thoughts about being on a TV show with Dee?
    - ☐ a. Those were very happy days for Mama.
    - ☐ b. Mama probably wishes she could be closer to Dee than she is.
    - ☐ c. Television is all that Mama has to think about.
    - ☐ d. Mama secretly wishes to be a popular performer.

Understanding Main Ideas

19. The story points out that the principal difference between Mama and Dee is that
    - ☐ a. Mama is an independent woman but Dee is not.
    - ☐ b. Dee is conscious of her heritage while Mama is not.
    - ☐ c. Mama doesn't see the value of an education; Dee does.
    - ☐ d. Mama has a high regard for her heritage; Dee really does not.

Recognizing Tone

20. The author writes: "Mama," Wangero said sweet as a bird. "Can I have these old quilts?" Which one of the following is a fair statement about this quotation?
    - ☐ a. Wangero tried to be very sweet so that Mama would give her the quilts.
    - ☐ b. Wangero has a very sweet, birdlike voice.
    - ☐ c. That was a wistful remark, like a mockingbird's song at twilight.
    - ☐ d. The author is referring to Wangero's nesting instinct inspired by the quilts.

21. The story ends shortly after Wangero and Hakim-a-barber have left. For the first time in the story, Maggie has a feeling of
  ☐ a. true longing.
  ☐ b. jealousy and anger.
  ☐ c. tranquility and contentment.
  ☐ d. personal fulfillment.

Recognizing Tone
22. When the author describes Dee reading to Mama and Maggie, Mama sounds
  ☐ a. tranquil and content.
  ☐ b. sarcastic.
  ☐ c. nostalgic.
  ☐ d. angry.

Appreciation of Literary Forms
23. An adjective describes a noun. Sometimes authors invent adjectives to enhance their descriptions. Which one of the following descriptions seems to contain an adjective that Alice Walker may have invented?
  ☐ a. steaming from the hog
  ☐ b. man-working hands
  ☐ c. blazed open by the flames
  ☐ d. in her shuffling way

Appreciation of Literary Forms
24. A simile is a direct comparison of unlike things. Which one of the following expressions is a simile?
  ☐ a. ". . . her own mother and father, tottering in weakly from backstage."
  ☐ b. ". . . the sweet gum tree she used to dig gum out of. . . ."
  ☐ c. ". . . her dress falling off her in little black papery flakes."
  ☐ d. ". . . my skin like an uncooked barley pancake. . . ."

Appreciation of Literary Forms
25. What does Mama mean when she says, "I have talked to them [white people] always with one foot raised in flight. . . ."?
  ☐ a. She was extremely distrustful, if not fearful, of white people.
  ☐ b. She would talk to whites as little as possible.
  ☐ c. White people had chased her on many occasions.
  ☐ d. Mama was probably referring to flight from slavery.

Now check your answers using the Answer Key at the back of the book. Make no mark for right answers. Correct any wrong answers you may have by putting a check mark (✓) in the box next to the right answer. Count the number of questions you answered correctly and plot the total on the Comprehension Scores Graph at the back of the book.

Next, look at the questions you answered incorrectly. What types of questions were they? Count the number you got wrong of each type and enter the numbers in the spaces below.

Recalling Specific Facts	_____
Organizing Facts	_____
Knowledge of Word Meanings	_____
Drawing a Conclusion	_____
Making a Judgment	_____
Making an Inference	_____
Understanding Characters	_____
Understanding Main Ideas	_____
Recognizing Tone	_____
Appreciation of Literary Forms	_____

Now use these numbers to fill in the Comprehension Skills Profile at the end of the book.

⸺ Extension Activities ⸺

Discussion Guide

Discussing Characterization

1. There are clues in the story that tell you how Mama regards Dee's character. There are also clues that tell you how Mama wishes Dee would be. Find both these kinds of clues and show how they provide insight into Mama's and Dee's characters.
2. Maggie and Dee are complete opposites. Why do you think Alice Walker put such different kinds of people into the story and made them sisters?
3. Alice Walker describes how Mama kills and eats meat. Why does Walker do that? What does that description accomplish in the story?

Discussing the Story

4. Mama sees her heritage in her immediate forebears and in the family history she knows. Wangero sees her heritage in her African ancestry. Who is right, in your opinion? Who and what do you consider to be part of *your* heritage?
5. Reread the passage that describes Dee reading to Mama and Maggie. Try to explain the possible reasons behind Mama's bitter feelings.
6. Mama is sarcastic about Wangero's hairstyle. She is even more sarcastic about Hakim-a-barber's hair. Why do hairstyles seem to be the cause of so much adverse criticism both in this story and in real life?

Discussing the Author's Work

7. Eudora Welty and Alice Walker are both Southerners writing about black women. Compare "A Worn Path" and "Everyday Use." How are they the same? How are they different?
8. Alice Walker has written many stories about black women and their problems. She often portrays men as silly—like Hakim-a-barber—or cruel, abusive, and unfeeling. Would a strong and likable male character help the story "Everyday Use," or would such a character detract from its meaning and effectiveness? Explain your opinions.
9. Alice Walker's stories are based on her black heritage. Bernard Malamud's stories are based on his Brooklyn-Jewish heritage. Frank O'Connor's stories are based on his Irish heritage. Still, there is meaning in all of these stories for everyone. Why do you think this is so?

Writing Exercise

The story ends just after Wangero and Hakim-a-barber leave. The author has never let you like these two characters for a moment all during the story. Write a conversation that takes place between Wangero and Hakim-a-barber as they are leaving.

- Write the conversation so that your readers will continue to dislike Wangero and Hakim-a-barber.
- Rewrite the conversation so that your readers will like Wangero and Hakim-a-barber a little better.

UNIT
Five

Unit Five

Introduction

What the Story Is About

Joseph Conrad often tells a story within a story. He will begin with a third-person narrator telling about a sailor or adventurer who is traveling in some mysterious and exotic place. Then the adventurer tells a tale about someone he knows and the story seems to slip into a first-person narration. It's an interesting technique and one that takes an expert storyteller like Conrad to manage well.

In "The Lagoon" an unnamed white adventurer is traveling in a large sampan (a flat-bottomed Chinese skiff) somewhere among the islands of the Malay archipelago of southeast Asia, also known as Indonesia. The time is about 1900 when the English, Dutch, and French were the active traders and colonial rulers in the area. The adventurer stops to spend the night with a Malay friend, Arsat, whom he has known from adventures in earlier days. Arsat's wife is dying of fever and he begins to reminisce about how he and his brother had stolen her from a local rajah, with tragic results. Arsat takes over the story with only brief interruptions from the third-person narrator—the story within a story.

Joseph Conrad, Jósef Teodor Konrad Korzeniowski, is considered one of the greatest novelists and prose stylists in English literature. What makes his talent remarkable is that he was born of Polish parents and spoke no English until he was twenty. He went to sea on French merchant ships when he was sixteen, sailed on an English ship for the first time when he was twenty-one, and successfully passed the exams for his master mariner's papers at the age of twenty-seven.

Conrad spent almost twenty years at sea, mostly on trading ships to Africa and southeast Asia. He wrote nothing until he was thirty-two, when he wrote *Almayer's Folly,* which was published in 1895. His stories focus on the seafarers, traders, adventurers, and people he knew in the lands he visited in his sailing days. There is usually some intense interaction in his tales between people of different cultures and different races, and he often discusses such things as ambition, greed, and exploitation of local populations and resources under the old colonial system.

The following passage that begins the Malay Arsat's story in "The Lagoon" is typical of Conrad:

> "Therefore I shall speak to you of love. Speak in the night. Speak before both night and love are gone—and the eye of day looks upon my sorrow and my shame; upon my blackened face; upon my burnt-up heart."

You will find out as you read the story what the love, the sorrow, and the shame are. After you read "The Lagoon," you may like to read one or more of Conrad's novels: *Lord Jim, Heart of Darkness, Typhoon,* and *Nostromo.*

What the Lesson Is About

Years ago there was a television show called "The Naked City" that was set in New York and always ended this way: "There are ten million stories in the naked city. This has been one of them."

What the statement was suggesting, of course, is that everyone has problems, and discussing these problems creates a story. In literature these problems are called *conflicts.* You may have conflicts with other people, with the rules of society, with the forces of nature, and even with yourself when you are filled with doubts about how to govern your actions.

Every story you have ever read, or ever will read, is based on a conflict or on a set of conflicts. This is because conflict is the heart of a story; it creates the interest and anticipation that keeps you reading. If there is no conflict, there is no story. In the lesson that follows "The Lagoon" you will examine the kinds of conflicts you most often encounter in your reading, and you will see how these conflicts work in the context of a story.

Keep the following questions in mind and try to answer them as you read. They will help you to understand what the conflicts are in "The Lagoon" and how they work to develop the story.

1. What conflicts does the character Arsat have to face in the story?

2. How do these conflicts create interest in the story?

3. What do you learn about Arsat from his conflicts and from the way he handles them?

4. The main conflict in a story often points to the main ideas and themes of the story. What questions do Arsat's conflicts raise in your mind?

The Lagoon

by Joseph Conrad

The white man, leaning with both arms over the roof of the little house in the stern of the boat, said to the steersman—

"We will pass the night in Arsat's clearing. It is late."

The Malay only grunted, and went on looking fixedly at the river. The white man rested his chin on his crossed arms and gazed at the wake of the boat. At the end of the straight avenue of forests cut by the intense glitter of the river, the sun appeared unclouded and dazzling, poised low over the water that shone smoothly like a band of metal. The forests, somber and dull, stood motionless and silent on each side of the broad stream. At the foot of big, towering trees, trunkless nipa palms rose from the mud of the bank, in bunches of leaves enormous and heavy, that hung unstirring over the brown swirl of eddies. In the stillness of the air every tree, every leaf, every bough, every tendril of creeper and every petal of minute blossoms seemed to have been bewitched into an immobility perfect and final. Nothing moved on the river but the eight paddles that rose flashing regularly, dipped together with a single splash; while the steersman swept right and left with a periodic and sudden flourish of his blade describing a glinting semicircle above his head. The churned-up water frothed alongside with a confused murmur. And the white man's canoe, advancing upstream in the short-lived disturbance of its own making, seemed to enter the portals of a land from which the very memory of motion had forever departed.

The white man, turning his back upon the setting sun, looked along the empty and broad expanse of the sea-reach. For the last three miles of its course the wandering, hesitating river, as if enticed irresistibly by the freedom of an open horizon, flows straight into the sea, flows straight to the east—to the east that harbors both light and darkness. Astern of the boat the repeated call of some bird, a cry discordant and feeble, skipped along over the smooth water and lost itself, before it could reach the other shore, in the breathless silence of the world.

The steersman dug his paddle into the stream, and held hard with stiffened arms, his body thrown forward. The water gurgled aloud; and suddenly the long straight reach seemed to pivot on its center, the forests swung in a semicircle, and the slanting beams of sunset touched the broadside of the canoe with a fiery glow, throwing the slender and distorted shadows of its crew upon the streaked glitter of the river. The white man turned to look ahead. The course of the boat had been altered at right-angles to the stream, and the carved dragon-head of its prow was pointing now at a gap in the fringing bushes of the bank. It glided through, brushing the overhanging twigs, and disappeared from the river like some slim and amphibious creature leaving the water for its lair in the forests.

The narrow creek was like a ditch: tortuous, fabulously deep; filled with gloom under the thin strip of pure and shining blue of the heaven. Immense trees soared up, invisible behind the festooned draperies of creepers. Here and there, near the glistening blackness of the water, a twisted root of some tall tree showed amongst the tracery of small ferns, black and dull, writhing and motionless, like an arrested snake. The short words of the paddlers reverberated loudly between the thick and somber walls of vegetation. Darkness oozed out from between the trees, through the tangled maze of the creepers, from behind the great fantastic and unstirring leaves; the darkness, mysterious and invincible; the darkness scented and poisonous of impenetrable forests.

The men poled in the shoaling water. The creek broadened, opening out into a wide sweep of a stagnant lagoon. The forests receded from the marshy bank, leaving a level strip of bright green, reedy grass to frame the reflected blueness of the sky. A fleecy pink cloud drifted high above, trailing the delicate coloring of its image under the floating leaves and the silvery blossoms of the lotus. A little house, perched on high poles, appeared black in the distance. Near it, two tall nibong palms, that seemed to have come out of the forests in the background, leaned slightly over the ragged roof, with a suggestion of sad tenderness and care in the droop of their leafy and soaring heads.

The steersman, pointing with his paddle, said, "Arsat is there. I see his canoe fast between the piles."

The polers ran along the sides of the boat, glancing over their shoulders at the end of the day's journey. They would have preferred to spend the night somewhere else than on this lagoon of weird aspect and ghostly reputation. Moreover, they disliked Arsat, first as a stranger, and also because he who repairs a ruined house, and dwells in it, proclaims that he is not afraid to live amongst the spirits that haunt the places abandoned by mankind. Such a man can disturb the course of fate by glances or words; while his familiar ghosts are not easy to propitiate by casual wayfarers upon whom they long to wreak the malice of their human master. White men care not for such things, being unbelievers and in league with the Father of Evil, who leads them unharmed through the invisible dangers of this world. To the warnings of the righteous they oppose an offensive pretense of disbelief. What is there to be done?

So they thought, throwing their weight on the end of their long poles. The big canoe glided on swiftly, noiselessly, and smoothly, towards Arsat's clearing, till, in a great rattling of poles thrown down, and the loud murmurs of "Allah be praised!" it came with a gentle knock against the crooked piles below the house.

The boatmen with uplifted faces shouted discordantly, "Arsat! O Arsat!" Nobody came. The white man began to climb the rude ladder giving access to the bamboo platform before the house. The juragan of the boat said sulkily, "We will cook in the sampan, and sleep on the water."

"Pass my blankets and the basket," said the white man, curtly.

He knelt on the edge of the platform to receive the bundle. Then the boat shoved off, and the white man, standing up, confronted Arsat, who had come out through the low door of his hut. He was a man young, powerful, with broad chest and muscular arms. He had nothing on but his sarong. His head was bare. His big, soft eyes stared eagerly at the white man, but his voice and demeanor were composed as he asked, without any words of greeting—

"Have you medicine, Tuan?"

"No," said the visitor in a startled tone. "No. Why? Is there sickness in the house?"

"Enter and see," replied Arsat, in the same calm manner, and turning short round, passed again through the small doorway. The white man, dropping his bundles, followed.

In the dim light of the dwelling he made out on a couch of

bamboos a woman stretched on her back under a broad sheet of red cotton cloth. She lay still, as if dead; but her big eyes, wide open, glittered in the gloom, staring upwards at the slender rafters, motionless and unseeing. She was in high fever, and evidently unconscious. Her cheeks were sunk slightly, her lips were partly open, and on the young face there was the ominous and fixed expression—the absorbed, contemplating expression of the unconscious who are going to die. The two men stood looking down at her in silence.

"Has she been long ill?" asked the traveler.

"I have not slept for five nights," answered the Malay, in a deliberate tone. "At first she heard voices calling her from the water and struggled against me who held her. But since the sun of today rose she hears nothing—she hears not me. She sees nothing. She sees not me—me!"

He remained silent for a minute, then asked softly—

"Tuan, will she die?"

"I fear so," said the white man, sorrowfully. He had known Arsat years ago, in a far country in times of trouble and danger, when no friendship is to be despised. And since his Malay friend had come unexpectedly to dwell in the hut on the lagoon with a strange woman, he had slept many times there, in his journeys up and down the river. He liked the man who knew how to keep faith in council and how to fight without fear by the side of his white friend. He liked him—not so much perhaps as a man likes his favorite dog—but still he liked him well enough to help and ask no questions, to think sometimes vaguely and hazily in the midst of his own pursuits, about the lonely man and the long-haired woman with audacious face and triumphant eyes, who lived together hidden by the forests—alone and feared.

The white man came out of the hut in time to see the enormous conflagration of sunset put out by the swift and stealthy shadows that, rising like a black and impalpable vapor above the treetops, spread over the heaven, extinguishing the crimson glow of floating clouds and the red brilliance of departing daylight. In a few moments all the stars came out above the intense blackness of the earth and the great lagoon gleaming suddenly with reflected lights resembled an oval patch of night sky flung down into the hopeless and abysmal night of the wilderness. The white man had some supper out of the basket, then collecting a few sticks that lay about the platform, made up a small fire, not for warmth, but for the sake of the smoke, which would keep off the mosquitoes. He wrapped himself in the blankets and sat with his back against the reed wall of the house, smoking thoughtfully.

Arsat came through the doorway with noiseless steps and squatted down by the fire. The white man moved his outstretched legs a little.

"She breathes," said Arsat in a low voice, anticipating the expected question. "She breathes and burns as if with a great fire. She speaks not; she hears not—and burns!"

He paused for a moment, then asked in a quiet, incurious tone—

"Tuan . . . will she die?"

The white man moved his shoulders uneasily and muttered in a hesitating manner—

"If such is her fate."

"No, Tuan," said Arsat, calmly. "If such is my fate. I hear, I see, I wait. I remember . . . Tuan, do you remember the old days? Do you remember my brother?"

"Yes," said the white man. The Malay rose suddenly and went in. The other, sitting still outside, could hear the voice in the hut. Arsat said: "Hear me! Speak!" His words were succeeded by a complete silence. "O Diamelen!" he cried, suddenly. After that cry there was a deep sigh. Arsat came out and sank down again in his old place.

They sat in silence before the fire. There was no sound within the house, there was no sound near them; but far away on the lagoon they could hear the voices of the boatmen ringing fitful and distinct on the calm water. The fire in the bows of the sampan shone faintly in the distance with a hazy red glow. Then it died out. The voices ceased. The land and the water slept invisible, unstirring and mute. It was as though there had been nothing left in the world but the glitter of stars streaming, ceaseless and vain, through the black stillness of the night.

The white man gazed straight before him into the darkness with wide-open eyes. The fear and fascination, the inspiration and the wonder of death—of death near, unavoidable, and unseen, soothed the unrest of his race and stirred the most indistinct, the most intimate of his thoughts. The ever-ready suspicion of evil, the gnawing suspicion that lurks in our hearts, flowed out into the stillness round him—into the stillness profound and dumb, and made it appear untrustworthy and infamous, like the placid and impenetrable mask of an unjustifiable violence. In that fleeting and powerful disturbance of his being the earth enfolded in the starlight peace became a shadowy country of inhuman strife, a battle-field of phantoms terrible and charming, august or ignoble, struggling ardently for the possession of our helpless hearts. An unquiet and mysterious country of inextinguishable desires and fears.

A plaintive murmur rose in the night; a murmur saddening and startling, as if the great solitudes of surrounding woods had tried to whisper into his ear the wisdom of their immense and lofty indifference. Sounds hesitating and vague floated in the air round him, shaped themselves slowly into words; and at last flowed on gently in a murmuring stream of soft and monotonous sentences. He stirred like a man waking up and changed his position slightly. Arsat, motionless and shadowy, sitting with bowed head under the stars, was speaking in a low and dreamy tone—

". . . for where can we lay down the heaviness of our trouble but in a friend's heart? A man must speak of war and of love. You, Tuan, know what war is, and you have seen me in time of danger seek death as other men seek life! A writing may be lost; a lie may be written; but what the eye has seen is truth and remains in the mind!"

"I remember," said the white man, quietly. Arsat went on with mournful composure—

"Therefore I shall speak to you of love. Speak in the night. Speak before both night and love are gone—and the eye of day looks upon my sorrow and my shame; upon my blackened face; upon my burnt-up heart."

A sigh, short and faint, marked an almost imperceptible pause, and then his words flowed on, without a stir, without a gesture.

"After the time of trouble and war was over and you went away from my country in the pursuit of your desires, which we, men of the islands, cannot understand, I and my brother became again, as we had been before, the sword-bearers of the Ruler. You know we were men of family, belonging to a ruling race, and more fit than any to carry on our right shoulder the emblem of power. And in the time of prosperity Si Dendring showed us favor, as we, in time of sorrow, had showed to him the faithfulness of our courage. It was a time of peace. A time of deer-hunts and cock-fights; of idle talks and foolish squabbles between men whose bellies are full and weapons are rusty. But the sower watched the young rice-shoots grow up without fear, and the traders came and went, departed lean and returned fat into the river of peace. They brought news, too. Brought lies and truth mixed together, so that no man knew when to rejoice and when to be sorry. We heard from them about you also. They had seen you here and had seen you there. And I was glad to hear, for I remember the stirring times, and I always remember you, Tuan, till the time came when my eyes could see nothing in the past, because they had looked upon the one who is dying there—in the house."

He stopped to exclaim in an intense whisper, "O Mara bahia! O Calamity!" then went on speaking a little louder:

"There's no worse enemy and no better friend than a brother, Tuan, for one brother knows another, and in perfect knowledge is strength for good or evil. I loved my brother. I went to him and told him that I could see nothing but one face, hear nothing but one voice. He told me: 'Open your heart so that she can see what is in it—and wait. Patience is wisdom. Inchi Midah may die or our Ruler may throw off his fear of a woman!' . . . I waited! . . . You remember the lady with the veiled face, Tuan, and the fear of our Ruler before her cunning and temper. And if she wanted her servant, what could I do? But I fed the hunger of my heart on short glances and stealthy words. I loitered on the path to the bathhouses in the daytime, and when the sun had fallen behind the forest I crept along the jasmine hedges of the women's courtyard. Unseeing, we spoke to one another through the scent of flowers, through the veil of leaves, through the blades of long grass that stood still before our lips; so great was our prudence, so faint was the murmur of our great longing. The time passed swiftly . . . and there were whispers amongst women—and our enemies watched— my brother was gloomy, and I began to think of killing and of a fierce death . . . We are of a people who take what they want—like you whites. There is a time when a man should forget loyalty and respect. Might and authority are given to rulers, but to all men is given love and strength and courage. My brother said, 'You shall take her from their midst. We are two who are like one.' And I answered, 'Let it be soon, for I find no warmth in sunlight that does not shine upon her.' Our time came when the Ruler and all the great people went to the mouth of the river to fish by torchlight. There were hundreds of boats, and on the white sand, between the water and the forests, dwellings of leaves were built for the households of the Rajahs. The smoke of cooking-fires was like a blue mist of the evening, and many voices rang in it joyfully. While they were making the boats ready to beat up the fish, my brother came to me and said, 'Tonight!' I looked to my weapons, and when the time came our canoe took its place in the circle of boats carrying the torches. The lights blazed on the water, but behind the boats there was darkness. When the shouting began and the excitement made them like mad we dropped out. The water swallowed our fire, and we floated back to the shore that was dark with only here and there the glimmer of embers. We could hear the talk of slave-girls amongst the sheds. Then we found a place deserted and silent. We waited there. She came. She came running along the shore, rapid and leaving no trace, like a leaf driven by the wind into the sea. My brother said gloomily, 'Go and take her; carry her into our boat.' I lifted her in my arms. She panted. Her heart was beating against my breast, I said, 'I take you from those people. You came to the cry of my heart, but my arms take you into my boat against the will of the great!' 'It is right,' said my brother. 'We are men who take what we want and can hold it against many. We should have taken her in daylight.' I said, 'Let us be off'; for since she was in my boat I began to think of our Ruler's many men. 'Yes. Let us be off,' said my brother. 'We are cast out and this boat is our country now—and the sea is our refuge.' He lingered with his foot on the shore, and I entreated him to hasten, for I remembered the strokes of her heart against my breast and thought that two men cannot withstand a hundred. We left, paddling downstream close to the bank; and as we passed by the creek where they were fishing, the great shouting had ceased, but the murmur of voices was loud like the humming of insects flying at noonday. The boats floated, clustered together, in the red light of torches, under a black roof of smoke; and men talked of their sport. Men that boasted, and praised, and jeered— men that would have been our friends in the morning, but on that night were already our enemies. We paddled swiftly past. We had no more friends in the country of our birth. She sat in the middle of the canoe with covered face; silent as she is now; unseeing as she is now—and I had no regret at what I was leaving because I could hear her breathing close to me—as I can hear her now."

He paused, listened with his ear turned to the doorway, then shook his head and went on:

"My brother wanted to shout the cry of challenge—one cry only—to let the people know we were freeborn robbers who trusted our arms and the great sea. And again I begged him in the name of our love to be silent. Could I not hear her breathing close to me? I knew the pursuit would come quick enough. My brother loved me. He dipped his paddle without a splash. He only said, 'There is half a man in you now—the other half is in that woman. I can wait. When you are a whole man again, you will come back with me here to shout defiance. We are sons of the same mother.' I made no answer. All my strength and all my spirit were in my hands that held the paddle—for I longed to be with her in a safe place beyond the reach of men's anger and of women's spite. My love was so great, that I thought it could guide me to a country where death was unknown, if I could only escape from Inchi Midah's fury and from our Ruler's sword. We paddled with haste, breathing through our teeth. The blades bit deep into the smooth water. We passed out of the river; we flew in clear channels amongst the shallows. We skirted the back coast; we skirted the sand beaches where the sea speaks in whispers to the land; and the gleam of white sand flashed back past our boat, so swiftly she ran upon the water. We spoke not. Only once I said, 'Sleep, Diamelen, for soon you may want all your strength.' I heard the sweetness of her voice, but I never turned my head. The sun rose and still we went on. Water fell from my face like rain from a cloud. We flew in the light and heat. I never looked back, but I knew that my brother's eyes, behind me, were looking steadily ahead, for the boat went as straight as a bushman's dart, when it leaves the end of the sumpitan. There was no better paddler, no better steersman than my brother. Many times, together, we had won races in that canoe. But we never had put out our strength as we did then—then, when for the last time we paddled together! There was no braver or stronger man in our country than my brother. I could not spare the strength to turn my head and look at him, but every moment I heard the hiss of his breath getting louder behind me. Still he did not speak. The sun was high. The heat clung to my back like a flame of fire. My ribs were ready to burst, but I could no longer get enough air into my chest. And then I felt I must cry out with my last breath, 'Let us rest!' . . . 'Good!' he answered; and his voice was firm. He was strong. He was brave. He knew not fear and no fatigue. . . . My brother!"

A murmur powerful and gentle, a murmur vast and faint; the murmur of trembling leaves, of stirring boughs, ran through the tangles depths of the forests, ran over the starry smoothness of the lagoon, and the water between the piles lapped the slimy timber once with a sudden splash. A breath of warm air touched the two men's faces and passed on with a mournful sound—a breath loud and short like an uneasy sigh of the dreaming earth.

Arsat went on in an even, low voice.

"We ran our canoe on the white beach of a little bay close to a long tongue of land that seemed to bar our road; a long wooded cape going far into the sea. My brother knew that place. Beyond the cape a river has its entrance, and through the jungle of that land there is a narrow path. We made a fire and cooked rice. Then we lay down to sleep on the soft sand in the shade of our canoe, while she watched. No sooner had I closed my eyes than I heard her cry of alarm. We leaped up. The sun was halfway down the sky already, and coming insight in the opening of the bay we saw a prau manned by many paddlers. We knew it at once; it was one of our Rajah's praus. They were watching the shore, and saw us. They beat the gong, and turned the head of the prau into the bay. I felt my heart become weak within my breast. Diamelen sat on the sand and covered her face. There was no escape by sea. My brother laughed. He had the gun you had given him, Tuan, before you went away, but there was only a handful of powder. He spoke to me quickly: 'Run with her along the path. I shall keep them back, for they have no firearms, and landing in the face of a man with a gun is certain death for some. Run with her. On the other side of that wood there is a fisherman's house—and a canoe. When I have fired all the shots I will follow. I am a great runner, and before they can come up we shall be gone. I will hold out as long as I can, for she is but a woman—that can neither run nor fight, but she has your heart in her weak hands.' He dropped behind the canoe. The prau was coming. She and I ran, and as we rushed along the path I heard shots. My brother fired—once—twice—and then the booming gong ceased. There was silence behind us. That neck of land is narrow. Before I heard my brother fire the third shot I saw the shelving shore, and I saw the water again; the mouth of a broad river. We crossed a grassy glade. We ran down to the water. I saw a low hut above the black mud, and a small canoe hauled up. I heard another shot behind me. I thought, 'That is his last charge.' We rushed down to the canoe; a man came running from the hut, but I leaped on him, and we rolled together in the mud. Then I got up, and he lay still at my feet. I don't know whether I had killed him or not. I and Diamelen pushed the canoe afloat. I heard yells behind me, and I saw my brother run across the glade. Many men were bounding after him, I took her in my arms and threw her into the boat, then leaped in myself. When I looked back I saw that my brother had fallen. He fell and was up again, but the men were closing around him. He shouted, 'I am coming!' The men were close to him. I looked. Many men. Then I looked at her. Tuan, I pushed the canoe! I pushed it into deep water. She was kneeling forward looking at me, and I said, 'Take your paddle,' while I struck the water with mine. Tuan, I heard him cry. I heard him cry my name twice; and I heard voices shouting, 'Kill! Strike!' I never turned back. I heard him calling my name again with a great shriek, as when life is going out together with the voice—and I never turned my head. My own name! . . . My brother! Three times he called—but I was not afraid of life. Was she not there in that canoe? And could I not with her find country where death is forgotten—where death is unknown!"

The white man sat up. Arsat rose and stood, an indistinct and silent figure above the dying embers of the fire. Over the lagoon a mist drifting and low had crept, erasing slowly the glittering images of the stars. And now a great expanse of white vapor covered the land: it flowed cold and gray in the darkness, eddied in the noiseless whirls round the tree-trunks and about the platform of the house, which seemed to float upon a restless and impalpable illusion of a sea. Only far away the tops of the trees stood outlined on the twinkle of heaven, like a somber and forbidding shore—a coast deceptive, pitiless and black.

Arsat's voice vibrated loudly in the profound peace. "I had her there! I had her! To get her I would have faced all mankind. But I had her—and—"

His words went out ringing into the empty distances. He paused, and seemed to listen to them dying away very far—beyond help and beyond recall. Then he said quietly—

"Tuan, I loved my brother."

A breath of wind made him shiver. High above his head, high above the silent sea of mist the drooping leaves of the palms rattled together with a mournful and expiring sound. The white man stretched his legs. His chin rested on his chest, and he murmured sadly without lifting his head—

"We all love our brothers."

Arsat burst out with an intense whispering violence—

"What did I care who died? I wanted peace in my own heart."

He seemed to hear a stir in the house—listened—then stepped in noiselessly. The white man stood up. A breeze was coming in fitful puffs. The stars shone paler as if they had retreated into the frozen depths of immense space. After a chill gust of wind there were a few seconds of perfect calm and absolute silence. Then from behind the black and wavy line of the forests a column of golden light shot up into the heavens and spread over the semicircle of the eastern horizon. The sun had risen. The mist lifted, broke into drifting patches, vanished into thin flying wreaths; and the unveiled lagoon lay, polished and black, in the heavy shadows at the foot of the wall of trees. A white eagle rose over it with a slanting and ponderous flight, reached the clear sunshine and appeared dazzlingly brilliant for a moment, then soaring higher, became a dark and motionless speck before it vanished into the blue as if it had left the earth forever. The white man, standing gazing upwards before the doorway, heard in the hut a confused and broken murmur of distracted words ending with a loud groan. Suddenly Arsat stumbled out with outstretched hands, shivered, and stood still for some time with fixed eyes. Then he said—

"She burns no more."

Before his face the sun showed its edge above the treetops rising steadily. The breeze freshened; a great brilliance burst upon the lagoon, sparkled on the rippling water. The forests came out of the clear shadows of the morning, became distinct, as if they had rushed nearer—to stop short in a great stir of leaves, of nodding boughs, of swaying branches. In the merciless sunshine the whisper of unconscious life grew louder, speaking in an incomprehensible voice round the dumb darkness of that human sorrow. Arsat's eyes wandered slowly, then stared at the rising sun.

"I can see nothing," he said half aloud to himself.

"There is nothing," said the white man, moving to the edge of the platform and waving his hand to his boat. A shout came faintly over the lagoon and the sampan began to glide toward the abode of the friend of ghosts.

"If you want to come with me, I will wait all the morning," said the white man, looking away upon the water.

"No, Tuan," said Arsat, softly. "I shall not eat or sleep in this house, but I must first see my road. Now I can see nothing—see nothing! There is no light and no peace in the world; but there is death—death for many. We are sons of the same mother—and I left him in the midst of enemies; but I am going back now."

He drew a long breath and went on in a dreamy tone:

"In a little while I shall see clear enough to strike—to strike. But she has died, and . . . now . . . darkness."

He flung his arms wide open, let them fall along his body, then stood still with unmoved face and stony eyes, staring at the sun. The white man got down into his canoe. The polers ran smartly along the sides of the boat, looking over their shoulders at the beginning of a weary journey. High in the stern, his head muffled up in white rags, the juragan sat moody, letting his paddle trail in the water. The white man, leaning with both arms over the grass roof of the little cabin, looked back at the shining ripple of the boat's wake. Before the sampan passed out of the lagoon into the creek he lifted his eyes. Arsat had not moved. He stood lonely in the searching sunshine; and he looked beyond the great light of a cloudless day into the darkness of a world of illusions.

Conflict

If a teenager cannot decide how to act among strangers, he or she is in conflict with the people he or she meets and with his or her own feelings. That conflict was the case in "The Garden Party" and the essence of the story. When an old woman struggles against obstacles on a long walk through a rural countryside, she is in conflict with nature and with the infirmities of old age. That conflict formed the basis of the story "A Worn Path." If Laura had felt no self-doubt, there would have been no point in telling about the garden party and its aftermath. If Phoenix Jackson had taken an uneventful stroll to the corner store to buy a pinwheel, there wouldn't have been a story there either.

Conflict is the essence of storytelling. Every story is built around conflict, or several conflicts, because conflict creates interest. People are interested in other people's problems. People like to learn how other people deal with problems. In fact, people often like to tell their own conflicts—tell their own stories—to an interested and sympathetic listener, because doing so sometimes helps them see their way through the conflicts to a solution.

When you read, you are, in a way, a sympathetic and interested listener to the problems of others. Sometimes you encounter familiar problems like Laura's self-doubt in "The Garden Party" and George's embarrassment in "A Summer's Reading." You also encounter problems in your reading that you may never have to face in your own life—hand-to-hand combat, mysterious murders, blizzards in the Arctic, or a doomed love affair in a strange and exotic land. Your interest in the stories centers on the way you see the conflicts affecting the characters, and on your need to know how the characters resolve their problems or work their way through them. These are the aspects of conflict that you will examine in the lesson:

1. Conflicts are found in literature and in life.
2. Conflicts arouse your interest and feelings.
3. Conflicts provide insight into the characters in a story.
4. Conflicts cause you to consider important ideas and themes in a story.

· 1 ·
Kinds of Conflict

Conflict that pits one person against another—one story character against another—is the most basic kind of conflict. It is also the easiest to identify. The main character in a story—called the *protagonist*—confronts an opponent, or *antagonist*. That is conflict between people. It can be physical combat, as when

Arsat's brother fights his pursuers, or it can be a combat of wits, words, or wills. Competition between two competing business people can involve a conflict of wits. A violent argument may involve a contest of both wits and words. Conflict between a parent and a child may become a conflict of wills.

Conflict that exists totally within a person is called inner conflict. It usually involves indecision, self-doubt, self-blame, or some intense emotion. Arsat, for example, lives with the memory of abandoning his brother. Maggie of "Everyday Use" suffered continually from feelings of self-doubt and inferiority.

When someone is in conflict with the manners, beliefs, customs, laws, or morals of a group of people, that person is in conflict with society. A criminal who has broken the law is an example of conflict with society. A person who acts contrary to the tenets of a religion is also in conflict with society. Even a different hairstyle or unusual clothing may declare a person to be in conflict with society. Arsat broke the rules when he abducted Diamelen and put himself in conflict with the society led by the local rajah.

Conflicts with nature frequently arise in stories. An adventure story may involve people against the sea or in conflict with an arctic blizzard. Combat with a shark or with a raging river also constitutes conflict with the forces of nature. Joseph Conrad was attracted to the power of the jungle and its effects on people who challenged it. In this story he doesn't use conflict with nature to develop the story, but he hints that it is there:

> Darkness oozed out from between the trees, through the tangled maze of the creepers, from behind the great fantastic and unstirring leaves; the darkness, mysterious and invincible; the darkness scented and poisonous of impenetrable forests.

Finally, people may be in conflict with fate, with the gods, or with the unknown. In the novel *Moby-Dick,* for instance, Captain Ahab challenges God and all the power in heaven to try to stop him in his pursuit of Moby-Dick, the great white whale. His pursuit puts him directly in conflict with God and with whatever unknown power or fate had made the whale his enemy. Notice how conflict with the unknown is used by Conrad in a rather difficult passage:

> The white man gazed straight before him into the darkness with wide-open eyes. The fear and fascination, the inspiration and the wonder of death—of death near, unavoidable, and unseen. . . . The ever-ready suspicion of evil, the gnawing suspicion that lurks in our hearts, flowed out into the stillness round him—into the stillness profound and dumb, and made it appear untrustworthy and in-famous, like the placid and impenetrable mask of an unjustifiable violence. In that fleeting and powerful disturbance of his being the

earth enfolded in the starlight peace became a shadowy country of inhuman strife, a battle-field of phantoms terrible and charming, august or ignoble, struggling ardently for the possession of our helpless hearts.

First Conrad speaks of conflict with the unknown—"the fear and fascination, the inspiration and the wonder of death." Then notice that he says the suspicion of evil "lurks in our hearts" and flows "out into the stillness." The stillness now wears a mask of unjustifiable violence, and it becomes "a shadowy country of inhuman strife, a battle-field of phantoms. . . . struggling ardently for the possession of our helpless hearts." The man's inner struggle makes him feel he is in conflict with a terrible unknown.

EXERCISE A

Read the following passage from the story and answer the questions that follow using the information you have learned in this part of the lesson.

They (the boatmen) would have preferred to spend the night somewhere else than on this lagoon of weird aspect and ghostly reputation. Moreover, they disliked Arsat, first as a stranger, and also because he who repairs a ruined house, and dwells in it, proclaims that he is not afraid to live amongst the spirits that haunt the places abandoned by mankind. . . . White men care not for such things, being unbelievers and in league with the Father of Evil, who leads them unharmed through the invisible dangers of this world.

1. Arsat is in conflict with his society because
   ☐ a. he lives on a ghostly lagoon.
   ☐ b. his house is ruined and disreputable.
   ☐ c. he has defied the local belief in spirits.
   ☐ d. he is considered abandoned by mankind.

2. The white man is also in conflict with this society. Copy the part of the sentence that tells you why.

_____

_____

_____

_____

Now check your answers using the Answer Key at the back of the book. Correct any wrong answers and review this part of the lesson if you do not understand why an answer is wrong.

· 2 ·

Conflict, Feeling, and Interest

Consider two parents who are talking about their children. One parent says, "My Marie was a smart girl from the first day she went to school. Even in kindergarten she got all As. She was captain of the debating team in high school, was elected to the honor society, received a scholarship to Princeton, and now she's a lawyer right out of law school making $90,000 a year."

You couldn't be blamed if you were to fall asleep during this recitation of achievement. Who's interested in a proud parent's bragging? Didn't Marie have to struggle for *anything* in her life? Here is the story from another parent: "Robert had a slow start in life. He was ill as a child so that most of his early schooling was done between stays in the hospital. He was determined to be like other children, however, and read a lot on his own. By the time he was able to enter regular classes at the age of eleven, he surprised his teachers with his extensive knowledge of literature and his ability to do complex mathematics."

The second story has human interest. It is about a child who has faced difficulties—conflicts—and has found a way to overcome them. You would also be interested in Robert's story if he were to have a brief, shining career in school, make many friends, and then succumb to his illness and die the day after graduation. Now the story pulls at your emotions. Either way, the story is interesting to listen to and to think about. What makes Robert's story interesting is his conflict and the emotions the conflict and its outcome arouse in listeners. Listeners tend to relate personally to Robert and to think how they might act under similar circumstances. Conflict functions the same way in good storytelling. If Arsat and Diamelen had simply eloped one night and lived happily ever after, the story would have no more interest than a wedding announcement in the newspaper. But when you add some powerful conflict to the tale, your interest is piqued, your emotions are aroused, and you have to know what's going to happen next:

> "I and Diamelen pushed the canoe afloat. I heard yells behind me, and I saw my brother run across the glade. Many men were bounding after him, I took her in my arms and threw her into the boat, then leaped in myself. When I looked back I saw that my brother had fallen. He fell and was up again, but the men were closing around him. He shouted, 'I am coming!' The men were close

to him. I looked. Many men. Then I looked at her. Tuan, I pushed the canoe! I pushed it into deep water. She was kneeling forward looking at me, and I said, 'Take your paddle,' while I struck the water with mine. Tuan, I heard him cry. I heard him cry my name twice; and I heard voices shouting 'Kill! Strike!' I never turned back. I heard him calling my name again with a great shriek, as when life is going out together with the voice—and I never turned my head. My own name! . . . My brother! Three times he called—but I was not afraid of life. Was she not there in that canoe? And could I not with her find a country where death is forgotten—where death is unknown!"

The reason that emotions and interest run so high in this part of the story is that you find yourself within two conflicts. There is the basic conflict between people—Arsat's brother fighting the pursuers and Arsat fleeing with Diamelen. Then Arsat is torn with inner conflict. Should he return to help his brother or escape with Diamelen? Because Arsat is the protagonist of the story, you identify with him. Because you are on his side you probably feel the same shock he does when he listens to his brother scream. At the same time, you probably sympathize with his yearning to spend his life with Diamelen in some peaceful place "where death is forgotten."

EXERCISE B

Read the following passage from the story and answer the questions that follow using the information you have learned in this part of the lesson.

Arsat's voice vibrated loudly in the profound peace. "I had her there! I had her! To get her I would have faced all mankind. But I had her—and—"

His words went out ringing into the empty distances. He paused, and seemed to listen to them dying away very far—beyond help and beyond recall. Then he said quietly—

"Tuan, I loved my brother."

. . . Arsat burst out with an intense whispering violence—

"What did I care who died? I wanted peace in my own heart."

1. Joseph Conrad brings your interest to bear on Arsat's inner conflict by leaving a sentence unfinished: "To get her I would have faced all mankind. But I had her—and—" Which one of the following phrases best completes Arsat's sentence and expresses the other half of his inner conflict?
   □ a. and I could not bring myself to give her up.
   □ b. and all thought of my brother left my mind.
   □ c. and I became a coward for the sake of a woman.
   □ d. and I was under her spell.

2. When a character in a story says one thing, but you know there is an opposite meaning the situation is called "dramatic irony." If the opposite meaning suggests a tragic turn of fate, it is called "tragic irony." What question does Arsat ask in the passage, relating to his inner conflict, that is interesting because you know he does not mean what he says—that it is tragically ironic?

   _____

   _____

   _____

Now check your answers using the Answer Key at the back of the book. Correct any wrong answers and review this part of the lesson if you do not understand why an answer is wrong.

· 3 ·
Conflict and Character

Hidden character traits tend to surface when a person is faced with a severe emotional crisis or some other kind of conflict. A soldier facing combat for the first time has been the basis of character studies in many war stories, some of which you may have read—*The Red Badge of Courage* and *All Quiet on the Western Front,* among others.

Lesser conflicts than war also reveal a person's character. In "Everyday Use" Maggie faced giving up the quilts that had been promised to her saying, " 'She can have them, Mama . . . I can 'member Grandma Dee without the quilts.' " Her reaction to the small conflict with her sister demonstrated a kind of nobility in Maggie that hadn't been seen before. In "A Summer's Reading" George reacted to his embarrassment by lying, reinforcing your impression of his weakness.

In "The Lagoon" you see several sides of Arsat's character in the course of the story. In the following passage, Arsat is anticipating trouble. How he reacts to the pressure of the moment clearly shows his inclination to be prudent at this time and perhaps even a bit cowardly in his brother's eyes.

> "My brother wanted to shout the cry of challenge—one cry only—to let the people know we were freeborn robbers who trusted our arms and the great sea. And again I begged him in the name of our love to be silent. Could I not hear her breathing close to me? I knew the pursuit would come quick enough. My brother loved me. He dipped his paddle without a splash. He only said, 'There is half a man in you now—the other half is in that woman. I can wait. When you are a whole man again, you will come back with me here to shout defiance. We are sons of the same mother.' I made no answer. All my strength and all my spirit were in my hands that held the paddle—for I longed to be with her in a safe place beyond the reach of men's anger and of women's spite."

Arsat had begun his story by reminding his white friend of their days together in combat: ". . . you have seen me in time of danger seek death as other men seek life!" But now you see Arsat avoiding combat at all costs. Because you are anxious to see Arsat escape to live happily ever after with his love, this caution may simply seem like good common sense. To his brother, however, Arsat is showing weakness: "There is half a man in you now, . . ." he says. The brother's reaction to the conflict of the moment may strike you as reckless; but you have to remember that this is not *your* society that is being told about in the story. It is the society in which Arsat, his brother, and Diamelen live, and it is in the context of that society that their characters must be judged.

EXERCISE C

Read the following passage from the story and answer the questions that follow using the information you have learned in this part of the lesson.

Arsat is telling about being in love with Diamelen:

> "But I fed the hunger of my heart on short glances and stealthy words. I loitered on the path to the bathhouses in the daytime, and when the sun had fallen behind the forest I crept along the jasmine

hedges of the women's courtyard. Unseeing, we spoke to one another through the scent of flowers, through the veil of leaves, through the blades of long grass that stood still before our lips; so great was our prudence, so faint was the murmur of our great longing. The time passed swiftly . . . and there were whispers amongst women—and our enemies watched—my brother was gloomy, and I began to think of killing and of a fierce death. . . . We are of a people who take what they want—like you whites. There is a time when a man should forget loyalty and respect. Might and authority are given to rulers, but to all men is given love and strength and courage."

1. Arsat apparently is not allowed to have Diamelen. How does this conflict seem to affect his character?
   ☐ a. It arouses all of his warrior instincts.
   ☐ b. It brings out the best in him.
   ☐ c. He becomes a love-sick boy.
   ☐ d. He takes a rational approach to life for the first time.

2. The continuing conflict brings about a change in Arsat. Copy the part of a sentence that begins to describe this change.

   _____

   _____

   _____

   _____

   _____

Now check your answers using the Answer Key at the back of the book. Correct any wrong answers and review this part of the lesson if you do not understand why an answer is wrong.

· 4 ·

Conflict and Main Ideas

Stories arise out of conflicts. To discover what the story is *really* about, it is important to examine those conflicts to find important ideas and themes. On one level you can say that "The Lagoon" is about Arsat falling in love with Diamelen, his elopement with her, his brother's death, and finally Diamelen's death. But what "The Lagoon" is *really* about is Arsat's conflicts throughout the story.

The story is about Arsat's breaking a social code by stealing Diamelen (conflict with society), and his yearning for peace and the comfort of love in "a country where death is unknown" (inner conflict). "The Lagoon" is also about an ironic fate—how Arsat took Diamelen to a safe place only to see her become sick and die (conflict with fate and the unknown). Those are themes in the story, and from those themes you can extract a number of ideas that the author is presenting.

One idea is that bad things are likely to happen when people disregard the rules of their society. Another idea is that gratifying a yearning doesn't always lead to happiness. There are other ideas that you will be able to find in the course of discussing the story, all centering on conflict. What ideas can you relate to the conflict expressed in the final passage of the story?

> The white man, leaning with both arms over the grass roof of the little cabin, looked back at the shining ripple of the boat's wake. Before the sampan passed out of the lagoon into the creek he lifted his eyes. Arsat had not moved. He stood lonely in the searching sunshine; and he looked beyond the great light of a cloudless day into the darkness of a world of illusions.

There are two conflicts in that passage: Arsat's loneliness and the struggle against the unknown—the "world of illusions." The idea suggested in the passage is one that appears in many of Conrad's stories. The world is never as it seems to be. No matter how you plan to satisfy your ambitions and your longings, things rarely work out the way you think they will. It's a very gloomy and pessimistic view of life.

One thing you want to keep in mind as you read a story and become involved in its conflicts is that the author has invented these conflicts to create a story that will present his other ideas to you. You do not have to accept the author's ideas as absolute truth. You are free to make up your own mind about them, to agree or disagree. Your own outlook on life, for instance, may be much rosier than Conrad's and more optimistic. Literature simply provides a forum for the discussion of ideas, which is why it is included as part of everyone's education.

EXERCISE D
Read the following passage from the story and answer the questions that follow using the information you have learned in this part of the lesson.

"If you want to come with me, I will wait all the morning," said the white man, looking away upon the water.

"No, Tuan," said Arsat, softly. "I shall not eat or sleep in this house, but I must first see my road. Now I can see nothing—see nothing! There is no light and no peace in the world; but there is death—death for many. We are sons of the same mother—and I left him in the midst of enemies; but I am going back now."

He drew a long breath and went on in a dreamy tone:

"In a little while I shall see clear enough to strike—to strike. But she has died, and . . . now . . . darkness."

1. In at least two places in the story Arsat says he thought he could find a country where death was unknown. That was an illusion. What does he want now?
   ☐ a. a new beginning
   ☐ b. revenge and death
   ☐ c. peace and light
   ☐ d. nothingness

2. What does Arsat say that means he cannot understand all that has happened or why things worked out the way they did?

   _____

   _____

Now check your answers using the Answer Key at the back of the book. Correct any wrong answers and review this part of the lesson if you do not understand why an answer is wrong.

Comprehension Questions

For each of the following statements or questions, select the option that best completes a statement or is the most accurate response to a question.

Recalling Specific Facts

1. The boatmen didn't want to spend the night in Arsat's clearing. Why not?
   - ☐ a. He was a stranger who lived in a ruined house he has repaired.
   - ☐ b. He had incurred the wrath of the Rajah and Inchi Midah.
   - ☐ c. They knew there was sickness there.
   - ☐ d. Arsat was known to be a man who had betrayed his brother.

Recalling Specific Facts

2. How had Arsat and the white man come to be friends?
   - ☐ a. They had been trading partners.
   - ☐ b. They had met on shipboard.
   - ☐ c. They were once enemies.
   - ☐ d. They had fought in a war together.

Recalling Specific Facts

3. What was the event that gave Arsat the opportunity to elope with Diamelen?
   - ☐ a. The Ruler was at war.
   - ☐ b. The women's compound was unguarded.
   - ☐ c. The Ruler and all the men were fishing.
   - ☐ d. Arsat and his brother created a diversion while Diamelen escaped.

Organizing Facts

4. What route did the boatmen take to get to Arsat's clearing?
   - ☐ a. They left the ocean to enter the lagoon.
   - ☐ b. A creek led from a river to the lagoon.
   - ☐ c. There was a sandbar that led to a bay and then to the lagoon.
   - ☐ d. The lagoon was found just beyond the coral reef of an atoll.

Organizing Facts

5. Arsat, his brother, and Diamelen were on a beach when they were discovered. Why were they there?
   - ☐ a. It was the country they had been looking for.
   - ☐ b. They were resting and eating.
   - ☐ c. They were driven there by the rajah's men.
   - ☐ d. Arsat's brother knew they would find a canoe there.

Organizing Facts

6. How did Arsat get the canoe in which he made his final escape with Diamelen?

 □ a. He bought it from a fisherman.

 □ b. His brother got it for him.

 □ c. It had been built and hidden in the bush for this purpose.

 □ d. He stole the canoe from a fisherman.

Knowledge of Word Meanings

7. You may not find the expression *sea-reach* in a modern dictionary, but you should be able to guess its meaning from the way it is used in the third paragraph at the beginning of the story. It most likely means

 □ a. the end of a river that is opening into the sea.

 □ b. where the sea reaches toward the land.

 □ c. a spit of land reaching out into the sea.

 □ d. a kind of fish like a sea urchin or a sea scallop.

Knowledge of Word Meanings

8. The creek "was like a ditch: tortuous, fabulously deep. . . ." This means the creek was

 □ a. too narrow and hard to navigate.

 □ b. difficult, and it had the fabulous quality of being deep.

 □ c. winding and very deep.

 □ d. very deep but dry like the Dry Tortugas.

Knowledge of Word Meanings

9. The lagoon was *stagnant.* What does *stagnant* mean?

 □ a. motionless

 □ b. turbulent

 □ c. odoriferous

 □ d. overgrown

Drawing a Conclusion

10. Before the trouble over Diamelen began, Arsat and his brother must have been

 □ a. soldiers of fortune.

 □ b. officers in the Ruler's guard or army.

 □ c. rulers in their own right.

 □ d. renegades or interlopers in a foreign land.

Drawing a Conclusion

11. Diamelen's position must have been that of
    - ☐ a. princess of the archipelago.
    - ☐ b. a rajah's daughter.
    - ☐ c. Inchi Midah's daughter.
    - ☐ d. a servant or slave.

Drawing a Conclusion

12. Considering the author's descriptions, the story must be set
    - ☐ a. on an atoll in the Pacific Ocean.
    - ☐ b. on an island in a great river.
    - ☐ c. on the edge of a tropical rain forest.
    - ☐ d. in the Amazon jungle.

Making a Judgment

13. What kind of story is "The Lagoon"?
    - ☐ a. a sea story
    - ☐ b. a love story
    - ☐ c. a fable
    - ☐ d. a historic romance

Making a Judgment

14. Arsat's brother's kind of bravery might best be called
    - ☐ a. reckless.
    - ☐ b. selfish.
    - ☐ c. calculated.
    - ☐ d. reasoned.

Making an Inference

15. Evidence in the story suggests that the religion of the country was
    - ☐ a. Christianity.
    - ☐ b. Hinduism.
    - ☐ c. Islamic.
    - ☐ d. voodooism.

Making an Inference

16. Arsat and Diamelen must have been living
    - ☐ a. as refugees a long way from home.
    - ☐ b. not far from where they were born.
    - ☐ c. at a white man's trading outpost.
    - ☐ d. in a place designated for exiles.

Understanding Characters

17. What is the function of the white man in the story?
    - ☐ a. He is the hero or protagonist.
    - ☐ b. He is the moving force behind the adventure.
    - ☐ c. He really has no part in the story at all.
    - ☐ d. He is an observer and listener.

Understanding Characters

18. Two emotions dominate Arsat as he tells his story. What are they?
    - ☐ a. hate and envy
    - ☐ b. anger and remorse
    - ☐ c. sorrow and shame
    - ☐ d. fear and longing

Understanding Main Ideas

19. Another title for the story could be
    - ☐ a. The River
    - ☐ b. A World of Darkness and Illusion
    - ☐ c. Far from It All
    - ☐ d. War and Remembrance

Understanding Main Ideas

20. Which one of the following expressions best sums up an important theme of the story?
    - ☐ a. two tragic loves
    - ☐ b. this weary life
    - ☐ c. thou shalt not steal
    - ☐ d. victory is for the brave

Understanding Main Ideas

21. What has eluded Arsat that he had thought he could find?
    - ☐ a. freedom from death
    - ☐ b. freedom from love
    - ☐ c. freedom from pursuit
    - ☐ d. freedom from want

Recognizing Tone

22. If you had to pick a dominant tone for the story from the following list, which one would be the best choice?

    ☐ a. hope
    ☐ b. courage
    ☐ c. awakening
    ☐ d. gloom

Recognizing Tone

23. Just before Arsat begins his tale, the author says, "A plaintive murmur rose in the night. . . ." What kind of tone does this establish?

    ☐ a. soft and mellow
    ☐ b. plain and musical
    ☐ c. sad and sorrowful
    ☐ d. fearful and evil

Appreciation of Literary Forms

24. Conrad uses personification frequently in his writing. This technique attributes human characteristics or actions to inanimate objects. Which one of the following is an example of personification?

    ☐ a. "The land and the water slept invisible, unstirring and mute."
    ☐ b. "The Malay only grunted and went on looking fixedly at the river."
    ☐ c. "The white man. . . . looked along the empty and broad expanse of the sea-reach."
    ☐ d. "The narrow creek was like a ditch. . . ."

Appreciation of Literary Forms

25. Great orators often use parallel phrases for emphasis. This happens when a word is repeated in some sort of listing. Which one of the following sentences from the story uses this technique?

    ☐ a. "Such a man can disturb the course of fate by glances or words; while his familiar ghosts are not easy to propitiate. . . ."
    ☐ b. "In the stillness of the air every tree, every leaf, every bough, every tendril of creeper and every petal . . . seemed to have been bewitched . . ."
    ☐ c. "She lay still, as if dead; but her big eyes, wide open, glittered in the gloom, staring upwards. . . ."
    ☐ d. "Arsat, motionless and shadowy, sitting with bowed head under the stars, was speaking in a low and dreamy tone—"

Now check your answers using the Answer Key at the back of the book. Make no mark for right answers. Correct any wrong answers you may have by putting a check mark (✓) in the box next to the right answer. Count the number of questions you answered correctly and plot the total on the Comprehension Scores Graph at the back of the book.

Next, look at the questions you answered incorrectly. What types of questions were they? Count the number you got wrong of each type and enter the numbers in the spaces below.

Recalling Specific Facts _____

Organizing Facts _____

Knowledge of Word Meanings _____

Drawing a Conclusion _____

Making a Judgment _____

Making an Inference _____

Understanding Characters _____

Understanding Main Ideas _____

Recognizing Tone _____

Appreciation of Literary Forms _____

Now use these numbers to fill in the Comprehension Skills Profile at the end of the book.

Extension Activities

Discussion Guide

Discussing Conflict

1. In their dramatic escape with Diamelen, Arsat and his brother paddle long and hard to get away. Reread that part of the story. What kinds of conflicts are in that passage?
2. Throughout the story the author describes the forest as enormous, motionless, silent, dark, indifferent. How do those descriptive words help set the scene and establish a mood for the conflicts that occur?
3. In novels the resolution of one conflict often creates a new conflict for the next chapter. That's how novels are made to move along from beginning to end. At the end of "The Lagoon" Arsat has decided to "go back." If this were a novel what new conflicts might come in the next few chapters?

Discussing the Story

4. If you were Arsat, how would you have handled his problems? What would you have done about your love for Diamelen? Would you have returned to help your brother? As you think about an answer, assume that you live under the same circumstances as Arsat.
5. Joseph Conrad is critical of white men in his story. For example, the Malay boatmen think white men are in league with the Father of Evil. Later, Arsat says of himself and his brother: " 'We are of a people who take what they want—like you whites.' " Why do you think Conrad put those comments into the story?
6. The story of Romeo and Juliet, written almost four hundred years ago, was a story of tragic love. "The Lagoon" is a story of tragic love. Why are tragic love stories popular? Do such things happen in real life?

Discussing the Author's Work

7. Some authors write descriptions that sound like poetry. Joseph Conrad is one of these authors. Katherine Mansfield who wrote "The Garden Party" is another. Consider the following passage from "The Lagoon" and do the following:
   a. Decide what is poetic about the passage.
   b. Try to rewrite the passage as a poem. (The poem has been started for you.)

> A murmur powerful and gentle, a murmur vast and faint; the murmur of trembling leaves, of stirring boughs, ran through the tangled depths of the forests, ran over the starry smoothness of the lagoon, and the water between the piles lapped the slimy timber once with a sudden splash. A breath of warm air touched

the two men's faces and passed on with a mournful sound—a breath loud and short like an uneasy sigh of the dreaming earth.

By a Lagoon

A murmur powerful and gentle,
A murmur vast and faint;
The murmur of trembling leaves . . .

8. In the lesson you learned that there is a gloomy and pessimistic view of life in Conrad's writing. What are some examples of that view of life in "The Lagoon"?
9. Conrad has spoken of "the darkness of a world of illusions" in others of his stories. What does he mean by that? Is his statement a realistic view of the world, in your opinion? Is Conrad more pessimistic about life than necessary?

Writing Exercise

Five situations are described below. Each represents a different kind of conflict. Write a few sentences for each situation that will serve as a summary for a story based on the conflict. Be sure to tell how each conflict is resolved—that is, how the story will end.

Conflict between people. Ed Bagley and Rutherford Thompson are opponents for a seat in Congress.

Conflict with society. Dana Ebersall and Martin Castillo are farmers who oppose the way their neighbors are endangering water supplies with pesticides, herbicides, and fertilizers. The neighbors and other people in town feel this is the way farming must be done and they refuse to change their ways.

Conflict with nature. In a period of drought, what little water is left to farmers Dana Ebersall and Martin Castillo is contaminated. They and their neighbors are faced with losing their farms.

Internal conflict. Sylvia Plummer is a cellist with a large symphony orchestra. She falls in love with Guy Holloway, a businessman whose job requires that he be away from home as much as six months a year. Sylvia can go with him if she wants to, but she is obliged to travel with the symphony if she wants to keep her job. Realizing that a marriage under such circumstances has little chance for survival, they must decide what to do.

Conflict with the unknown. Francie Allbright is desperately poor. The way she chooses to rise from poverty is by investing five dollars a week in a lottery. She hits the jackpot. Does she find happiness and financial security, or does something else happen?

UNIT
Six

Unit Six

Introduction

What the Story Is About

"The Guest" is set in a tiny mountain village in Algeria in the mid-1950s. To understand fully what happens in the story, you should know a bit about the situation in Algeria at that time. Algeria is a country in northern Africa, directly across the Mediterranean Sea from France. Except for a fertile belt of land bordering the northern seacoast, the country is hilly, rocky, and barren. The majority of the people are descended from Berber tribesmen and Arabs; they speak Arabic and they are Moslems.

In 1830 France invaded and took control of Algeria. Until 1962 France was in charge of the political and economic life of the country. European colonists moved in, and by the first half of the twentieth century a large minority—about a million people—were Europeans, mostly French.

The native Algerians were caught up in the wave of nationalism that swept Africa after World War II, and in 1954 the National Liberation Front was formed to fight for independence from France. A bitter struggle followed in which many French and many more Algerians lost their lives. The revolt was settled in 1962 when France agreed to withdraw, and the largest part of the French population of Algeria left as well.

During the 130 years of French occupation, many generations of French-speaking people were born in Algeria and thought of the country as their home. Daru, the hero, or protagonist, of "The Guest" is one of these people. He is not an important person in the French colonial community; he is just a country schoolteacher teaching Arab children in a remote and desolate part of the country. Algeria has become his home and he loves it.

In the rising spirit of nationalism and the impending revolt of the 1950s, Daru is forced by the colonial police to face his identity as "one of us"—a Frenchman—as opposed to "one of them"—an Arab. Against Daru's will, the local police give him an Arab prisoner to deliver to jail. The man is not charged with a political or revolutionary crime but with killing a relative in a family squabble. The Arab will be brought to the French police headquarters, which angers the local people who feel that the French have no right to administer justice in their country. Whether he wants to be or not, Daru is "one of us," and the Arab prisoner is "one of them." Daru's dilemma—what to do with the prisoner—is the conflict of the story.

Like Daru, author Albert Camus was born into a French-Algerian family of very moderate means. He was educated in Algerian schools and graduated from the University of Algiers. He is considered one of the most important thinkers and authors of the twentieth century, and for his achievements he received the Nobel Prize for literature in 1957.

Because his work often proposes that there is a strong element of absurdity in the human condition, he is identified with the existential movement in literature and philosophy, but he himself denied that he adhered to this school of thought. Existentialists believe that an individual must make his or her own decisions with no way of knowing what the correct choices are. Each person is responsible for his or her own behavior, actions, beliefs, and decisions. The existentialists believe that a person's responsibility for himself or herself results in feelings of loneliness and insecurity.

That existentialist idea is most apparent in Camus's famous novel *L'Étranger (The Stranger)* which was published in 1942. You will also find an expression of this idea in "The Guest," as the schoolteacher Daru becomes caught in a series of circumstances that he is powerless to control. One thing that separates Camus from the existentialists, however, is that his protagonists, though aware of the absurd conditions in which they become enmeshed, nevertheless rebel against their circumstances in a way that has an important meaning of its own. Daru, as you will read, acts with human compassion as he tries to extract himself from a situation he would rather not be involved in—even though the results of his actions are far from what he expects.

What the Lesson Is About

The lesson that follows "The Guest" is about plot. Plot is the arrangement of events and actions in a story. A plot logically connects the actions of a story by assuring that each action causes or leads into the next action—from the beginning, to the middle, to the end of the story.

Plot is important because it brings order to a story and keeps your interest by enticing you to see what will happen next—what will be the result of an action that has just occurred. When you understand the way an author has structured a plot, it is easier to understand the characters' relationships and the ideas that the author has woven into the story.

Keep the following questions in mind as you read "The Guest." They will help you to focus on how Camus develops his plot.

1. What events at the beginning of the story tell you who is involved in the story and what is going on?

2. What thoughts go through Daru's mind that represent struggles or conflicts that affect the course of the story?

3. Where, near the end of the story, is there a final important action or turning point that you are sure must lead at last to the story's outcome?

4. How does the story turn out? That is, how are the conflicts and the actions brought to some conclusion in the end?

The Guest

by Albert Camus

The schoolmaster was watching the two men climb toward him. One was on horseback, the other on foot. They had not yet tackled the abrupt rise leading to the schoolhouse built on the hillside. They were toiling onward, making slow progress in the snow, among the stones, on the vast expanse of the high, deserted plateau. From time to time the horse stumbled. Without hearing anything yet, he could see the breath issuing from the horse's nostrils. One of the men, at least, knew the region. They were following the trail although it had disappeared days ago under a layer of dirty white snow. The schoolmaster calculated that it would take them half an hour to get onto the hill. It was cold; he went back into the school to get a sweater.

He crossed the empty, frigid classroom. On the blackboard the four rivers of France, drawn with four different colored chalks, had been flowing toward their estuaries for the past three days. Snow had suddenly fallen in mid-October after eight months of drought without the transition of rain, and the twenty pupils, more or less, who lived in the villages scattered over the plateau had stopped coming. With fair weather they would return. Daru now heated only the single room that was his lodging, adjoining the classroom and giving also onto the plateau to the east. Like the classroom windows, his window looked to the south too. On that side the school was a few kilometers from the point where the plateau began to slope toward the south. In clear weather could be seen the purple mass of the mountain range where the gap opened onto the desert.

Somewhat warmed, Daru returned to the window from which he had first seen the two men. They were no longer visible. Hence they must have tackled the rise. The sky was not so dark, for the snow had stopped falling during the night. The morning had opened with a dirty light which had scarcely become brighter as the ceiling of clouds lifted. At two in the afternoon it seemed as if the day were merely beginning. But still this was better than those three days when the thick snow was falling amidst unbroken darkness with little gusts of wind that rattled the double door of the classroom. Then Daru had spent long hours in his room, leaving it only to go to the shed and feed the chickens or get some coal. Fortunately the delivery truck from Tadjid, the nearest village to the north, had brought his supplies two days before the blizzard. It would return in forty-eight hours.

Besides, he had enough to resist a siege, for the little room was cluttered with bags of wheat that the administration left as a stock to distribute to those of his pupils whose families had suffered from the drought. Actually they had all been victims because they were all poor. Every day Daru would distribute a ration to the children. They had missed it, he knew, during these bad days. Possibly one of the fathers or big brothers would come this afternoon and he could supply them with grain. It was just a matter of carrying them over to the next harvest. Now shiploads of wheat were arriving from France and the worst was over. But it would be hard to forget that poverty, that army of ragged ghosts wandering in the sunlight, the plateaus burned to a cinder month after month, the earth shriveled up little by little, literally scorched, every stone bursting into dust under one's foot. The sheep had died then by thousands and even a few men, here and there, sometimes without anyone's knowing.

In contrast with such poverty, he who lived almost like a monk in his remote schoolhouse, nonetheless satisfied with the little he had and with the rough life, had felt like a lord with his white-washed walls, his narrow couch, his unpainted shelves, his well, and his weekly provision of water and food. And suddenly this snow, without warning, without the foretaste of rain. This is the way the region was, cruel to live in, even without men—who didn't help matters either. But Daru had been born here. Everywhere else, he felt exiled.

He stepped out onto the terrace in front of the schoolhouse. The two men were now halfway up the slope. He recognized the horse-man as Balducci, the old gendarme he had known for a long time. Balducci was holding on the end of a rope an Arab who was walking behind him with hands bound and head lowered. The gendarme waved a greeting to which Daru did not reply, lost as he was in contemplation of the Arab dressed in a faded blue jellaba, his feet in sandals but covered with socks of heavy raw wool, his head surmounted by a narrow, short *chèche.* They were approaching. Balducci was holding back his horse in order not to hurt the Arab, and the group was advancing slowly.

Within earshot, Balducci shouted: "One hour to do the three kilometers from El Ameur!" Daru did not answer. Short and square in his thick sweater, he watched them climb. Not once had the Arab raised his head. "Hello," said Daru when they got up onto the terrace. "Come in and warm up." Balducci painfully got down from his horse without letting go of the rope. From under his bristling mustache he smiled at the schoolmaster. His little dark eyes, deep-set under a tanned forehead, and his mouth surrounded with wrinkles made him look attentive and studious. Daru took the bridle, led the horse to the shed, and came back to the two men, who were now waiting for him in the school. He led them into his room. "I am going to heat up the classroom," he said. "We'll be more comfortable there." When he entered the room again, Balducci was on the couch. He had undone the rope tying him to the Arab, who had squatted near the stove. His hands still bound, the *chèche* pushed back on his head, he was looking toward the window. At first Daru noticed only his huge lips, fat, smooth, almost Negroid; yet his nose was straight, his eyes were dark and full of fever. The *chèche* revealed an obstinate forehead and, under the weathered skin now rather discolored by the cold, the whole face had a restless and rebellious look that struck Daru when the Arab, turning his face toward him, looked him straight in the eyes. "Go into the other room," said the schoolmaster, "and I'll make you some mint tea." "Thanks," Balducci said. "What a chore! How I long for retirement." And addressing his prisoner in Arabic: "Come on, you." The Arab got up and, slowly, holding his bound wrists in front of him, went into the classroom.

With the tea, Daru brought a chair. But Balducci was already enthroned on the nearest pupil's desk and the Arab had squatted against the teacher's platform facing the stove, which stood between the desk and the window. When he held out the glass of tea to the prisoner, Daru hesitated at the sight of his bound hands. "He might perhaps be untied." "Sure," said Balducci. "That was for the trip." He started to get to his feet. But Daru, setting the glass on the floor, had knelt beside the Arab. Without saying anything, the Arab watched him with his feverish eyes. Once his hands were free, he rubbed his swollen wrists against each other, took the glass of tea, and sucked up the burning liquid in swift little sips.

"Good," said Daru. "And where are you headed?"

Balducci withdrew his mustache from the tea. "Here, son."

"Odd pupils! And you're spending the night?"

"No. I'm going back to El Ameur. And you will deliver this fellow to Tinguit. He is expected at police headquarters."

Balducci was looking at Daru with a friendly little smile.

"What's this story?" asked the schoolmaster. "Are you pulling my leg?"

"No, son. Those are the orders."

"The orders? I'm not . . ." Daru hesitated, not wanting to hurt the old Corsican. "I mean, that's not my job."

"What! What's the meaning of that? In wartime people do all kinds of jobs."

"Then I'll wait for the declaration of war!"

Balducci nodded.

"O.K. But the orders exist and they concern you too. Things are brewing, it appears. There is talk of a forthcoming revolt. We are mobilized, in a way."

Daru still had his obstinate look.

"Listen, son," Balducci said. "I like you and you must understand. There's only a dozen of us at El Ameur to patrol throughout the whole territory of a small department and I must get back in a hurry. I was told to hand this guy over to you and return without delay. He couldn't be kept there. His village was beginning to stir; they wanted to take him back. You must take him to Tinguit tomorrow before the day is over. Twenty kilometers shouldn't faze a husky fellow like you. After that, all will be over. You'll come back to your pupils and your comfortable life."

Behind the wall the horse could be heard snorting and pawing the earth. Daru was looking out the window. Decidedly, the weather was clearing and the light was increasing over the snowy plateau. When all the snow was melted, the sun would take over again and once more would burn the fields of stone. For days, still, the unchanging sky would shed its dry light on the solitary expanse where nothing had any connection with man.

"After all," he said, turning around toward Balducci, "what did he do?" And, before the gendarme had opened his mouth, he asked: "Does he speak French?"

"No, not a word. We had been looking for him for a month, but they were hiding him. He killed his cousin."

"Is he against us?"

"I don't think so. But you can never be sure."

"Why did he kill?"

"A family squabble, I think. One owed the other grain, it seems. It's not at all clear. In short, he killed his cousin with a billhook. You know, like a sheep, *kreezk!*"

Balducci made the gesture of drawing a blade across his throat and the Arab, his attention attracted, watched him with a sort of anxiety. Daru felt a sudden wrath against the man, against all men with their rotten spite, their tireless hates, their blood lust.

But the kettle was singing on the stove. He served Balducci more tea, hesitated, then served the Arab again, who, a second time, drank avidly. His raised arms made the jellaba fall open and the schoolmaster saw his thin, muscular chest.

"Thanks, kid," Balducci said. "And now, I'm off."

He got up and went toward the Arab, taking a small rope from his pocket.

"What are you doing?" Daru asked dryly.

Balducci, disconcerted, showed him the rope.

"Don't bother."

The old gendarme hesitated. "It's up to you. Of course, you are armed?"

"I have my shotgun."

"Where?"

"In the trunk."

"You ought to have it near your bed."

"Why? I have nothing to fear."

"You're crazy, son. If there's an uprising, no one is safe, we're all in the same boat."

"I'll defend myself. I'll have time to see them coming."

Balducci began to laugh, then suddenly the mustache covered the white teeth. "You'll have time? O.K. That's just what I was saying. You have always been a little cracked. That's why I like you, my son was like that."

At the same time he took out his revolver and put it on the desk.

"Keep it; I don't need two weapons from here to El Ameur."

The revolver shone against the black paint of the table. When the gendarme turned toward him, the schoolmaster caught the smell of leather and horseflesh.

"Listen, Balducci," Daru said suddenly, "every bit of this disgusts me, and first of all your fellow here. But I won't hand him over. Fight, yes, if I have to. But not that."

The old gendarme stood in front of him and looked at him severely.

"You're being a fool," he said slowly. "I don't like it either. You don't get used to putting a rope on a man even after years of it, and you're even ashamed—yes, ashamed. But you can't let them have their way."

"I won't hand him over," Daru said again.

"It's an order, son, and I repeat it."

"That's right. Repeat to them what I've said to you: I won't hand him over."

Balducci made a visible effort to reflect. He looked at the Arab and at Daru. At last he decided.

"No, I won't tell them anything. If you want to drop us, go ahead; I'll not denounce you. I have an order to deliver the prisoner and I'm doing so. And now you'll just sign this paper for me."

"There's no need. I'll not deny that you left him with me."

"Don't be mean with me. I know you'll tell the truth. You're from hereabouts and you are a man. But you must sign, that's the rule."

Daru opened his drawer, took out a little square bottle of purple ink, the red wooden penholder with the "sergeant-major" pen he used for making models of penmanship, and signed. The gendarme carefully folded the paper and put it into his wallet. Then he moved toward the door.

"I'll see you off," Daru said.

"No," said Balducci. "There's no use being polite. You insulted me."

He looked at the Arab, motionless in the same spot, sniffed peevishly, and turned away toward the door. "Good-by, son," he said. The door shut behind him. Balducci appeared suddenly outside the window and then disappeared. His footsteps were muffled by the snow. The horse stirred on the other side of the wall and several chickens fluttered in fright. A moment later Balducci reappeared outside the window leading the horse by the bridle. He walked toward the little rise without turning around and disappeared from sight with the horse following him. A big stone could be heard bouncing down. Daru walked back toward the prisoner, who, without stirring, never took his eyes off him. "Wait," the schoolmaster said in Arabic and went toward the bedroom. As he was going through the door, he had a second thought, went to the desk, took the revolver, and stuck it in his pocket. Then, without looking back, he went into his room.

For some time he lay on his couch watching the sky gradually close over, listening to the silence. It was this silence that had seemed painful to him during the first days here, after the war. He had requested a post in the little town at the base of the foothills separating the upper plateaus from the desert. There, rocky walls, green and black to the north, pink and lavender to the south, marked the frontier of eternal summer. He had been named to a post farther north, on the plateau itself. In the beginning, the solitude and the silence had been hard for him on these wastelands peopled only by stones. Occasionally, furrows suggested cultivation, but they had been dug to uncover a certain kind of stone good for building. The only plowing here was to harvest rocks. Elsewhere a thin layer of soil accumulated in the hollows would be scraped out to enrich paltry village gardens. This is the way it was: bare rock covered three quarters of the region. Towns sprang up, flourished, then disappeared; men came by, loved one another or fought bitterly, then died. No one in this desert, neither he nor his guest, mattered. And yet, outside this desert neither of them, Daru knew, could have really lived.

When he got up, no noise came from the classroom. He was amazed at the unmixed joy he derived from the mere thought that the Arab might have fled and that he would be alone with no decision to make. But the prisoner was there. He had merely stretched out between the stove and the desk. With eyes open, he was staring at the ceiling. In that position, his thick lips were particularly noticeable, giving him a pouting look. "Come," said Daru. The Arab got up and followed him. In the bedroom, the schoolmaster pointed to a chair near the table under the window.

The Arab sat down without taking his eyes off Daru.

"Are you hungry?"

"Yes," the prisoner said.

Daru set the table for two. He took flour and oil, shaped a cake in a frying-pan, and lighted the little stove that functioned on bottled gas. While the cake was cooking, he went out to the shed to get cheese, eggs, dates, and condensed milk. When the cake was done he set it on the window sill to cool, heated some condensed milk diluted with water, and beat up the eggs into an omelette. In one of his motions he knocked against the revolver stuck in his right pocket. He set the bowl down, went into the classroom, and put the revolver in his desk drawer. When he came back to the room, night was falling. He put on the light and served the Arab. "Eat," he said. The Arab took a piece of the cake, lifted it eagerly to his mouth, and stopped short.

"And you?" he asked.

"After you. I'll eat too."

The thick lips opened slightly. The Arab hesitated, then bit into the cake determinedly.

The meal over, the Arab looked at the schoolmaster. "Are you the judge?"

"No, I'm simply keeping you until tomorrow."

"Why do you eat with me?"

"I'm hungry."

The Arab fell silent. Daru got up and went out. He brought back a folding bed from the shed, set it up between the table and the stove, perpendicular to his own bed. From a large suitcase which, upright in a corner, served as a shelf for papers, he took two blankets and arranged them on the camp bed. Then he stopped, felt useless, and sat down on his bed. There was nothing more to do or to get ready. He had to look at this man. He looked at him, therefore, trying to imagine his face bursting with rage. He couldn't do so. He could see nothing but the dark yet shining eyes and the animal mouth.

"Why did you kill him?" he asked in a voice whose hostile tone surprised him.

The Arab looked away. "He ran away. I ran after him."

He raised his eyes to Daru again and they were full of a sort of woeful interrogation. "Now what will they do to me?"

"Are you afraid?"

He stiffened, turning his eyes away.

"Are you sorry?"

The Arab stared at him openmouthed. Obviously he did not understand. Daru's annoyance was growing. At the same time he felt awkward and self-conscious with his big body wedged between the two beds.

"Lie down there," he said impatiently. "That's your bed."

The Arab didn't move. He called to Daru:

"Tell me!"

The schoolmaster looked at him.

"Is the gendarme coming back tomorrow?"

"I don't know."

"Are you coming with us?"

"I don't know. Why?"

The prisoner got up and stretched out on top of the blankets, his feet toward the window. The light from the electric bulb shone straight into his eyes and he closed them at once.

"Why?" Daru repeated, standing beside the bed.

The Arab opened his eyes under the blinding light and looked at him, trying not to blink.

"Come with us," he said.

In the middle of the night, Daru was still not asleep. He had gone to bed after undressing completely; he generally slept naked. But when he suddenly realized that he had nothing on, he hesitated. He felt vulnerable and the temptation came to him to put his clothes back on. Then he shrugged his shoulders; after all, he wasn't a child and, if need be, he could break his adversary in two. From his bed he could observe him, lying on his back, still motionless with his eyes closed under the harsh light. When Daru turned out the light, the darkness seemed to coagulate all of a sudden. Little by little, the night came back to life in the window where the starless sky was stirring gently. The schoolmaster soon made out the body lying at his feet. The Arab still did not move, but his eyes seemed open. A faint wind was prowling around the schoolhouse. Perhaps it would drive away the clouds and the sun would reappear.

During the night the wind increased. The hens fluttered a little and then were silent. The Arab turned over on his side with his back to Daru, who thought he heard him moan. Then he listened for his guest's breathing, become heavier and more regular. He listened to that breath so close to him and mused without being able to go to sleep. In this room where he had been sleeping alone for a year, this presence bothered him. But it bothered him also by imposing on him a sort of brotherhood he knew well but refused to accept in the present circumstances. Men who share the same rooms, soldiers or prisoners, develop a strange alliance as if, having cast off their armor with their clothing, they fraternized every evening, over and above their differences, in the ancient community of dream and fatigue. But Daru shook himself; he didn't like such musings, and it was essential to sleep.

A little later, however, when the Arab stirred slightly, the schoolmaster was still not asleep. When the prisoner made a second move, he stiffened, on the alert. The Arab was lifting himself slowly on his arms with almost the motion of a sleepwalker. Seated upright in bed, he waited motionless without turning his head toward Daru, as if he were listening attentively. Daru did not stir; it had just occurred to him that the revolver was still in the drawer of his desk. It was better to act at once. Yet he continued to observe the prisoner, who, with the same slithery motion, put his feet on the ground, waited again, then began to stand up slowly. Daru was about to call out to him when the Arab began to walk, in a quite natural but extraordinarily silent way. He was heading toward the door at the end of the room that opened into the shed. He lifted the latch with precaution and went out, pushing the door behind him but without shutting it. Daru had not stirred. "He is running away," he merely thought. "Good riddance!" Yet he listened attentively. The hens were not fluttering; the guest must be on the plateau. A faint sound of water reached him, and he didn't know what it was until the Arab again stood framed in the doorway, closed the door carefully, and came back to bed without a sound. Then Daru turned his back on him and fell asleep. Still later he seemed, from the depths of his sleep, to hear furtive steps around the schoolhouse. "I'm dreaming! I'm dreaming!" he repeated to himself. And he went on sleeping.

When he awoke, the sky was clear; the loose window let in a cold, pure air. The Arab was asleep, hunched up under the blankets now, his mouth open, utterly relaxed. But when Daru shook him, he started dreadfully, staring at Daru with wild eyes as if he had never seen him and such a frightened expression that the schoolmaster stepped back. "Don't be afraid. It's me. You must eat." The Arab nodded his head and said yes. Calm had returned to his face, but his expression was vacant and listless.

The coffee was ready. They drank it seated together on the folding bed as they munched their pieces of the cake. Then Daru led the Arab under the shed and showed him the faucet where he washed. He went back into the room, folded the blankets and the bed, made his own bed and put the room in order. Then he went through the classroom and out onto the terrace. The sun was already rising in the blue sky; a soft, bright light was bathing the deserted plateau. On the ridge the snow was melting in spots. The stones were about to reappear. Crouched on the edge of the plateau, the schoolmaster looked at the deserted expanse. He thought of Balducci. He had hurt him, for he had sent him off in a way as if he didn't want to be associated with him. He could still hear the gendarme's farewell and, without knowing why, he felt strangely empty and vulnerable. At that moment, from the other side of the schoolhouse, the prisoner coughed. Daru listened to him almost despite himself and then, furious, threw a pebble that whistled through the air before sinking into the snow. That man's stupid crime revolted him, but to hand him over was contrary to honor. Merely thinking of it made him smart with humiliation. And he cursed at one and the same time his own people who had sent him this Arab and the Arab too who had dared to kill and not managed to get away. Daru got up, walked in a circle on the terrace, waited motionless, and then went back into the schoolhouse.

The Arab, leaning over the cement floor of the shed, was washing his teeth with two fingers. Daru looked at him and said: "Come." He went back into the room ahead of the prisoner. He slipped a hunting-jacket on over his sweater and put on walking-shoes. Standing, he waited until the Arab had put on his *chèche* and sandals. They went into the classroom and the schoolmaster pointed to the exit, saying: "Go ahead." The fellow didn't budge. "I'm coming," said Daru. The Arab went out. Daru went back into the room and made a package of pieces of rusk, dates, and sugar. In the classroom, before going out, he hesitated a second in front of his desk, then crossed the threshold and locked the door. "That's the way," he said. He started toward the east, followed by the prisoner. But, a short distance from the schoolhouse, he thought he heard a slight sound behind them. He retraced his steps and examined the surroundings of the house; there was no one there. The Arab watched him without seeming to understand. "Come on," said Daru.

They walked for an hour and rested beside a sharp peak of lime-stone. The snow was melting faster and faster and the sun was drinking up the puddles at once, rapidly cleaning the plateau, which gradually dried and vibrated like the air itself. When they resumed walking, the ground rang under their feet. From time to time a bird rent the space in front of them with a joyful cry. Daru breathed in deeply the fresh morning light. He felt a sort of rapture before the vast familiar expanse, now almost entirely yellow under its dome of blue sky. They walked an hour more, descending toward the south. They reached a level height made up of crumbly rocks. From there on, the plateau sloped down, eastward toward a low plain where there were a few spindly trees and, to the south, toward outcroppings of rock that gave the landscape a chaotic look.

Daru surveyed the two directions. There was nothing but the sky on the horizon. Not a man could be seen. He turned toward the Arab, who was looking at him blankly. Daru held out the package to him. "Take it," he said. "There are dates, bread, and sugar. You can hold out for two days. Here are a thousand francs too." The Arab took the package and the money but kept his full hands at chest level as if he didn't know what to do with what was being given him. "Now look," the schoolmaster said as he pointed in the direction of the east, "there's the way to Tinguit. You have a two-hour walk. At Tinguit you'll find the administration and the police. They are expecting you." The Arab looked toward the east, still holding the package and the money against his chest. Daru took his elbow and turned him rather roughly toward the south. At the foot of the height on which they stood could be seen a faint path. "That's the trail across the plateau. In a day's walk from here you'll find pasturelands and the first nomads. They'll take you in and shelter you according to their law." The Arab had now turned toward Daru and a sort of panic was visible in his expression. "Listen," he said. Daru shook his head: "No, be quiet. Now I'm leaving you." He turned his back on him, took two long steps in the direction of the school, looked hesitantly at the motionless Arab, and started off again. For a few minutes he heard nothing but his own step resounding on the cold ground and did not turn his head. A moment later, however, he turned around. The Arab was still there on the edge of the hill, his arms hanging now, and he was looking at the schoolmaster. Daru felt something rise in his throat. But he swore with impatience, waved vaguely, and started off again. He had already gone some distance when he again stopped and looked. There was no longer anyone on the hill.

Daru hesitated. The sun was now rather high in the sky and was beginning to beat down on his head. The schoolmaster retraced his steps, at first somewhat uncertainly, then with decision. When he reached the little hill, he was bathed in sweat. He climbed it as fast as he could and stopped, out of breath, at the top. The rock-fields to the south stood out sharply against the blue sky, but on the plain to the east a steamy heat was already rising. And in that slight haze, Daru, with heavy heart, made out the Arab walking slowly on the road to prison.

A little later, standing before the window of the classroom, the schoolmaster was watching the clear light bathing the whole surface of the plateau, but he hardly saw it. Behind him on the blackboard, among the winding French rivers, sprawled the clumsily chalked-up words he had just read: "You handed over our brother. You will pay for this." Daru looked at the sky, the plateau, and, beyond, the invisible lands stretching all the way to the sea. In this vast landscape he had loved so much, he was alone.

Plot

A well-ordered series of *connected* events in a story comprises the plot. A plot is not just a summary of the story or a list of events; it is an *arrangement* of the events in such a way that one incident leads naturally, or sensibly, to another. The ordering of events and actions helps make a story interesting and believable because you become absorbed in the logical flow of things. You also become anxious to see the results of the actions, or what will happen next.

A good story unravels in a way that makes sense, with ideas and events connected to one another, usually in a cause and effect relationship. Strange elements do not materialize in the setting without a reason. Characters act in a reasonable way, given the circumstances of the story. If, for example, the hero in a movie thriller is seen heading for certain death in a fiery crash and suddenly and unbelievably escapes, the plot must be considered badly flawed. Contrived solutions were created in ancient Greek drama. Just when events were at their worst, a god would descend from heaven to set things right again. The device was called *deus ex machina,* or god from the machine, because the actor playing the god was actually lowered onto the stage by a pulley arrangement. It is considered bad plotting because there is no sensible, logical, or believable connection between one action and the next.

Order does not occur spontaneously in a story; it is imposed by the author. The author selects and arranges events so that the story progresses along a well-planned course to a logical conclusion. A classic story structure is as follows: The beginning of a story, the *exposition,* introduces the main characters, the setting, and the situation. The exposition tells you the time, the place, and the initial action of the story. The writer then begins to develop the main *conflict* in the story. Other, lesser, conflicts often develop as well. The conflicts intensify as one action leads to another, until the story reaches a point of highest tension and greatest interest called the *climax*. At the climax some action often occurs that signals a turning point in the story, which is usually referred to as a *crisis*. Then there is a period of falling action as the story winds down to its conclusion or *resolution.*

You may recall in "The Garden Party" that the climax and turning point came when Laura viewed the body of the dead carter. She fled the scene and the action wound down to the resolution of the story as she walked home with her brother. In "Everyday Use" the turning point came when Mama refused to give Dee the quilts. Dee left in a huff and the story approached its resolution with Mama and Maggie quietly sitting in the yard.

You will study the way that Albert Camus uses these four elements of plot in "The Guest":

1. **Exposition.** The author uses exposition to introduce the setting, the main characters, and the situation that will lead to the conflicts of the plot.
2. **Conflicts and complications.** The plot develops; that is, the story unfolds in an interesting way as the characters deal with their conflicts and the complications that arise from their actions.
3. **Crisis and climax.** The conflicts and complications of the story become more intense until a high point in the action or a turning point is reached.
4. **Resolution.** The story winds down to its end.

· I ·
The Exposition

A story most often begins with an exposition in which the author "exposes" or introduces some basic facts about the setting, the characters, and the general situation around which the story will develop. That is the most common way for a story to begin, but some authors use variations of the technique. A story can begin in the present and switch to the past. An author may develop an exposition slowly over a number of chapters. But even in these cases an author must do something at the very beginning of the story to orient you to what is happening in the story and to what the story will deal with. If this doesn't happen soon after the story begins you will quickly become confused and lose interest.

Albert Camus uses a conventional exposition in "The Guest" that goes on for about five paragraphs. Readers are immediately introduced to the schoolmaster, Daru, and you get a distant view, with him, of the two other characters in the story winding their way up a hillside. What important information do you find in the following passage that prepares you to understand the story?

> The schoolmaster was watching the two men climb toward him. One was on horseback, the other on foot. They had not yet tackled the abrupt rise leading to the schoolhouse built on the hillside. They were toiling onward, making slow progress in the snow, among the stones, on the vast expanse of the high, deserted plateau. . . . One of the men, at least, knew the region. They were following the trail although it had disappeared days ago under a layer of dirty white snow.

The picture that is shown to you in that paragraph is of a man at the top of a barren snow-covered hill watching two others climb slowly toward him. These men, it will develop, will be the main characters of the story. A feeling or tone also begins to develop that will dominate the story. The landscape is cold, rocky, and deserted. Travel seems difficult and tedious. It's not a very nice place, and the whole scene makes you want to shiver.

Camus also uses the exposition to capture your interest. He doesn't tell you much about the visitors who are climbing the hill. He tells you just enough to make you wonder about them. Daru is plainly the most important character—the protagonist—since you are watching the action from his place at the top of the hill. But what is a schoolmaster doing in this place? Why are the two people plodding through the snow to visit him? The author has already begun to design the plot in such a way to make you wonder, What will happen next? He knows that you will stay with the story at least until you meet the visitors and find out what they want, and by then new questions will arise as the conflict of the story begins.

Certain elements of exposition continue to appear throughout the story, but you can usually tell where the main exposition ends, because the conflict and action begin. In "The Guest" the main exposition ends before you meet the two visitors. After describing the poor country, the poverty of the people, and Daru's modest living quarters, Camus says:

> In contrast with such poverty, he [Daru] who lived almost like a monk in his remote schoolhouse, nonetheless satisfied with the little he had and with the rough life, had felt like a lord with his whitewashed walls, his narrow couch, his unpainted shelves, his well, and his weekly provision of water and food. And suddenly this snow, without warning, without the foretaste of rain. This is the way the region was, cruel to live in, even without men—who didn't help matters either. But Daru had been born here. Everywhere else, he felt exiled.
>
> He stepped out onto the terrace in front of the schoolhouse. The two men were now halfway up the slope. He recognized the horseman as Balducci, the old gendarme he had known for a long time. Balducci was holding on the end of a rope an Arab who was walking behind him with hands bound and head lowered.

The exposition continues while Daru—and you—wait for the visitors to arrive. In the final paragraph of the exposition you learn how Daru feels about living in isolation and in such modest circumstances. It's interesting that he actually feels like a lord with the little that he has. As modest as it is, he is master here. It is where he was born and he would feel like an exile anywhere else. This is a hint about the ironic turn events will take as the conflict of the story unfolds.

The action begins as Daru steps out onto the terrace and recognizes Balducci who is leading an Arab prisoner. As the story will reveal, this will mark the end of Daru's control over his own affairs in his isolated domain, and it will also threaten Daru with the need to leave his home and become an exile.

EXERCISE A

Read the following passage from the story and answer the questions that follow using the information you have learned in this part of the lesson.

Besides, he had enough to resist a siege, for the little room was cluttered with bags of wheat that the administration left as a stock to distribute to those of his pupils whose families had suffered from the drought. Actually they had all been victims because they were all poor. Every day Daru would distribute a ration to the children. They had missed it, he knew, during these bad days. Possibly one of the fathers or big brothers would come this afternoon and he could supply them with grain. It was just a matter of carrying them over to the next harvest. Now shiploads of wheat were arriving from France and the worst was over. But it would be hard to forget that poverty, that army of ragged ghosts wandering in the sunlight. . . .

1. That passage is part of the exposition that tells how Daru feels about the local people, and it sets a tone that makes you feel the same way. That feeling is one of
   ☐ a. disgust for such backward people.
   ☐ b. unease in anticipation of a siege.
   ☐ c. sympathy for the suffering of the people.
   ☐ d. overwhelming responsibility in a difficult task.

2. One of the problems in the story will be the conflict between the local people and the colonial authorities. Copy at least one sentence or part of a sentence from the paragraph that tells how the colonial power is helping the people.

   _____

   _____

   _____

   _____

*Now check your answers using the Answer Key at the back of the book.
Correct any wrong answers and review this part of the lesson if you do not
understand why an answer is wrong.*

·2·
Conflict and Complication

In the lesson that followed "The Lagoon," you learned how conflict is used in
a story to move it along. You learned that without conflict there would be no
story—it would just be a recitation of unrelated events. If Balducci and his
prisoner had simply stopped to have tea and warm themselves before moving
on and out of Daru's life, there would be no interest in the story, nothing to think
about, and no reason to read it. But this is not the case.

You are led to believe in the exposition that Daru is leading a rather
uncomplicated life before Balducci's visit, and he lives in harmony with the
people. He teaches their children and feeds them in time of need. Now Balducci
and the authorities have complicated Daru's life by ordering him to deliver a
prisoner to the police in a nearby town. It is a complication because the new
situation—the action recorded in the story—has created several conflicts for
Daru. The first is reflected in this excerpt:

> "Good," said Daru. "And where are you headed?"
> Balducci withdrew his mustache from the tea. "Here, son."
> "Odd pupils! And you're spending the night?"
> "No. I'm going back to El Ameur. And you will deliver this fellow
> to Tinguit. He is expected at police headquarters." Balducci was
> looking at Daru with a friendly little smile.
> "What's this story?" asked the schoolmaster. "Are you pulling
> my leg?"
> "No, son. Those are the orders."
> "The orders? I'm not . . ." Daru hesitated, not wanting to hurt
> the old Corsican. "I mean, that's not my job."
> "What! What's the meaning of that? In wartime people do all
> kinds of jobs."
> "Then I'll wait for the declaration of war!"
> Balducci nodded.
> "O.K. But the orders exist and they concern you too. Things are
> brewing, it appears. There is talk of a forthcoming revolt. We are
> mobilized, in a way."
> Daru still had his obstinate look.

The exposition painted a picture of Daru as a benevolent schoolmaster who helped the French authorities to help the people. The Arabs were his people in a sense because he was born here among them. The story is now complicated by the fact that Daru must turn policeman against his will. "I'm not . . ." Daru hesitated. . . . "I mean, that's not my job."

What had Daru wanted to say he is *not?* Living among the Arabs, teaching them, and feeding them, perhaps he was about to blurt out, "I'm not one of you." But not wanting to hurt the gendarme, who was an old friend, he simply protested, "I mean, that's not my job." The political situation has created an inner conflict for Daru, and has drawn a line between *them,* the Arabs, and *us,* the French. You see these two pronouns appearing frequently in the story from here on. Until now Daru has lived comfortably as part of both worlds. He would like things to remain this way. He doesn't want to take sides in the coming struggle. But with the arrival of Balducci and his orders, Daru must make his own decisions and live with the results of those decisions.

Typically, stories become more complicated as they move along, as one conflict is dealt with and leads to another. If the Arab was simply a political prisoner, it would have been easy for Daru to decide to let him go. "After all, what did he do?" Daru asks. It turns out that the Arab is a murderer.

> Daru felt a sudden wrath against the man, against all men with
> their rotten spite, their tireless hates, their blood lust.

Nevertheless, Daru tells Balducci he won't hand the Arab over to the police.

> "It's an order, son, and I repeat it."
> "That's right. Repeat to them what I've said to you: I won't hand
> him over."
> Balducci made a visible effort to reflect. He looked at the Arab
> and at Daru. At last he decided.
> "No, I won't tell them anything. If you want to drop us, go ahead;
> I'll not denounce you. I have an order to deliver the prisoner and
> I'm doing so. And now you'll just sign this paper for me."

Balducci leaves and Daru's real conflict begins. He has to decide what to do with the prisoner. Daru also has to decide if he is one of *us* or one of *them,* a choice he would rather not make. And what about the Arab? "Is he against *us?*" They don't know. As one conflict leads to another, the story becomes increasingly more complicated as it moves along. Daru and the Arab pass a night together. At first they are suspicious of one another. Daru isn't sure if the Arab will attack him in an effort to escape. The Arab doesn't know what to expect from Daru. But the two develop a kind of trust and even a friendship, and in the morning, instead of escaping as Daru would have wished, the Arab is still there.

He apparently has decided he will not escape so as not to put Daru at odds with the authorities. Far from solving Daru's conflict, the Arab unknowingly has complicated things even more.

The term for this increasing complication in a story, caused by the continuing progression of conflicts, is called "rising action." The rising action of a plot continues until the author feels that the action must finally take a turn toward the end of the story. What will Daru do? What will the Arab do? How will it all work out? What are the moral and philosophical problems that are raised by these conflicts, and how can they be solved?

EXERCISE B

Read the following passage from the story and answer the questions that follow using the information you have learned in this part of the lesson.

Daru is waiting for the Arab prisoner just before they leave on their journey:

> Crouched on the edge of the plateau, the schoolmaster looked at the deserted expanse. He thought of Balducci. He had hurt him, for he had sent him off in a way as if he didn't want to be associated with him. He could still hear the gendarme's farewell and, without knowing why, he felt strangely empty and vulnerable. At that moment, from the other side of the schoolhouse, the prisoner coughed. . . . That man's stupid crime revolted him, but to hand him over was contrary to honor. Merely thinking of it made him smart with humiliation. And he cursed at one and the same time his own people who had sent him this Arab and the Arab too who had dared to kill and not managed to get away.

1. Daru is angry. What is the conflict that has made him feel this way?
   - ☐ a. Daru realizes he should never have accepted a schoolmaster's post among the Arabs.
   - ☐ b. Daru is angry at having been drawn into this situation by both the Arab and his own people.
   - ☐ c. If the weather had not turned cold and snowy he would not be in this position.
   - ☐ d. Listening to the Arab cough, Daru decides he can't deliver a sick man to the police.

2. How has the conflict with Balducci affected Daru's feelings? Copy the part of the sentence that tells you.

_____

_____

Now check your answers using the Answer Key at the back of the book. Correct any wrong answers and review this part of the lesson if you do not understand why an answer is wrong.

· 3 ·
Crisis and Climax

The plot structure of stories is often a classic or typical pattern that is used by many authors and consists of the elements of exposition, conflicts and complications, rising action, crisis and climax, and the resolution.

It would make things easy for students of literature if all stories were laid out in such a neat pattern, but they aren't. Stories vary widely in style and form, so it is important to keep in mind that this discussion of the pattern of a plot is simply a general outline of how most stories are constructed. An author may provide elements of exposition throughout a story, for example, instead of limiting them to the beginning. In novels there may be two or more parallel plots that the author only brings together at the end of the book. In some books there is a crisis and a climax in almost every chapter.

However, it is a rare story that doesn't have all of the elements of plot in some form. There must be a satisfactory exposition if you are to understand the situation in the story. There must be conflicts to move the plot along and to maintain your interest. At some point the story must finally turn toward its end. It is a story's turning point that will be discussed in this part of the lesson.

Because of the conflicts, the situation in a story becomes more and more complicated. The complication makes up the rising action. A point is finally reached where the action can rise no higher. This can either be a high point of interest or a high point of emotional excitement where you finally must be told what will happen to the protagonist.

A *climax* is a high point of interest or excitement. A *crisis* is a turning point in a story that occurs when a decision is made or something happens to turn a story toward its end. Crisis and climax can, and often do, occur together.

A war story, for example, may build in excitement as two armies gather and deploy for battle. The battle itself is likely to be the high point or climax of the story. At some point the tide turns against one side or the other and this will be the crisis or turning point of the story. From here on the action and excitement will be less intense as the story winds down to its outcome or resolution.

In stories with less violent action than a war story, the main character's life may become more and more complicated until a decision must be made. This will be a climax in the story. How will the protagonist resolve the mess he or she is in? The decision he or she makes will turn the story (the crisis) toward its conclusion.

In "The Guest" you have seen that the conflicts and complications began to build with the arrival of Balducci and the Arab prisoner. The plot became even more complicated as a kind of bond developed between Daru and the Arab.

> But it bothered him also by imposing on him a sort of brotherhood he knew well but refused to accept in the present circumstances. Men who share the same rooms, soldiers or prisoners, develop a strange alliance as if, having cast off their armor with their clothing, they fraternized every evening, over and above their differences, in the ancient community of dream and fatigue. But Daru shook himself; he didn't like such musings. . . .

Daru is bothered by the relationship that is building between himself and the Arab. He doesn't want that to happen; he wants to be objective and not to think about it. But, the author points out, the alliance that develops between two people who share a room and share food is going to be a problem for Daru.

Tension builds after this passage when Daru sees his guest slowly rise from his bed, and he realizes he has left the revolver in his desk. Will the Arab turn on him? Will there be a struggle? Will he escape and solve Daru's problem? No—the Arab just steps outside to relieve himself and returns to bed. They rise the next morning, share breakfast, and wash, just like old friends. The climax of the story has not yet come. Daru must still decide what to do with his new "friend," the murderer.

In building a plot, an author often plans several events that make you sense that a climax in the action is imminent, but it turns out that it is just a further complication. Camus does this a second time when he leads you to believe that Daru has solved his problem by making a choice about what to do with his prisoner.

> Daru surveyed the two directions. There was nothing but the sky on the horizon. Not a man could be seen. He turned toward the Arab, who was looking at him blankly. Daru held out the package

to him. "Take it," he said. "There are dates, bread, and sugar. You can hold out for two days. Here are a thousand francs too."

It seems that the turning point or crisis has come. Daru has decided not only to free the prisoner but also to give him food and money to help his escape. The conflict, however, has been passed to the Arab. Now *he* must decide what to do. The story is still rising toward its final climax and final crisis when it is the *Arab* rather than Daru who makes the decision that turns the story toward its conclusion.

> Daru hesitated. . . . The schoolmaster retraced his steps, at first somewhat uncertainly, then with decision. When he reached the little hill, he was bathed in sweat. He climbed it as fast as he could and stopped, out of breath, at the top. . . . And in that slight haze, Daru, with heavy heart, made out the Arab walking slowly on the road to prison.

That is the real turning point or crisis of the story. Apparently the Arab had undergone the same conflicts as Daru. The Arab finally chooses to save Daru from setting himself against his own people. From this point on, the story moves rather quietly toward its conclusion, so it is also the story's climax. The author has only one more point to make in the story which will be discussed in the fourth part of the lesson.

EXERCISE C

Read the following passage from the story and answer the questions that follow using the information you have learned in this part of the lesson.

> The Arab had now turned toward Daru and a sort of panic was visible in his expression. "Listen," he said. Daru shook his head: "No, be quiet. Now I'm leaving you." He turned his back on him, took two long steps in the direction of the school, looked hesitantly at the motionless Arab, and started off again.

1. Why is there a brief rising conflict between Daru and the Arab?
   - ☐ a. Daru is set on freeing the Arab, but the Arab isn't sure he wants to be freed.
   - ☐ b. The Arab is suspicious that Daru is tricking him into an even worse situation than he is in now.
   - ☐ c. It seems that Daru doesn't understand the risk involved in turning the Arab into the desert alone.
   - ☐ d. The Arab knows his family will take revenge on Daru no matter what he does.

2. Copy the sentence that tells you that it is now the Arab who is experiencing an inner conflict that will carry the story to an even higher climax.

_____

_____

_____

Now check your answers using the Answer Key at the back of the book. Correct any wrong answers and review this part of the lesson if you do not understand why an answer is wrong.

·4·

The Resolution

The resolution of a story brings it to its end. Resolution is also called *falling action* because the conflicts and their resulting actions are descending from the high point of the story's climax. At this point, the main conflicts of the story are over, or *resolved*. The term *resolution* can be misleading because it seems to suggest that all of the problems of the story are solved and the characters live happily ever after. That is not necessarily the case. Many stories end tragically with the action descending to the death of the protagonist or to some other unhappy conclusion. Sometimes that kind of resolution is called a *catastrophe*. You saw an example of this in "The Lagoon." There were two stories, you recall— a story within a story. One story ended with the death of Arsat's brother; the other story ended with the death of Diamelen, and Arsat's resolve to seek revenge for his brother and certain death for himself.

In "The Guest" the story seems to have arrived at a resolution when the Arab disappears from the crest of the hill. All the conflicts apparently have ended. But once again, the author suddenly brings you back to a new high point of excitement when Daru wonders what choice the Arab has made and races back to the hilltop.

The real resolution of the story begins as Daru realizes the whole business is now out of his hands. The main conflict of the story has ended, even though it is not the way Daru had intended.

> The rock-fields to the south stood out sharply against the blue sky,

but on the plain to the east a steamy heat was already rising. And in that slight haze, Daru, with heavy heart, made out the Arab walking slowly on the road to prison.

The climax of the story extended over the entire episode where Daru and the Arab experience a kind of contest of wills over what the Arab will do. The crisis or turning point comes when the Arab makes his decision and Daru discovers what it is. Then, the resolution of the plot begins:

And in that slight haze, Daru, with heavy heart, made out the Arab walking slowly on the road to prison.

The main conflict of the story has been what to do with the Arab—how to set him free without Daru having to choose between being "one of them," or "one of us." The Arab finally takes the problem out of Daru's hands by making a decision on his own to go to jail. There is no more story to tell that involves this conflict, and so the story must soon end. You will see in the excerpt in Exercise D that the action has indeed wound down from the high point of the climax. But you will also notice that Camus resolves the story with a final ironic twist, as many authors like to do, in order to emphasize a main idea.

EXERCISE D

Read the following passage from the story and answer the questions that follow using the information you have learned in this part of the lesson.

A little later, standing before the window of the classroom, the schoolmaster was watching the clear light bathing the whole surface of the plateau, but he hardly saw it. Behind him on the blackboard, among the winding French rivers, sprawled the clumsily chalked-up words he had just read: "You handed over our brother. You will pay for this." Daru looked at the sky, the plateau, and, beyond, the invisible lands stretching all the way to the sea. In this vast landscape he had loved so much, he was alone.

1. You can often see where a new story might begin where the story you have been reading ends. This story ends with the Arab on his way to prison and Daru standing in his classroom. What is clearly the new conflict that can lead to a new story—"The Guest II," so to speak?
   ☐ a. Daru must plan for the return of his pupils now that the weather is better.

☐ b. The Arab might change his mind and return to the schoolhouse.

☐ c. Balducci will learn what Daru has done and will return to arrest Daru.

☐ d. The Arabs will try to take revenge against Daru for something he has not done.

2. Daru had not wanted to make a choice between the French authorities and the Arabs. The ironic twist that ends the story is that he is now at odds with both communities. What is the phrase that emphasizes this idea?

_____

Now check your answers using the Answer Key at the back of the book. Correct any wrong answers and review this part of the lesson if you do not understand why an answer is wrong.

Comprehension Questions

For each of the following statements or questions, select the option that best completes a statement or is the most accurate response to a question.

Recalling Specific Facts

1. Why did Daru have so much wheat?
   - ☐ a. It was the custom in the country to use schoolhouses for storage.
   - ☐ b. Since he received no salary, Daru supported himself this way.
   - ☐ c. This was an emergency food supply for the region because of a drought.
   - ☐ d. It was a supply he was supposed to use in case of a siege.

Recalling Specific Facts

2. What did Balducci give to Daru before leaving him?
   - ☐ a. his revolver
   - ☐ b. nothing but advice
   - ☐ c. handcuffs
   - ☐ d. a message for Tinguit

Organizing Facts

3. How far had Balducci traveled from El Ameur with the prisoner walking behind?
   - ☐ a. two days travel
   - ☐ b. twenty kilometers or about 15 miles
   - ☐ c. the story doesn't say
   - ☐ d. three kilometers or less than two miles

Organizing Facts

4. Daru asked the Arab, "Why did you kill him?" What was the Arab's reason?
   - ☐ a. It was self-defense.
   - ☐ b. It was a matter of honor.
   - ☐ c. He ran away.
   - ☐ d. He stole from me.

Knowledge of Word Meanings

5. The Arab was wearing a *chèche*. This is a French word, but you don't need a French dictionary to understand its meaning. You should be able to tell what the word means from the way it is used in the story. What is it?
   - ☐ a. a necklace
   - ☐ b. a kind of headdress
   - ☐ c. a loose robe
   - ☐ d. sandals

Knowledge of Word Meanings

6. Balducci was an old *gendarme*. What is a *gendarme?*
   - ☐ a. an army sergeant
   - ☐ b. a policeman
   - ☐ c. the local administrator
   - ☐ d. a colonial rancher

Drawing a Conclusion

7. The part of the country where the story takes place can best be described as
   - ☐ a. a desert.
   - ☐ b. a rocky wasteland.
   - ☐ c. tropical.
   - ☐ d. snowbound mountains.

Drawing a Conclusion

8. Balducci was a man who
   - ☐ a. didn't believe in doing things according to rules.
   - ☐ b. was opposed to Daru's feelings.
   - ☐ c. hated Arabs.
   - ☐ d. believed in rules and orders.

Making a Judgment

9. How did Daru feel about his life in the schoolhouse?
   - ☐ a. He was always lonely.
   - ☐ b. He was content.
   - ☐ c. He would leave one day.
   - ☐ d. He felt more Arab than French.

Making a Judgment

10. How did the Arab seem to feel when he first met Daru?
    - ☐ a. He seemed fearful and suspicious.
    - ☐ b. He trusted Daru at once.
    - ☐ c. He was numb with fright.
    - ☐ d. He felt a strange bond with Daru.

Making a Judgment

11. How did Balducci feel about Daru's attitude toward delivering the prisoner?
    - ☐ a. He shrugged it off.
    - ☐ b. He was offended.
    - ☐ c. He became angry.
    - ☐ d. He found it funny.

Making an Inference

12. You are not told either Balducci's age or Daru's age. But can you guess from clues in the story what their relative ages are?
    - ☐ a. Balducci is younger.
    - ☐ b. Balducci is a bit older.
    - ☐ c. They are about the same age.
    - ☐ d. Balducci is much older.

Making an Inference

13. You can infer from the story that Daru
    - ☐ a. lived as much in fear of the French as of the Arabs.
    - ☐ b. was uneasy being alone among Arabs.
    - ☐ c. would feel uncomfortable living anywhere else.
    - ☐ d. had never thought of living anywhere else.

Making an Inference

14. From the way Daru guarded his prisoner you may infer that he
    - ☐ a. hoped the prisoner would escape.
    - ☐ b. had decided not to disappoint Balducci after all.
    - ☐ c. wasn't at all nervous about his "guest."
    - ☐ d. knew there was no doubt the prisoner would escape.

Understanding Characters

15. Daru felt
    - ☐ a. he could not trust either the Arabs or the French.
    - ☐ b. that Balducci represented a dying empire.
    - ☐ c. at odds with the French and the Arab murderer.
    - ☐ d. a lack of caring for what would become of the French or the Arabs.

Understanding Character

16. As they spent time together, Daru and the Arab
    □ a. became more and more aware of their differences.
    □ b. totally understood one another.
    □ c. began to look inward rather than outward.
    □ d. began to feel a kind of attachment.

Understanding Character

17. From what you have read about him, it is fair to say that Daru
    □ a. hated to be the cause of harm to anyone, unless it was a matter of self-defense.
    □ b. had a deep-seated fear of reality and would have escaped himself if it were possible.
    □ c. felt that sooner or later he would come under siege at the hands of his Arab neighbors.
    □ d. was a deeply religious and patriotic person.

Understanding Main Ideas

18. The author suggests in the story that
    □ a. colonialism is wrong no matter how benevolent it may seem.
    □ b. no matter how you try to control the outcome of a situation, it is impossible to know what will happen.
    □ c. no matter what the circumstances, the police should stay within their own sphere.
    □ d. people living in harsh environments under near-starvation conditions are not responsible for their actions.

Understanding Main Ideas

19. Another point that the author makes in the story is that
    □ a. everyone always has the best intentions.
    □ b. reasoning is sometimes not a good substitute for anger.
    □ c. good intentions and actions do not always produce good results.
    □ d. good is better than evil because it is nicer.

Recognizing Tone

20. "In this vast landscape he had loved so much, he was alone." How does this make you feel?
    □ a. somewhat uncomfortable
    □ b. a bit sad
    □ c. angry
    □ d. offended

Recognizing Tone

21. "Listen," he [the Arab] said. Daru shook his head: "No, be quiet. Now I'm leaving you." At that point in the story, both Daru and the Arab seem
    ☐ a. agitated.
    ☐ b. disappointed.
    ☐ c. angry.
    ☐ d. frightened.

Recognizing Tone

22. ". . . the plateau . . . vibrated like the air itself. . . . the ground rang under their feet. From time to time a bird rent the space in front of them with a joyful cry." The feeling in this passage is
    ☐ a. understated.
    ☐ b. exhilarating.
    ☐ c. overstated.
    ☐ d. debilitating.

Appreciation of Literary Forms

23. Near the beginning of the story the author refers to "that army of ragged ghosts wandering in the sunlight." Who are "the ghosts" in this metaphor?
    ☐ a. the drought-stricken people
    ☐ b. the French colonials
    ☐ c. Algerians in general
    ☐ d. early settlers

Appreciation of Literary Forms

24. Camus uses this simile in referring to Daru: ". . . he who lived almost like a monk. . . ." What does the author mean?
    ☐ a. It was as if Daru lived alone in a cave.
    ☐ b. Daru had no contact with other people.
    ☐ c. Daru lived a very plain and simple life.
    ☐ d. He felt it was a very lonely existence.

Appreciation of Literary Forms

25. When the Arab first arrived, he watched Daru "with feverish eyes." This meant that the Arab
    ☐ a. was ill from traveling at the end of a rope.
    ☐ b. had a frightened or frenzied look on his face.
    ☐ c. had very black eyes as someone does who has a fever.
    ☐ d. was looking at Daru with great hatred.

Now check your answers using the Answer Key at the back of the book. Make no mark for right answers. Correct any wrong answers you may have by putting a check mark (✓) in the box next to the right answer. Count the number of questions you answered correctly and plot the total on the Comprehension Scores Graph at the back of the book.

Next, look at the questions you answered incorrectly. What types of questions were they? Count the number you got wrong of each type and enter the numbers in the spaces below.

Recalling Specific Facts	_____
Organizing Facts	_____
Knowledge of Word Meanings	_____
Drawing a Conclusion	_____
Making a Judgment	_____
Making an Inference	_____
Understanding Characters	_____
Understanding Main Ideas	_____
Recognizing Tone	_____
Appreciation of Literary Forms	_____

Now use these numbers to fill in the Comprehension Skills Profile at the end of the book.

Extension Activities

Discussion Guide

Discussing Plot

1. Camus omits some information from the plot exposition that might help you to understand the story. For example, he never names the country, Algeria. He doesn't say how old Daru is. You must infer these things from clues in the story or from knowledge about Camus and his work. Why do you think authors don't tell you *everything* you might like to know in an exposition?

2. Stories are said to be "a slice of life." "The Guest" is less than twenty-four hours in Daru's life. Compare this with other stories you have read in this book and with other novels and short stories you know. How is it possible to write two stories that are about the same length, when one covers less than a day and one covers weeks, months, or years? (For example, how large a "slice of life" does "The Lagoon" cover?)

3. The conflicts in a story "drive" the plot or move it along. You can usually find a cause and effect relationship in this movement of the plot. Give an example of how a conflict in "The Guest" caused something to happen.

Discussing the Story

4. When Daru says he won't hand over the Arab to the French authorities, Balducci says: "I don't like it either. You don't get used to putting a rope on a man even after years of it, and you're even ashamed—yes, ashamed. But you can't let them have their way." If you were a police officer, how would you feel about putting handcuffs or chains on someone?

5. When Balducci leaves he says to Daru: "There's no use being polite. You insulted me." It is not entirely clear why Balducci feels insulted. Why do you think he feels insulted?

6. The author tells you Daru's thoughts: "That man's stupid crime revolted him [Daru], but to hand him [the Arab] over was contrary to honor. Merely thinking of it made him smart with humiliation. And he cursed at one and the same time his own people who had sent him this Arab and the Arab too who had dared to kill and not managed to get away."
   - Why do you think Daru's honor is offended?
   - The crime revolts Daru, yet he is upset that the Arab has not managed to get away. What is troubling Daru, in your opinion?

Discussing the Author's Work

7. Camus wrote in French, so obviously this story has been translated by someone. These are not the author's original words.

- Some of the dialogue (the conversations) sound artificial or stilted. Find some of this dialogue and tell how an author writing in English might write the conversation.
- Some people say that in order to really understand a story you must read it in its original language. What do you think a story might lose in translation?

8. The bare, rocky landscape seems to play an important role in the story. How does Camus use this landscape to emphasize ideas he presents in the story?

9. Camus was a French-Algerian. How does this show in the story? Do you think the story shows him to be more sympathetic with one side or the other in the fight for independence—with the French or the Algerians?

Writing Exercise

1. Reread the last paragraph of the story which serves as the resolution of the plot. There is a new conflict in the resolution that could be the beginning of a new story.

2. Write a plot outline for a new story based on this conflict. Include the following information in your outline:
   - Tell what you will include in the exposition.
   - Describe at least two major conflicts that will occur in the story.
   - Describe at least two actions that are caused by the conflicts.
   - What action will mark the climax of the story?
   - How will the story be resolved?

3. Optional: Write a short story based on your plot outline.

UNIT
Seven

Unit Seven

Introduction

What the Story Is About

Between the ages of four and ten, Truman Capote lived with a family of older cousins in Alabama. The household consisted of three elderly ladies and a bachelor brother. One of the three ladies, a shy, retiring person named Sook Faulk, was in charge of Truman, whom she called Buddy. He liked to call her his "friend." The two were extremely fond of each other, feeling themselves kindred spirits in many ways in spite of the vast difference in their ages.

"A Christmas Memory" is set in the early 1930s in a big old house in Monroeville, Alabama, where Truman Capote lived with Miss Sook, as she was called, and other cousins. This is the same town, incidentally, that would become the setting for *To Kill a Mockingbird* by Truman's childhood friend Harper Lee, in which Truman Capote appeared as the bright little boy Dill who was shuffled from one relative to the next, just as young Truman was.

As you read of the spare country living and the very modest Christmas gifts exchanged in the household, you may get the impression that Truman Capote's family was poor. Quite the opposite was true. Though Miss Sook scrounged for pennies and wore hand-me-down clothes, the other two ladies ran a dry-goods business and other enterprises in town. Their brother owned and operated several large cotton farms. He supervised his farms on horseback, because he refused to have anything to do with cars or other newfangled machinery, even though he could well afford them. Together, the family income and holdings must have been substantial.

The story is about the last Christmas that Truman spent with his friend Miss Sook and the good times they had preparing for it. "A Christmas Memory" is his favorite story, the author has said, because it is true. This and another story about himself and Miss Sook, "The Thanksgiving Visitor," have been published as small gift books that are always popular during the holiday season. Both stories have been made into movies for television that are shown over and over again at Christmastime. Their popularity continues to attract new audiences, and old audiences never tire of them.

Much of Truman Capote's writing is "true" in that his stories frequently relate to experiences he has had, and he often appears in the stories himself in either a major or a minor role. Another type of writing that Capote has done is reportage—accounts of events during his travels and observations about prominent people. Each type of story makes fascinating reading in its own way because of the author's talent for making people and places come alive. Capote was one of the most unusual people to appear on the literary scene in the mid-twentieth century, and he was an expert at descriptive technique, which is why his story was chosen to illustrate a lesson on the use of language in literature.

After reading "A Christmas Memory," you may want to read "The Thanksgiving Visitor," which sheds more light on the Monroeville household. Then you will surely want to read *In Cold Blood*, which the author called "a nonfiction novel." It is a detailed study of a particularly brutal murder committed in a small midwestern town that shows how the murder affected the lives of the people involved—the murderers, the officer who brought them to justice, and the relatives and friends of the victims.

The story of Truman Capote's life is as interesting as his stories and novels. If you would like to find out more about this fascinating writer, read *Capote: A Biography* by Gerald Clark (Simon & Schuster, 1988).

What the Lesson Is About

The lesson that follows the story points out how authors use language in the same way that artists use lines and colors on a canvas. Just as an artist draws lines that lead your eye and uses colors and shadings to affect your feelings, writers use words to lead your mind and use their choices and arrangements of words to appeal to your senses.

Writers use many techniques to create vivid images in your mind. Some writers are better at their trade than others, as you have surely noticed in comparing stories you have liked with those you have not liked. As a craftsman with words, Truman Capote was among the best.

In the lesson you will learn how he uses words to make you *see* the characters of the story and their world. You will also learn how he uses the "tricks" of his trade to make you *feel* the same way he does about the story he is telling.

The following questions will help you to see for yourself how Truman Capote uses language in "A Christmas Memory." Keep the questions in mind and try to answer them in the course of your reading:

1. Authors often use unusual comparisons. For example, Truman Capote says of an old baby buggy: ". . . the wheels wobble like a drunkard's legs." How many other interesting or unusual comparisons can you find?

2. How does the author use the sounds of words to paint pictures that capture your attention and appeal to your senses? As you read, look for sounds that are repeated ("porch pots") and words that portray sounds (whoosh).

3. Readers like to "hear" characters in a story talk. How does the author help you to *hear* and *see* the characters in the conversations that appear in "A Christmas Memory"?

4. Can you find unusual, colorful, or interesting ways in which the author has used language in the story? For example, instead of saying, "There is frost on the lawn," the author says, "Frozen rime lusters the grass."

A Christmas Memory

by Truman Capote

*I*magine a morning in late November. A coming of winter morning more than twenty years ago. Consider the kitchen of a spreading old house in a country town. A great black stove is its main feature; but there is also a big round table and a fireplace with two rocking chairs placed in front of it. Just today the fireplace commenced its seasonal roar.

A woman with shorn white hair is standing at the kitchen window. She is wearing tennis shoes and a shapeless gray sweater over a summery calico dress. She is small and sprightly, like a bantam hen; but, due to a long youthful illness, her shoulders are pitifully hunched. Her face is remarkable—not unlike Lincoln's, craggy like that, and tinted by sun and wind; but it is delicate too, finely boned, and her eyes are sherry-colored and timid. "Oh my," she exclaims, her breath smoking the windowpane, "it's fruitcake weather!"

The person to whom she is speaking is myself. I am seven; she is sixty-something. We are cousins, very distant ones, and we have lived together—well, as long as I can remember. Other people inhabit the house, relatives; and though they have power over us, and frequently make us cry, we are not, on the whole, too much aware of them. We are each other's best friend. She calls me Buddy, in memory of a boy who was formerly her best friend. The other Buddy died in the 1880s, when she was still a child. She is still a child.

"I knew it before I got out of bed," she says, turning away from the window with a purposeful excitement in her eyes. "The courthouse bell sounded so cold and clear. And there were no birds singing; they've gone to warmer country, yes indeed. Oh, Buddy, stop stuffing biscuit and fetch our buggy. Help me find my hat. We've thirty cakes to bake."

It's always the same: a morning arrives in November, and my friend, as though officially inaugurating the Christmas time of year that exhilarates her imagination and fuels the blaze of her heart, announces: "It's fruitcake weather! Fetch our buggy. Help me find my hat."

The hat is found, a straw cartwheel corsaged with velvet roses out-of-doors has faded: it once belonged to a more fashionable relative. Together, we guide our buggy, a dilapidated baby carriage, out to the garden and into a grove of pecan trees. The buggy is mine; that is, it was bought for me when I was born. It is made of wicker, rather unraveled, and the wheels wobble like a drunkard's legs. But it is a faithful object; springtimes, we take it to the woods and fill it with flowers, herbs, wild fern for our porch pots; in the summer, we pile it with picnic paraphernalia and sugar-cane fishing poles and roll it down to the edge of a creek; it has its winter uses, too: as a truck for hauling firewood from the yard to the kitchen, as a warm bed for Queenie, our tough little orange and white rat terrier who has survived distemper and two rattlesnake bites. Queenie is trotting beside it now.

Three hours later we are back in the kitchen hulling a heaping buggyload of windfall pecans. Our backs hurt from gathering them: how hard they were to find (the main crop having been shaken off the trees and sold by the orchard's owners, who are not us) among their concealing leaves, the frosted, deceiving grass. Caarackle! A cheery crunch, scraps of miniature thunder sound as the shells collapse and the golden mound of sweet oily ivory meat mounts in the milk-glass bowl. Queenie begs to taste, and now and again my friend sneaks her a mite, though insisting we deprive ourselves. "We mustn't, Buddy. If we start, we won't stop. And there's scarcely enough as there is. For thirty cakes." The kitchen is growing dark. Dusk turns the window into a mirror: our reflections mingle with the rising moon as we work by the fireside in the firelight. At last, when the moon is quite high, we toss the final hull into the fire and, with joined sighs, watch it catch flame. The buggy is empty, the bowl is brimful.

We eat our supper (cold biscuits, bacon, blackberry jam) and discuss tomorrow. Tomorrow the kind of work I like best begins: buying. Cherries and citron, ginger and vanilla and canned Hawaiian pineapple, rinds and raisins and walnuts and whiskey and oh, so much flour, butter, so many eggs, spices, flavorings: why, we'll need a pony to pull the buggy home.

But before these purchases can be made, there is the question of money. Neither of us has any. Except for skinflint sums persons in the house occasionally provide (a dime is considered very big money); or what we earn ourselves from various activities: holding rummage sales, selling buckets of hand-picked blackberries, jars of homemade jam and apple jelly and peach preserves, rounding up flowers for funerals and weddings. Once we won seventy-ninth prize, five dollars, in a national football contest. Not that we know a fool thing about football. It's just that we enter any contest we hear about: at the moment our hopes are centered on the fifty-thousand-dollar Grand Prize being offered to name a new brand of coffee (we suggested "A.M."; and, after some hesitation, for my friend thought it perhaps sacrilegious, the slogan "A.M.! Amen!"). To tell the truth, our only *really* profitable enterprise was the Fun and Freak Museum we conducted in a back-yard woodshed two summers ago. The Fun was a stereopticon with slide views of Washington and New York lent us by a relative who had been to those places (she was furious when she discovered why we'd borrowed it); the Freak was a three-legged biddy chicken hatched by one of our own hens. Everybody hereabouts wanted to see that biddy: we charged grownups a nickel, kids two cents. And took in a good twenty dollars before the museum shut down due to the decease of the main attraction.

But one way and another we do each year accumulate Christmas savings, a Fruitcake Fund. These moneys we keep hidden in an ancient bead purse under a loose board under the floor under a chamber pot under my friend's bed. The purse is seldom removed from this safe location except to make a deposit, or, as happens every Saturday, a withdrawal; for on Saturdays I am allowed ten cents to go to the picture show. My friend has never been to a picture show, nor does she intend to: "I'd rather hear you tell the story, Buddy. That way I can imagine it more. Besides, a person my age shouldn't squander their eyes. When the Lord comes, let me see him clear." In addition to never having seen a movie, she has never: eaten in a restaurant, traveled more than five miles from home, received or sent a telegram, read anything except funny papers and the Bible, worn cosmetics, cursed, wished someone harm, told a lie on purpose, let a hungry dog go hungry. Here are a few things she has done, does do: killed with a hoe the biggest rattlesnake ever seen in this county (sixteen rattles), dip snuff (secretly), tame hummingbirds (just try it) till they balance on her finger, tell ghost stories (we both believe in ghosts) so tingling they chill you in July, talk to herself, take walks in the rain, grow the prettiest japonicas in town, know the recipe for every sort of old-time Indian cure, including a magical wart-remover.

Now, with supper finished, we retire to the room in a faraway part of the house where my friend sleeps in a scrap-quilt-covered iron bed painted rose pink, her favorite color. Silently, wallowing in the pleasures of conspiracy, we take the bead purse from its secret place and spill its contents on the scrap quilt. Dollar bills, tightly rolled and green as May buds. Somber fifty-cent pieces, heavy enough to weight a dead man's eyes. Lovely dimes, the liveliest coin, the one that really jingles. Nickels and quarters, worn smooth as creek pebbles. But mostly a hateful heap of bitter-odored pennies. Last summer others in the house contracted to pay us a penny for every twenty-five flies we killed. Oh, the carnage of August: the flies that flew to heaven! Yet it was not work in which we took pride. And, as we sit counting pennies, it is as though we were back tabulating dead flies. Neither of us has a head for figures; we count slowly, lose track, start again. According to her calculations, we have $12.73. According to mine, exactly $13. "I do hope you're wrong, Buddy. We can't mess around with thirteen. The cakes will fall. Or put somebody in the cemetery. Why, I wouldn't dream of getting out of bed on the thirteenth." This is true: she always spends thirteenths in bed. So, to be on the safe side, we subtract a penny and toss it out the window.

Of the ingredients that go into our fruitcakes, whiskey is the most expensive, as well as the hardest to obtain: State laws forbid its sale. But everybody knows you can buy a bottle from Mr. Haha Jones. And the next day, having completed our more prosaic shopping, we set out for Mr. Haha's business address, a "sinful" (to quote public opinion) fish-fry and dancing cafe down by the river. We've been there before, and on the same errand; but in previous years our dealings have been with Haha's wife, an iodine-dark Indian woman with brassy peroxided hair and a dead-tired disposition. Actually, we've never laid eyes on the husband, though we've heard that he's an Indian too. A giant with razor scars across his cheeks. They call him Haha because he's so gloomy, a man who never laughs. As we approach his cafe (a large log cabin festooned inside and out with chains of garish-gay naked light bulbs and standing by the river's muddy edge under the shade of river trees where moss drifts through the branches like gray mist) our steps slow down. Even Queenie stops prancing and sticks close by. People have been murdered in Haha's cafe. Cut to pieces. Hit on the head. There's a case coming up in court next month. Naturally these goings-on happen at night when the colored lights cast crazy patterns and the victrola wails. In the daytime Haha's is shabby and deserted. I knock at the door, Queenie barks, my friend calls: "Mrs. Haha, ma'am? Anyone to home?"

Footsteps. The door opens. Our hearts overturn. It's Mr. Haha Jones himself! And he *is* a giant; he does have scars; he *doesn't* smile. No, he glowers at us through Satan-tilted eyes and demands to know: "What you want with Haha?"

For a moment we are too paralyzed to tell. Presently my friend half-finds her voice, a whispery voice at best: "If you please, Mr. Haha, we'd like a quart of your finest whiskey."

His eyes tilt more. Would you believe it? Haha is smiling! Laughing, too. "Which one of you is a drinkin' man?"

"It's for making fruitcakes, Mr. Haha. Cooking."

This sobers him. He frowns. "That's no way to waste good whiskey." Nevertheless, he retreats into the shadowed cafe and seconds later appears carrying a bottle of daisy yellow unlabeled liquor. He demonstrates its sparkle in the sunlight and says: "Two dollars."

We pay him with the nickels and dimes and pennies. Suddenly, jangling the coins in his hand like a fistful of dice, his face softens. "Tell you what," he proposes, pouring the money back into our bead purse, "just send me one of them fruitcakes instead."

"Well," my friend remarks on our way home, "there's a lovely man. We'll put an extra cup of raisins in *his* cake."

The black stove, stoked with coal and firewood, glows like a lighted pumpkin. Eggbeaters whirl, spoons spin round in bowls of butter and sugar, vanilla sweetens the air, ginger spices it; melting, nose-tingling odors saturate the kitchen, suffuse the house, drift out to the world on puffs of chimney smoke. In four days our work is done. Thirty-one cakes, dampened with whiskey, bask on window sills and shelves.

Who are they for?

Friends. Not necessarily neighbor friends: indeed, the larger share are intended for persons we've met maybe once, perhaps not at all. People who've struck our fancy. Like President Roosevelt. Like the Reverend and Mrs. J. C. Lucey, Baptist missionaries to Borneo who lectured here last winter. Or the little knife grinder who comes through town twice a year. Or Abner Packer, the driver of the six o'clock bus from Mobile, who exchanges waves with us every day as he passes in a dust-cloud whoosh. Or the young Wistons, a California couple whose car one afternoon broke down outside the house and who spent a pleasant hour chatting with us on the porch (young Mr. Wiston snapped our picture, the only one we've ever had taken). Is it because my friend is shy with everyone *except* strangers that these strangers, and merest acquaintances, seem to us our truest friends? I think yes. Also, the scrapbooks we keep of thank-you's on White House stationery, time-to-time communications from California and Borneo, the knife grinder's penny post cards, make us feel connected to eventful worlds beyond the kitchen with its view of a sky that stops.

Now a nude December fig branch grates against the window. The kitchen is empty, the cakes are gone; yesterday we carted the last of them to the post office, where the cost of stamps turned our purse inside out. We're broke. That rather depresses me, but my friend insists on celebrating—with two inches of whiskey left in Haha's bottle. Queenie has a spoonful in a bowl of coffee (she likes her coffee chicory-flavored and strong). The rest we divide between a pair of jelly glasses. We're both quite awed at the prospect of drinking straight whiskey; the taste of it brings screwed-up expressions and sour shudders. But by and by we begin to sing, the two of us singing different songs simultaneously. I don't know the words to mine, just: *Come on along, come on along, to the darktown strutters' ball.* But I can dance: that's what I mean to be, a tap dancer in the movies. My dancing shadow rollicks on the walls; our voices rock the chinaware; we giggle: as if unseen hands were tickling us. Queenie rolls on her back, her paws plow the air, something like a grin stretches her black lips. Inside myself, I feel warm and sparky as those crumbling logs, carefree as the wind in the chimney. My friend waltzes round the stove, the hem of her poor calico skirt pinched between her fingers as though it were a party dress: *Show me the way to go home,* she sings, her tennis shoes squeaking on the floor. *Show me the way to go home.*

Enter: two relatives. Very angry. Potent with eyes that scold, tongues that scald. Listen to what they have to say, the words tumbling together into a wrathful tune: "A child of seven! whiskey on his breath! are you out of your mind? feeding a child of seven! must be loony! road to ruination! Remember Cousin Kate? Uncle Charlie? Uncle Charlie's brother-in-law? shame! scandal! humiliation! kneel, pray, beg the Lord!"

Queenie sneaks under the stove. My friend gazes at her shoes, her chin quivers, she lifts her skirt and blows her nose and runs to her room. Long after the town has gone to sleep and the house is silent except for the chimings of clocks and the sputter of fading fires, she is weeping into a pillow already as wet as a widow's handkerchief.

"Don't cry," I say, sitting at the bottom of her bed and shivering despite my flannel nightgown that smells of last winter's cough syrup, "don't cry," I beg, teasing her toes, tickling her feet, "you're too old for that."

"It's because," she hiccups, "I *am* too old. Old and funny."

"Not funny. Fun. More fun than anybody. Listen. If you don't stop crying you'll be so tired tomorrow we can't go cut a tree."

She straightens up. Queenie jumps on the bed (where Queenie is not allowed) to lick her cheeks. "I know where we'll find real pretty trees, Buddy. And holly, too. With berries as big as your eyes. It's way off in the woods. Farther than we've ever been. Papa used to bring us Christmas trees from there: carry them on his shoulder. That's fifty years ago. Well, now: I can't wait for morning."

Morning. Frozen rime lusters the grass; the sun, round as an orange and orange as hot-weather moons, balances on the horizon, burnishes the silvered winter woods. A wild turkey calls. A renegade hog grunts in the undergrowth. Soon, by the edge of knee-deep, rapid-running water, we have to abandon the buggy. Queenie wades the stream first, paddles across barking complaints at the swiftness of the current, the pneumonia-making coldness of it. We follow, holding our shoes and equipment (a hatchet, a burlap sack) above our heads. A mile more: of chastising thorns, burs and briers that catch at our clothes; of rusty pine needles brilliant with gaudy fungus and molted feathers. Here, there, a flash, a flutter, an ecstasy of shrillings remind us that not all the birds have flown south. Always, the path unwinds through lemony sun pools and pitch vine tunnels. Another creek to cross: a disturbed armada of speckled trout froths the water round us, and frogs the size of plates practice belly flops; beaver workmen are building a dam. On the farther shore, Queenie shakes herself and trembles. My friend shivers, too: not with cold but enthusiasm. One of her hat's ragged roses sheds a petal as she lifts her head and inhales the pine-heavy air. "We're almost there; can you smell it, Buddy?" she says, as though we were approaching an ocean.

And, indeed, it is a kind of ocean. Scented acres of holiday trees, prickly-leafed holly. Red berries shiny as Chinese bells: black crows swoop upon them screaming. Having stuffed our burlap sacks with enough greenery and crimson to garland a dozen windows, we set about choosing a tree. "It should be," muses my friend, "twice as tall as a boy. So a boy can't steal the star." The one we pick is twice as tall as me. A brave handsome brute that survives thirty hatchet strokes before it keels with a creaking rending cry. Lugging it like a kill, we commence the long trek out. Every few yards we abandon the struggle, sit down and pant. But we have the strength of triumphant huntsmen; that and the tree's virile, icy perfume revive us, goad us on. Many compliments accompany our sunset return along the red clay road to town; but my friend is sly and noncommittal when passers-by praise the treasure perched in our buggy: what a fine tree and where did it come from? "Yonderways," she murmurs vaguely. Once a car stops and the rich mill owner's lazy wife leans out and whines: "Giveya two-bits cash for that ol tree." Ordinarily my friend is afraid of saying no; but on this occasion she promptly shakes her head: "We wouldn't take a dollar." The mill owner's wife persists. "A dollar, my foot! Fifty cents. That's my last offer. Goodness, woman, you can get another one." In answer, my friend gently reflects: "I doubt it. There's never two of anything."

Home: Queenie slumps by the fire and sleeps till tomorrow, snoring loud as a human.

A trunk in the attic contains: a shoebox of ermine tails (off the opera cape of a curious lady who once rented a room in the house), coils of frazzled tinsel gone gold with age, one silver star, a brief rope of dilapidated, undoubtedly dangerous candy-like light bulbs. Excellent decorations, as far as they go, which isn't far enough: my friend wants our tree to blaze "like a Baptist window," droop with weighty snows of ornament. But we can't afford the made-in-Japan splendors at the five-and-dime. So we do what we've always done: sit for days at the kitchen table with scissors and crayons and stacks of colored paper. I make sketches and my friend cuts them out: lots of cats, fish too (because they're easy to draw), some apples, some watermelons, a few winged angels devised from saved-up sheets of Hershey-bar tin foil. We use safety pins to attach these creations to the tree; as a final touch, we sprinkle the branches with shredded cotton (picked in August for this purpose). My friend, surveying the effect, clasps her hands together. "Now honest, Buddy. Doesn't it look good enough to eat?" Queenie tries to eat an angel.

After weaving and ribboning holly wreaths for all the front windows, our next project is the fashioning of family gifts. Tie-dye scarves for the ladies, for the men a home-brewed lemon and licorice and aspirin syrup to be taken "at the first Symptoms of a Cold and after Hunting." But when it comes time for making each other's gift, my friend and I separate to work secretly. I would like to buy her a pearl-handled knife, a radio, a whole pound of chocolate-covered cherries (we tasted some once, and she always swears: "I could live on them, Buddy, Lord yes I could—and that's not taking His name in vain"). Instead, I am building her a kite. She would like to give me a bicycle (she's said so on several million occasions: "If only I could, Buddy. It's bad enough in life to do without something *you* want; but confound it, what gets my goat is not being able to give somebody something you want *them* to have. Only one of these days I will, Buddy. Locate you a bike. Don't ask how. Steal it, maybe"). Instead, I'm fairly certain that she is building me a kite—the same as last year, and the year before: the year before that we exchanged slingshots. All of which is fine by me. For we are champion kite-fliers who study the wind like sailors; my friend, more accomplished than I, can get a kite aloft when there isn't enough breeze to carry clouds.

Christmas Eve afternoon we scrape together a nickel and go to the butcher's to buy Queenie's traditional gift, a good gnawable beef bone. The bone, wrapped in funny paper, is placed high in the tree near the silver star. Queenie knows it's there. She squats at the foot of the tree staring up in a trance of greed: when bedtime arrives she refuses to budge. Her excitement is equaled by my own. I kick the covers and turn my pillow as though it were a scorching summer's night. Somewhere a rooster crows: falsely, for the sun is still on the other side of the world.

"Buddy, are you awake?" It is my friend, calling from her room, which is next to mine; and an instant later she is sitting on my bed holding a candle. "Well, I can't sleep a hoot," she declares. "My mind's jumping like a jack rabbit. Buddy, do you think Mrs. Roosevelt will serve our cake at dinner?" We huddle in the bed, and she squeezes my hand I-love-you. "Seems like your hand used to be so much smaller. I guess I hate to see you grow up. When you're grown up, will we still be friends?" I say always. "But I feel so bad, Buddy. I wanted to give you a bike. I tried to sell my cameo Papa gave me. Buddy—" she hesitates, as though embarrassed—"I made you another kite." Then I confess that I made her one, too; and we laugh. The candle burns too short to hold. Out it goes, exposing the starlight, the stars spinning at the window like a visible caroling that slowly, slowly daybreak silences. Possibly we doze; but the beginnings of dawn splash us like cold water: we're up, wide-eyed and wandering while we wait for others to waken. Quite deliberately my friend drops a kettle on the kitchen floor. I tap-dance in front of closed doors. One by one the household emerges, looking as though they'd like to kill us both; but it's Christmas, so they can't. First, a gorgeous breakfast: just everything you can imagine—from flapjacks and fried squirrel to hominy grits and honey-in-the-comb. Which puts everyone in a good humor except my friend and I. Frankly, we're so impatient to get at the presents we can't eat a mouthful.

Well, I'm disappointed. Who wouldn't be? With socks, a Sunday school shirt, some handkerchiefs, a hand-me-down sweater and a year's subscription to a religious magazine for children. *The Little Shepherd*. It makes me boil. It really does.

My friend has a better haul. A sack of Satsumas, that's her best present. She is proudest, however, of a white wool shawl knitted by her married sister. But she *says* her favorite gift is the kite I built her. And it *is* very beautiful; though not as beautiful as the one she made me, which is blue and scattered with gold and green Good Conduct stars; moreover, my name is painted on it, "Buddy."

"Buddy, the wind is blowing."

The wind is blowing, and nothing will do till we've run to a pasture below the house where Queenie has scooted to bury her bone (and where, a winter hence, Queenie will be buried, too.) There, plunging through the healthy waist-high grass, we unreel our kites, feel them twitching at the string like sky fish as they swim into the wind. Satisfied, sun-warmed we sprawl in the grass and peel Satsumas and watch our kites cavort. Soon I forget the socks and hand-me-down sweater. I'm as happy as if we'd won the fifty-thousand-dollar Grand Prize in the coffee-naming contest.

"My, how foolish I am!" my friend cries, suddenly alert, like a woman remembering too late she has biscuits in the oven. "You know what I've always thought?" she asks in a tone of discovery, and not smiling at me but a point beyond. "I've always thought a body would have to be sick and dying before they saw the Lord. And I imagined that when He came it would be like looking at the Baptist window: pretty as colored glass with the sun pouring through, such a shine you don't know it's getting dark. And it's been a comfort: to think of that shine taking away all the spooky feeling. But I'll wager it never happens. I'll wager at the very end a body realizes the Lord has already shown Himself. That things as they are"—her hand circles in a gesture that gathers clouds and kites and grass and Queenie pawing earth over her bone—"just what they've always seen, was seeing Him. As for me, I could leave the world with today in my eyes."

This is our last Christmas together.

Life separates us. Those who Know Best decide that I belong in a military school. And so follows a miserable succession of bugle-blowing prisons, grim reveille-ridden summer camps. I have a new home, too. But it doesn't count. Home is where my friend is, and there I never go.

And there she remains, puttering around the kitchen. Alone with Queenie. Then alone. ("Buddy dear," she writes in her wild hard-to-read script, "yesterday Jim Macy's horse kicked Queenie bad. Be thankful she didn't feel much. I wrapped her in a Fine Linen sheet and rode her in the buggy down to Simpson's pasture where she can be with all her Bones . . ."). For a few Novembers she continues to bake her fruitcakes single-handed; not as many, but some: and, of course, she always sends me "the best of the batch."

Also, in every letter she encloses a dime wadded in toilet paper: "See a picture show and write me the story." But gradually in her letters she tends to confuse me with her other friend, the Buddy who died in the 1880s; more and more thirteenths are not the only days she stays in bed: a morning arrives in November, a leafless birdless coming of winter morning, when she cannot rouse herself to exclaim: "Oh, my, it's fruitcake weather!"

And when that happens, I know it. A message saying so merely confirms a piece of news some secret vein had already received, severing me from an irreplaceable part of myself, letting it loose like a kite on a broken string. That is why, walking across a school campus on this particular December morning, I keep searching the sky. As if I expected to see, rather like hearts, a lost pair of kites hurrying toward heaven.

· Use of Language ·

Whenever you make an effort to describe something in a different or unusual way, chances are you will use "figurative" expressions:

"My feelings were on an express train speeding away with me."
"The old oak was a tower of strength."
"My mind was made up as neat as Granny's bed."
"The exam was a mind-blaster."
"I've seen bigger fish than that in a sardine can."

You could have simply said, "What a tiny fish you caught" or "That sure was a tough exam." But such simple expressions are often not enough to express your real feelings. They lack the impact of more descriptive language.

Poets and authors use figurative and descriptive language to express in a short space feelings and impressions that a string of adjectives cannot capture. "How like a winter hath my absence been from thee," Shakespeare wrote, because like winter, being apart from a lover made him feel cold, barren, and forsaken. Winter also seems bleak, hostile, and endless. All this is conveyed in the comparison, "How like a winter. . . ."

Figurative language is words and phrases used in unusual ways to create vivid images, to emphasize certain ideas, or to compare dissimilar things. Figurative language uses "figures of speech." Figures of speech include comparisons, exaggerations, understatement, sarcasm or irony, repetitions of sounds, and so on. *Descriptive language* can include figures of speech, but it also refers to unusual and picturesque choices of words. In the following lesson you will read examples from Truman Capote's "A Christmas Memory" to examine four ways that authors use descriptive and figurative language in their writing:

1. Authors use unusual comparisons to create vivid pictures in your mind.
2. Authors use the sounds and rhythms of words for emphasis and for communicating feeling.
3. Authors use dialogue (conversation) and dialect to help you "hear" and "see" the characters in a story.
4. Authors choose colorful and unusual words to create vivid descriptions.

· 1 ·
Using Comparisons

The three most common forms of comparison used in literature are *simile* (SIM-uh-lee), *metaphor* (MET-uh-for), and *personification*. You will look at these one at a time.

A simile is a direct comparison between dissimilar things. The comparison is always introduced by *like* or *as*. In fact, the easiest way to identify a simile is to look for these two words. Just be sure the expression is a comparison.

In "A Christmas Memory" the author compares Miss Sook to a small hen: "She is small and sprightly, *like* a bantam hen." You know that an elderly lady is nothing like a bantam hen. Yet, as the author points out, both are small and sprightly. You can picture Miss Sook's alert eyes as she takes in her surroundings with quick henlike turns of the head. Also notice the attitude or feeling that the simile conveys. A bantam hen is small, harmless, and vulnerable, and so is Miss Sook.

One word of caution. Be careful how you use the words *like* and *as* to identify a simile. "The sun was rising as I got out of bed," is not a simile. Neither is "I like a morn in June." The *like* or *as* must introduce a comparison of unlike, or dissimilar, things: "The sun is like a giant orange in the morning sky."

A metaphor also compares unlike things. In a metaphor, however, the comparison is not announced by *like* or *as*. The comparison is implied. "The sun is a giant orange in the morning sky." This time the writer states flatly that the sun *is* an orange, not *like* one. You are left to interpret the author's real meaning—that the sun resembles an orange in some ways.

You can turn to William Shakespeare's sonnets again for an example. Just as he compared a lover's absence to winter in the simile you read earlier, he also compared winter to old age in the following metaphor:

> That time of year thou mayst in me behold
> When yellow leaves, or none, or few, do hang
> Upon those boughs which shake against the cold,
> Bare ruined choirs where late the sweet birds sang.

Notice that Shakespeare never makes a *direct* comparison between his age and the dreary season. He describes bare trees, a cold feeling, and the missed song of birds. "I am the same as this dreary season," is *implied* in an indirect way, which makes the lines of verse a metaphor.

Truman Capote used a lovely combination of similes and metaphors to describe his feelings when he heard that his friend had died:

> . . . a morning arrives in November, a leafless birdless coming of winter morning, when she cannot rouse herself to exclaim: "Oh, my, it's fruitcake weather!"
>
> And when that happens, I know it. A message saying so merely confirms a piece of news some secret vein had already received, severing from me an irreplaceable part of myself, letting it loose like a kite on a broken string. That is why, walking across a school

campus on this particular December morning, I keep searching the sky. As if I expected to see, rather like hearts, a lost pair of kites hurrying toward heaven.

To convey the idea that Buddy and his friend were kindred spirits, Capote uses both simile and metaphor. Using a simile, he compares losing his friend to cutting the string on a kite. He builds on this image by turning the whole paragraph into a metaphor. (This is sometimes called "an extended metaphor.")

The kites, he implies, are the kindred souls of the two friends. Buddy imagines his soul hurrying toward heaven with the soul of his friend, and he expresses a feeling of double loss. He has lost his friend in death and feels lost himself without her. That feeling would be almost impossible to describe without using a metaphoric comparison.

Personification is a third way that is used to make comparisons. Personification is a figure of speech in which animals and inanimate objects are given human qualities or characteristics. "As we approached, the cave opened its awful maw to devour us." A cave doesn't have a mouth (maw) and it doesn't eat; the comparison makes the cave seem alive.

People often personify their pets; that is, people try to make their pets seem like people. Consider this description from "At the Bay" by Katherine Mansfield. In the story she uses personification to describe a dog that is assisting a shepherd with his flock of sheep:

> Behind them [the sheep] an old sheep-dog, his soaking paws covered with sand, ran along with his nose to the ground, but carelessly, as if thinking, of something else. And then the shepherd himself appeared. . . . The old dog cut an ancient caper or two and then drew up sharp, ashamed of his levity, and walked a few dignified paces by his master's side.

The dog is personified in that he is made to seem like an old man walking along letting his mind wander from his job. He does a little jig (cuts a caper) and is at once ashamed of himself for showing a lack of seriousness on the job, and he walks on with greater dignity. The author makes it seem that the animal is behaving and thinking like a person, and this comparison through personification helps you understand the scene better and the way the author feels about it.

As Buddy and his "friend" go to find a Christmas tree in "A Christmas Memory," the author uses a great deal of personification. They meet a "renegade" hog. Queenie barks "complaints" about crossing a cold stream. There is an "ecstasy" of shrillings from birds and a school of trout is described as if they were a small navy—"a disturbed armada of speckled trout."

Dogs don't complain, hogs aren't renegades, and trout don't form navies. Those are things people do and feel, and so the comparisons are personifications.

EXERCISE A

Read the following passage from "A Christmas Memory" and answer the questions that follow using the information you have learned in this part of the lesson.

> And, indeed, it [the grove of trees] is a kind of ocean. Scented acres of holiday trees, prickly-leafed holly. Red berries shiny as Chinese bells: black crows swoop upon them screaming. Having stuffed our burlap sacks with enough greenery and crimson to garland a dozen windows, we set about choosing a tree. . . . The one we pick is twice as tall as me. A brave handsome brute that survives thirty hatchet strokes before it keels with a creaking rending cry. Lugging it like a kill, we commence the long trek out. Every few yards we abandon the struggle, sit down and pant.

1. The tree is compared to a brave handsome brute who keels over with a rending cry. This is an example of
   ☐ a. a simile.
   ☐ b. personification.
   ☐ c. a metaphor.
   ☐ d. a direct or implied comparison.

2. The author compares the successful hunt for the tree with a successful hunt for wild game. On the lines below, copy the sentence that contains the simile which makes this comparison.

   _____

   _____

Now check your answers using the Answer Key at the back of the book. Correct any wrong answers and review this part of the lesson if you do not understand why an answer is wrong.

· 2 ·
The Sounds of Words

As languages developed, certain words were invented to imitate sounds. In English-speaking countries people say that a rooster crows *cock-a-doodle-doo.* In France people say that a rooster crows *co-co-ri-co.* Both words attempt to imitate a rooster's piercing cry.

The sounds of words can also convey meanings and feelings in subtler ways. The word *soft,* for example, sounds soft, while *hard* with a harsh *rrr* followed by a striking *duh* sound, sounds hard.

In his tales of horror and suspense, Edgar Allan Poe often used words with many long vowel sounds to send shivers down your spine. Watch for all the *oh, ah,* and *ai* sounds in these lines from "The Tell-Tale Heart" that make you hear the *groans* and feel the *mortal terror:*

> I knew it was the groan of mortal terror. It was not a groan of pain or of grief—oh no!—it was the low stifled sound that arises from the bottom of the soul when overcharged with awe.

Authors sometimes use their words to create a kind of cadence to pace or regulate the way you read. Sometimes the flow of words and sentences becomes so rhythmical that it is almost like poetry, as you saw in some of the passages from Joseph Conrad's "The Lagoon."

Notice how Truman Capote uses cadence in a combination of long and short sentences, or short phrases, when he wants to emphasize or call your attention to something:

> The person to whom she is speaking is myself. I am seven; she is sixty-something. We are cousins, very distant ones, and we have lived together—well, as long as I can remember. Other people inhabit the house, relatives; and though they have power over us, and frequently make us cry, we are not, on the whole, too much aware of them. We are each other's best friend. She calls me Buddy, in memory of a boy who was formerly her best friend. The other Buddy died in the 1880s, when she was still a child. She is still a child.

In that passage the author separates long sentences with short ones. There are three things the author wants you to take special notice of, and he gives you that information in the shortest sentences:

> "I am seven; she is sixty-something."
> "We are each other's best friend."
> "She is still a child."

Authors often repeat sounds to achieve special effects, as Truman Capote does when he describes the Christmas tree falling: ". . . it keels with a creaking rending cry." There are three *"kuh"* sounds in a row—*keels, creaking, cry.* This is called *alliteration.* In the short phrase, the author uses both alliteration and cadence to reproduce the sight and sound of a tree falling. The cadence is slowed with long *ee* sounds to imitate the slow way that a tree begins to topple when it is cut down (keels, creaking). Notice how different the phrase sounds and how different the effect is when you simply say, ". . . the tree fell with a cry."

When the pronunciation of a word imitates its meaning, it is called *onomatopoeia* (ahn-uh-mat-uh-PEE-uh): *buzzing, whish, slam, bang, boom, sizzle.* Sometimes repeating sounds (alliteration) and onomatopoeia are used together as in this phrase from an old song: "The buzzing of the bees in the cigarette trees, by the soda water fountain. . . ."

The sounds of some words and expressions appeal to the senses in other ways, as you have seen with the words *hard* and *soft.* The word *gloomy* conveys feeling better than the word *sad.* When you use *luscious* or *scrumptious* to describe golden pancakes with runny melted butter and maple syrup, you get a delicious chewy feeling that you don't get with the word *tasty.*

Truman Capote doesn't use much onomatopoeia in "A Christmas Memory," but there are a few examples: Dimes *jingle,* when he and his friend count their money; the victrola *wails* at Mr. Haha's place; and Mr. Haha *jangles* the coins in his hand. (Somehow it seems appropriate that coins *jingle* for Buddy but *jangle* in Haha's big fist.) Then there is the description of Buddy and his friend making fruitcakes. The words Capote chooses do not imitate sounds, but they certainly give a feeling of the frenzied, fragrant goings-on:

> The black stove, stoked with coal and firewood, glows like a lighted pumpkin. Eggbeaters whirl, spoons spin round in bowls of butter and sugar, vanilla sweetens the air, ginger spices it; melting, nose-tingling odors saturate the kitchen, suffuse the house, drift out to the world on puffs of chimney smoke.

EXERCISE B

Read the following passage from "A Christmas Memory" and answer the questions that follow using the information you have learned in this part of the lesson.

> Three hours later we are back in the kitchen hulling a heaping buggyload of windfall pecans. . . . Caarackle! A cheery crunch, scraps of miniature thunder sound as the shells collapse and the golden mound of sweet oily ivory meat mounts in the milk-glass

bowl. . . . The kitchen is growing dark. Dusk turns the window into a mirror: our reflections mingle with the rising moon as we work by the fireside in the firelight. At last, when the moon is quite high, we toss the final hull into the fire and, with joined sighs, watch it catch flame. The buggy is empty, the bowl is brimful.

1. What kinds of sound effects does the author use when he says: ". . . hulling a heaping buggyload of windfall pecans. . . . Caarackle! A cheery crunch. . . ."?
   ☐ a. simile and metaphor
   ☐ b. personification and cliche
   ☐ c. alliteration and onomatopoeia
   ☐ d. stridency and nuance

2. Lines of poetry usually have a cadence. Here is a familiar line from a Christmas poem: "The stockings were hung by the chimney with care." The cadence of the line is:

   The stóckings were húng by the chímney with cáre.

   Which sentence in the last part of the paragraph has been given the same cadence by Truman Capote? Copy it on the line below.

   _____

   _____

Now check your answers using the Answer Key at the back of the book. Correct any wrong answers and review this part of the lesson if you do not understand why an answer is wrong.

· 3 ·
Dialogue and Dialect

Stories are about people (or animals that resemble people), and readers like to *hear* what these characters sound like when they talk. A good writer uses words to create "a voice" for his or her characters.

Each writer controls dialogue differently, but you know instinctively when conversation—dialogue—is done well and when it is not. In Ernest Hemingway's novels, for example, you find pages of dialogue where you begin to feel that you are reading a play script. Truman Capote, on the other hand, just sprinkles his stories with conversation.

It is very difficult to imitate regional patterns of speech—dialect—on a printed page, and many authors wisely do not attempt it. They prefer to set the scene and allow you to fill in for yourself what you imagine to be the appropriate sound for that location.

The characters in "A Christmas Memory" are people from a small town. If you know that Capote is writing about the part of his childhood spent in Alabama, you might want to imagine a soft southern accent even though the author doesn't try to reproduce this sound on the page. Capote reproduces some of Miss Sook's expressions: "It's fruitcake weather! Fetch our buggy. Help me find my hat."

The language suits the character, and so you can *hear* her speak. In another passage the author effectively uses snippets of conversation. It is the only time you hear the "relatives," but it's enough to leave a lasting impression of their scolding, impatient voices and attitudes. Buddy and his friend are a bit tipsy from drinking the last of Mr. Haha's whiskey, and their noise attracts the attention of others in the house. Capote sets the scene as if it were a play.

> Enter: two relatives. Very angry. Potent with eyes that scold, tongues that scald. Listen to what they have to say, the words tumbling together into a wrathful tune: "A child of seven! whiskey on his breath! are you out of your mind? feeding a child of seven! must be loony! road to ruination! remember Cousin Kate? Uncle Charlie? Uncle Charlie's brother-in-law? shame! scandal! humiliation! kneel, pray, beg the Lord!"

"Listen to what they have to say," the author instructs you. Then he describes how the words sound: "the words tumbling together into a wrathful tune." The bits of conversation, running together in a long sentence, let you hear how the words do indeed tumble together. You are aware of angry eyes and mouths, which are the likely focal points for the attention of a frightened seven-year-old child.

EXERCISE C

Read the following passage from "A Christmas Memory" and answer the questions that follow using the information you have learned in this part of the lesson.

> In the daytime Haha's is shabby and deserted. I knock at the door, Queenie barks, my friend calls: "Mrs. Haha, ma'am? Anyone to home?"
>
> Footsteps. The door opens. Our hearts overturn. It's Mr. Haha Jones himself! . . . he glowers at us through Satan-tilted eyes and

demands to know: "What you want with Haha?"

For a moment we are too paralyzed to tell. Presently my friend half-finds her voice, a whispery voice at best: "If you please, Mr. Haha, we'd like a quart of your finest whiskey."

His eyes tilt more. Would you believe it? Haha is smiling! Laughing, too. "Which one of you is a drinkin' man?"

1. You can tell from the way the author records the conversation that the characters go from fear to
   ☐ a. relief.
   ☐ b. terror.
   ☐ c. nervousness.
   ☐ d. anxiety.

2. Incorrect grammar in one sentence of the dialogue allows you to "hear" that Mr. Haha has an accent. Write that sentence here.

   _____

   Something that the "friend" says near the beginning of the conversation marks her speech as uneducated. Write that part of the dialogue here.

   _____

Now check your answers using the Answer Key at the back of the book. Correct any wrong answers and review this part of the lesson if you do not understand why an answer is wrong.

·4·
Colorful Descriptions

You probably know the kind of morning in summer when it is still hot and humid from the day before, but there is no sunshine. It is a gray day and rain is expected. Your mood matches the weather. As you leave your house you meet a neighbor and the conversation goes like this:

"Sure is a gray day. Hot and humid too."
"Sure is. Probably have some rain before long."

An undescriptive conversation like that is enough to communicate what you have to say about the day because both of you are experiencing the same feelings induced by the awful weather. An author describing the same scene to an unseen audience of readers faces a different problem, however.

Using words only, the author must convey the feelings created by the weather and perhaps create a mood for the action which is about to occur. Here is how mystery writer P. D. James describes a dreary morning in her novel *The Black Tower:*

> The next morning was airless and sultry, inducing headache, the sky a tent of stained calico ponderous with unspilt rain.

No doubt you identified her comparison in the form of a metaphor: "the sky a tent of stained calico . . ." But the *color* of the description comes from the adjectives the author has chosen so carefully: *airless and sultry; stained calico; ponderous.*

Adjectives are the paints on an author's palette. Just as the colors in a painting help you see and feel a scene as the artist wants you to, an author's adjectives produce sensations in you that are needed to understand and enjoy a story. Truman Capote was a master at coloring his prose. Here are a few examples from "A Christmas Memory." The colorful adjectives are in italics.

> "She is small and *sprightly.* . . ."
>
> ". . . the *concealing* leaves, the *frosted, deceiving* grass." (Did you notice the personification here?)
>
> ". . . the *golden* mound of *sweet oily ivory* meat. . . ."

All of those color words help you to see and feel what the author wants you to see and feel. When you read *sprightly* you see a woman lively and full of life. You have the experience of the search for nuts that are hidden in the grass and fallen leaves—*concealing* leaves and *deceiving* grass. And if you happen to like the expensive, mouth-watering, buttery taste of pies and cakes made with pecans, the description of the *sweet oily ivory* meat will certainly appeal to you.

Authors also choose their action words—verbs—very carefully to give feeling to the action they are describing. For example, when Buddy and his friend take out their money to count it, Capote says they were "*wallowing* in the pleasure of conspiracy." The verb *wallow* describes the feeling of the moment as well as the action. See if you can find the descriptive verbs in this passage. (One of the verbs used is a metaphor.)

> It's always the same: a morning arrives in November, and my friend, as though officially inaugurating the Christmas time of year that exhilarates her imagination and fuels the blaze of her heart, announces: "It's fruitcake weather!"

The friend does not begin the Christmas season, she *inaugurates* it. That suggests much more fanfare, much more importance than simply starting something. The time of year does more than stimulate her imagination; it "*exhilarates* her imagination and *fuels* the blaze of her heart" (the metaphor).

EXERCISE D

Read the following passage from "A Christmas Memory" and answer the questions that follow using the information you have learned in this part of the lesson.

> Silently, wallowing in the pleasures of conspiracy, we take the bead purse from its secret place and spill its contents on the scrap quilt. Dollar bills, tightly rolled and green as May buds. Somber fifty-cent pieces, heavy enough to weight a dead man's eyes. Lovely dimes, the liveliest coin, worn smooth as creek pebbles. But mostly a hateful heap of bitter-odored pennies. Last summer others in the house contracted to pay us a penny for every twenty-five flies we killed. Oh, the carnage of August: the flies that flew to heaven! Yet it was not work in which we took pride. And, as we sit counting pennies, it is as though we were back tabulating dead flies.

1. The adjective *somber* in "somber fifty-cent pieces" makes the expression
   - ☐ a. a metaphor.
   - ☐ b. onomatopoeia.
   - ☐ c. a simile.
   - ☐ d. personification.

2. List at least three colorful adjectives that you find in the passage.

   _____

   _____

   Copy at least one colorful simile that begins with an adjective.

   _____

   _____

Find at least one colorful expression in the passage that begins with a descriptive verb.

_____

_____

Capote also uses colorful *nouns* in his story. Can you find the colorful noun he uses in a metaphor to describe the number of flies that were killed.

_____

Now check your answers using the Answer Key at the back of the book. Correct any wrong answers and review this part of the lesson if you do not understand why an answer is wrong.

Comprehension Questions

For each of the following statements or questions, select the option that best completes a statement or is the most accurate response to a question.

Recalling Specific Facts

1. The narrator's friend calls him "Buddy" after
   - ☐ a. her father.
   - ☐ b. an old lover.
   - ☐ c. a relative.
   - ☐ d. a child who had died.

Recalling Specific Facts

2. The main attraction in the Fun and Freak Museum was a
   - ☐ a. tap dancer.
   - ☐ b. slide viewer.
   - ☐ c. three-legged chicken.
   - ☐ d. two-headed turtle.

Recalling Specific Facts

3. The fruitcakes are for
   - ☐ a. members of the family.
   - ☐ b. strangers or near strangers.
   - ☐ c. a church bake sale.
   - ☐ d. close friends.

Organizing Facts

4. What is the first job for the old buggy in fruitcake weather?
   - ☐ a. going to the store
   - ☐ b. going to Haha's
   - ☐ c. gathering pecans
   - ☐ d. hauling a tree

Organizing Facts

5. The relatives made Buddy's friend cry. What activity did Buddy then suggest that restored her good spirits?
   - ☐ a. baking fruitcakes
   - ☐ b. going to Haha's place
   - ☐ c. going to cut a tree
   - ☐ d. finding windfall pecans

Organizing Facts

6. What is Buddy doing as the story ends?
   - ☐ a. walking on a school campus
   - ☐ b. flying kites
   - ☐ c. reading a letter from his friend
   - ☐ d. returning for his friend's funeral

Knowledge of Word Meanings

7. Which of the following best defines *decease* in ". . . the museum shut down due to the *decease* of the main attraction"?
   - ☐ a. disappearance
   - ☐ b. death
   - ☐ c. illness
   - ☐ d. theft

Knowledge of Word Meanings

8. ". . . my friend is sly and *noncommittal* when passers-by praise the treasure perched in our buggy: what a fine tree and where did it come from? 'Yonderways,' she murmurs vaguely." In that sentence *noncommittal* means
   - ☐ a. rude.
   - ☐ b. suspicious.
   - ☐ c. hostile.
   - ☐ d. evasive.

Knowledge of Word Meanings

9. ". . . the Christmas time of year *exhilarates* her imagination and fuels the blaze of her heart. . . ." What does *exhilarates* mean?
   - ☐ a. overshadows
   - ☐ b. stimulates
   - ☐ c. dulls
   - ☐ d. portends

Drawing a Conclusion

10. Buddy's friend spends the thirteenth day of each month in bed. She throws out a penny so they won't have an even $13 to spend. Those facts lead you to conclude that she is
    - ☐ a. cautious.
    - ☐ b. feebleminded.
    - ☐ c. scatterbrained.
    - ☐ d. superstitious.

Drawing a Conclusion

11. After the scene with Haha Jones, you must conclude that he is
    - ☐ a. not as fierce as he seems.
    - ☐ b. completely without morals.
    - ☐ c. unfeeling and humorless.
    - ☐ d. a bit foolish.

Drawing a Conclusion

12. For Buddy, the years spent in military schools and camps were
    - ☐ a. acceptable.
    - ☐ b. total misery.
    - ☐ c. a good lesson in self-discipline.
    - ☐ d. revealing and instructive.

Making a Judgment

13. The scolding that Buddy's friend received for drinking some of the fruitcake whiskey was probably
    - ☐ a. more harsh than was necessary.
    - ☐ b. well deserved.
    - ☐ c. totally undeserved.
    - ☐ d. not really important for the relatives.

Making a Judgment

14. The decision to send Buddy to a military school was probably
    - ☐ a. unfortunate.
    - ☐ b. wise.
    - ☐ c. necessary.
    - ☐ d. generous.

Making an Inference

15. The author refers to "the relatives" and "other people in the house." That leads you to infer that
    - ☐ a. the family is close-knit.
    - ☐ b. these people are fond of Buddy and his friend.
    - ☐ c. the people are always unkind and abusive.
    - ☐ d. Buddy doesn't consider them very important.

Making an Inference

16. As you read about Buddy and his friend, you are likely to infer that they
    □ a. live in a private world.
    □ b. are involved in their community.
    □ c. have little in common with each other.
    □ d. suffer from a "generation gap."

Understanding Characters

17. Buddy's friend might best be described as
    □ a. crotchety.
    □ b. shrewd.
    □ c. childlike.
    □ d. domineering.

Understanding Characters

18. In the years after Buddy goes away, his friend
    □ a. becomes bitter and resentful.
    □ b. remains lively and spirited.
    □ c. lapses into contentment.
    □ d. becomes frail and confused.

Understanding Main Ideas

19. For Buddy and his friend making fruitcakes, finding a Christmas tree, making decorations, and putting Queenie's bone in the tree are all
    □ a. games.
    □ b. traditions.
    □ c. imaginary adventures.
    □ d. required by relatives.

Understanding Main Ideas

20. Buddy's friend speaks twice about seeing the Lord. She comes to believe that people see the Lord in
    □ a. things as they are.
    □ b. revelations at Christmastime.
    □ c. the window of the Baptist church.
    □ d. wishes of the heart.

Understanding Main Ideas

21. One reason that Buddy and his friend were so close is that they
    - ☐ a. were shy and lonely people who turned to each other for companionship.
    - ☐ b. were forced to look after one another by other members of the family.
    - ☐ c. were both a bit peculiar and recognized this trait in one another.
    - ☐ d. had a mutual interest in Christmas and in kite flying that served to bring them together.

Recognizing Tone

22. "Oh my," she exclaims . . . "it's fruitcake weather!" The story opens with an air of
    - ☐ a. wistful sadness.
    - ☐ b. foreboding.
    - ☐ c. excitement and anticipation.
    - ☐ d. comic expectation.

Recognizing Tone

23. The author's tone as he tells the story might best be described as
    - ☐ a. comic.
    - ☐ b. antagonistic.
    - ☐ c. wistful.
    - ☐ d. sarcastic.

Appreciation of Literary Forms

24. ". . . the stars spinning at the window like a visible caroling that slowly, slowly daybreak silences." That phrase is an example of both
    - ☐ a. simile and metaphor.
    - ☐ b. simile and personification.
    - ☐ c. onomatopoeia and syncopation.
    - ☐ d. metaphor and alliteration.

Appreciation of Literary Forms

25. Which of the following expressions is a simile?
    - ☐ a. hulling a heaping buggyload of windfall pecans
    - ☐ b. it has its winter uses, too: as a truck for hauling firewood
    - ☐ c. it is a faithful object
    - ☐ d. the wheels wobble like a drunkard's legs

Now check your answers using the Answer Key at the back of the book. Make no mark for right answers. Correct any wrong answers you may have by putting a check mark (✓) in the box next to the right answer. Count the number of questions you answered correctly and plot the total on the Comprehension Scores Graph at the back of the book.

Next, look at the questions you answered incorrectly. What types of questions were they? Count the number you got wrong of each type and enter the numbers in the spaces below.

Recalling Specific Facts _____

Organizing Facts _____

Knowledge of Word Meanings _____

Drawing a Conclusion _____

Making a Judgment _____

Making an Inference _____

Understanding Characters _____

Understanding Main Ideas _____

Recognizing Tone _____

Appreciation of Literary Forms _____

Now use these numbers to fill in the Comprehension Skills Profile at the end of the book.

Extension Activities

Discussion Guide

Discussing the Author's Use of Language

1. Truman Capote began "A Christmas Memory" with these two sentences: "Imagine a morning in late November. A coming of winter morning more than twenty years ago." How does Capote use language to create a better opening for the story than this example: "It was a morning in November more than twenty years ago?"

2. You use figures of speech all the time in everyday conversation: "The runners were off like a shot." " Every night my cat meets his friends for choir practice." Why do people use figurative language? Why do authors carefully choose figures of speech for their stories?

3. Many great orators use metaphors and other figures of speech:

   William Jennings Bryan: "You shall not crucify mankind upon a cross of gold." Martin Luther King: "I have been to the mountaintop. . . ."

   One of the most moving and most memorable speeches ever given was Abraham Lincoln's Gettysburg Address, which at first glance seems extremely simple and plain. Find and reread the Gettysburg Address. What is so special about its language that makes it one of the greatest documents of all time? What is there about the language in "A Christmas Memory" that can be called simple but effective and memorable?

Discussing the Story

4. Socks, handkerchiefs, and a homemade kite are not what most people would call a memorable Christmas. Why do you think this Christmas was so memorable to Truman Capote that he would write a story about it? Can you think of a special time in your own life or some small thing that stands out in your memory?

5. Why do you think Buddy and his friend use their savings every Christmas to make fruitcakes for people they hardly know? Find Buddy's explanation in the story. Do you agree with him?

6. There are hints in the story that Buddy's friend is "different" in some way. Buddy says that at sixty-something she is still a child. A relative in the house calls her "loony." What do you think? Is Buddy's friend mentally retarded? old and foolish? or something else? Explain your opinion.

Discussing the Author's Work

7. Because Truman Capote is famous for turning true events into "stories," it is difficult to know whether or not to call them fiction or nonfiction. Author Alex Haley called this kind of writing *faction* (fact and fiction)—like his own novel *Roots*. To what extent do you think all storytelling is "faction"?

8. The narrator begins the story by saying that the events happened more than twenty years ago. Yet he tells the story in the present tense as if it were happening right now: "A woman with shorn white hair *is* standing at the kitchen window. . . . I *am* seven; she *is* sixty-something." What effect does the use of the present tense create?

9. The very last sentence of the story shifts to the past tense: "As if I *expected* to see, rather like hearts, a lost pair of kites hurrying toward heaven." Why do you think the author shifts to the past tense at the end of the story?

10. Why do you think so many authors dig into their childhoods to find material for their stories? (Katherine Mansfield, "The Garden Party"; Frank O'Connor, "My Oedipus Complex")

Writing Exercise

Choose *one* holiday tradition that is important to you—decorating a Christmas tree, shopping for presents, receiving presents, or a holiday meal. Write a paragraph or two describing this tradition.

Use descriptive and figurative language to describe the feelings—sights, sounds, smells, sensations—that make the tradition special for you. Try to use several similes, perhaps a metaphor, alliteration, onomatopoeia, and descriptive adjectives.

UNIT
Eight

Unit Eight

Introduction

What the Story Is About

Among fans of Gothic horror stories, "The Black Cat" has always ranked as a favorite. Gothic tales originated in England in the middle of the eighteenth century with the publication of Horace Walpole's novel *The Castle of Otranto*. The style quickly became a favorite among readers and Walpole's classic was soon followed by others including the very famous *Frankenstein* by Mary Wollstonecraft Shelley.

Gothic tales are so named because the early stories were usually set in gloomy Gothic castles. They were frequently filled with dank dungeons, secret passageways, ghosts, empty suits of armor come to life, tortures, gruesome murders, screams, moans, and groans—all the things that send delightful shivers down the reader's spine.

"The Black Cat" is not set in an old European castle, yet it possesses many of the elements of a Gothic tale—horror, evil, terror, cruelty, ghostly visions, murder, and the required groans and screams. As the story begins, the narrator addresses you from a jail cell (this is a first-person narration). He will be hanged in the morning for murder and he is unburdening his soul by telling how he got to be where he is. His tale is not a story for the fainthearted.

You have probably read works by Edgar Allan Poe before. In fact, it is difficult to go very far in school without reading something Poe has written. He is still a very popular and well-known author. His poems include: "The Raven," "The Bells," "Annabel Lee," "Lenore," and "Eldorado." He is credited with writing the world's first detective stories: "The Murders in the Rue Morgue" and "The Purloined Letter." And best known of all are his Gothic stories: "The Tell-Tale Heart," "The Pit and the Pendulum," "The Mask of the Red Death," "The Cask of Amontillado," and "The Black Cat," which you are about to read.

Poe was born in Boston, Massachusetts, in 1809. His father deserted the family and his mother died when Poe was about three years old. He was raised by the Allans. Like the main character in "The Black Cat," he brought many problems on himself because he was an alcoholic. After being expelled from West Point for breaking too many rules, Poe spent most of his adult life in poverty. He barely earned a living editing newspapers and writing literary reviews. His masterpiece poems and stories never earned him much money. Poe lived a tortured life, and it is a wonder that he accomplished as much as he did. He was an innovator in his time and has been called "the finest of fine artists" by those writers who followed and learned from him.

The end came for Poe in 1849, when he was found unconscious in a Baltimore street. Poe died a few days later. He was forty.

"I dwelt alone in a world of moan," he said in his poem "Eulalie." As you read "The Black Cat," see if you think this image of his life is reflected in the author's tone and in the mood of the story.

What the Lesson Is About

The lesson that follows the story is about tone and mood. All writing has a tone to it, just as your voice has a tone when you speak. You will find that tone changes throughout a story just as your tone and manner of speaking change throughout a conversation.

The way you feel at any given time describes your mood. How an author feels from time to time about the story he is writing is called the author's mood. The author imparts this mood to you through the tone he designs for the story. Tone is sometimes called the author's "attitude," or the reflection of his or her attitude toward the story situation, the characters, and the ideas he or she is presenting. Tone and mood, as you will see, work very closely together.

The following questions will help you to focus on the tones and moods you will encounter in "The Black Cat." Keep the questions in mind and try to answer them as you read:

1. The narrator of the story is speaking directly to you. Just as any other speaker, the narrator must have a tone to his "voice." What is the tone of the narrator's "voice" and how does it feel to "listen" to him?

2. The author's tone and the resulting mood of the story change from time to time. Where do these changes occur and how do tone and mood change?

3. Story elements affect the tone and mood of a story. How do the characters and the settings of the story make you feel?

4. What words and expressions create a certain tone for the story and affect your mood as you read?

The Black Cat

by Edgar Allan Poe

For the most wild, yet mostly homely narrative which I am about to pen, I neither expect nor solicit belief. Mad indeed would I be to expect it, in a case where my very senses reject their own evidence. Yet, mad am I not—and very surely do I not dream. But tomorrow I die, and today I would unburden my soul. My immediate purpose is to place before the world, plainly, succinctly, and without comment, a series of mere household events. In their consequences, these events have terrified—have tortured—have destroyed me. Yet I will not attempt to expound them. To me, they have presented little but Horror—to many they will seem less terrible than *baroques*. Hereafter, perhaps, some intellect may be found which will reduce my phantasm to the common-place—some intellect more calm, more logical and far less excitable than my own, which will perceive, in the circumstances I detail with awe, nothing more than an ordinary succession of very natural causes and effects.

From my infancy I was noted for the docility and humanity of my disposition. My tenderness of heart was even so conspicuous as to make me the jest of my companions. I was especially fond of animals, and was indulged by my parents with a great variety of pets. With these I spent most of my time, and never was so happy as when feeding and caressing them. This peculiarity of character grew with my growth, and, in my manhood, I derived from it one of my principal sources of pleasure. To those who have cherished an affection for a faithful and sagacious dog, I need hardly be at the trouble of explaining the nature or the intensity of the gratification thus derivable. There is something in the unselfish and self-sacrificing love of a brute, which goes directly to the heart of him who has had frequent occasion to test the paltry friendship and gossamer fidelity of mere *Man*.

I married early and was happy to find in my wife a disposition not uncongenial with my own. Observing my partiality for domestic pets, she lost no opportunity of procuring those of the most agreeable kind. We had birds, gold fish, a fine dog, rabbits, a small monkey, and *a cat.*

This latter was a remarkably large and beautiful animal, entirely black, and sagacious to an astonishing degree. In speaking of his intelligence, my wife, who at heart was not a little tinctured with superstition, made frequent allusion to the ancient popular notion, which regarded all black cats as witches in disguise. Not that she was ever *serious* upon this point—and I mention the matter at all for no better reason than that it happens, just now, to be remembered.

Pluto—this was the cat's name—was my favorite pet and playmate. I alone fed him, and he attended me wherever I went about the house. It was even with difficulty that I could prevent him from following me through the streets.

Our friendship lasted, in this manner, for several years, during which my general temperament and character—through the instrumentality of the Fiend Intemperance—had (I blush to confess it) experienced a radical alteration for the worse. I grew, day by day, more moody, more irritable, more regardless of the feelings of others. I suffered myself to use intemperate language to my wife. At length, I even offered her personal violence. My pets, of course, were made to feel the change in my disposition. I not only neglected, but ill-used them. For Pluto, however, I still retained sufficient regard to restrain me from maltreating him, as I made no scruple of maltreating the rabbits, the monkey, or even the dog, when by accident, or through affection, they came in my way. But my disease grew upon me—for what disease is like Alcohol!—and at length even Pluto, who was now becoming old, and consequently somewhat peevish—even Pluto began to experience the effects of my ill temper.

One night, returning home, much intoxicated, from one of my haunts about town, I fancied that the cat avoided my presence. I seized him; when, in his fright at my violence, he inflicted a slight wound upon my hand with his teeth. The fury of a demon instantly possessed me. I knew myself no longer. My original soul seemed, at once, to take its flight from my body; and a more than fiendish malevolence, gin-nurtured, thrilled every fibre of my frame. I took from my waistcoat-pocket a penknife, opened it, grasped the poor beast by the throat, and deliberately cut one of its eyes from the socket! I blush, I burn, I shudder, while I pen the damnable atrocity.

When reason returned with the morning—when I had slept off the fumes of the night's debauch—I experienced a sentiment half of horror, half of remorse, for the crime of which I had been guilty; but it was, at best, a feeble and equivocal feeling, and the soul remained untouched. I again plunged into excess, and soon drowned in wine all memory of the deed.

In the meantime the cat slowly recovered. The socket of the lost eye presented, it is true, a frightful appearance, but he no longer appeared to suffer any pain. He went about the house as usual, but, as might be expected, fled in extreme terror at my approach. I had so much of my old heart left, as to be at first grieved by this evident dislike on the part of a creature which had once so loved me. But this feeling soon gave place to irritation. And then came, as if to my final and irrevocable overthrow, the spirit of PERVERSENESS. Of this spirit philosophy takes no account. Yet I am not more sure that my soul lives, than I am that perverseness is one of the primitive impulses of the human heart—one of the indivisible primary faculties, or sentiments, which give direction to the character of Man. Who has not, a hundred times, found himself committing a vile or a silly action, for no other reason than because he knows he should *not?* Have we not a perpetual inclination, in the teeth of our best judgment, to violate that which is *Law,* merely because we understand it to be such? This spirit of perverseness, I say, came to my final overthrow. It was this unfathomable longing of the soul *to vex itself*—to offer violence to its own nature— to do wrong for the wrong's sake only—that urged me to continue and finally to consummate the injury I had inflicted upon the unoffending brute. One morning, in cold blood, I slipped a noose about his neck and hung it to the limb of a tree;—hung it with the tears streaming from my eyes, and with the bitterest remorse at my heart;—hung it *because* I knew that it had loved me, and *because* I felt it had given me no reason of offense;—hung it *because* I knew that in so doing I was committing a sin—a deadly sin that would so jeopardize my immortal soul as to place it—if such a thing were possible—even beyond the reach of the infinite mercy of the Most Merciful and Most Terrible God.

On the night of the day on which this cruel deed was done, I was aroused from sleep by the cry of fire. The curtains of my bed were in flames. The whole house was blazing. It was with great difficulty that my wife, a servant, and myself, made our escape from the conflagration. The destruction was complete. My entire worldly wealth was swallowed up, and I resigned myself thenceforward to despair.

I am above the weakness of seeking to establish a sequence of cause and effect, between the disaster and the atrocity. But I am detailing a chain of facts—and wish not to leave even a possible link imperfect. On the day succeeding the fire, I visited the ruins. The walls, with one exception, had fallen in. This exception was found in a compartment wall, not very thick, which stood about the middle of the house, and against which had rested the head of my bed. The plastering had here, in great measure, resisted the action of the fire—a fact which I attributed to its having been recently spread. About this wall a dense crowd were collected, and many persons seemed to be examining a particular portion of it with very minute and eager attention. The words "strange!" "singular!" and other similar expressions, excited my curiosity. I approached and saw, as if graven in *bas-relief* upon the white surface, the figure of a gigantic *cat*. The impression was given with an accuracy truly marvelous. There was a rope about the animal's neck.

When I first beheld this apparition—for I could scarcely regard it as less—my wonder and my terror were extreme. But at length reflection came to my aid. The cat, I remembered, had been hung in a garden adjacent to the house. Upon the alarm of fire, this garden had been immediately filled by the crowd—by some one of whom the animal must have been cut from the tree and thrown, through an open window, into my chamber. This had probably been done with the view of arousing me from sleep. The falling of other walls had compressed the victim of my cruelty into the substance of the freshly-spread plaster; the lime of which, with the flames, and the *ammonia* from the carcass, had then accomplished the portraiture as I saw it.

Although I thus readily accounted to my reason, if not altogether to my conscience, for the startling fact just detailed, it did not the less fail to make a deep impression upon my fancy. For months I could not rid myself of the phantasm of the cat; and, during this period, there came back into my spirit a half-sentiment that seemed, but was not, remorse. I went so far as to regret the loss of the animal, and to look about me, among the vile haunts which I now habitually frequented, for another pet of the same species, and of somewhat similar appearance, with which to supply its place.

One night as I sat, half stupefied, in a den of more than infamy, my attention was suddenly drawn to some black object, reposing upon the head of one of the immense hogsheads of Gin, or of Rum, which constituted the chief furniture of the apartment. I had been looking steadily at the top of this hogshead for some minutes, and what now caused me surprise was the fact that I had not sooner perceived the object thereupon. I approached it, and touched it with my hand. It was a black cat—a very large one—fully as large as Pluto, and closely resembling him in every respect but one. Pluto had not a white hair upon any portion of his body; but this cat had a large, although indefinite splotch of white, covering nearly the whole region of the breast.

Upon my touching him, he immediately arose, purred loudly, rubbed against my hand, and appeared delighted with my notice. This, then, was the very creature of which I was in search. I at once offered to purchase it of the landlord; but this person made no claim to it—knew nothing of it—had never seen it before.

I continued my caresses, and, when I prepared to go home, the animal evinced a disposition to accompany me. I permitted it to do so; occasionally stooping and patting it as I proceeded. When it reached the house it domesticated itself at once, and became immediately a great favorite with my wife.

For my own part, I soon found a dislike to it arising within me. This was just the reverse of what I had anticipated; but I know not how or why it was—its evident fondness for myself rather disgusted and annoyed me. By slow degrees, these feelings of disgust and annoyance rose into the bitterness of hatred. I avoided the creature; a certain sense of shame, and the remembrance of my former deed of cruelty, preventing me from physically abusing it. I did not, for some weeks, strike, or otherwise violently ill use it; but gradually—very gradually—I came to look upon it with unutterable loathing, and to flee silently from its odious presence, as from the breath of a pestilence.

What added, no doubt, to my hatred of the beast, was the discovery, on the morning after I brought it home, that, like Pluto, it also had been deprived of one of its eyes. This circumstance, however, only endeared it to my wife, who, as I have already said, possessed, in a high degree, that humanity of feeling which had once been my distinguishing trait, and the source of many of my simplest and purest pleasures.

With my aversion to this cat, however, its partiality for myself seemed to increase. It followed my footsteps with a pertinacity which it would be difficult to make the reader comprehend. Whenever I sat, it would crouch beneath my chair, or spring upon my knees, covering me with its loathsome caresses. If I arose to walk it would get between my feet and thus nearly throw me down, or, fastening its long and sharp claws in my dress, clamber, in this manner, to my breast. At such times, although I longed to destroy it with a blow, I was yet withheld from so doing, partly by a memory of my former crime, but chiefly—let me confess it at once—by absolute *dread* of the beast.

This dread was not exactly a dread of physical evil—and yet I should be at a loss how otherwise to define it. I am almost ashamed to own—yes, even in this felon's cell, I am almost ashamed to own—that the terror and horror with which the animal inspired me, had been heightened by one of the merest chimaeras it would be possible to conceive. My wife had called my attention, more than once, to the character of the mark of white hair, of which I have spoken, and which constituted the sole visible difference between the strange beast and the one I had destroyed. The reader will remember that this mark, although large, had been originally very indefinite; but, by slow degrees—degrees nearly imperceptible, and which for a long time my Reason struggled to reject as fanciful—it had, at length, assumed a rigorous distinctness of outline. It was now the representation of an object that I shudder to name—and for this, above all, I loathed, and dreaded, and would have rid myself of the monster *had I dared*—it was now, I say, the image of a hideous—ghastly thing—of the GALLOWS!—oh, mournful and terrible engine of Horror and of Crime—of Agony and of Death!

And now was I indeed wretched beyond the wretchedness of mere Humanity. And *a brute beast*—whose fellow I had contemptuously destroyed—*a brute beast* to work out for *me*—for me a man, fashioned in the image of the High God—so much of insufferable wo! Alas! neither by day nor by night knew I the blessing of Rest any more! During the former the creature left me no moment alone; and, in the latter, I started, hourly, from dreams of unutterable fear, to find the hot breath of *the thing* upon my face, and its vast weight—an incarnate Night-Mare that I had no power to shake off—incumbent eternally upon my *heart!*

Beneath the pressure of torments such as these, the feeble remnant of the good within me succumbed. Evil thoughts became my sole intimates—the darkest and most evil of thoughts. The moodiness of my usual temper increased to hatred of all things and of all mankind; while, from the sudden, frequent, and ungovernable outbursts of a fury to which I now blindly abandoned myself, my uncomplaining wife, alas! was the most usual and the most patient of sufferers.

One day she accompanied me, upon some household errand, into the cellar of the old building which our poverty compelled us to inhabit. The cat followed me down the steep stairs, and, nearly throwing me headlong, exasperated me to madness. Uplifting an axe, and forgetting, in my wrath, the childish dread which had hitherto stayed my hand, I aimed a blow at the animal which, of course, would have proved instantly fatal had it descended as I wished. But this blow was arrested by the hand of my wife. Goaded, by the interference, into a rage more than demoniacal, I withdrew my arm from her grasp and buried the axe in her brain. She fell dead upon the spot, without a groan.

This hideous murder accomplished, I set myself forthwith, and with entire deliberation, to the task of concealing the body. I knew that I could not remove it from the house, either by day or by night, without the risk of being observed by the neighbors. Many projects entered my mind. At one period I thought of cutting the corpse into minute fragments, and destroying them by fire. At another, I resolved to dig a grave for it in the floor of the cellar. Again, I deliberated about casting it in the well in the yard—about packing it in a box, as if merchandise, with the usual arrangements, and so getting a porter to take it from the house. Finally I hit upon what I considered a far better expedient than either of these. I determined to wall it up in the cellar—as the monks of the middle ages are recorded to have walled up their victims.

For a purpose such as this the cellar was well adapted. Its walls were loosely constructed, and had lately been plastered throughout with a rough plaster, which the dampness of the atmosphere had prevented from hardening. Moreover, in one of the walls was a projection, caused by a false chimney, or fireplace, that had been filled up, and made to resemble the rest of the cellar. I made no doubt that I could readily displace the bricks at this point, insert the corpse, and wall the whole up as before, so that no eye could detect anything suspicious.

And in this calculation I was not deceived. By means of a crowbar I easily dislodged the bricks, and, having carefully deposited the body against the inner wall, I propped it in that position, while, with little trouble, I re-laid the whole structure as it originally stood. Having procured mortar, sand, and hair, with every possible precaution, I prepared a plaster which could not be distinguished from the old, and with this I very carefully went over the new brick-work. When I had finished, I felt satisfied that all was right. The wall did not present the slightest appearance of having been disturbed. The rubbish on the floor was picked up with the minutest care. I looked around triumphantly, and said to myself—"Here at least, then, my labor has not been in vain."

My next step was to look for the beast which had been the cause of so much wretchedness; for I had, at length, firmly resolved to put it to death. Had I been able to meet with it, at the moment, there could have been no doubt of its fate; but it appeared that the crafty animal had been alarmed at the violence of my previous anger, and forbore to present itself in my present mood. It is impossible to describe, or to imagine, the deep, the blissful sense of relief which the absence of the detested creature occasioned in my bosom. It did not make its appearance during the night—and thus for one night at least, since its introduction into the house, I soundly and tranquilly slept; aye, *slept* even with the burden of murder upon my soul!

The second and the third day passed, and still my tormentor came not. Once again I breathed as a freeman. The monster, in terror, had fled the premises forever! I should behold it no more! My happiness was supreme! The guilt of my dark deed disturbed me but little. Some few inquiries had been made, but these had been readily answered. Even a search had been instituted—but of course nothing was to be discovered I looked upon my future felicity as secured.

Upon the fourth day of the assassination, a party of the police came, very unexpectedly, into the house, and proceeded again to make rigorous investigation of the premises. Secure, however, in the inscrutability of my place of concealment, I felt no embarrassment whatever. The officers bade me accompany them in their search. They left no nook or corner unexplored. At length, for the third of fourth time, they descended into the cellar. I quivered not in a muscle. My heart beat calmly as that of one who slumbers in innocence. I walked the cellar from end to end. I folded my arms upon my bosom, and roamed easily to and fro. The police were thoroughly satisfied and prepared to depart. The glee at my heart was too strong to be restrained. I burned to say if but one word, by way of triumph, and to render doubly sure their assurance of my guiltlessness.

"Gentlemen," I said at last, as the party ascended the steps, "I delight to have allayed your suspicions. I wish you all health, and a little more courtesy. By the bye, gentlemen, this—this is a very well-constructed house." (In the rabid desire to say something easily, I scarcely knew what I uttered at all.)—"I may say an *excellently* well-constructed house. These walls—are you going, gentlemen—these walls are solidly put together"; and here, through the mere frenzy of bravado, I rapped heavily, with a cane which I held in my hand, upon the very portion of the brick-work behind which stood the corpse of the wife of my bosom.

But may God shield and deliver me from the fangs of the Arch-Fiend! No sooner had the reverberation of my blows sunk into silence, than I was answered by a voice from within the tomb!—by a cry, at first muffled and broken, like the sobbing of a child, and then quickly swelling into one long, loud, and continuous scream, utterly anomalous and inhuman—a howl—a wailing shriek, half of horror and half of triumph, such as might have arisen only out of hell, conjointly from the throats of the damned in their agony and of the demons that exult in the damnation.

Of my own thoughts it is folly to speak. Swooning, I staggered to the opposite wall. For one instant the party upon the stairs remained motionless, through extremity of terror and of awe. In the next, a dozen stout arms were toiling at the wall. It fell bodily. The corpse, already greatly decayed and clotted with gore, stood erect before the eyes of the spectators. Upon its head, with red extended mouth and solitary eye of fire, sat the hideous beast whose craft had seduced me into murder, and whose informing voice had consigned me to the hangman. I had walled the monster up within the tomb!

Tone and Mood

People produce an amazing range of emotions when they speak. A harsh tone, or attitude, signals fear or anger. A gentle tone may inspire confidence or affection. A stirring speech can provoke listeners in a way the speaker desires—excite people to action, influence their feelings toward an issue, or even incite hatred.

Other things besides the human voice register tone. Places create tone, too. Think of the tone you find in a church as opposed to the tone in your home or in a football stadium. A clown or mime can project tone through soundless actions. People can create tones, or attitudes, by their actions: one person is severe while another is flighty; the mere presence of one person makes you feel good about yourself while another makes you feel fearful or insecure.

Tone carries with it a *mood*. Mood describes the feeling or emotion that the tone of a voice, a place, or a person inspires. Mood refers to the atmosphere that surrounds an incident or scene. In church your mood may be solemn or reflective. The tone of football competition brings a mood of excitement and high spirits.

Tone and mood are interactive because both involve feelings. Tone is the manner, or attitude, that carries or conveys a feeling. Mood is the feeling itself.

Tone and mood work together in a story this way: An author feels a certain way about an idea, a character or some action in the story and expresses this mood, or feeling, through a tone imparted to the story. You sense the tone as you read, and recognize the mood that it creates. The author's tone conveys the mood of the story. It is not unusual, however, for readers to respond in different ways to the tone of a story.

For example, most people find a sort of morbid interest or fascination in the horrors of "The Black Cat," while others, more sensitive to cruelty and violence, find the brutality totally repelling. Tone and mood, therefore, result from an interaction between an author and a reader that reflects the feelings of both.

This lesson focuses on four aspects of tone and mood.

1. You will look at the relationship between tone and mood in the story.
2. You will examine changes in tone and mood as the story progresses.
3. You will see how settings and characters influence tone and mood in a story.
4. You will see how the author's choice of words influences tone and mood in a story.

· I ·
Tone and Mood

Tone and mood resist separation and precise definition. Scholars have been debating for years the similarities and the distinctions between them. Still, there is no denying that tone and mood exist. You have only to compare any two stories you have read in this book to recognize that each story has a different sound, a different "air" about it, and a different effect on you. As you read, you experience tone and mood at work, and like the other elements of a story, they are controlled by the author.

Perhaps the best way to explore tone and mood is to plunge right into a story and see what kinds of feelings you sense there. The following passage is from the opening paragraph of "The Black Cat." What feeling does the author convey to you through the story's narrator?

> For the most wild, yet mostly homely narrative which I am about to pen, I neither expect nor solicit belief. Mad indeed would I be to expect it, in a case where my very senses reject their own evidence. Yet, mad am I not—and very surely do I not dream. But tomorrow I die, and today I would unburden my soul. My immediate purpose is to place before the world, plainly, succinctly, and without comment, a series of mere household events. In their consequences, these events have terrified—have tortured—have destroyed me.

From the tone of the opening lines, you get the impression that you are listening to a very rational and intelligent man who is about to explain a series of bizarre events. He talks about writing an account like a scientist might keep a journal. He says he will tell you the story plainly and succinctly, in the manner of a well-organized investigator. Yet you feel a little uneasy because of all the talk of dreams, madness, death, torture, and terror. The author deliberately causes you to approach this story with mixed emotions. Who is this man who talks so rationally about horror and dying? He seems decent enough. Perhaps he is someone who has been falsely accused and is facing an unjust sentence. This will be a strange tale.

Poe has imparted a tone—a certain attitude—to the story. The feelings that you experience from his writing are the story's mood. Poe has communicated his feelings to you through the vehicle of tone and mood.

EXERCISE A

Read the following passage from the story and answer the questions that follow using the information you have learned in this part of the lesson.

The police are just leaving after examining the cellar:

> "Gentlemen," I said at last, as the party ascended the steps, "I delight to have allayed your suspicions. I wish you all health, and

a little more courtesy. By the bye, gentlemen, this—this is a very well-constructed house." (In the rabid desire to say something easily, I scarcely knew what I uttered at all.)—"I may say an *excellently* well-constructed house. These walls—are you going, gentlemen—these walls are solidly put together"; and here, through the mere frenzy of bravado, I rapped heavily, with a cane which I held in my hand, upon the very portion of the brick-work behind which stood the corpse of the wife of my bosom.

1. Pretend that the narrator is speaking to you in person. What can you determine about his mood as expressed by the tone of his voice and his manner?
   - ☐ a. He feels completely calm because he has the situation under control.
   - ☐ b. He is satisfied with his cleverness and is feeling proud of himself.
   - ☐ c. He is feeling extremely nervous and is trying to mask it with rambling conversation.
   - ☐ d. He is filled with remorse because of what he has done to his dear wife.

2. One sentence, and especially one word within that sentence, describes the narrator's *real* mood. Write the sentence and circle the word that most accurately describes the narrator's mood at this point.

   _____

   _____

   _____

Now check your answers using the Answer Key at the back of the book. Correct any wrong answers and review this part of the lesson if you do not understand why an answer is wrong.

·2·
Changing Tones and Moods

As you know from personal experience, moods can change rather quickly. It is possible to be deliriously happy one minute and very sad the next, depending on changing circumstances. Moods also change as the atmosphere or tone of your surroundings changes. Think of attending a church wedding. As you meet friends and relatives outside the church everyone is joking and laughing. The mood is light and happy. Yet as soon as you go inside the church you quiet down and become serious and subdued. The atmosphere or tone of the church impresses the company with the more solemn aspects of the occasion and the mood becomes quiet and reflective.

For a story to be realistic, there must be changing moods and tones, just as there are in the course of everyday living. The difference between changing tones and moods in real life and in a story, however, is that in real life the changes usually occur randomly while in a story the changes are carefully planned by the author to produce particular effects.

In the following passages from the story, notice how the tone grows from an almost clinical explanation of growing alcoholism to an expression of horror and revulsion.

> Pluto—this was the cat's name—was my favorite pet and playmate. . . .
>
> Our friendship lasted, in this manner, for several years, during which my general temperament and character—through the instrumentality of the Fiend Intemperance—had (I blush to confess it) experienced a radical alteration for the worse. I grew, day by day, more moody, more irritable, more regardless of the feelings of others. . . . My pets, of course, were made to feel the change in my disposition. I not only neglected, but ill-used them. For Pluto, however, I still retained sufficient regard to restrain me from maltreating him, as I made no scruple of maltreating the rabbits, the monkey, or even the dog. . . . But my disease grew upon me— for what disease is like Alcohol!—and at length . . . even Pluto began to experience the effects of my ill temper.

The beginning of the passage sounds as if a doctor is describing a patient's symptoms. By midparagraph, however, the tone has changed—it is more serious. You begin to feel concerned (your mood) about a person who is so sick that he begins to abuse helpless animals. By the end of the paragraph the narrator sounds despairing as his alcoholism begins to take complete charge of him. In the next passage you begin to experience the horror of his alcohol-induced state:

> One night, returning home, much intoxicated, from one of my haunts about town, I fancied that the cat avoided my presence. I seized him; when, in his fright at my violence, he inflicted a slight wound upon my hand with his teeth. The fury of a demon instantly possessed me. I knew myself no longer. My original soul seemed,

at once, to take its flight from my body; and a more than fiendish malevolence, gin-nurtured, thrilled every fibre of my frame. I took from my waistcoat-pocket a penknife, opened it, grasped the poor beast by the throat, and deliberately cut one of its eyes from the socket! I blush, I burn, I shudder, while I pen the damnable atrocity.

When you read this passage aloud, the style of writing almost forces you to read faster and louder until at the end you pant and shout with his agonizing memory of the terrible deed. The tone has changed along with the narrator's deteriorating mood. At the end you share with him a terrible revulsion at what he has done.

EXERCISE B

Read the following passage from the story and answer the questions that follow using the information you have learned in this part of the lesson.

The narrator meets the new cat:

I continued my caresses, and, when I prepared to go home, the animal evinced a disposition to accompany me. I permitted it to do so; occasionally stooping and patting it as I proceeded. When it reached the house it domesticated itself at once, and became immediately a great favorite with my wife.

For my own part, I soon found a dislike to it arising within me. . . . By slow degrees, these feelings of disgust and annoyance rose into the bitterness of hatred. I avoided the creature; a certain sense of shame, and the remembrance of my former deed of cruelty, preventing me from physically abusing it. . . . but gradually—very gradually—I came to look upon it with unutterable loathing, and to flee silently from its odious presence, as from the breath of a pestilence.

1. The mood in the two paragraphs changes from
   ☐ a. affection to hatred.
   ☐ b. happiness to sadness.
   ☐ c. soberness to drunkenness.
   ☐ d. anger to contentment.

2. Copy a phrase from the paragraphs that conveys a tender mood. Then copy a phrase that conveys a harsh mood.

_____

_____

Now check your answers using the Answer Key at the back of the book.
Correct any wrong answers and review this part of the lesson if you do not
understand why an answer is wrong.

· 3 ·
Setting, Character, Tone, and Mood

As you have seen, people and places convey a certain tone and put you in a corresponding mood—a church compared to a football stadium; a stern boss compared to an old friend.

Writers know that certain settings and certain kinds of characters will produce certain feelings in readers. Author Eudora Welty, for example, knew that if she put a poor, old black woman in an office with a condescending white secretary there would be a feeling of tension. By putting George in a small room during a hot summer, author Bernard Malamud created a stifling atmosphere in "A Summer's Reading." Albert Camus created a feeling of loneliness by setting "The Guest" on a barren, isolated hillside and by having as his main character a man who preferred isolation.

The fact that the main character in "The Black Cat" is a convicted murderer waiting to be hanged immediately puts you in a suspicious and curious mood as you look forward to reading the gory details. The view of the narrator as a child, however, makes you feel warm and sympathetic toward him:

> From my infancy I was noted for the docility and humanity of my disposition. My tenderness of heart was even so conspicuous as to make me the jest of my companions. I was especially fond of animals, and was indulged by my parents with a great variety of pets. With these I spent most of my time, and never was so happy as when feeding and caressing them.

However, Poe quickly frees you of the feeling that the narrator is a man who deserves your sympathy. The character soon becomes a drunken monster and you tend to shudder as you wonder what horror he is going to commit next. How the character is described clearly influences your feelings toward him.

In a Gothic tale much of the action takes place at night. "The Black Cat" has its nighttime settings, too. The narrator mutilates his cat at night. He finds his new cat at night in one of his infamous haunts. And there is this nighttime scene:

> On the night of the day on which this cruel deed was done, I was aroused from sleep by the cry of fire. The curtains of my bed were in flames. The whole house was blazing. . . . My entire worldly wealth was swallowed up, and I resigned myself thenceforward to despair. . . .
>
> On the day succeeding the fire, I visited the ruins. The walls, with one exception, had fallen in. This exception was found in a compartment wall. . . . which stood about the middle of the house, and against which had rested the head of my bed. . . . About this wall a dense crowd were collected, and many persons seemed to be examining a particular portion of it. . . . The words "strange!" "singular!" and other similar expressions, excited my curiosity. I approached and saw, as if graven in *bas-relief* [a form of raised sculpture] upon the white surface, the figure of a gigantic *cat*. The impression was given with an accuracy truly marvelous. There was a rope about the animal's neck.

Nighttime, fire, and total ruin make an ideal setting for a Gothic tale. They create just the right mood for the next day's discovery of the ghostly image. There is no doubt in your mind that there are scary supernatural events afoot here. In the following paragraph the narrator says:

> When I first beheld this apparition—for I could scarcely regard it as less—my wonder and my terror were extreme.

Wonder and terror indeed!—which is just how you would feel if you came home one night to find one of your evil deeds engraved on your bedroom wall.

EXERCISE C
Read the following passage from the story and answer the questions that follow using the information you have learned in this part of the lesson.

> One day she [his wife] accompanied me, upon some household errand, into the cellar of the old building which our poverty compelled us to inhabit. The cat followed me down the steep stairs, and, nearly throwing me headlong, exasperated me to madness.

Uplifting an axe, and forgetting, in my wrath, the childish dread which had hitherto stayed my hand, I aimed a blow at the animal which, of course, would have proved instantly fatal had it descended as I wished. But this blow was arrested by the hand of my wife. Goaded, by the interference into a rage more than demoniacal, I withdrew my arm from her grasp and buried the axe in her brain.

1. How does the author make you feel about the main character at this point in the story?
    □ a. You tend to feel sympathetic toward his extreme mental illness.
    □ b. You can understand how an animal can be infuriating at times.
    □ c. You realize that extreme poverty can drive a person to madness.
    □ d. You are frightened and revolted by his madness and cruelty.

2. What do you recognize in the setting as being a place in a Gothic tale where you can typically expect some horrifying event to occur?

_____

Now check your answers using the Answer Key at the back of the book. Correct any wrong answers and review this part of the lesson if you do not understand why an answer is wrong.

· 4 ·

Language, Tone, and Mood

You have probably remarked upon Poe's rather elegant and even pompous-sounding language as you were reading "The Black Cat." You may have also remarked upon how long some of his sentences are:

> When reason returned with the morning—when I had slept off the fumes of the night's debauch [corruption]—I experienced a sentiment half of horror, half of remorse, for the crime of which I had been guilty; but it was, at best, a feeble and equivocal feeling, and the soul remained untouched.

That old style of writing, not likely to be used by anyone writing today, is particularly suited to creating the proper tone and mood for a Gothic tale. It is heavy and ornate as were the medieval castles where so many horror stories have been set. The style of writing is as heavy as the burden that the narrator in "The Black Cat" keeps talking about.

And now was I indeed wretched beyond the wretchedness of mere Humanity. And *a brute beast*—whose fellow I had contemptuously destroyed—*a brute beast* to work out for *me*—for me a man, fashioned in the image of the High God—so much of insufferable wo! Alas! neither by day nor by night knew I the blessing of Rest any more! During the former the creature left me no moment alone; and, in the latter, I started, hourly, from dreams of unutterable fear, to find the hot breath of *the thing* upon my face, and its vast weight—an incarnate Night-Mare that I had no power to shake off—incumbent eternally upon my *heart!*

The tone of the story varies between the narrator's moods. At first, he appears very reasonable, logical, and scientific, but he soon becomes very depressed. Those personality changes are typical of the mood swings of a mentally ill person suffering from manic depression, and Poe has captured it superbly in words. In the paragraph just quoted notice words that convey the feeling either of heaviness or of depression: *wretchedness, contemptuously, insufferable wo, unutterable fear, vast weight, an incarnate Night-Mare, incumbent eternally.*

The last sentence of the paragraph is so long it can leave you gasping for breath when you read it aloud. It must be read slowly and somberly. Notice how Poe breaks up the sentences with commas, semicolons, exclamation points, and dashes to drag it out and slow it down even beyond the effect of his lengthy words. He puts words in italics and capitalizes words to emphasize them. The poor cat becomes *the thing*—making it seem like an evil, alien, unexplainable object. The author uses exaggeration, talking of the cat's "vast weight."

The word *incarnate* means that the cat gave living form to his nightmares. It is a word you would expect to find in a sermon or in a funeral oration. The expression *incumbent eternally* provides a similar tone—it makes you feel the never-ending burden upon the man's chest, as if he is laid in his grave with this *thing* weighting him down.

The effect of the author's language in this passage and elsewhere throughout the story is to heighten the emotional impact of the narrator's tale. The choice of words produces a tone that is heavy and demented. The mood is gloomy.

EXERCISE D

Read the following passage from the story and answer the questions that follow using the information you have learned in this part of the lesson.

But may God shield and deliver me from the fangs of the Arch-Fiend! No sooner had the reverberation of my blows sunk into

silence, than I was answered by a voice from within the tomb!—
by a cry, at first muffled and broken, like the sobbing of a child,
and then quickly swelling into one long, loud, and continuous
scream, utterly anomalous [of uncertain nature] and inhuman—a
howl—a wailing shriek, half of horror and half of triumph, such as
might have arisen only out of hell, conjointly from the throats of
the damned in their agony and of the demons that exult in the
damnation.

1. The way the author describes the shriek from the "tomb" makes the tone of
the paragraph terrifying and also
   □ a. mystifying.
   □ b. childlike.
   □ c. unearthly.
   □ d. reverberating.

2. Write down as many words and phrases as you can find that make the
passage seem like a nightmare.

_____

_____

_____

_____

*Now check your answers using the Answer Key at the back of the book.
Correct any wrong answers and review this part of the lesson if you do not
understand why an answer is wrong.*

Comprehension Questions

For each of the following statements or questions, select the option that best completes a statement or is the most accurate response to a question.

Recalling Specific Facts

1. One wall remained standing after the fire. On this wall could be seen
   - ☐ a. the figure of the Arch-Fiend.
   - ☐ b. a skull and crossbones.
   - ☐ c. a cat.
   - ☐ d. a cross and shroud.

Recalling Specific Facts

2. The patch of white on the breast of the second black cat grew to resemble
   - ☐ a. the first cat.
   - ☐ b. the letter P for Pluto.
   - ☐ c. a gallows.
   - ☐ d. an axe.

Organizing Facts

3. The fire which destroyed the narrator's house occurred the night
   - ☐ a. after he hanged Pluto.
   - ☐ b. he found the new cat in a tavern.
   - ☐ c. he murdered his wife.
   - ☐ d. after he cut out Pluto's eye.

Organizing Facts

4. When and where did the murder occur?
   - ☐ a. in the yard, immediately after the fire
   - ☐ b. in the new quarters sometime after the fire
   - ☐ c. on the cellar stairs just before the fire
   - ☐ d. in the new house just after a drunken evening

Knowledge of Word Meanings

5. "There is something in the unselfish and self-sacrificing of a brute, which goes directly to the heart of him who has had frequent occasion to test the *paltry* friendship and *gossamer* fidelity of mere Man." What do *paltry* and *gossamer* mean?
   - ☐ a. valuable and sincere
   - ☐ b. faithful and long-lasting
   - ☐ c. deceitful and vain
   - ☐ d. worthless and flimsy

294   THE BLACK CAT

Knowledge of Word Meanings

6. ". . . through the mere *frenzy of bravado,* I rapped heavily with a cane . . . upon . . . the brick-work. . . ." What is a *frenzy of bravado?*
   □ a. reasoned heroism
   □ b. wild pretense at bravery
   □ c. strong defiance
   □ d. whining cowardice

Drawing a Conclusion

7. As you think about the story, the second black cat that followed the narrator home was probably
   □ a. just a stray.
   □ b. the Arch-Fiend.
   □ c. the reincarnation of Pluto.
   □ d. Pluto himself, who hadn't really died.

Drawing a Conclusion

8. What seemed to be the source of all the narrator's problems?
   □ a. a physical breakdown
   □ b. split personality
   □ c. stress
   □ d. alcoholism

Making a Judgment

9. When the police went to the narrator's house, the narrator's behavior can be said to have been
   □ a. rude.
   □ b. hostile.
   □ c. irrational.
   □ d. suspicious.

Making a Judgment

10. Along with his other faults, the narrator can be called
    □ a. cowardly.
    □ b. mean and miserly.
    □ c. a wife beater.
    □ d. power mad.

Making a Judgment

11. The cat that replaces Pluto serves to
    - ☐ a. remind the narrator of his cruelty.
    - ☐ b. comfort the narrator in his troubles.
    - ☐ c. turn the narrator's wife against him.
    - ☐ d. reform the narrator from his cruel ways.

Making an Inference

12. It is safe to say that the black cat was
    - ☐ a. a scapegoat for the narrator's problems.
    - ☐ b. the real cause of the narrator's problems.
    - ☐ c. of no real significance in the story.
    - ☐ d. a symbol of injustice in the story.

Making an Inference

13. While the narrator is preparing his wife's tomb, he seems
    - ☐ a. remorseful as he thinks back on all his crimes.
    - ☐ b. to be intentionally leaving clues so that the crime will be discovered.
    - ☐ c. really impressed with the excellent construction of the building.
    - ☐ d. more concerned with proper masonry than with his crime.

Making an Inference

14. After the narrator began to focus on the white marking on the second cat, he
    - ☐ a. finally lost all control of himself.
    - ☐ b. was full of remorse for what he had done to Pluto.
    - ☐ c. regained his composure in order to plan the murder.
    - ☐ d. realized the significance of the image on the wall.

Understanding Characters

15. The narrator calls himself "perverse." Evidence of that comes when he kills Pluto because
    - ☐ a. he felt the cat contained an evil spirit.
    - ☐ b. the cat was always underfoot.
    - ☐ c. he knew he had no reason to do it.
    - ☐ d. his wife loved the cat.

Understanding Characters

16. The story is an account of a man who
    ☐ a. was inherently evil all of his life.
    ☐ b. becomes obsessed with cats as evil creatures.
    ☐ c. turns to alcohol to replace his earlier love of animals.
    ☐ d. undergoes a severe personality change.

Understanding Characters

17. The narrator's wife can be characterized as
    ☐ a. unable to understand the cause of her husband's problem.
    ☐ b. patient and long suffering.
    ☐ c. shrewish in her attempts to reform her husband.
    ☐ d. not really in love with her husband.

Understanding Main Ideas

18. Poetic justice is defined as an outcome of a story in which a vice is punished and a virtue is rewarded usually in a particularly ironic or appropriate manner. What is the element of poetic justice in this story?
    ☐ a. Alcohol destroys brain; brain destroys man.
    ☐ b. Man kills wife; wife accuses man.
    ☐ c. Crime is committed; justice is done.
    ☐ d. Man kills cat; cat kills man.

Understanding Main Ideas

19. Which one of the following best describes the principal theme of the story?
    ☐ a. revelations about cruelty to animals
    ☐ b. the rise and fall of humanity
    ☐ c. alcoholism and a man's descent into insanity
    ☐ d. belief in cats as a symbol of witchcraft

Recognizing Tone

20. The narrator sees the gallows in the white mark on the cat. ". . . it was now, I say, the image of a hideous—ghastly thing—of the GALLOWS!—oh, mournful and terrible engine of Horror and of Crime—of Agony and of Death!" The tone of this passage expresses
    ☐ a. terrible fear.
    ☐ b. cowardice.
    ☐ c. utter disgust.
    ☐ d. remorse and repentance.

Recognizing Tone

21. When the narrator talks to the police, his conversation sounds
    ☐ a. clever.
    ☐ b. logical.
    ☐ c. friendly.
    ☐ d. nervous.

Recognizing Tone

22. The story ends on a note of
    ☐ a. fear and anxiety.
    ☐ b. horror and terror.
    ☐ c. relief and comfort.
    ☐ d. triumph and relief.

Appreciation of Literary Forms

23. In at least two places the narrator compares the qualities of a *brute beast* and man. Why does the author use the expression *brute beast* instead of saying animal or cat?
    ☐ a. The expression suggests a comparison between the intelligence and values of people and those of animals.
    ☐ b. It is an old form of expression probably derived from the biblical story of Daniel in the lion's den.
    ☐ c. The words are used to create a tone of fear and terror in the story.
    ☐ d. The expression is more interesting than simply saying cat or animal.

Appreciation of Literary Forms

24. You recall that personification means that human qualities are given to animals or inanimate objects. Which one of the following quotations from the story is an example of personification?
    ☐ a. ". . . the party upon the stairs remained motionless. . . ."
    ☐ b. ". . . through extremity of terror and of awe. . . ."
    ☐ c. ". . . the beast whose craft had seduced me into murder. . . ."
    ☐ d. ". . . a dozen stout arms were toiling at the wall. . . ."

Appreciation of Literary Forms

25. The literary term for using an expression of exaggeration to achieve a special effect is called *hyperbole* (heye-PUHR-buh-lee). Which one of the following expressions from the story is hyperbole?
    ☐ a. ". . . a brute beast—whose fellow I had contemptuously destroyed. . . ."
    ☐ b. ". . . for me a man, fashioned in the image of the High God. . . ."
    ☐ c. ". . . its [the cat's] vast weight . . . incumbent eternally upon my heart!"
    ☐ d. "Alas! neither by day nor by night knew I the blessing of Rest. . . ."

Now check your answers using the Answer Key at the back of the book. Make no mark for right answers. Correct any wrong answers you may have by putting a check mark (✓) in the box next to the right answer. Count the number of questions you answered correctly and plot the total on the Comprehension Scores Graph at the back of the book.

Next, look at the questions you answered incorrectly. What types of questions were they? Count the number you got wrong of each type and enter the numbers in the spaces below.

Recalling Specific Facts   _____

Organizing Facts   _____

Knowledge of Word Meanings   _____

Drawing a Conclusion   _____

Making a Judgment   _____

Making an Inference   _____

Understanding Characters   _____

Understanding Main Ideas   _____

Recognizing Tone   _____

Appreciation of Literary Forms   _____

Now use these numbers to fill in the Comprehension Skills Profile at the end of the book.

Extension Activities

Discussion Guide

Discussing Tone and Mood

1. Here is a passage from "The Black Cat" as Poe wrote it, followed by a simplified version. Why does Poe's version have a tone that creates a mood, while the translation is flat—without any tone or mood?

> One night, returning home, much intoxicated, from one of my haunts about town, I fancied that the cat avoided my presence. I seized him; when, in his fright at my violence, he inflicted a slight wound upon my hand with his teeth. The fury of a demon instantly possessed me.

> One night, when I came home drunk from my favorite bar, I thought the cat was avoiding me. I grabbed him, and because he was frightened he bit me. I became insanely angry.

2. The author changes the tone and mood of the story from time to time. Sometimes it is mild and reasonable. Other times it is morbid and gloomy, or mad and violent. In some horror stories there are even moments of humor. What would be the result if an author maintained just one mood throughout a story?

3. "The Black Cat" is a Gothic tale. Is it possible to have a horror story in a modern setting and still create the proper tone and mood? For example, how can you develop a tone and mood that will turn an ordinary home into a setting for a horror story? Think of some examples from books you have read, movies you have seen, or even true stories from news accounts.

Discussing the Story

4. How do you account for the narrator's behavior when the police arrive? Why do you think he calls attention to the wall where his wife's body is concealed?

5. Why do black cats appear so often in mystery and horror stories? There have been books and articles written throughout history about cats. You may want to research the history of cats and tell how they have been regarded at various times and in various places around the world.

6. Can you find a message in the story relating to violence against women? How is the situation of the wife in the story (about 1850) similar to problems faced by some women today? How is her situation different?

Discussing the Author's Work

7. Poe used Gothic conventions in many of his stories. Gothic conventions include morbid concerns such as murder, horror, mystery, decay, evil, magic,

and the supernatural. Gothic settings typically include fens, bogs, ruins, cemeteries, and so on. Gothic characters include evil princes, "ruined" men, and deranged or deformed creatures. How many of the Gothic conventions can you find in "The Black Cat"? You may want to read another Poe story and look for other Gothic conventions.

8. Poe uses a first-person point of view in the story. You see things through the eyes and mind of the narrator who tells his own story. How is it possible to get a true picture of the character if he is telling about himself?

9. Poe's use of language is not the style that writers use today—even for horror stories. Nevertheless, people who like a good scary story still love to listen to stories told in Poe's style. How does this language make a good horror story?

Writing Exercise

1. Write a paragraph that describes something or someone familiar—your home, a room, a pet, a friend. Give the description a pleasant, cheerful tone.

2. Write a second paragraph describing the same place, person, or thing—but this time give the description a tone that makes it unpleasant or frightening.

UNIT
Nine

Unit Nine

Introduction

What the Story Is About

Emily Grierson may be one of the strangest women you will meet in literature. But to tell you just *how* strange she had become over the years would spoil the very unusual ending of the story. The time is the 1930s or thereabouts, and Emily has just passed away at the age of seventy-four. It is the occasion of her death that prompts the narrator of the story to tell you about her.

Emily is the last of the Griersons, an aristocratic family of the Old South. With her death the last vestiges of the pre-Civil War society and its aristocracy have passed from the town of Jefferson forever. "Alive," you are told, "Miss Emily had been a tradition, a duty, and a care" for the town, and the narrator goes on to describe what the old tradition was like. It is not a pretty picture.

William Faulkner was one of the great American authors of modern times, having won the Nobel Prize for literature and many other national and international honors. He was a Southerner, born in New Albany, Mississippi, in 1897. He attended the University of Mississippi in Oxford, and he lived in Oxford for the rest of his life. Faulkner often uses a first-person narrator who is supposedly a witness to the events and a character in the story. Sometimes more than one character in a story speaks to you, presenting you with various points of view.

Faulkner himself was descended from the Southern aristocracy. His family was ruined by the Civil War. He used Mississippi, its history, and its people, to observe human nature; and he used them, as he said in his Nobel acceptance speech, "to create out of the materials of the human spirit something which did not exist before."

Faulkner created an entire county in Mississippi out of pure imagination and filled it with people who appear again and again in his stories. Colonel Sartoris, for example, who is a minor character in "A Rose for Emily," appears as the main character in a novel titled *Sartoris*. The county was called Yoknapatawpha County, and the county seat, Jefferson (a copy of his native Oxford), is where most of his stories are set. It is where Emily Grierson lived and died.

There is a detailed map of Yoknapatawpha County, which appeared in one of Faulkner's novels in 1951, and genealogies of the families who "lived" there had been developed with great care. The map is labeled "Jefferson, Yoknapatawpha County, Mississippi. Area 2400 square miles. Population: Whites 6298; Negroes 9313. William Faulkner, sole owner and proprietor." Yoknapatawpha County is one of the most famous places in literature.

Faulkner stories are influenced by the past, and by the effects of the past on the present. Emily Grierson was a character out of the past who endured into modern times. She was so much a part of the past that she was a symbol of another age and another culture, which the people of Jefferson recalled with an uncertain longing and nostalgia. They attempted to make the past a better world in their minds than it actually was.

The narrator says that Emily, as a symbol of the past, was "dear and inescapable." But as you read the story, try to decide what Faulkner is really saying about the past through the character of Emily.

What the Lesson Is About

The lesson that follows the story shows how authors use symbols to express ideas and themes.

Symbols are not vague or abstract ideas that artists and writers only understand. Quite the contrary—symbols are all around us everyday. Our country's flag is a symbol. The familiar statue of a blindfolded woman seen in courthouses, with sword in one hand and scales in the other, reminds us that justice strives to be blind to all but the truth (the blindfold), weighs the evidence (the scales), and enforces justice (the sword). Schools adopt symbols for their athletic teams to show how superior they are—lions, eagles, panthers, cowboys, and so on.

People can be symbols, too. A police officer is a symbol of the authority of the law. A principal is a symbol of authority in school. A grandmother or grandfather may be a symbol of some value, memory, or tradition that is important in your family. As you will see, Emily Grierson is a symbol in the story you are about to read.

Keep the following questions in mind and try to answer them as you read. They will help you to focus on certain symbols as they develop in the story.

1. What do some elements of the setting seem to symbolize in the story—Emily's house and furniture, for example?
2. How are characters in the story used as symbols? What do the characters symbolize?
3. How do situations in the story symbolize relationships between the past and the present?
4. How does Faulkner manipulate symbols to have them represent ideas he wants to present?

A Rose for Emily

by William Faulkner

I

When Miss Emily Grierson died, our whole town went to her funeral: the men through a sort of respectful affection for a fallen monument, the women mostly out of curiosity to see the inside of her house, which no one save an old manservant—a combined gardener and cook—had seen in at least ten years.

It was a big, squarish frame house that had once been white, decorated with cupolas and spires and scrolled balconies in the heavily lightsome style of the seventies, set on what had once been our most select street. But garages and cotton gins had encroached and obliterated even the august names of that neighborhood; only Miss Emily's house was left, lifting its stubborn and coquettish decay above the cotton wagons and the gasoline pumps—an eyesore among eyesores. And now Miss Emily had gone to join the representatives of those august names where they lay in the cedar-bemused cemetery among the ranked and anonymous graves of Union and Confederate soldiers who fell at the battle of Jefferson.

Alive, Miss Emily had been a tradition, a duty, and a care; a sort of hereditary obligation upon the town, dating from that day in 1894 when Colonel Sartoris, the mayor—he who fathered the edict that no Negro woman should appear on the streets without an apron—remitted her taxes, the dispensation dating from the death of her father on into perpetuity. Not that Miss Emily would have accepted charity. Colonel Sartoris invented an involved tale to the effect that Miss Emily's father had loaned money to the town, which the town, as a matter of business, preferred this way of repaying. Only a man of Colonel Sartoris' generation and thought could have invented it, and only a woman could have believed it.

When the next generation, with its more modern ideas, became mayors and aldermen, this arrangement created some little dissatisfaction. On the first of the year they mailed her a tax notice.

February came, and there was no reply. They wrote her a formal letter, asking her to call at the sheriff's office at her convenience. A week later the mayor wrote her himself, offering to call or to send his car for her, and received in reply a note on paper of an archaic shape, in a thin, flowing calligraphy in faded ink, to the effect that she no longer went out at all. The tax notice was also enclosed, without comment.

They called a special meeting of the Board of Aldermen. A deputation waited upon her, knocked at the door through which no visitor had passed since she ceased giving china-painting lessons eight or ten years earlier. They were admitted by the old Negro into a dim hall from which a stairway mounted into still more shadow. It smelled of dust and disuse—a close, dank smell. The Negro led them into the parlor. It was furnished in heavy, leather-covered furniture. When the Negro opened the blinds of one window, they could see that the leather was cracked; and when they sat down, a faint dust rose sluggishly about their thighs, spinning with slow motes in the single sun-ray. On a tarnished gilt easel before the fireplace stood a crayon portrait of Miss Emily's father.

They rose when she entered—a small, fat woman in black, with a thin gold chain descending to her waist and vanishing into her belt, leaning on an ebony cane with a tarnished gold head. Her skeleton was small and spare; perhaps that was why what would have been merely plumpness in another was obesity in her. She looked bloated, like a body long submerged in motionless water, and of that pallid hue. Her eyes, lost in the fatty ridges of her face, looked like two small pieces of coal pressed into a lump of dough as they moved from one face to another while the visitors stated their errand.

She did not ask them to sit. She just stood in the door and listened quietly until the spokesman came to a stumbling halt. Then they could hear the invisible watch ticking at the end of the gold chain.

Her voice was dry and cold. "I have no taxes in Jefferson. Colonel Sartoris explained it to me. Perhaps one of you can gain access to the city records and satisfy yourselves."

"But we have. We are the city authorities, Miss Emily. Didn't you get a notice from the sheriff, signed by him?"

"I received a paper, yes," Miss Emily said. "Perhaps he considers himself the sheriff. . . . I have no taxes in Jefferson."

"But there is nothing on the books to show that, you see. We must go by the—"

"See Colonel Sartoris. I have no taxes in Jefferson."

"But, Miss Emily—"

"See Colonel Sartoris." (Colonel Sartoris had been dead almost ten years.) "I have no taxes in Jefferson. Tobe!" The Negro appeared. "Show these gentlemen out."

II

So she vanquished them, horse and foot, just as she had vanquished their fathers thirty years before about the smell. That was two years after her father's death and a short time after her sweetheart—the one we believed would marry her—had deserted her. After her father's death she went out very little; after her sweetheart went away, people hardly saw her at all. A few of the ladies had the temerity to call, but were not received, and the only sign of life about the place was the Negro man—a young man then—going in and out with a market basket.

"Just as if a man—any man—could keep a kitchen properly," the ladies said; so they were not surprised when the smell developed. It was another link between the gross, teeming world and the high and mighty Griersons.

A neighbor, a woman, complained to the mayor, Judge Stevens, eighty years old.

"But what will you have me do about it, madam?" he said.

"Why, send her word to stop it," the woman said. "Isn't there a law?"

"I'm sure that won't be necessary," Judge Stevens said. "It's probably just a snake or a rat that nigger of hers killed in the yard. I'll speak to him about it."

The next day he received two more complaints, one from a man who came in diffident deprecation. "We really must do something about it, Judge. I'd be the last one in the world to bother Miss Emily, but we've got to do something." That night the Board of Aldermen met—three gray-beards and one younger man, a member of the rising generation.

"It's simple enough," he said. "Send her word to have her place cleaned up. Give her a certain time to do it in, and if she don't . . ."

"Dammit, sir," Judge Stevens said, "will you accuse a lady to her face of smelling bad?"

So the next night, after midnight, four men crossed Miss Emily's lawn and slunk about the house like burglars, sniffing along the base of the brickwork and at the cellar openings while one of them performed a regular sowing motion with his hand out of a sack slung from his shoulder. They broke open the cellar door and sprinkled lime there, and in all the outbuildings. As they recrossed the lawn, a window that had been dark was lighted and Miss Emily sat in it, the light behind her, and her upright torso motionless as that of an idol. They crept quietly across the lawn and into the shadow of the locusts that lined the street. After a week or two the smell went away.

That was when people had begun to feel really sorry for her. People in our town, remembering how old lady Wyatt, her great-aunt, had gone completely crazy at last, believed that the Griersons held themselves a little too high for what they really were. None of the young men were quite good enough for Miss Emily and such. We had long thought of them as a tableau; Miss Emily a slender figure in white in the background, her father a spraddled silhouette in the foreground, his back to her and clutching a horsewhip, the two of them framed by the back-flung front door. So when she got to be thirty and was still single, we were not pleased exactly, but vindicated; even with insanity in the family she wouldn't have turned down all of her chances if they had really materialized.

When her father died, it got about that the house was all that was left to her; and in a way, people were glad. At last they could pity Miss Emily. Being left alone, and a pauper, she had become humanized. Now she too would know the old thrill and the old despair of a penny more or less.

The day after his death all the ladies prepared to call at the house and offer condolence and aid, as is our custom. Miss Emily met them at the door, dressed as usual and with no trace of grief on her face. She told them that her father was not dead. She did that for three days, with the ministers calling on her, and the doctors, trying to persuade her to let them dispose of the body. Just as they were about to resort to law and force, she broke down, and they buried her father quickly.

We did not say she was crazy then. We believed she had to do that. We remembered all the young men her father had driven away, and we knew that with nothing left, she would have to cling to that which had robbed her, as people will.

III

She was sick for a long time. When we saw her again, her hair was cut short, making her look like a girl, with a vague resemblance to those angels in colored church windows—sort of tragic and serene.

The town had just let the contracts for paving the sidewalks, and in the summer after her father's death they began to work. The construction company came with niggers and mules and machinery, and a foreman named Homer Barron, a Yankee—a big, dark, ready man, with a big voice and eyes lighter than his face. The little boys would follow in groups to hear him cuss the niggers, and the niggers singing in time to the rise and fall of picks. Pretty soon he knew everybody in town. Whenever you heard a lot of laughing anywhere about the square, Homer Barron would be in the center of the group. Presently we began to see him and Miss Emily on Sunday afternoons driving in the yellow-wheeled buggy and the matched team of bays from the livery stable.

At first we were glad that Miss Emily would have an interest, because the ladies all said, "Of course a Grierson would not think seriously of a Northerner, a day laborer." But there were still others, older people, who said that even grief could not cause a real lady to forget *noblesse oblige*—without calling it *noblesse oblige*. They just said, "Poor Emily. Her kinsfolk should come to her." She had some kin in Alabama; but years ago her father had fallen out with them over the estate of old lady Wyatt, the crazy woman, and there was no communication between the two families. They had not even been represented at the funeral.

And as soon as the old people said, "Poor Emily," the whispering began. "Do you suppose it's really so?" they said to one another. "Of course it is. What else could . . ." This behind their hands; rustling of craned silk and satin behind jalousies closed upon the sun of Sunday afternoon as the thin, swift clop-clop-clop of the matched team passed: "Poor Emily."

She carried her head high enough—even when we believed that she was fallen. It was as if she demanded more than ever the recognition of her dignity as the last Grierson; as if it had wanted that touch of earthiness to reaffirm her imperviousness. Like when she bought the rat poison, the arsenic. That was over a year after they had begun to say "Poor Emily," and while the two female cousins were visiting her.

"I want some poison," she said to the druggist. She was over thirty then, still a slight woman, though thinner than usual, with cold, haughty black eyes in a face the flesh of which was strained across the temples and about the eye sockets as you imagine a lighthouse-keeper's face ought to look. "I want some poison," she said.

"Yes, Miss Emily. What kind? For rats and such? I'd recom—"

"I want the best you have. I don't care what kind."

The druggist named several. "They'll kill anything up to an elephant. But what you want is—"

"Arsenic," Miss Emily said. "Is that a good one?"

"Is . . . arsenic? Yes, ma'am. But what you want—"

"I want arsenic."

The druggist looked down at her. She looked back at him, erect, her face like a strained flag. "Why, of course," the druggist said. "If that's what you want. But the law requires you to tell what you are going to use it for."

Miss Emily just stared at him, her head tilted back in order to look him eye for eye, until he looked away and went and got the arsenic and wrapped it up. The Negro delivery boy brought her the package; the druggist didn't come back. When she opened the package at home there was written on the box, under the skull and bones: "For rats."

IV

So the next day we all said, "She will kill herself"; and we said it would be the best thing. When she had first begun to be seen with Homer Barron, we had said, "She will marry him." Then we said, "She will persuade him yet," because Homer himself had remarked—he liked men, and it was known that he drank with the younger men in the Elk's Club—that he was not a marrying man. Later we said, "Poor Emily," behind the jalousies as they passed on Sunday afternoon in the glittering buggy, Miss Emily with her head high and Homer Barron with his hat cocked and a cigar in his teeth, reins and whip in a yellow glove.

Then some of the ladies began to say that it was a disgrace to the town and a bad example to the young people. The men did not want to interfere, but at last the ladies forced the Baptist minister—Miss Emily's people were Episcopal—to call upon her. He would never divulge what happened during that interview, but he refused to go back again. The next Sunday they again drove about the streets, and the following day the minister's wife wrote to Miss Emily's relations in Alabama.

So she had blood-kin under her roof again and we sat back to watch developments. At first nothing happened. Then we were sure that they were to be married. We learned that Miss Emily had been to the jeweler's and ordered a man's toilet set in silver, with the letters H. B. on each piece. Two days later we learned that she had bought a complete outfit of men's clothing, including a nightshirt, and we said, "They are married." We were really glad. We were glad because the two female cousins were even more Grierson than Miss Emily had ever been.

So we were not surprised when Homer Barron—the streets had been finished some time since—was gone. We were a little disappointed that there was not a public blowing-off, but we believed that he had gone on to prepare for Miss Emily's coming, or to give her a chance to get rid of the cousins. (By that time it was a cabal, and we were all Miss Emily's allies to help circumvent the cousins.) Sure enough, after another week they departed. And, as we had expected all along, within three days Homer Barron was back in town. A neighbor saw the Negro man admit him at the kitchen door at dusk one evening.

And that was the last we saw of Homer Barron. And of Miss Emily for some time. The Negro man went in and out with the market basket, but the front door remained closed. Now and then we would see her at a window for a moment, as the men did that night when they sprinkled the lime, but for almost six months she did not appear on the streets. Then we knew that this was to be expected too; as if that quality of her father which had thwarted her woman's life so many times had been too virulent and too furious to die.

When we next saw Miss Emily, she had grown fat and her hair was turning gray. During the next few years it grew grayer and grayer until it attained an even pepper-and-salt iron-gray, when it ceased turning. Up to the day of her death at seventy-four it was still that vigorous iron-gray, like the hair of an active man.

From that time on her front door remained closed, save for a period of six or seven years, when she was about forty, during which she gave lessons in china-painting. She fitted up a studio in one of the downstairs rooms, where the daughters and grand-daughters of Colonel Sartoris' contemporaries were sent to her with the same regularity and in the same spirit that they were sent to church on Sundays with a twenty-five-cent piece for the collection plate. Meanwhile her taxes had been remitted.

Then the newer generation became the backbone and the spirit of the town, and the painting pupils grew up and fell away and did not send their children to her with boxes of color and tedious brushes and pictures cut from the ladies' magazines. The front door closed upon the last one and remained closed for good. When the town got free postal delivery, Miss Emily alone refused to let them fasten the metal numbers above her door and attach a mailbox to it. She would not listen to them.

Daily, monthly, yearly we watched the Negro grow grayer and more stooped, going in and out with the market basket. Each December we sent her a tax notice, which would be returned by the post office a week later, unclaimed. Now and then we would see her in one of the downstairs windows—she had evidently shut up the top floor of the house—like the carven torso of an idol in a niche, looking or not looking at us, we could never tell which. Thus she passed from generation to generation—dear, inescapable, impervious, tranquil, and perverse.

And so she died. Fell ill in the house filled with dust and shadows, with only a doddering Negro man to wait on her. We did not even know she was sick; we had long since given up trying to get any information from the Negro. He talked to no one, probably not even to her, for his voice had grown harsh and rusty, as if from disuse.

She died in one of the downstairs rooms, in a heavy walnut bed with a curtain, her gray head propped on a pillow yellow and moldy with age and lack of sunlight.

V

The Negro met the first of the ladies at the front door and let them in, with their hushed, sibilant voices and their quick, curious glances, and then he disappeared. He walked right through the house and out the back and was not seen again.

The two female cousins came at once. They held the funeral on the second day, with the town coming to look at Miss Emily beneath a mass of bought flowers, with the crayon face of her father musing profoundly above the bier and the ladies sibilant and macabre; and the very old men—some in their brushed Confederate uniforms—on the porch and the lawn, talking of Miss Emily as if she had been a contemporary of theirs, believing that they had danced with her and courted her perhaps, confusing time with its mathematical progression, as the old do, to whom all the past is not a diminishing road, but, instead, a huge meadow which no winter ever quite touches, divided from them now by the narrow bottle-neck of the most recent decade of years.

Already we knew that there was one room in that region above stairs which no one had seen in forty years, and which would have to be forced. They waited until Miss Emily was decently in the ground before they opened it.

The violence of breaking down the door seemed to fill this room with pervading dust. A thin, acrid pall as of the tomb seemed to lie everywhere upon this room decked and furnished as for a bridal: upon the valance curtains of faded rose color, upon the rose-shaded lights, upon the dressing table, upon the delicate array of crystal and the man's toilet things backed with tarnished silver, silver so tarnished that the monogram was obscured. Among them lay a collar and tie, as if they had just been removed, which, lifted, left upon the surface a pale crescent in the dust. Upon a chair hung the suit, carefully folded; beneath it the two mute shoes and the discarded socks.

The man himself lay in the bed.

For a long while we just stood there, looking down at the profound and fleshless grin. The body had apparently once lain in the attitude of an embrace, but now the long sleep that outlasts love, that conquers even the grimace of love, had cuckolded him. What was left of him, rotted beneath what was left of the nightshirt, had become inextricable from the bed in which he lay;

and upon him and upon the pillow beside him lay that even coating of the patient and biding dust.

Then we noticed that in the second pillow was the indentation of a head. One of us lifted something from it, and leaning forward, that faint and invisible dust dry and acrid in the nostrils, we saw a long strand of iron-gray hair.

Symbolism

A very simple definition of a symbol is an image, object, or person that represents something other or more important than itself. A flag, in itself, is a piece of colored cloth. Yet it stands for a country, a state, a school, a business, or any number of other things that people want it to represent. A flag flown at half-staff is just a piece of cloth lowered halfway down a pole; but it signifies the death of someone important—someone mourned by everyone.

A teacher at home watching a football game is just another football fan. But a teacher in a classroom symbolizes leadership and a level of knowledge in one or more academic subjects. A doctor on the golf course may be just another golfer, but in the operating room she may represent hope for a desperately ill person.

So *things* can be symbols, *people* can be symbols, and *actions* or situations can be symbols. Symbols abound in everyday life—in music, painting, architecture, literature, sculpture and many other human endeavors. Arches and spires symbolize a church's heavenly mission. Certain refrains in such musical compositions as Sibelius's *Finlandia* and Chopin's *Polonaise* represent the spirit and patriotism of the Finnish and Polish people.

In early literature legends featured heroes, heroines, and villains who symbolized good and evil forces at work in the world. Many of the adventures of the gods in myths represent the creation and fertility of the earth. Oceans have been used to symbolize eternity or the origin of life; voyages are frequently used to represent the idea of life as a journey from birth to death. A simple, long-suffering character in a story may represent the average person who struggles through an average life.

Much of William Faulkner's work is concerned with time and the changes that time brings to people, places, institutions, and traditions. He frequently looks to the past to explain the present. Therefore, many of his stories use people, places, and actions as symbols that help to make connections between the past and the present. In this lesson you will examine the following aspects of symbolism in Faulkner's story:

1. Settings can become symbols in stories.
2. Characters may be used as symbols in stories.
3. Symbolism develops through story situations and actions.
4. Authors control the symbols they use.

· 1 ·

Elements of Setting as Symbols

You probably remember the familiar nursery rhyme "Rockabye Baby," but you may not know that when it was written, hundreds of years ago, it was riddled with political symbols.

> Rockabye baby on the treetop,
> When the wind blows the cradle will rock;
> When the bough breaks the cradle will fall,
> And down will come baby, bough, cradle and all.

The baby was a symbol of a king of England. The tree was a symbol of the royal family tree, the line of descent. The wind was the wind of a coming revolt that would rock the cradle (the throne) and cause the downfall of the king, his throne, and the entire branch of the royal line—baby, bough, cradle and all. In a time when people could be imprisoned for expressing feelings against the monarchy, they resorted to using *things* to stand for something else—symbols. It was safer, a short but very effective way to make a point, and it was more entertaining for the listeners than reciting a whole political history.

Authors use symbols in a similar way. For instance, using a symbol is a shorter, more intriguing, and often more meaningful way to portray a family's background than to relate a long, boring family history. Houses are frequently used as symbols because they so intimately relate to the people that live in them. In "The Lagoon" Arsat's house had a ghostly reputation because it had been restored by a stranger. In "The Guest" the lonely schoolhouse on the hillside was a perfect representation of the loneliness and isolation that pervaded the story. You have probably noticed how Faulkner uses Miss Emily's house to connect the past to the present:

> It was a big, squarish frame house that had once been white, decorated with cupolas and spires and scrolled balconies in the heavily lightsome style of the seventies, set on what had once been our most select street. But garages and cotton gins had encroached and obliterated even the august names of that neighborhood; only Miss Emily's house was left, lifting its stubborn and coquettish decay above the cotton wagons and the gasoline pumps—an eyesore among eyesores. And now Miss Emily had gone to join the representatives of those august names where they lay in the cedar-bemused cemetery among the ranked and anonymous graves of Union and Confederate soldiers who fell at the battle of Jefferson.

The author covers long periods of time and the changes during that time through the use of symbolism. The entire setting is symbolic of changes that occurred in Jefferson in two or more generations since the Civil War. The house was an anachronism—a thing out of its proper time and place, like Miss Emily herself. Now, with Emily gone, the old house will probably go too. The house and

Emily's death both symbolize the last vestiges of an era and a way of life that is over at last.

The house symbolizes the ornate luxury of the late Victorian era; the garages and cotton gins symbolize the passage of time. The house is in decay—"coquettish decay"—the author says, just as former times and its people are gone but are remembered in an attractive and beguiling way.

How is the setting of the interior house used in a similar way in the passage in Exercise A?

EXERCISE A

Read the following passage from the story and answer the questions that follow using the information you have learned in this part of the lesson.

> They called a special meeting of the Board of Aldermen. A deputation waited upon her, knocked at the door through which no visitor had passed since she ceased giving china-painting lessons eight or ten years earlier. They were admitted by the old Negro into a dim hall from which a stairway mounted into still more shadow. It smelled of dust and disuse—a close, dank smell. The Negro led them into the parlor. It was furnished in heavy, leather-covered furniture. When the Negro opened the blinds of one window, they could see that the leather was cracked; and when they sat down, a faint dust rose sluggishly about their thighs, spinning with slow motes in the single sun-ray. On a tarnished gilt easel before the fireplace stood a crayon portrait of Miss Emily's father.

1. Which of the elements of the setting best symbolize the passage of time?
   - ☐ a. the door and the hallway
   - ☐ b. the blinds and the sun-ray
   - ☐ c. the dust and the cracked leather
   - ☐ d. the stairway and shadows

2. What is the symbol of a past generation that the author includes in the passage?

   _____

   _____

   _____

Now check your answers using the Answer Key at the back of the book. Correct any wrong answers and review this part of the lesson if you do not understand why an answer is wrong.

· 2 ·

Characters as Symbols

Emily Grierson is the central character of the story and she is also the dominant symbol for a number of ideas. In the following paragraphs she symbolizes old aristocratic traditions. As time goes on and ideas change, however, the town's attitude towards its traditions is changing. Who else seems to be a character symbol in this passage?

> Alive, Miss Emily had been a tradition, a duty, and a care; a sort of hereditary obligation upon the town, dating from that day in 1894 when Colonel Sartoris, the mayor—he who fathered the edict that no Negro woman should appear on the streets without an apron—remitted her taxes, the dispensation [arrangement] dating from the death of her father on into perpetuity [forever]. Not that Miss Emily would have accepted charity. Colonel Sartoris invented an involved tale to the effect that Miss Emily's father had loaned money to the town, which the town, as a matter of business, preferred this way of repaying. Only a man of Colonel Sartoris' generation and thought could have invented it, and only a woman could have believed it.

> When the next generation, with its more modern ideas, became mayors and aldermen, this arrangement created some little dissatisfaction.

Since 1894 the narrator tells you, Miss Emily "had been a tradition, a duty, and a care. . . ." You almost expect him to add, "like the town's Confederate war memorial and the cemetery with its honored dead." Like the war memorial and the graves of the soldiers, Emily symbolized the past. Just as the town looks after these other symbols, the town looks after Emily and cares for her.

Colonel Sartoris and the younger aldermen are the other character symbols in the passage—one representing an old way of thinking and doing things, the other the newer ways. The Colonel's gallant treatment of Emily seems as out of place today as his edict that black women must wear aprons on the street. Time has passed by both Emily and the Colonel. They are symbols of another era. How is Emily, the character symbol, made to appear in the passage in Exercise B?

EXERCISE B

Read the following passage from the story and answer the questions that follow using the information you have learned in this part of the lesson.

> They rose when she entered—a small, fat woman in black, with a thin gold chain descending to her waist and vanishing into her belt, leaning on an ebony cane with a tarnished gold head. Her skeleton was small and spare; perhaps that was why what would have been merely plumpness in another was obesity in her. She looked bloated, like a body long submerged in motionless water, and of that pallid hue.

1. Like the past, Miss Emily is represented as appearing to be
   ☐ a. dead and decaying.
   ☐ b. dear and inescapable.
   ☐ c. domineering but dependable.
   ☐ d. plump and comfortable.

2. What is the image that the author uses to make you shudder at this representation of the past?

   _____

   _____

   _____

Now check your answers using the Answer Key at the back of the book. Correct any wrong answers and review this part of the lesson if you do not understand why an answer is wrong.

· 3 ·

Symbols in Situations and Actions

Just as objects and characters are used symbolically, actions are used symbolically when they have meanings outside themselves. In some cultures dances are symbolic, with the movements of the dance representing bravery, a plea for rain, comfort for the sick, thanks for a good harvest, and so on. Parts of religious ceremonies are symbolic. Breaking and eating bread, for example, have important symbolic significance in ceremonies of both the Christian and Jewish religions.

As you read in the introduction, a journey in a novel is sometimes used to symbolize a journey through life or a quest for knowledge. In "The Guest" the actions of Daru, the Arab, and the unknown hand that scrawled a threat on the blackboard, combined to symbolize the irrationality of life. What might Emily's relationship with Homer Barron symbolize?

> At first we were glad that Miss Emily would have an interest, because the ladies all said, "Of course a Grierson would not think seriously of a Northerner, a day laborer." But there were still others, older people, who said that even grief could not cause a real lady to forget *noblesse oblige*—without calling it *noblesse oblige*. They just said, "Poor Emily. . . ."
>
> She carried her head high enough—even when we believed that she was fallen. It was as if she demanded more than ever the recognition of her dignity as the last Grierson; as if it had wanted that touch of earthiness to reaffirm her imperviousness.

The expression *noblesse oblige* refers to the obligations and noble behavior that is expected of persons of high rank of birth. The expression is used when talking about people of the aristocracy, and a class structure with an aristocracy did exist in the South until the end of the Civil War. Emily was a remnant of that aristocracy and the ladies of the town of lower rank were happy to be able to gossip about her apparent fall. The symbolism of Emily's and Homer's relationship once again points to an ambivalence of wanting to hang on to old ways even as times are changing. How is this shown in another way in the passage in Exercise C?

EXERCISE C
Read the following passage from the story and answer the questions that follow using the information you have learned in this part of the lesson.

> When her father died, it got about that the house was all that was left to her; and in a way, people were glad. At last they could pity Miss Emily. Being left alone, and a pauper, she had become humanized. Now she too would know the old thrill and the old despair of a penny more or less.

The day after his death all the ladies prepared to call at the house and offer condolence and aid, as is our custom. Miss Emily met them at the door, dressed as usual and with no trace of grief on her face. She told them that her father was not dead. She did that for three days, with the ministers calling on her, and the doctors, trying to persuade her to let them dispose of the body. Just as they were about to resort to law and force, she broke down, and they buried her father quickly.

1. Emily told people that her father was not dead. What might that action symbolize?
   - ☐ a. The action may symbolize Emily's reluctance to conform with town customs.
   - ☐ b. The action is symbolic of the pressure a town places on its aristocracy.
   - ☐ c. The action indicates that Emily has probably inherited the strain of family insanity.
   - ☐ d. The action is probably symbolic of Emily's reluctance to break with the past.

2. Find at least one sentence in the passage that tells you the townspeople were actually pleased to see the passing of their aristocracy.

   _____

   _____

   _____

   _____

Now check your answers using the Answer Key at the back of the book. Correct any wrong answers and review this part of the lesson if you do not understand why an answer is wrong.

· 4 ·
Controlling Symbols

Because there is nothing that goes into their stories that authors do not have a hand in controlling, you can expect that they also control the symbolism they choose to use. Emily, for example, is a symbol of the aristocracy of the Old South. There are a number of ways Faulkner could have chosen to present this symbol. If she had been portrayed as tall, stately, loved, and respected, you would have to say that Faulkner viewed the old aristocracy existing into the present as a respected and beloved institution. What he did, however, was present the symbol as a rotting corpse:

> She looked bloated, like a body long submerged in motionless water, and of that pallid hue.

When Faulkner introduced Colonel Sartoris, also a symbol of the old aristocracy, he could have just told about the gracious remission of Emily's taxes. That would have presented a nostalgic view of an old-time officer and gentleman of the Confederacy. But the author added a qualification that gives an entirely different twist to that symbol. In one sentence Faulkner makes him a foolish old man:

> . . . Colonel Sartoris, the mayor—he who fathered the edict that no Negro woman should appear on the streets without an apron. . . .

You recall in the lesson accompanying "The Black Cat" that in creating tone and mood for a story there is a certain degree of interaction between authors and their readers. Readers bring their own attitudes and feelings to a story, so that while one person may find a morbid fascination in the destruction of a cat, someone else may be repelled by the image. The same is true with symbols. For example, most people look on the flag (a symbol) of their country with pride; but in another country the same flag may symbolize the greatest treachery, and the people rejoice to see it burned in the street. Despite the way that Faulkner presents Emily and Colonel Sartoris as symbols, some readers with strong feelings for the old Confederacy may find an enduring graciousness and nobility in these characters that survives their physical and mental decay.

Readers may even discover symbolism that the author was not entirely conscious of injecting into a story. For example, Homer Barron was a Yankee. Did the author make him a Northerner to add symbolic meaning to the story, or was it just a way to give the local gossips a juicier scandal to enjoy? If you remember history, there was a period after the Civil War when Yankee carpetbaggers went to the South in droves to exploit the defeated Confederacy politically and commercially. Was the encounter between Homer and Emily symbolic of the rape of the South by carpetbaggers? Does Homer's and Emily's macabre affair symbolize the way both factions died in time?

You shouldn't carry this kind of search for meaning too far in a study of literature, because it can detract from the more fundamental enjoyments of reading. Yet these questions always arise as you think about a story, and they can become substance for stimulating discussions and lively arguments.

Read the following passage from the story and answer the questions that
follow using the information you have learned in this part of the lesson.

> Now and then we would see her in one of the downstairs win-
> dows—she had evidently shut up the top floor of the house—like the
> carven torso of an idol in a niche, looking or not looking at us, we
> could never tell which. Thus she passed from generation to genera-
> tion—dear, inescapable, impervious, tranquil, and perverse.

1. In comparing Emily to "the carven torso of an idol in a niche," Faulkner
   makes her seem like
   ☐ a. a person to be worshiped for her good qualities.
   ☐ b. a dead god from some ancient time.
   ☐ c. a work of art standing on a pedestal.
   ☐ d. an ideal for the world to follow.

2. How does the author tell you that traditions from the past create mixed
   feelings in people? He says in a phrase of six words that traditions are loved,
   they are unavoidable in our society, they are impossible to break with, they
   serve to steady our lives, and at the same time they may work against people.
   Find and copy the six-word phrase.

   _____

   _____

   _____

Now check your answers using the Answer Key at the back of the book.
Correct any wrong answers and review this part of the lesson if you do not
understand why an answer is wrong.

Comprehension Questions

For each of the following statements or questions, select the option that best completes a statement or is the most accurate response to a question.

Recalling Specific Facts

1. Emily and her father had
   - ☐ a. no close family ties.
   - ☐ b. traditionally close family ties.
   - ☐ c. great concern for the opinions of family members.
   - ☐ d. no relatives they could call upon for help.

Recalling Specific Facts

2. At the time of her death, Emily's hair was
   - ☐ a. a vigorous black.
   - ☐ b. pure white.
   - ☐ c. iron-gray.
   - ☐ d. dyed blond.

Recalling Specific Facts

3. What was the one occupation Emily had for a few years that earned some money?
   - ☐ a. giving piano lessons
   - ☐ b. tutoring
   - ☐ c. sewing
   - ☐ d. giving china-painting lessons

Organizing Facts

4. When Emily's father died he left her
   - ☐ a. quite enough to live on.
   - ☐ b. the Grierson fortune.
   - ☐ c. very little.
   - ☐ d. enough to maintain the old life-style.

Organizing Facts

5. Emily began seeing Homer Barron
   - ☐ a. long before her father died.
   - ☐ b. just before her father died.
   - ☐ c. shortly after her father died.
   - ☐ d. many years after her father died.

Organizing Facts

6. The townspeople thought Emily had married Homer Barron when
   ☐ a. she was seen riding with him in the buggy.
   ☐ b. he was seen entering her house.
   ☐ c. her relatives came to her.
   ☐ d. she bought a toilet set and nightshirt.

Knowledge of Word Meanings

7. "But garages and cotton gins had *encroached* and *obliterated* even the *august* names of that neighborhood." That sentence means the garages and cotton gins had
   ☐ a. made the prominent houses more outstanding by contrast.
   ☐ b. reduced the prominent people to poverty.
   ☐ c. intruded on and forced out the old and well-known families.
   ☐ d. destroyed the last vestiges of decency in the neighborhood.

Knowledge of Word Meanings

8. The townspeople thought of Emily and her father as a *tableau* framed in the open doorway of their house. A *tableau* is a
   ☐ a. large statue.
   ☐ b. vivid vision.
   ☐ c. striking scene or picture.
   ☐ d. stone engraving.

Knowledge of Word Meanings

9. If dust is dry and *acrid* in the nostrils, it is dry and
   ☐ a. irritating.
   ☐ b. fragrant.
   ☐ c. tickling.
   ☐ d. like acrylic.

Drawing a Conclusion

10. As you review what the author tells you, you can conclude that the smell around Emily's house was caused by
   ☐ a. age and neglect.
   ☐ b. a dead rat or snake.
   ☐ c. moldy rugs and furniture.
   ☐ d. a decaying body.

Drawing a Conclusion
11. You may conclude from the story that the townspeople
    - ☐ a. were secretly pleased to hear of Emily's problems.
    - ☐ b. were troubled by Emily's problems.
    - ☐ c. cared about Emily and worried about her.
    - ☐ d. didn't think one way or another about Emily's troubles.

Drawing a Conclusion
12. Whenever Emily had contact with the town fathers, you would have to say
    - ☐ a. they always had the upper hand.
    - ☐ b. she always intimidated them.
    - ☐ c. they deferred to her judgment.
    - ☐ d. she had the law on her side.

Making a Judgment
13. When Emily told the Aldermen to see Colonel Sartoris about her taxes, it showed that she
    - ☐ a. still had a friend in her own generation.
    - ☐ b. didn't have a clear idea of the passage of time.
    - ☐ c. had made enemies among the Aldermen.
    - ☐ d. knew her rights as a leading citizen.

Making a Judgment
14. By keeping company with Homer Barron, Emily violated rules of
    - ☐ a. law and civic responsibility.
    - ☐ b. love and marriage.
    - ☐ c. class and moral propriety.
    - ☐ d. honesty and loyalty to the town.

Making an Inference
15. Right after Emily died, her old servant walked out the back door and disappeared. That was probably because he
    - ☐ a. had known about Homer's fate for years.
    - ☐ b. had been a slave and saw his chance for freedom.
    - ☐ c. was basically disloyal to Emily.
    - ☐ d. was Emily's accomplice.

Making an Inference

16. The indentation in the pillow and the gray hair found there at the end of the story strongly suggest that Emily had

☐ a. smothered her lover with the pillow.

☐ b. been in bed with the skeleton.

☐ c. not visited the room for years.

☐ d. tried unsuccessfully to get rid of the body.

Understanding Characters

17. Emily's servant Tobe is

☐ a. actually the hero of the story.

☐ b. an important main character.

☐ c. of no consequence to the story.

☐ d. an important minor character.

Understanding Characters

18. The very old men who attended Emily's funeral in their Confederate uniforms were character symbols who represented

☐ a. a blurring of time between two eras.

☐ b. the townspeople's faith in a resurgent Confederacy.

☐ c. all the beaus Emily danced with as a girl.

☐ d. the father image that Emily had lost years before.

Understanding Main Ideas

19. In various ways throughout the story you are made to feel that, for the townspeople, Emily represents

☐ a. a liability.

☐ b. a tax cheater.

☐ c. a tradition.

☐ d. an insoluble problem.

Understanding Main Ideas

20. An idea that keeps appearing in the story is that clinging to the past

☐ a. is necessary so as not to repeat past mistakes in the future.

☐ b. can be destructive.

☐ c. preserves historical values.

☐ d. assures continuity.

Understanding Main Ideas

21. Another title for the story might be
    ☐ a. "The Sound and the Fury."
    ☐ b. "The End of an Era."
    ☐ c. "Stubborn Is As Stubborn Does."
    ☐ d. "Jefferson Days."

Recognizing Tone

22. The author compares Colonel Sartoris's courtly treatment of Emily with his decree that black women must wear aprons on the street. That indicates that the author
    ☐ a. is being critical of the Colonel.
    ☐ b. views the Colonel with great good humor.
    ☐ c. is simply reporting the facts objectively.
    ☐ d. is angry and bitter about the whole situation.

Recognizing Tone

23. By using a citizen of Jefferson as the narrator of the story, the author has made it sound
    ☐ a. official, like a police investigation.
    ☐ b. whining, complaining, and outraged.
    ☐ c. smug and condescending.
    ☐ d. conversational and gossipy.

Appreciation of Literary Forms

24. An expression that contains words that contradict each other is known as an oxymoron. An example is "the icy fires of hell." Which one of the following expressions from the story contains an oxymoron?
    ☐ a. ". . . a sort of respectful affection for a fallen monument. . . ."
    ☐ b. ". . . in the heavily lightsome style of the seventies. . . ."
    ☐ c. ". . . the august names of that neighborhood. . . ."
    ☐ d. ". . . an eyesore among eyesores . . ."

Appreciation of Literary Forms

25. The author says: "Only Miss Emily's house was left, lifting its *stubborn and coquettish decay* above the cotton wagons and the gasoline pumps. . . ." The expression in italics is an example of
    ☐ a. a simile.
    ☐ b. exaggeration.
    ☐ c. a metaphor.
    ☐ d. personification.

Now check your answers using the Answer Key at the back of the book. Make no mark for right answers. Correct any wrong answers you may have by putting a check mark (✓) in the box next to the right answer. Count the number of questions you answered correctly and plot the total on the Comprehension Scores Graph at the back of the book.

Next, look at the questions you answered incorrectly. What types of questions were they? Count the number you got wrong of each type and enter the numbers in the spaces below.

Recalling Specific Facts	_____
Organizing Facts	_____
Knowledge of Word Meanings	_____
Drawing a Conclusion	_____
Making a Judgment	_____
Making an Inference	_____
Understanding Characters	_____
Understanding Main Ideas	_____
Recognizing Tone	_____
Appreciation of Literary Forms	_____

Now use these numbers to fill in the Comprehension Skills Profile at the end of the book.

Extension Activities

Discussion Guide

Discussing Symbolism

1. How is Emily's father a character symbol in the story?
2. In the Bible, Genesis 3:19, it says ". . . for dust thou art, and unto dust shalt thou return." How is that idea reflected in the symbolism of the story?
3. William Faulkner often used symbolism in the titles of his stories. What might be the symbolism of the rose in the title "A Rose for Emily"? If you think there is no symbolism in it, explain why you think not. (Some suggestions: Roses are sometimes given in tribute. A rose may be a sign of love. Roses are sent to funerals. An excellent person or a beautiful woman may be called a rose.)

Discussing the Story

4. When Emily's father died, she refused at first to admit he was dead. The story narrator said: "We believed she had to do that . . . she would have to cling to that which had robbed her, as people will." How may you connect that statement with the shocking end of the story?
5. When the townspeople thought Emily was "fallen," did they mean socially, morally, or what? Do you think they wanted her to fall, even though she was their "tradition, duty and care"?
6. Why was Emily a "hereditary obligation" for the people when it seems that she had done nothing special for the town?

Discussing the Author's Work

7. How would the feeling of the story change if Faulkner told the story using a third-person narrator, rather than a first-person narrator who is one of the townspeople?
8. There are many passages in the story that appeal to the senses—hearing, smelling, seeing, touching. Find and reread some of those passages and explain what effect they have on the story.
9. Read this sentence from the story: "The construction company came with niggers and mules and machinery, and a foreman named Homer Barron, a Yankee . . ." Everywhere else in the story Faulkner says "Negro" when referring to black people. Why do you think he uses the objectionable term "nigger" here?

Writing Exercise

Think about some familiar objects, places, people, and activities that have symbolic meaning for you. Use three or four sentences to describe why you regard each of these things as a symbol. Here are some possibilities:

Objects and places: a plain gold ring, the ocean, a mountain, your home, a badge or medal, an animal

People: the president or prime minister, your parents, an entertainer or sports figure, an old person, a friend

Actions or situations: a war, a ceremony, a dance, a sports event, a first kiss

UNIT
Ten

Unit Ten

Introduction

What the Story Is About

"The Kugelmass Episode" may be one of the most improbable and impossible stories you will ever read, and one of the funniest. Sidney Kugelmass is a middle-aged professor of humanities at City College of New York—uptown branch, he hastens to point out, which is just a touch more prestigious than the downtown or suburban branches. (City College is now called City University of New York). Kugelmass is unhappy, neurotic, and anxiety ridden, mostly because his life has turned out just the way he planned it.

He is married to Daphne whom he describes as a troglodyte (cave dweller) who has swollen up like a beach ball. Kugelmass has a preference for women who are young, beautiful, sensual, and exciting. "She had promise," is the nicest thing Kugelmass can tell his analyst about Daphne. Kugelmass had married Daphne for her money in order to help meet alimony and child support payments to his first wife. He now finds his life with Daphne frustrating. Compassion for the feelings of others is not a high priority for Kugelmass.

"I'm a man who needs romance. I need softness, I need flirtation," Kugelmass whines to Dr. Mandel. "I'm an analyst, not a magician," Dr. Mandel replies.

At that point Kugelmass decides that a magician is exactly what he does need. It will take a magician to put a little romance in his life without Daphne finding out about it. A few weeks later The Great Persky, a small-time magician in Brooklyn, telephones Kugelmass. Persky promises that for a double sawbuck ($20) he will project Kugelmass into any novel he chooses, where he can "carry on as much as he likes" with the beautiful heroine of the story.

Kugelmass chooses to meet Emma Bovary in the classic nineteenth-century French novel *Madame Bovary* by Gustave Flaubert. Emma is young, beautiful, and sensuous—all the things that Kugelmass has told his analyst he wants in a woman. In the novel Emma Bovary is bored with her marriage to a stodgy doctor, and she has been romantically involved with two other men, Léon and Rodolphe.

Persky works his magic well and manages to get Kugelmass into the book at a point when Dr. Bovary is away from home and between the appearances of Léon and Rodolphe. "By showing up in the right chapters, I've got the situation knocked," says Kugelmass.

Emma finds Kugelmass exciting, and the romantic encounters that follow are all that he ever dreamed. Intrigued by Kugelmass's stories of twentieth-century marvels, such as Hollywood, fast cars, and muscular football players, Emma decides that she wants to return to New York with her new lover. She is sure she can become a great actress and win an Academy Award.

Persky works his magic again, and Emma and Kugelmass arrive in the

Bovary carriage at the Plaza Hotel where Kugelmass has reserved a suite for the weekend. Once in New York, however, the same fate that always plagues Kugelmass takes control once more.

The story is pure fantasy and just the kind of hilarious fun that you can expect from Woody Allen's fertile imagination. Most people think of Woody Allen as only an actor and director, but he was a writer long before he was either of those, and he still writes, or collaborates in writing, the screenplays for his films.

"The Kugelmass Episode" first appeared in *The New Yorker* magazine and was published again in *Prize Stories, 1978, The O. Henry Awards*. Because the story contains some trendy slang and references to places familiar to New Yorkers, you may find it helpful to review the following words and expressions that are listed in the order in which they appear in the story:

kugel (as in Kugelmass). a pudding made of noodles, bread, or potatoes

trade quips at "21". Club 21, a tony New York restaurant

It's the emess. the truth; on the level

the ball and chain. Kugelmass's wife

Rupert Murdoch. a wealthy publisher of newspapers and magazines

Women's Wear Daily. the newspaper of the fashion industry

FAO Schwarz. a large and famous toy store

the Sherry. the Sherry Netherland, a New York hotel where celebrities often stay

Halston, Saint Laurent, Ralph Lauren. well-known fashion designers

the Guggenheim. a famous art museum in New York

SoHo. a trendy district of nightspots just below New York City's Greenwich Village

Dom Pérignon and black eggs. an expensive brand of French champagne and black caviar

Comp Lit. Comparative Literature; often a required college English course

International Herald Tribune. an American newspaper published in France

The Monkey in Portnoy's Complaint. a promiscuous young woman in the book by Philip Roth

What the Lesson Is About

The lesson that follows the story is about humor and satire. People like to laugh, which is why you usually find a book of humor on the national best-seller list. Humor is whatever is funny or amusing in a situation and evokes laughter.

Satire is a kind of writing in which certain aspects of human behavior, customs, or human weaknesses are ridiculed by the writer.

Woody Allen uses both humor and satire in "The Kugelmass Episode." Keep the following questions in mind as you read. They will help you understand how authors use humor and satire to make you laugh and to make you think.

1. When you find something funny in the story, what is it that makes you laugh?

2. Which parts of the story seem the funniest to you, and *why* do you find them so funny?

3. Which parts of the story are just for fun? When does the author use humor and satire to be critical of society and the way people behave?

4. Are there parts of the story that seem more disturbing than funny to you?

The Kugelmass Episode

by Woody Allen

Kugelmass, a professor of humanities at City College, was unhappily married for the second time. Daphne Kugelmass was an oaf. He also had two dull sons by his first wife, Flo, and was up to his neck in alimony and child support.

"Did I know it would turn out so badly?" Kugelmass whined to his analyst one day. "Daphne had promise. Who suspected she'd let herself go and swell up like a beach ball? Plus she had a few bucks, which is not in itself a healthy reason to marry a person, but it doesn't hurt, with the kind of operating nut I have. You see my point?"

Kugelmass was bald and as hairy as a bear, but he had soul.

"I need to meet a new woman," he went on. "I need to have an affair. I may not look the part, but I'm a man who needs romance. I need softness, I need flirtation. I'm not getting younger, so before it's too late I want to make love in Venice, trade quips at '21,' and exchange coy glances over red wine and candlelight. You see what I'm saying?"

Dr. Mandel shifted in his chair and said, "An affair will solve nothing. You're so unrealistic. Your problems run much deeper."

"And also this affair must be discreet," Kugelmass continued. "I can't afford a second divorce. Daphne would really sock it to me."

"Mr. Kugelmass—"

"But it can't be anyone at City College, because Daphne also works there. Not that anyone on the faculty at CCNY is any great shakes, but some of those coeds . . ."

"Mr. Kugelmass—"

"Help me. I had a dream last night. I was skipping through a meadow holding a picnic basket and the basket was marked 'Options.' And then I saw there was a hole in the basket."

"Mr. Kugelmass, the worst thing you could do is act out. You must simply express your feelings here, and together we'll analyze them. You have been in treatment long enough to know there is no overnight cure. After all, I'm an analyst, not a magician."

"Then perhaps what I need is a magician," Kugelmass said, rising from his chair. And with that he terminated his therapy.

A couple of weeks later, while Kugelmass and Daphne were moping around in their apartment one night like two pieces of old furniture, the phone rang.

"I'll get it," Kugelmass said. "Hello."

"Kugelmass?" a voice said. "Kugelmass, this is Persky."

"Who?"

"Persky. Or should I say The Great Persky?"

"Pardon me?"

"I hear you're looking all over town for a magician to bring a little exotica into your life? Yes or no?"

"Sh-h-h," Kugelmass whispered. "Don't hang up. Where are you calling from, Persky?"

Early the following afternoon, Kugelmass climbed three flights of stairs in a broken-down apartment house in the Bushwick section of Brooklyn. Peering through the darkness of the hall, he found the door he was looking for and pressed the bell. I'm going to regret this, he thought to himself.

Seconds later, he was greeted by a short, thin, waxy-looking man.

"*You're* Persky the Great?" Kugelmass said.

"The Great Persky. You want a tea?"

"No, I want romance. I want music. I want love and beauty."

"But not tea, eh? Amazing. OK, sit down."

Persky went to the back room, and Kugelmass heard the sounds of boxes and furniture being moved around. Persky reappeared, pushing before him a large object on squeaky roller-skate wheels. He removed some old silk handkerchiefs that were lying on its top and blew away a bit of dust. It was a cheap-looking Chinese cabinet, badly lacquered.

"Persky," Kugelmass said, "what's your scam?"

"Pay attention," Persky said. "This is some beautiful effect. I developed it for a Knights of Pythias date last year, but the booking fell through. Get into the cabinet."

"Why, so you can stick it full of swords or something?"

"You see any swords?"

Kugelmass made a face and, grunting, climbed into the cabinet. He couldn't help noticing a couple of ugly rhinestones glued onto the raw plywood just in front of his face. "If this is a joke," he said.

"Some joke. Now, here's the point. If I throw any novel into this cabinet with you, shut the doors, and tap it three times, you will find yourself projected into that book."

Kugelmass made a grimace of disbelief.

"It's the emess," Persky said. "My hand to God. Not just a novel, either. A short story, a play, a poem. You can meet any of the women created by the world's best writers. Whoever you dreamed of. You could carry on all you like with a real winner. Then when you've had enough you give a yell, and I'll see you're back here in a split second."

"Persky, are you some kind of outpatient?"

"I'm telling you it's on the level," Persky said.

Kugelmass remained skeptical. "What are you telling me—that this cheesy homemade box can take me on a ride like you're describing?"

"For a double sawbuck."

Kugelmass reached for his wallet. "I'll believe this when I see it," he said.

Persky tucked the bills in his pants pocket and turned toward his bookcase. "So who do you want to meet? Sister Carrie? Hester Prynne? Ophelia? Maybe someone by Saul Bellow? Hey, what about Temple Drake? Although for a man your age she'd be a workout."

"French. I want to have an affair with a French lover."

"Nana?"

"I don't want to have to pay for it."

"What about Natasha in *War and Peace*?"

"I said French. I know! What about Emma Bovary? That sounds to me perfect."

"You got it, Kugelmass. Give me a holler when you've had enough." Persky tossed in a paperback copy of Flaubert's novel.

"You sure this is safe?" Kugelmass asked as Persky began shutting the cabinet doors.

"Safe. Is anything safe in this crazy world?" Persky rapped three times on the cabinet and then flung open the doors.

Kugelmass was gone. At the same moment, he appeared in the

bedroom of Charles and Emma Bovary's house at Yonville. Before him was a beautiful woman, standing alone with her back turned to him as she folded some linen. I can't believe this, thought Kugelmass, staring at the doctor's ravishing wife. This is uncanny. I'm here. It's her.

Emma turned in surprise. "Goodness, you startled me," she said. "Who are you?" She spoke in the same fine English translation as the paperback.

It's simply devastating, he thought. Then, realizing that it was he whom she had addressed, he said, "Excuse me. I'm Sidney Kugelmass. I'm from City College. A professor of humanities. CCNY? Uptown. I—oh, boy!"

Emma Bovary smiled flirtatiously and said, "Would you like a drink? A glass of wine, perhaps?"

She is beautiful, Kugelmass thought. What a contrast with the troglodyte who shared his bed! He felt a sudden impulse to take this vision into his arms and tell her she was the kind of woman he had dreamed of all his life.

"Yes, some wine," he said hoarsely. "White. No, red. No, white. Make it white."

"Charles is out for the day," Emma said, her voice full of playful implication.

After the wine, they went for a stroll in the lovely French countryside. "I've always dreamed that some mysterious stranger would appear and rescue me from the monotony of this crass rural existence," Emma said, clasping his hand. They passed a small church. "I love what you have on," she murmured. "I've never seen anything like it around here. It's so . . . so modern."

"It's called a leisure suit," he said romantically. "It was marked down." Suddenly he kissed her. For the next hour they reclined under a tree and whispered together and told each other deeply meaningful things with their eyes. Then Kugelmass sat up. He had just remembered he had to meet Daphne at Bloomingdale's. "I must go," he told her. "But don't worry, I'll be back."

"I hope so," Emma said.

He embraced her passionately, and the two walked back to the house. He held Emma's face cupped in his palms, kissed her again, and yelled, "OK, Persky! I got to be at Bloomingdale's by three-thirty."

There was an audible pop, and Kugelmass was back in Brooklyn.

"So? Did I lie?" Persky asked triumphantly.

"Look, Persky, I'm right now late to meet the ball and chain at Lexington Avenue, but when can I go again? Tomorrow?"

"My pleasure. Just bring a twenty. And don't mention this to anybody."

"Yeah. I'm going to call Rupert Murdoch."

Kugelmass hailed a cab and sped off to the city. His heart danced on point. I am in love, he thought, I am the possessor of a wonderful secret. What he didn't realize was that at this very moment students in various classrooms across the country were saying to their teachers, "Who is this character on page 100? A bald Jew is kissing Madame Bovary?" A teacher in Sioux Falls, South Dakota, sighed and thought, Jesus, these kids, with their pot and acid. What goes through their minds!

Daphne Kugelmass was in the bathroom-accessories department at Bloomingdale's when Kugelmass arrived breathlessly.

"Where've you been?" she snapped. "It's four-thirty."

"I got held up in traffic," Kugelmass said.

Kugelmass visited Persky the next day, and in a few minutes was again passed magically to Yonville. Emma couldn't hide her excitement at seeing him. The two spent hours together, laughing and talking about their different backgrounds. Before Kugelmass left, they made love. "My God, I'm doing it with Madame Bovary!" Kugelmass whispered to himself. "Me, who failed freshman English."

As the months passed, Kugelmass saw Persky many times and developed a close and passionate relationship with Emma Bovary. "Make sure and always get me into the book before page 120," Kugelmass said to the magician one day. "I always have to meet her before she hooks up with this Rodolphe character."

"Why?" Persky asked. "You can't beat his time?"

"Beat his time. He's landed gentry. Those guys have nothing better to do than flirt and ride horses. To me, he's one of those faces you see in the pages of *Women's Wear Daily*. With the Helmut Berger hairdo. But to her he's hot stuff."

"And her husband suspects nothing?"

"He's out of his depth. He's a lacklustre little paramedic who's thrown in his lot with a jitterbug. He's ready to go to sleep by ten, and she's putting on her dancing shoes. Oh, well . . . See you later."

And once again Kugelmass entered the cabinet and passed instantly to the Bovary estate at Yonville. "How you doing, cupcake?" he said to Emma.

"Oh, Kugelmass," Emma sighed. "What I have to put up with. Last night at dinner, Mr. Personality dropped off to sleep in the middle of the dessert course. I'm pouring my heart out about Maxim's and the ballet, and out of the blue I hear snoring."

"It's OK, darling. I'm here now," Kugelmass said, embracing her. I've earned this, he thought, smelling Emma's French perfume and burying his nose in her hair. I've suffered enough. I've paid enough analysts. I've searched till I'm weary. She's young and nubile, and I'm here a few pages after Léon and just before Rodolphe. By showing up during the correct chapters, I've got the situation knocked.

Emma, to be sure, was just as happy as Kugelmass. She had been starved for excitement, and his tales of Broadway night life, of fast cars and Hollywood and TV stars, enthralled the young French beauty.

"Tell me again about O. J. Simpson," she implored that evening, as she and Kugelmass strolled past Abbé Bournisien's church.

"What can I say? The man is great. He sets all kinds of rushing records. Such moves. They can't touch him."

"And the Academy Awards?" Emma said wistfully. "I'd give anything to win one."

"First you've got to be nominated."

"I know. You explained it. But I'm convinced I can act. Of course, I'd want to take a class or two. With Strasberg maybe. Then, if I had the right agent—"

"We'll see, we'll see. I'll speak to Persky."

That night, safely returned to Persky's flat, Kugelmass brought up the idea of having Emma visit him in the big city.

"Let me think about it," Persky said. "Maybe I could work it. Stranger things have happened." Of course, neither of them could think of one.

"Where the hell do you go all the time?" Daphne Kugelmass barked at her husband as he returned home late that evening. "You got a chippie stashed somewhere?"

"Yeah, sure, I'm just the type," Kugelmass said wearily. "I was with Leonard Popkin. We were discussing Socialist agriculture in Poland. You know Popkin. He's a freak on the subject."

"Well, you've been very odd lately," Daphne said. "Distant. Just don't forget about my father's birthday. On Saturday?"

"Oh, sure, sure," Kugelmass said, heading for the bathroom.

"My whole family will be there. We can see the twins. And Cousin Hamish. You should be more polite to Cousin Hamish—he likes you."

"Right, the twins," Kugelmass said, closing the bathroom door and shutting out the sound of his wife's voice. He leaned against it and took a deep breath. In a few hours, he told himself, he would be back in Yonville again, back with his beloved. And this time, if all went well, he would bring Emma back with him.

At three-fifteen the following afternoon, Persky worked his wizardry again. Kugelmass appeared before Emma, smiling and eager. The two spent a few hours at Yonville with Binet and then remounted the Bovary carriage. Following Persky's instructions, they held each other tightly, closed their eyes, and counted to ten. When they opened them, the carriage was just drawing up at the side door of the Plaza Hotel, where Kugelmass had optimistically reserved a suite earlier in the day.

"I love it! It's everything I dreamed it would be," Emma said as she swirled joyously around the bedroom, surveying the city from their window. "There's FAO Schwarz. And there's Central Park, and the Sherry is which one? Oh, there—I see. It's too divine."

On the bed there were boxes from Halston and Saint Laurent. Emma unwrapped a package and held up a pair of black velvet pants against her perfect body.

"The slacks suit is by Ralph Lauren," Kugelmass said. "You'll look like a million bucks in it. Come on, sugar, give us a kiss."

"I've never been so happy!" Emma squealed as she stood before the mirror. "Let's go out on the town. I want to see *Chorus Line* and the Guggenheim and this Jack Nicholson character you always talk about. Are any of his flicks showing?"

"I cannot get my mind around this," a Stanford professor said. "First a strange character named Kugelmass, and now she's gone from the book. Well, I guess the mark of a classic is that you can reread it a thousand times and always find something new."

The lovers passed a blissful weekend. Kugelmass had told Daphne he would be away at a symposium in Boston and would return Monday. Savoring each moment, he and Emma went to the movies, had dinner in Chinatown, passed two hours at a discothèque, and went to bed with a TV movie. They slept till noon on Sunday, visited SoHo, and ogled celebrities at Elaine's. They had caviar and champagne in their suite on Sunday night and talked until dawn. That morning, in the cab taking them to Persky's apartment, Kugelmass thought, It was hectic, but worth it. I can't bring her here too often, but now and then it will be a charming contrast with Yonville.

At Persky's, Emma climbed into the cabinet, arranged her new boxes of clothes neatly around her, and kissed Kugelmass fondly. "My place next time," she said with a wink. Persky rapped three times on the cabinet. Nothing happened.

"Hmm," Persky said, scratching his head. He rapped again, but still no magic. "Something must be wrong," he mumbled.

"Persky, you're joking!" Kugelmass cried. "How can it not work?"

"Relax, relax. Are you still in the box, Emma?"

"Yes."

Persky rapped again—harder this time.

"I'm still here, Persky."

"I know, darling. Sit tight."

"Persky, we *have* to get her back," Kugelmass whispered. "I'm a married man, and I have a class in three hours. I'm not prepared for anything more than a cautious affair at this point."

"I can't understand it," Persky muttered. "It's such a reliable little trick."

But he could do nothing. "It's going to take a little while," he said to Kugelmass. "I'm going to have to strip it down. I'll call you later."

Kugelmass bundled Emma into a cab and took her back to the Plaza. He barely made it to his class on time. He was on the phone all day, to Persky and to his mistress. The magician told him it might be several days before he got to the bottom of the trouble.

"How was the symposium?" Daphne asked him that night.

"Fine, fine," he said, lighting the filter end of a cigarette.

"What's wrong? You're as tense as a cat."

"Me? Ha, that's a laugh. I'm as calm as a summer night. I'm just going to take a walk." He eased out the door, hailed a cab, and flew to the Plaza.

"This is no good," Emma said. "Charles will miss me."

"Bear with me, sugar," Kugelmass said. He was pale and sweaty. He kissed her again, raced to the elevators, yelled at Persky over a pay phone in the Plaza lobby, and just made it home before midnight.

"According to Popkin, barley prices in Kraków have not been this stable since 1971," he said to Daphne, and smiled wanly as he climbed into bed.

The whole week went by like that.

On Friday night, Kugelmass told Daphne there was another symposium he had to catch, this one in Syracuse. He hurried back to the Plaza, but the second weekend there was nothing like the first. "Get me back into the novel or marry me," Emma told Kugelmass. "Meanwhile, I want to get a job or go to class, because watching TV all day is the pits."

"Fine. We can use the money," Kugelmass said. "You consume twice your weight in room service."

"I met an off-Broadway producer in Central Park yesterday, and he said I might be right for a project he's doing," Emma said.

"Who is this clown?" Kugelmass asked.

"He's not a clown. He's sensitive and kind and cute. His name's Jeff Something-or-Other, and he's up for a Tony."

Later that afternoon, Kugelmass showed up at Persky's drunk.

"Relax," Persky told him. "You'll get a coronary."

"Relax. The man says relax. I've got a fictional character stashed in a hotel room, and I think my wife is having me tailed by a private shamus."

"OK, OK. We know there's a problem." Persky crawled under the cabinet and started banging on something with a large wrench.

"I'm like a wild animal," Kugelmass went on. "I'm sneaking around town, and Emma and I have had it up to here with each other. Not to mention a hotel tab that reads like the defense budget."

"So what should I do? This is the world of magic," Persky said. "It's all nuance."

"Nuance, my foot. I'm pouring Dom Pérignon and black eggs into this little mouse, plus her wardrobe, plus she's enrolled at the Neighborhood Playhouse and suddenly needs professional photos.

Also, Persky, Professor Fivish Kopkind, who teaches Comp Lit and who has always been jealous of me, has identified me as the sporadically appearing character in the Flaubert book. He's threatened to go to Daphne. I see ruin and alimony; jail. For adultery with Madame Bovary, my wife will reduce me to beggary."

"What do you want me to say? I'm working on it night and day. As far as your personal anxiety goes, that I can't help you with. I'm a magician, not an analyst."

By Sunday afternoon, Emma had locked herself in the bathroom and refused to respond to Kugelmass's entreaties. Kugelmass stared out the window at the Wollman Rink and contemplated suicide. Too bad this is a low floor, he thought, or I'd do it right now. Maybe if I ran away to Europe and started life over . . . Maybe I could sell the *International Herald Tribune,* like those young girls used to.

The phone rang. Kugelmass lifted it to his ear mechanically.

"Bring her over," Persky said. "I think I got the bugs out of it."

Kugelmass's heart leaped. "You're serious?" he said. "You got it licked?"

"It was something in the transmission. Go figure."

"Persky, you're a genius. We'll be there in a minute. Less than a minute."

Again the lovers hurried to the magician's apartment, and again Emma Bovary climbed into the cabinet with her boxes. This time there was no kiss. Persky shut the doors, took a deep breath, and tapped the box three times. There was the reassuring popping noise, and when Persky peered inside, the box was empty. Madame Bovary was back in her novel. Kugelmass heaved a great sigh of relief and pumped the magician's hand.

"It's over," he said. "I learned my lesson. I'll never cheat again, I swear it." He pumped Persky's hand again and made a mental note to send him a necktie.

Three weeks later, at the end of a beautiful spring afternoon, Persky answered his doorbell. It was Kugelmass, with a sheepish expression on his face.

"OK, Kugelmass," the magician said. "Where to this time?"

"It's just this once," Kugelmass said. "The weather is so lovely, and I'm not getting any younger. Listen, you've read *Portnoy's Complaint*? Remember The Monkey?"

"The price is now twenty-five dollars, because the cost of living is up, but I'll start you off with one freebie, due to all the trouble I caused you."

"You're good people," Kugelmass said, combing his few remaining hairs as he climbed into the cabinet again. "This'll work all right?"

"I hope. But I haven't tried it much since all that unpleasantness."

"Sex and romance," Kugelmass said from inside the box. "What we go through for a pretty face."

Persky tossed in a copy of *Portnoy's Complaint* and rapped three times on the box. This time, instead of a popping noise there was a dull explosion, followed by a series of crackling noises and a shower of sparks. Persky leaped back, was seized by a heart attack, and dropped dead. The cabinet burst into flames, and eventually the entire house burned down.

Kugelmass, unaware of this catastrophe, had his own problems. He had not been thrust into *Portnoy's Complaint,* or into any other novel, for that matter. He had been projected into an old textbook, *Remedial Spanish,* and was running for his life over a barren, rocky terrain as the word *tener* ("to have")—a large and hairy irregular verb—raced after him on its spindly legs.

Humor and Satire

Many people do not realize that there is an art to writing good humor. In literature humor is whatever is funny or amusing in a situation and may evoke laughter. The response to humor can range from boisterous laughter to a reluctant smile at some all-too-recognizable human weakness.

Like any art, humor that is successful requires talent, intelligence, sensitivity to the world and the people in it, and a deep insight into human behavior, motives, and feelings. The humorist must have an ability to take a familiar situation and make it funny by changing or twisting it to create delighted surprise and laughter.

Humor takes a variety of forms. You will generally find something to laugh at, chuckle at, or smile over in most fiction and drama. Without some lighter moments, a story may become too oppressive to continue reading. William Shakespeare was well aware of the importance of humor—in his most moving tragedies you will find relief in the form of comic scenes and funny lines. No matter how desperate the circumstances in a Dickens novel, there will always be comic characters whose actions relieve the tension for a while. That technique is called, appropriately enough, comic relief.

In the stories you have read so far in this book there are very few without something to chuckle over. For example, the tone of "The Garden Party" is serious, but you have to smile over Laura's clumsy conversation with the workman and her preoccupation with her hat. In "A Worn Path" Phoenix Jackson's expressions and her encounter with a scarecrow also make you smile. The antics of Larry and his father in "My Oedipus Complex" make the whole story funny. There is a warm sort of humor in "A Christmas Memory" as Buddy and his friend prepare for Christmas—especially when they meet Haha Jones.

Woody Allen sets out to create a story that is funny; this makes him a humorist. He also makes you think a bit about our society and the behavior of people; this makes him a satirist. In this lesson you will recognize the elements of humor that Woody Allen uses in "The Kugelmass Episode":

1. Humor and surprise work together to make people laugh.
2. There are "rules" used to create humor.
3. Satire is the serious side of humor.
4. Everything that causes laughter may not be funny.

· I ·

Humor and Surprise

Using surprise is one of the oldest, most popular, and most dependable ways of making people laugh. Surprise is, in fact, basic to all humor. Surprise adds an unexpected twist to a story. Of course, surprise must be pleasant and non-threatening. It is not funny to be surprised with bad news.

A pie in the face, ten clowns emerging from a tiny auto, a talking horse, and a funny punch line to a joke are all variations of surprise humor. What surprise makes this love scene funny?

> After the wine, they went for a stroll in the lovely French countryside. "I've always dreamed that some mysterious stranger would appear and rescue me from the monotony of this crass rural existence," Emma said, clasping his hand. They passed a small church. "I love what you have on," she murmured. "I've never seen anything like it around here. It's so . . . so modern."
>
> "It's called a leisure suit," he said romantically. "It was marked down."

Kugelmass is in a romantic setting with the exotic Emma. You expect that their conversation will explore love and the beautiful scenery. What you read is a surprising exchange about Kugelmass's cheap leisure suit. Emma calls him "a mysterious stranger," someone who should be tall, dark, and handsome. But, in one sentence, Woody Allen presents a man who, far from a dashing lover, is a foolish man in marked down and outdated clothing.

The surprise in humor often involves the ridiculous. Pratfalls in slapstick comedy, the famous "Who's on First" routine of the late Abbott and Costello, and clowns in outlandish costumes are funny because they are ludicrous, illogical, and ridiculous. The premise of "The Kugelmass Episode" is ridiculous. You cannot help but smile when you think of yourself in any novel of your choice. Here is the passage where the premise of the story is established.

> "It's the emess," Persky said. "My hand to God. Not just a novel, either. A short story, a play, a poem. You can meet any of the women created by the world's best writers. Whoever you dreamed of. You could carry on all you like with a real winner. Then when you've had enough you give a yell, and I'll see you're back here in a split second."

You know the premise is impossible, illogical, and ridiculous. It becomes funny, however, when you picture yourself in an English class where your teacher has the powers of The Great Persky. Get into a box and presto!—instead of reading Shakespeare you find yourself on the balcony with Juliet or strolling the streets of Verona arm-in-arm with Romeo.

EXERCISE A

Read the following passage from the story and answer the questions that follow using the information you have learned in this part of the lesson.

> Kugelmass hailed a cab and sped off to the city. His heart danced on point. I am in love, he thought, I am the possessor of a wonderful secret. What he didn't realize was that at this very moment students in various classrooms across the country were saying to their teachers, "Who is this character on page 100? A bald Jew is kissing Madame Bovary?"

1. What is the ridiculous premise in this passage that makes it funny?
   - ☐ a. Everyone is reading Madame Bovary.
   - ☐ b. Kugelmass has a wonderful secret.
   - ☐ c. Kugelmass is in love.
   - ☐ d. Kugelmass appears as a character in the novel.

2. Persky has told Kugelmass not to mention what happened. Kugelmass says he is "the possessor of a wonderful secret." Copy the sentences that describe the surprise that you know about but Kugelmass does not.

_____

_____

_____

_____

_____

_____

Now check your answers using the Answer Key at the back of the book. Correct any wrong answers and review this part of the lesson if you do not understand why an answer is wrong.

· 2 ·

Creating Humor

There are certain do's and don'ts "rules" that apply to writing humor. Rules are not absolute and many good humorists violate them, but the rules apply often enough to list them.

- Good humor must relate to the audience for which it is intended. The situation must be familiar enough for audiences to recognize and understand.
- The best humor will stimulate your imagination. It will appeal to your sense of the ridiculous.
- Good humor is fresh and spontaneous. People do not laugh at tired old jokes or at humor that is prolonged and labored. The premise or idea supporting the joke must be fresh and funny.
- You are generally made to feel a bit superior to the object of the humor. That is why comedians often make themselves the target of their own jokes.
- You cannot be made to feel sorry for the character involved in the humor. When you begin to feel sorry for the character, or if you are upset by the situation, the story will not be funny. Neither can humor be overserious or threatening. If you pity the character, the situation is no longer humorous.

Let's see how Woody Allen uses humor in a passage from "The Kugelmass Episode." The story itself is based on a humorous premise: Kugelmass can be projected into a book of his choice in order to dally with its heroine.

> Kugelmass, a professor of humanities at City College, was unhappily married for the second time. Daphne Kugelmass was an oaf. He also had two dull sons by his first wife, Flo, and was up to his neck in alimony and child support.
>
> "Did I know it would turn out so badly?" Kugelmass whined to his analyst one day. "Daphne had promise. Who suspected she'd let herself go and swell up like a beach ball? Plus she had a few bucks, which is not in itself a healthy reason to marry a person, but it doesn't hurt, with the kind of operating nut I have. You see my point?"
>
> Kugelmass was bald and as hairy as a bear, but he had soul.
>
> "I need to meet a new woman," he went on. "I need to have an affair. I may not look the part, but I'm a man who needs romance. . . . I'm not getting younger, so before it's too late I want to make love in Venice, trade quips at '21,' and exchange coy glances over red wine and candlelight. You see what I'm saying?"

Do you feel a little superior to Kugelmass? He calls Daphne an oaf when, in fact, he is the oaf. He complains about Daphne's appearance when he himself is "bald and as hairy as a bear." At the same time he expresses a secret urge that most people can identify with—everyone wants to "cut loose from time to time," to be wild, and to have exciting adventures—as long as they do not get caught.

The scene between the main character of a story and his psychoanalyst is a Woody Allen specialty. You are likely to see a similar scene in most of his movies. Few humorists describe that scene so well.

Woody Allen has never hesitated to tell about his many visits to analysts. He is himself a short, owlish little man; he is well on the way to becoming bald and as "hairy as a bear," and he has had many well-publicized relationships with women. So in some ways the author is making himself the target of his jokes about Kugelmass. "What would it be like," he seems to be saying, "if an unattractive little guy like me could somehow be free to dally with the most beautiful women created by the world's best writers?" It is a highly original approach to humor that jostles the imagination.

While Woody Allen's humor appeals to audiences everywhere, it is obvious that it works best with New Yorkers who know "21", Bloomingdales, The Plaza, City College, and other topical references to New York City. But his humor may not sit well with those distressed by the way Kugelmass treats women. Nevertheless, most people can find humor in the poetic justice that comes to such a man: doomed to spend eternity being pursued by irregular verbs in a Spanish grammar book—just as he has been pursuing women.

EXERCISE B

Read the following passage from the story and answer the questions that follow using the information you have learned in this part of the lesson.

Kugelmass was gone. At the same moment, he appeared in the bedroom of Charles and Emma Bovary's house at Yonville. Before him was a beautiful woman, standing alone with her back turned to him as she folded some linen. I can't believe this, thought Kugelmass, staring at the doctor's ravishing wife. This is uncanny. I'm here. It's her.

Emma turned in surprise. "Goodness, you startled me," she said. "Who are you?" She spoke in the same fine English translation as the paperback.

It's simply devastating, he thought. Then, realizing that it was he whom she had addressed, he said, "Excuse me. I'm Sidney Kugelmass. I'm from City College. A professor of humanities. CCNY? Uptown. I—oh, boy!"

Emma Bovary smiled flirtatiously and said, "Would you like a drink? A glass of wine, perhaps?"

1. One thing that makes this passage humorous is that the author is having fun with
   - ☐ a. English courses and an English teacher.
   - ☐ b. French manners and customs.
   - ☐ c. Emma Bovary and her husband, Charles.
   - ☐ d. magic and magicians.

2. Readers can put their imaginations to work and identify with the humor in the passage when it shows what it would be like if dreams were to suddenly come true. Copy the sentences that describe Kugelmass's dream coming true.

   _____

   _____

   _____

   _____

   _____

Now check your answers using the Answer Key at the back of the book. Correct any wrong answers and review this part of the lesson if you do not understand why an answer is wrong.

· 3 ·

Satire: The Serious Side of Humor

Satire adds a critical or instructive tone to humor that may range from mild and playful to bitter or sarcastic and ironic. You can see the difference between humor and satire rather easily if you think about some popular comic strips. "Peanuts," "Garfield," and "Blondie" are all examples of humor that almost never has a critical or instructive tone. The situations are all fun for fun's sake—kids falling asleep in school or losing ball games 99 to 0, a cat who eats too much, or a likable bumbler who runs into the mailman on his way to catch a bus.

The comic "Doonesbury," on the other hand, qualifies as satire because it is highly critical of government authority and current weaknesses in society. The humor is often sharp, biting, and serious. It's object is not just to entertain but also to inform readers of author Gary Trudeau's opinions. "Small Society," "The Wizard of Id," "Cathy," "For Better or for Worse," and "B.C." are other examples of comics where the humor often contains a message or a lesson. Humor derived from satire is used to make a point as well as to entertain.

It is not hard to distinguish humor from satire in "The Kugelmass Episode." Persky and his magic box and Kugelmass actually appearing in the novel are ridiculous and funny. The episode with the psychoanalyst is another matter. Here you can see Woody Allen commenting on people who have spent years in expensive psychoanalysis:

> "I need to meet a new woman," he went on. "I need to have an affair. . . . I want to make love in Venice, trade quips at '21,' and exchange coy glances over red wine and candlelight. You see what I'm saying?"
>
> Dr. Mandel shifted in his chair and said, "An affair will solve nothing. You're so unrealistic. Your problems run much deeper."
>
> "And also this affair must be discreet," Kugelmass continued. "I can't afford a second divorce. Daphne would really sock it to me. . . ."
>
> "Mr. Kugelmass, the worst thing you could do is act out. You must simply express your feelings here, and together we'll analyze them. You have been in treatment long enough to know there is no overnight cure. After all, I'm an analyst, not a magician."
>
> "Then perhaps what I need is a magician," Kugelmass said, rising from his chair. And with that he terminated his therapy.

The author is pointing out how someone may attempt to use psychoanalysis to justify self-indulgence. The analyst here does not offer any real advice or help; he delivers platitudes that seem to be designed to keep the patient coming back for more years of expensive treatments: "Mr. Kugelmass, the worst thing you could do is act out. You must simply express your feelings here, and together we'll analyze them. . . . After all, I'm an analyst, not a magician." Apparently the two of them have been analyzing Kugelmass's "problem" for years without admitting that Kugelmass is simply a louse who deserves the trouble he brings upon himself.

Finally realizing that he is not getting the license for promiscuity that he is seeking, Kugelmass ends his therapy and finds a magician. A sure mark of satire is the use of irony—the contrast between appearance and reality or between what is expected to happen and what actually happens. In the following passage Woody Allen has set up Kugelmass for an ironic twist to come later when Persky cannot get Emma back into her book:

> "I'm like a wild animal," Kugelmass went on. "I'm sneaking around town, and Emma and I have had it up to here with each other. . . ."

"What do you want me to say?" [Persky replied.] "I'm working on it night and day. As far as your personal anxiety goes, that I can't help you with. I'm a magician, not an analyst."

The satiric lesson hidden in the humor is that Kugelmass must conquer his own anxieties. Neither analyst nor magician can solve his problems for him.

EXERCISE C

Read the following passage from the story and answer the questions that follow using the information you have learned in this part of the lesson.

Madame Bovary was back in her novel. Kugelmass heaved a great sigh of relief and pumped the magician's hand.

"It's over," he said. "I learned my lesson. I'll never cheat again, I swear it. . . ."

Three weeks later, at the end of a beautiful spring afternoon, Persky answered his doorbell. It was Kugelmass, with a sheepish expression on his face.

"OK, Kugelmass," the magician said. "Where to this time?"

"It's just this once," Kugelmass said. "The weather is so lovely, and I'm not getting any younger. Listen, you've read *Portnoy's Complaint*? Remember The Monkey? . . ."

"Sex and romance," Kugelmass said from inside the box. "What we go through for a pretty face."

1. One lesson satirically taught in the story is that
   ☐ a. people rarely reform from bad habits as a result of a bad experience.
   ☐ b. you can depend on a magician more than you can depend on an analyst.
   ☐ c. when you are burned once you are twice cautious.
   ☐ d. in spring a young man's fancy turns to thoughts of love.

2. Copy the sentence that makes a satiric comment on the lengths people will go to in pursuit of pleasure.

_____

_____

_____

Now check your answers using the Answer Key at the back of the book. Correct any wrong answers and review this part of the lesson if you do not understand why an answer is wrong.

·4·

Understanding Humor

Most people laugh at pleasant surprises, ridiculous situations, comic characters, or even their own follies and foibles. Yet humor is very personal—not everyone finds the same things funny.

People can laugh at their own foibles, but they do not like poking fun at their racial or ethnic identities unless it is done with tact and without malice. Neither do people laugh at situations they know nothing about. If people do not understand the humor, they do not "get the joke."

Good satire is not so bitter that it is hurtful or offensive. Satire should be thought-provoking; it should point out the foolishness of certain ideas, customs, or human weaknesses by exaggerating them. As you have learned, humor derived from satire is used to make a point as well as to entertain you.

Some people may find certain kinds of humor abrasive because of unpleasant experiences they may have had. Women, for example, who have been treated in the same way that Kugelmass treats Daphne will probably not find Kugelmass's complaints about her very funny. It is not really amusing to hear her called a troglodyte except that the statement reflects Kugelmass's own ridiculous personality.

People must be able to respond to humor instantly and spontaneously or it loses its effect. Allen uses the following joke that you may not have appreciated because it is a bit difficult to respond to without giving it some thought.

> "Help me. I had a dream last night. I was skipping through a meadow holding a picnic basket and the basket was marked 'Options.' And then I saw there was a hole in the basket."

You might chuckle at Kugelmass's dream when you realize you can interpret the dream just as well as Dr. Mandel the analyst: Kugelmass does not have many "options" left in his life. His options are running out.

Sometimes an author will intentionally make a character objectionable so that the humor comes when the character gets what he or she deserves, as Kugelmass does. When he gets what he wants—Emma—and he is stuck with supporting her on champagne and caviar at the Plaza Hotel, the situation is funny because Kugelmass gets exactly what he deserves.

EXERCISE D

Read the following passage from the story and answer the questions that follow using the information you have learned in this part of the lesson.

Kugelmass and Persky are discussing Emma and her husband:

> "And her husband suspects nothing?" [Persky asks.]
>
> "He's out of his depth. He's a lacklustre little paramedic who's thrown in his lot with a jitterbug. He's ready to go to sleep by ten, and she's putting on her dancing shoes. Oh, well . . . See you later."
>
> And once again Kugelmass entered the cabinet and passed instantly to the Bovary estate at Yonville. "How you doing, cupcake?" he said to Emma.
>
> "Oh, Kugelmass," Emma sighed. "What I have to put up with. Last night at dinner, Mr. Personality dropped off to sleep in the middle of the dessert course. I'm pouring my heart out about Maxim's and the ballet, and out of the blue I hear snoring."

1. Emma is bored with her husband. Why does her husband have good reason to be bored with *her?*
   ☐ a. Emma is not as beautiful as Kugelmass thinks she is.
   ☐ b. Charles Bovary is a doctor and doctors get bored easily.
   ☐ c. Emma is only interested in having fun.
   ☐ d. The novel *Madame Bovary* is a long and boring book.

2. Kugelmass talks about Emma's husband in much the same way that he talks about Daphne. Nor does he have a very high opinion of Emma except for her romantic favors. Copy the sentence that tells you this.

   _____

   _____

   _____

Now check your answers using the Answer Key at the back of the book. Correct any wrong answers and review this part of the lesson if you do not understand why an answer is wrong.

———— Comprehension Questions ————

For each of the following statements or questions, select the option that best completes a statement or is the most accurate response to a question.

Recalling Specific Facts

1. Dr. Mandel was
   - ☐ a. Emma Bovary's husband.
   - ☐ b. a professor.
   - ☐ c. Kugelmass's analyst.
   - ☐ d. a theatrical producer.

Recalling Specific Facts

2. Emma spoke to Kugelmass in
   - ☐ a. fine English.
   - ☐ b. French and English.
   - ☐ c. the original French.
   - ☐ d. English with a French accent.

Organizing Facts

3. While Kugelmass was dallying with Emma, Daphne
   - ☐ a. didn't suspect a thing.
   - ☐ b. was busy with her own life.
   - ☐ c. didn't care what her husband was doing.
   - ☐ d. was suspicious of her husband.

Organizing Facts

4. When Persky's machine broke down, Emma
   - ☐ a. went into hiding.
   - ☐ b. was returned to the Plaza.
   - ☐ c. stayed with Persky.
   - ☐ d. went to another hotel.

Knowledge of Word Meanings

5. Kugelmass said that Daphne's money helped him with his kind of *operating nut*. This slang business expression in this context seems to mean
   - ☐ a. psychological problems.
   - ☐ b. expenses.
   - ☐ c. escapades.
   - ☐ d. life insurance.

Knowledge of Word Meanings

6. Kugelmass thinks his wife is having him tailed by a *private shamus*. This is slang for a
   □ a. credit agency.
   □ b. clergyman.
   □ c. divorce lawyer.
   □ d. hired detective.

Drawing a Conclusion

7. After you get to know Kugelmass and Emma, you may conclude that
   □ a. neither one can ever be satisfied with their lives.
   □ b. they are both contented and happy people.
   □ c. they are a good influence on one another.
   □ d. they can each find happiness if they try.

Drawing a Conclusion

8. You can conclude from the story that Kugelmass
   □ a. has learned his lesson after his experience with Emma.
   □ b. will probably never change.
   □ c. will probably return to his therapist.
   □ d. has a new lease on life.

Making a Judgment

9. Kugelmass considers his marriage to Daphne
   □ a. better than some marriages.
   □ b. all right considering the money.
   □ c. challenging.
   □ d. dull.

Making a Judgment

10. Dr. Mandel says, "I'm not a magician." Persky says, "I'm not an analyst." Those statements suggest that
    □ a. neither one can solve Kugelmass's problem.
    □ b. together they can probably help Kugelmass.
    □ c. Kugelmass won't cooperate fully.
    □ d. they really do not want to help Kugelmass.

Making a Judgment
11. What seems to be the only thing that Kugelmass wants in his life?
   □ a. romance
   □ b. financial security
   □ c. excitement and danger
   □ d. a date with a coed

Making an Inference
12. Charles is identified as Emma's husband. It is left to readers to infer that Léon and Rodolphe are her
   □ a. servants.
   □ b. lovers.
   □ c. guards.
   □ d. relatives.

Making an Inference
13. Emma meets an off-Broadway producer in Central Park. She says he is sensitive and kind. Knowing Emma as you do, you can infer he probably
   □ a. wants to take advantage of her just as Kugelmass has.
   □ b. is a producer who has a part for a French beauty.
   □ c. is another one of Persky's clients.
   □ d. is just another friendly stranger.

Making an Inference
14. When Emma was unable to return to her novel, the relationship with Kugelmass
   □ a. became strained.
   □ b. warmed.
   □ c. deepened.
   □ d. became informal.

Understanding Characters
15. A good word to describe Kugelmass is
   □ a. big-hearted.
   □ b. open.
   □ c. selfish.
   □ d. crazy.

Understanding Characters

16. We can describe Emma as
    - ☐ a. intelligent and bright.
    - ☐ b. sloppy and careless.
    - ☐ c. shallow and fickle.
    - ☐ d. sympathetic and understanding.

Understanding Characters

17. When Emma arrives in New York, she
    - ☐ a. becomes sophisticated.
    - ☐ b. retains her dignity.
    - ☐ c. becomes morose and withdrawn.
    - ☐ d. acts like a stage-struck girl.

Understanding Main Ideas

18. After getting what he wanted from Emma, Kugelmass
    - ☐ a. figured Daphne wasn't so bad after all.
    - ☐ b. came to love her.
    - ☐ c. became tired of her.
    - ☐ d. wanted someone more sensible.

Understanding Main Ideas

19. It becomes clear that Kugelmass
    - ☐ a. will never be satisfied.
    - ☐ b. wants a permanent relationship.
    - ☐ c. is really afraid of women.
    - ☐ d. prefers foreign women to all others.

Recognizing Tone

20. When Kugelmass considers suicide or running away to Europe, the tone of the story
    - ☐ a. becomes threatening.
    - ☐ b. remains humorous.
    - ☐ c. becomes moralistic.
    - ☐ d. turns serious.

Recognizing Tone

21. Emma said that watching TV all day is the pits. This is apt to strike you funny because
    - ☐ a. the use of slang is always comical.
    - ☐ b. authors rarely use slang.
    - ☐ c. the expression is unexpected from a Frenchwoman.
    - ☐ d. watching TV all day is a common human failing.

Recognizing Tone

22. During the time that Persky's machine was broken, the tone of the story and Kugelmass's demeanor became
    - ☐ a. complex.
    - ☐ b. blasé.
    - ☐ c. frantic.
    - ☐ d. intuitive.

Appreciation of Literary Forms

23. "Kugelmass was bald and as hairy as a bear. . . ." That sentence contains
    - ☐ a. a simile.
    - ☐ b. a metaphor.
    - ☐ c. personification.
    - ☐ d. understatement.

Appreciation of Literary Forms

24. When Emma calls her husband Mr. Personality she is being
    - ☐ a. generous.
    - ☐ b. sarcastic.
    - ☐ c. descriptive.
    - ☐ d. antagonistic.

Appreciation of Literary Forms

25. The story ends with Kugelmass trapped in a grammar book. His situation can be called
    - ☐ a. poetic justice.
    - ☐ b. an abstraction.
    - ☐ c. personification.
    - ☐ d. understatement of facts.

Now check your answers using the Answer Key at the back of the book. Make no mark for right answers. Correct any wrong answers you may have by putting a check mark (✓) in the box next to the right answer. Count the number of questions you answered correctly and plot the total on the Comprehension Scores Graph at the back of the book.

Next, look at the questions you answered incorrectly. What types of questions were they? Count the number you got wrong of each type and enter the numbers in the spaces below.

Recalling Specific Facts _____

Organizing Facts _____

Knowledge of Word Meanings _____

Drawing a Conclusion _____

Making a Judgment _____

Making an Inference _____

Understanding Characters _____

Understanding Main Ideas _____

Recognizing Tone _____

Appreciation of Literary Forms _____

Now use these numbers to fill in the Comprehension Skills Profile at the end of the book.

Extension Activities

Discussion Guide

Discussing Humor and Satire

1. What makes Persky a funny character?
2. Kugelmass is bald, hairy, middle-aged, and unsure of himself. Would the story be as funny if the main character were handsome, young, dashing, and clever?
3. Who and what is Woody Allen satirizing in the story? What sorts of human weaknesses does he satirize?

Discussing the Story

4. All of the characters in the story, except for Emma, are Jewish. What is the difference between this story and jokes that deride Jews, blacks, Poles, Italians, and other ethnic groups?
5. Humor is funniest when you can identify with the main character. In a way, you are laughing at yourself as well as at the character. In what ways can most people identify with Kugelmass?
6. How does the fact that Kugelmass is a professor of humanities help make the story funnier than if he were a businessman?

Discussing the Author's Work

7. Woody Allen uses New York City as a setting for this story as he does for many of his movies. What ingredient does New York add to a funny story?
8. Conversations among the characters in the story contain modern slang. Even Emma Bovary uses modern slang expressions. In between the conversations the author uses correct narrative English. Why do you suppose Woody Allen wrote the story that way? What would change if the story were told as a first-person narrative?
9. Many people feel that Woody Allen has a special insight into human nature. What is it about this story that would indicate it comes from a person who has a fertile imagination and insight into human nature? If you have seen any of Woody Allen's movies, include them in your discussion.

Writing Exercise

The following jokes are missing the punch lines that give them surprise endings and funny twists. Write a punch line for each joke. There are many possible funny endings, so you can have some fun by having different people read their jokes aloud.

It is very difficult to write humor that others find funny, so you will probably find this exercise more difficult than it first seems. If possible, work in teams of three writers. (Professional comedians usually have teams of writers who work together to produce funny material.)

- "Bob is divorcing Ethel because of a bowl of cereal."
  "That's silly. Why would anyone get a divorce over a bowl of cereal?"
- "The Congress has just solved the energy crisis."
  "They did? How?"
- A comic birthday card: I wanted to give you a pair of alligator cowboy boots for your birthday, but
- "I gave my (girlfriend/boyfriend) a rare talking bird for (her/his) birthday that cost me more than a thousand dollars."
  "That was very generous of you. Did (she/he) like it?"

UNIT
Eleven

Unit Eleven

Introduction

What the Story Is About

You may find "Sonny's Blues" one of the most challenging stories in this collection of short stories. To understand the story you have to allow yourself to experience the themes that the author has woven into the story's framework. The story is about two brothers. One is a schoolteacher living a conventional life, while the other is a musician embroiled in a struggle to come to terms with a profound inner conflict. Sonny, the younger brother, is a jazz pianist who has used heroin to relieve what he perceives as his suffering.

The music called *blues* is considered the heart of jazz, and because Sonny plays the blues, this is one level of meaning of the title "Sonny's Blues." A deeper meaning of the title lies in the fact that jazz, with blues at its center, originated in the work songs, field chants, sorrow songs, hymns, and spirituals sung by black American slaves in the nineteenth century. Blues and jazz, therefore, originated in suffering and were first used to give expression to that suffering. How the blues relates to Sonny's suffering and, through him, to millions of black Americans in similar circumstances, is the major theme of the story.

Author James Baldwin was born and raised in New York City's Harlem and became the literary spokesman for urban black Americans in the generation following Richard Wright, the author of *Native Son*. Wright was the example and guiding light for the young Baldwin, encouraging and helping him at the beginning of his literary career.

Baldwin's father was a Pentecostal minister in New York, and Baldwin himself preached in church as a teenager but gave it up by the time he graduated from high school, when he turned to writing. You will notice his familiarity with the church in Harlem in "Sonny's Blues" and with the preachers and gospel singers who organize instant congregations in the streets.

Baldwin's first novel, *Go Tell It on the Mountain*, was published in 1953 while the author was living as an expatriate in France. The novel was based closely on Baldwin's early religious experiences in Harlem, with his life there, and with the lives of family members in the South before they moved to Harlem during the great migration north by southern blacks following World War I.

Other books by Baldwin that you will enjoy include *Another Country, Tell Me How Long the Train's Been Gone,* his famous collection of essays *Notes of a Native Son,* and *The Fire Next Time, Blues for Mr. Charlie,* and *Giovanni's Room.*

What the Lesson Is About

The lesson that follows the story deals with finding themes in literature. When you want to tell what a story, a play, a poem, or a piece of music is *really* about, you talk in terms of its themes. For example, you can say that "The Kugelmass Episode" is about a professor who is projected into a novel. But if you talk in terms of the story's *themes,* you would have to say it's about selfishness and self-indulgence. "A Rose for Emily" is about an old woman who murdered her lover and hid the crime for years. But its *theme* deals with the passing of time and the changes in the South.

A theme is the underlying message or central idea of a piece of writing. A theme is the *major* idea that controls or dominates a work. As you read "Sonny's Blues," you will notice that certain ideas occur again and again. Foremost is the idea of suffering and seeking release from that suffering, which is suggested in the title. The author also repeatedly talks about feeling trapped, seeking freedom, living in darkness, and being afraid. Those are other themes that are tied to the unifying major theme of the story.

Authors express themes through the elements of fiction that you have been studying: characters, conflicts and action, and images. Keep the following questions in mind and try to answer them as you read. They will help you identify the story's themes and understand the ways that James Baldwin expresses them.

1. Both Sonny and his older brother have deep feelings that are expressed as inner conflicts in the story. What ideas are expressed in these conflicts?

2. What ideas emerge in actions and conversations (dialogue) involving the characters?

3. How do the characters in the story seem to be representations of ideas?

4. How does the author express his ideas in the images or descriptions he uses to tell the story?

Sonny's Blues

by James Baldwin

*J*read about it in the paper, in the subway, on my way to work. I read it, and I couldn't believe it, and I read it again. Then perhaps I just stared at it, at the newsprint spelling out his name, spelling out the story. I stared at it in the swinging lights of the subway car, and in the faces and bodies of the people, and in my own face, trapped in the darkness which roared outside.

It was not to be believed, and I kept telling myself that, as I walked from the subway station to the high school. And at the same time I couldn't doubt it. I was scared, scared for Sonny. He became real to me again. A great block of ice got settled in my belly and kept melting there slowly all day long, while I taught my classes algebra. It was a special kind of ice. It kept melting, sending trickles of ice water all up and down my veins, but it never got less. Sometimes it hardened and seemed to expand until I felt my guts were going to come spilling out or that I was going to choke or scream. This would always be at a moment when I was remembering some specific thing Sonny had once said or done.

When he was about as old as the boys in my classes, his face had been bright and open, there was a lot of copper in it; and he'd had wonderfully direct brown eyes, and great gentleness and privacy. I wondered what he looked like now. He had been picked up, the evening before, in a raid on an apartment downtown, for peddling and using heroin.

I couldn't believe it: but what I mean by that is that I couldn't find any room for it anywhere inside me. I had kept it outside me for a long time. I hadn't wanted to know. I had had suspicions, but I didn't name them, I kept putting them away. I told myself that Sonny was wild, but he wasn't crazy. And he'd always been a good boy, he hadn't ever turned hard or evil or disrespectful, the way kids can, so quick, so quick, especially in Harlem. I didn't want to believe that I'd ever see my brother going down, coming to nothing, all that light in his face gone out, in the condition I'd already seen so many others. Yet it had happened and here I was, talking about algebra to a lot of boys who might, every one of them for all I knew, be popping off needles every time they went to the head. Maybe it did more for them than algebra could.

I was sure that the first time Sonny had ever had horse, he couldn't have been much older than these boys were now. These boys, now, were living as we'd been living then, they were growing up with a rush and their heads bumped abruptly against the low ceiling of their actual possibilities. They were filled with rage. All they really knew were two darknesses, the darkness of their lives, which was now closing in on them, and the darkness of the movies, which had blinded them to that other darkness, and in which they now, vindictively, dreamed, at once more together than they were at any other time, and more alone.

When the last bell rang, the last class ended, I let out my breath. It seemed I'd been holding it for all that time. My clothes were wet— I may have looked as though I'd been sitting in a steam bath, all dressed up, all afternoon. I sat alone in the classroom a long time. I listened to the boys outside, downstairs, shouting and cursing and laughing. Their laughter struck me for perhaps the first time. It was not the joyous laughter which—God knows why—one associates with children. It was mocking and insular, its intent was to denigrate. It was disenchanted, and in this, also, lay the authority of their curses. Perhaps I was listening to them because I was thinking about my brother and in them I heard my brother. And myself.

One boy was whistling a tune, at once very complicated and very simple, it seemed to be pouring out of him as though he were a bird, and it sounded very cool and moving through all that harsh, bright air, only just holding its own through all those other sounds.

I stood up and walked over to the window and looked down into the courtyard. It was the beginning of the spring, and the sap was rising in the boys. A teacher passed through them every now and again, quickly, as though he or she couldn't wait to get out of that courtyard, to get those boys out of their sight and off their minds. I started collecting my stuff. I thought I'd better get home and talk to Isabel.

The courtyard was almost deserted by the time I got downstairs. I saw this boy standing in the shadow of a doorway, looking just like Sonny. I almost called his name. Then I saw that it wasn't Sonny, but somebody we used to know, a boy from around our block. He'd been Sonny's friend. He'd never been mine, having been too young for me, and, anyway, I'd never liked him. And now, even though he was a grown-up man, he still hung around that block, still spent hours on the street corners, was always high and raggy. I used to run into him from time to time, and he'd often work around to asking me for a quarter or fifty cents. He always had some real good excuse, too, and I always gave it to him, I don't know why.

But now, abruptly, I hated him. I couldn't stand the way he looked at me, partly like a dog, partly like a cunning child. I wanted to ask him what the hell he was doing in the school courtyard.

He sort of shuffled over to me, and he said, "I see you got the papers. So you already know about it."

"You mean about Sonny? Yes, I already know about it. How come they didn't get you?"

He grinned. It made him repulsive and it also brought to mind what he'd looked like as a kid. "I wasn't there. I stay away from them people."

"Good for you." I offered him a cigarette and I watched him through the smoke. "You come all the way down here just to tell me about Sonny?"

"That's right." He was sort of shaking his head and his eyes looked strange, as though they were about to cross. The bright sun deadened his damp dark brown skin and it made his eyes look yellow and showed up the dirt in his conked hair. He smelled funky. I moved a little away from him and I said, "Well, thanks. But I already know about it and I got to get home."

"I'll walk you a little ways," he said. We started walking. There were a couple of kids still loitering in the courtyard and one of them said good night to me and looked strangely at the boy beside me.

"What're you going to do?" he asked me. "I mean, about Sonny?"

"Look. I haven't seen Sonny for over a year, I'm not sure I'm going to do anything. Anyway, what the hell *can* I do?"

"That's right," he said quickly, "ain't nothing you can do. Can't much help old Sonny no more, I guess."

It was what I was thinking and so it seemed to me he had no right to say it.

"I'm surprised at Sonny, though," he went on—he had a funny way of talking, he looked straight ahead as though he were talking to himself—"I thought Sonny was a smart boy, I thought he was too smart to get hung."

"I guess he thought so, too," I said sharply, "and that's how he got hung. And how about you? You're pretty goddamn smart, I bet."

Then he looked directly at me, just for a minute. "I ain't smart," he said. "If I was smart, I'd have reached for a pistol a long time ago."

"Look. Don't tell *me* your sad story, if it was up to me, I'd give you one." Then I felt guilty—guilty, probably, for never having supposed that the poor bastard *had* a story of his own, much less a sad one, and I asked, quickly, "What's going to happen to him now?"

He didn't answer this. He was off by himself someplace.

"Funny thing," he said, and from his tone we might have been discussing the quickest way to get to Brooklyn, "when I saw the papers this morning, the first thing I asked myself was if I had anything to do with it. I felt sort of responsible."

I began to listen more carefully. The subway station was on the corner, just before us, and I stopped. He stopped, too. We were in front of a bar and he ducked slightly, peering in, but whoever he was looking for didn't seem to be there. The juke box was blasting away with something black and bouncy, and I half watched the barmaid as she danced her way from the juke box to her place behind the bar. And I watched her face as she laughingly responded to something someone said to her, still keeping time to the music. When she smiled one saw the little girl, one sensed the doomed, still-struggling woman beneath the battered face of the semi-whore.

"I never *give* Sonny nothing," the boy said finally, "but a long time ago I come to school high and Sonny asked me how it felt." He paused, I couldn't bear to watch him, I watched the barmaid, and I listened to the music which seemed to be causing the pavement to shake. "I told him it felt great." The music stopped, the barmaid paused and watched the juke box until the music began again. "It did."

All this was carrying me someplace I didn't want to go. I certainly didn't want to know how it felt. It filled everything, the people, the houses, the music, the dark, quicksilver barmaid, with menace; and this menace was their reality.

"What's going to happen to him now?" I asked again.

"They'll send him away someplace and they'll try to cure him." He shook his head. "Maybe he'll even think he's kicked the habit. Then they'll let him loose"—he gestured, throwing his cigarette into the gutter. "That's all."

"What do you mean, that's *all?*"

But I knew what he meant.

"I *mean,* that's *all.*" He turned his head and looked at me, pulling down the corners of his mouth. "Don't you know what I mean?" he asked, softly.

"How the hell *would* I know what you mean?" I almost whispered it, I don't know why.

"That's right," he said to the air, "how would *he* know what I mean?" He turned toward me again, patient and calm, and yet I somehow felt him shaking, shaking as though he were going to fall apart. I felt that ice in my guts again, the dread I'd felt all afternoon; and again I watched the barmaid, moving about the bar, washing glasses, and singing. "Listen. They'll let him out and then it'll just start over again. That's what I mean."

"You mean—they'll let him out. And then he'll just start working his way back in again. You mean he'll never kick the habit. Is that what you mean?"

"That's right," he said, cheerfully. "*You* see what I mean."

"Tell me," I said at last, "why does he want to die? He must want to die, he's killing himself, why does he want to die?"

He looked at me in surprise. He licked his lips. "He don't want to die. He wants to live. Don't nobody want to die, ever."

Then I wanted to ask him—too many things. He could not have answered, or if he had, I could not have borne the answers. I started walking. "Well, I guess it's none of my business."

"It's going to be rough on old Sonny," he said. We reached the subway station. "This is your station?" he asked. I nodded. I took one step down. "Damn!" he said, suddenly. I looked up at him. He grinned again. "Damn it if I didn't leave all my money home. You ain't got a dollar on you, have you? Just for a couple of days, is all."

All at once something inside gave and threatened to come pouring out of me. I didn't hate him any more. I felt that in another moment I'd start crying like a child.

"Sure," I said. "Don't sweat." I looked in my wallet and didn't have a dollar, I only had a five. "Here," I said. "That hold you?"

He didn't look at it—he didn't want to look at it. A terrible, closed look came over his face, as though he were keeping the number on the bill a secret from him and me. "Thanks," he said, and now he was dying to see me go. "Don't worry about Sonny. Maybe I'll write him or something."

"Sure," I said. "You do that. So long."

"Be seeing you," he said. I went on down the steps.

And I didn't write Sonny or send him anything for a long time. When I finally did, it was just after my little girl died, and he wrote me back a letter which made me feel like a bastard.

Here's what he said:

Dear brother,

You don't know how much I needed to hear from you. I wanted to write you many a time but I dug how much I must have hurt you and so I didn't write. But now I feel like a man who's been trying to climb up out of some deep, real deep and funky hole and just saw the sun up there, outside. I got to get outside.

I can't tell you much about how I got here. I mean I don't know how to tell you. I guess I was afraid of something or I was trying to escape from something and you know I have never been very strong in the head (smile). I'm glad Mama and Daddy are dead and can't see what's happened to their son and I swear if I'd known what I was doing I would never have hurt you so, you and a lot of other fine people who were nice to me and who believed in me.

I don't want you to think it had anything to do with me being a musician. It's more than that. Or maybe less than that. I can't get anything straight in my head down here and I try not to think about what's going to happen to me when I get outside again. Sometime I think I'm going to flip and *never* get outside and sometime I think I'll come straight back. I tell you one thing, though, I'd rather blow my brains out than go through this again. But that's what they all say, so they tell me. If I tell you when I'm coming to New York and if you could meet me, I sure would appreciate it. Give my love to Isabel and the kids and I was sure sorry to hear about little Gracie. I wish I could be like Mama and say the Lord's will be done, but I don't know it seems to me that trouble is the one thing that never does get stopped and I don't know what good it does to blame it on the Lord. But maybe it does some good if you believe it.

Your brother,
Sonny

Then I kept in constant touch with him and I sent him whatever I could and I went to meet him when he came back to New York. When I saw him, many things I thought I had forgotten came flooding back to me. This was because I had begun, finally, to wonder about Sonny, about the life that Sonny lived inside. This life, whatever it was, had made him older and thinner and it had deepened the distant stillness in which he had always moved. He looked very unlike my baby brother. Yet, when he smiled, when we shook hands, the baby brother I'd never known looked out from the depths of his private life, like an animal waiting to be coaxed into the light.

"How you been keeping?" he asked me.

"All right. And you?"

"Just fine." He was smiling all over his face. "It's good to see you again."

"It's good to see you."

The seven years' difference in our ages lay between us like a chasm: I wondered if these years would ever operate between us as a bridge. I was remembering, and it made it hard to catch my breath, that I had been there when he was born; and I had heard the first words he had ever spoken. When he started to walk, he walked from our mother straight to me. I caught him just before he fell when he took the first steps he ever took in this world.

"How's Isabel?"

"Just fine. She's dying to see you."

"And the boys?"

"They're fine, too. They're anxious to see their uncle."

"Oh, come on. You know they don't remember me."

"Are you kidding? Of course they remember you."

He grinned again. We got into a taxi. We had a lot to say to each other, far too much to know how to begin.

As the taxi began to move, I asked, "You still want to go to India?"

He laughed. "You still remember that. Hell, no. This place is Indian enough for me."

"It used to belong to them," I said.

And he laughed again. "They damn sure knew what they were doing when they got rid of it."

Years ago, when he was around fourteen, he'd been all hipped on the idea of going to India. He read books about people sitting on rocks, naked, in all kinds of weather, but mostly bad, naturally, and walking barefoot through hot coals and arriving at wisdom. I used to say that it sounded to me as though they were getting away from wisdom as fast as they could. I think he sort of looked down on me for that.

"Do you mind," he asked, "if we have the driver drive alongside the park? On the west side—I haven't seen the city in so long."

"Of course not," I said. I was afraid that I might sound as though I were humoring him, but I hoped he wouldn't take it that way.

So we drove along, between the green of the park and the stony, lifeless elegance of hotels and apartment buildings, toward the vivid, killing streets of our childhood. These streets hadn't changed, though housing projects jutted up out of them now like rocks in the middle of a boiling sea. Most of the houses in which we had grown up had vanished, as had the stores from which we had stolen, the basements in which we had first tried sex, the rooftops from which we had hurled tin cans and bricks. But houses exactly like the houses of our past yet dominated the landscape, boys exactly like the boys we once had been found themselves smothering in these houses, came down into the streets for light and air and found themselves encircled by disaster. Some escaped the trap, most didn't. Those who got out always left something of themselves behind, as some animals amputate a leg and leave it in the trap. It might be said, perhaps, that I had escaped, after all, I was a schoolteacher; or that Sonny had, he hadn't lived in Harlem for years. Yet, as the cab moved uptown through streets which seemed, with a rush, to darken with dark people, and as I covertly studied Sonny's face, it came to me that what we both were seeking through our separate cab windows was that part of ourselves which had been left behind. It's always at the hour of trouble and confrontation that the missing member aches.

We hit 110th Street and started rolling up Lenox Avenue. And I'd known this avenue all my life, but it seemed to me again, as it had seemed on the day I'd first heard about Sonny's trouble, filled with a hidden menace which was its very breath of life.

"We almost there," said Sonny.

"Almost." We were both too nervous to say anything more.

We live in a housing project. It hasn't been up long. A few days after it was up it seemed uninhabitably new, now, of course, it's already rundown. It looks like a parody of the good, clean, faceless life—God knows the people who live in it do their best to make it a parody. The beat-looking grass lying around isn't enough to make their lives green, the hedges will never hold out the streets, and they know it. The big windows fool no one, they aren't big enough to make space out of no space. They don't bother with the windows, they watch the TV screen instead. The playground is most popular with the children who don't play at jacks, or skip rope, or roller skate, or swing, and they can be found in it after dark. We moved in partly because it's not too far from where I teach, and partly for the kids; but it's really just like the houses in which Sonny and I grew up. The same things happen, they'll have the same things to remember. The moment Sonny and I started into the house I had the feeling that I was simply bringing him back into the danger he had almost died trying to escape.

Sonny has never been talkative. So I don't know why I was sure he'd be dying to talk to me when supper was over the first night. Everything went fine, the oldest boy remembered him, and the youngest boy liked him, and Sonny had remembered to bring something for each of them; and Isabel, who is really much nicer than I am, more open and giving, had gone to a lot of trouble about dinner and was genuinely glad to see him. And she'd always been able to tease Sonny in a way that I haven't. It was nice to see her face so vivid again and to hear her laugh and watch her make Sonny laugh. She wasn't, or, anyway, she didn't seem to be, at all uneasy or embarrassed. She chatted as though there were no subject which had to be avoided and she got Sonny past his first, faint stiffness. And thank God she was there, for I was filled with that icy dread again. Everything I did seemed awkward to me, and everything I said sounded freighted with hidden meaning. I was trying to remember everything I'd heard about dope addiction and I couldn't help watching Sonny for signs. I wasn't doing it out of malice. I was trying to find out something about my brother. I was dying to hear him tell me he was safe.

"Safe!" my father grunted, whenever Mama suggested trying to move to a neighborhood which might be safer for children. "Safe, hell! Ain't no place safe for kids, nor nobody."

He always went on like this, but he wasn't, ever, really as bad as he sounded, not even on weekends, when he got drunk. As a matter of fact, he was always on the lookout for "something a little better," but he died before he found it. He died suddenly, during a drunken weekend in the middle of the war, when Sonny was fifteen. He and Sonny hadn't ever got on too well. And this was partly because Sonny was the apple of his father's eye. It was because he loved Sonny so much and was frightened for him, that he was always fighting with him. It doesn't do any good to fight with Sonny. Sonny just moves back, inside himself, where he can't be reached. But the principal reason that they never hit it off is that they were so much alike. Daddy was big and rough and loud-talking, just the opposite of Sonny, but they both had—that same privacy.

Mama tried to tell me something about this, just after Daddy died. I was home on leave from the army.

This was the last time I ever saw my mother alive. Just the same, this picture gets all mixed up in my mind with pictures I had of her when she was younger. The way I always see her is the way she used to be on a Sunday afternoon, say, when the old folks were talking after the big Sunday dinner. I always see her wearing pale blue. She'd be sitting on the sofa. And my father would be sitting in the easy chair, not far from her. And the living room would be full of church folks and relatives. There they sit, in chairs all around the living room, and the night is creeping up outside, but nobody knows it yet. You can see the darkness growing against the windowpanes and you hear the street noises every now and again, or maybe the jangling beat of a tambourine from one of the churches close by, but it's real quiet in the room. For a moment nobody's talking, but every face looks darkening, like the sky outside. And my mother rocks a little from the waist, and my father's eyes are closed. Everyone is looking at something a child can't see. For a minute they've forgotten the children. Maybe a kid is lying on the rug, half asleep. Maybe somebody's got a kid in his lap and is absent-mindedly stroking the kid's head. Maybe there's a kid, quiet and big-eyed, curled up in a big chair in the corner. The silence, the darkness coming, and the darkness in the faces frighten the child obscurely. He hopes that the hand which strokes his forehead will never stop—will never die. He hopes that there will never come a time when the old folks won't be sitting around the living room, talking about where they've come from, and what they've seen, and what's happened to them and their kinfolk.

But something deep and watchful in the child knows that this is bound to end, is already ending. In a moment someone will get up and turn on the light. Then the old folks will remember the children and they won't talk any more that day. And when light fills the room, the child is filled with darkness. He knows that every time this happens he's moved just a little closer to that darkness outside. The darkness outside is what the old folks have been talking about. It's what they've come from. It's what they endure. The child knows that they won't talk any more because if he knows too much about what's happened to *them,* he'll know too much too soon, about what's going to happen to *him.*

The last time I talked to my mother, I remember I was restless. I wanted to get out and see Isabel. We weren't married then and we had a lot to straighten out between us.

There Mama sat, in black, by the window. She was humming an old church song, *Lord, you brought me from a long ways off.* Sonny was out somewhere. Mama kept watching the streets.

"I don't know," she said, "if I'll ever see you again, after you go off from here. But I hope you'll remember the things I tried to teach you."

"Don't talk like that," I said, and smiled. "You'll be here a long time yet."

She smiled, too, but she said nothing. She was quiet for a long time. And I said, "Mama, don't you worry about nothing. I'll be writing all the time, and you be getting the checks. . . ."

"I want to talk to you about your brother," she said, suddenly. "If anything happens to me, he ain't going to have nobody to look out for him."

"Mama," I said, "ain't nothing going to happen to you *or* Sonny. Sonny's all right. He's a good boy and he's got good sense."

"It ain't a question of his being a good boy," Mama said, "nor of his having good sense. It ain't only the bad ones, nor yet the dumb ones that gets sucked under." She stopped, looking at me. "Your Daddy once had a brother," she said, and she smiled in a way that made me feel she was in pain. "You didn't never know that, did you?"

"No," I said. "I never knew that," and I watched her face.

"Oh, yes," she said, "your Daddy had a brother." She looked out of the window again. "I know you never saw your Daddy cry. But *I* did—many a time, through all these years."

I asked her, "What happened to his brother? How come nobody's ever talked about him?"

This was the first time I ever saw my mother look old.

"His brother got killed," she said, "when he was just a little younger than you are now. I knew him. He was a fine boy. He was maybe a little full of the devil, but he didn't mean nobody no harm."

Then she stopped, and the room was silent, exactly as it had sometimes been on those Sunday afternoons. Mama kept looking out into the streets.

"He used to have a job in the mill," she said, "and, like all young folks, he just liked to perform on Saturday nights. Saturday nights, him and your father would drift around to different places, go to dances and things like that, or just sit around with people they knew, and your father's brother would sing, he had a fine voice, and play along with himself on his guitar. Well, this particular Saturday night, him and your father was coming home from some place, and they were both a little drunk and there was a moon that night, it was bright like day. Your father's brother was feeling kind of good, and he was whistling to himself, and he had his guitar slung over his shoulder. They was coming down a hill, and beneath them was a road that turned off from the highway. Well, your father's brother, being always kind of frisky, decided to run down this hill, and he did, with that guitar banging and clanging behind him, and he ran across the road, and he was making water behind a tree. And your father was sort of amused at him and he was still coming down the hill, kind of slow. Then he heard a car motor and that same minute his brother stepped from behind the tree, into the road, in the moonlight. And he started to cross the road. And your father started to run down the hill, he says he don't know why. This car was full of white men. They was all drunk, and when they seen your father's brother they let out a great whoop and holler and they aimed the car straight at him. They was having fun, they just wanted to scare him, the way they do sometimes, you know. But they was drunk. And I guess the boy, being drunk, too, and scared, kind of lost his head. By the time he jumped it was too late. Your father says he heard his brother scream when the car rolled over him, and he heard the wood of that guitar when it give, and he heard them strings go flying, and he heard them white men shouting, and the car kept on a-going and it ain't stopped till this day. And, time your father got down the hill, his brother weren't nothing but blood and pulp."

Tears were gleaming on my mother's face. There wasn't anything I could say.

"He never mentioned it," she said, "because I never let him mention it before you children. Your Daddy was like a crazy man that night and for many a night thereafter. He says he never in his life seen anything as dark as that road after the lights of that car had gone away. Weren't nothing, weren't nobody on that road, just your Daddy and his brother and that busted guitar. Oh, yes. Your Daddy never did really get right again. Till the day he died he weren't sure but that every white man he saw was the man that killed his brother."

She stopped and took out her handkerchief and dried her eyes and looked at me.

"I ain't telling you all this," she said, "to make you scared or bitter or to make you hate nobody. I'm telling you this because you got a brother. And the world ain't changed."

I guess I didn't want to believe this. I guess she saw this in my face. She turned away from me, toward the window again, searching those streets.

"But I praise my Redeemer," she said at last, "that he called your Daddy home before me. I ain't saying it to throw no flowers at myself, but, I declare, it keeps me from feeling too cast down to know I helped your father get safely through this world. Your father always acted like he was the roughest, strongest man on earth. And everybody took him to be like that. But if he hadn't had me there—to see his tears!"

She was crying again. Still, I couldn't move. I said, "Lord, Lord, Mama, I didn't know it was like that."

"Oh, honey," she said, "there's a lot that you don't know. But you are going to find out." She stood up from the window and came over to me. "You got to hold on to your brother," she said, "and don't let him fall, no matter what it looks like is happening to him and no matter how evil you gets with him. You going to be evil with him many a time. But don't you forget what I told you, you hear?"

"I won't forget," I said. "Don't you worry, I won't forget. I won't let nothing happen to Sonny."

My mother smiled as though she were amused at something she saw in my face. Then, "You may not be able to stop nothing from happening. But you got to let him know you's *there.*"

Two days later I was married, and then I was gone. And I had a lot of things on my mind and I pretty well forgot my promise to Mama until I got shipped home on a special furlough for her funeral.

And, after the funeral, with just Sonny and me alone in the empty kitchen, I tried to find out something about him.

"What do you want to do?" I asked him.

"I'm going to be a musician," he said.

For he had graduated, in the time I had been away, from dancing to the juke box to finding out who was playing what, and what they were doing with it, and he had bought himself a set of drums.

"You mean, you want to be a drummer?" I somehow had the feeling that being a drummer might be all right for other people but not for my brother Sonny.

"I don't think," he said, looking at me very gravely, "that I'll ever be a good drummer. But I think I can play a piano."

I frowned. I'd never played the role of the older brother quite so seriously before, had scarcely ever, in fact, *asked* Sonny a damn thing. I sensed myself in the presence of something I didn't really know how to handle, didn't understand. So I made my frown a little deeper as I asked: "What kind of musician do you want to be?"

He grinned. "How many kinds do you think there are?"

"Be *serious,*" I said.

He laughed, throwing his head back, and then looked at me. "I *am* serious."

"Well, then, for Christ's sake, stop kidding around and answer a serious question. I mean, do you want to be a concert pianist, you want to play classical music and all that, or—or what?" Long before I finished he was laughing again. "For Christ's *sake,* Sonny!"

He sobered, but with difficulty. "I'm sorry. But you sound so—*scared!*" And he was off again.

"Well, you may think it's funny now, baby, but it's not going to be so funny when you have to make your living at it, let me tell you *that.*" I was furious because I knew he was laughing at me and I didn't know why.

"No," he said, very sober now, and afraid, perhaps, that he'd hurt me, "I don't want to be a classical pianist. That isn't what interests me. I mean"—he paused, looking hard at me, as though his eyes would help me to understand, and then gestured helplessly, as though perhaps his hand would help—"I mean, I'll have a lot of studying to do, and I'll have to study *everything*, but I mean, I want to play *with*—jazz musicians." He stopped. "I want to play jazz," he said.

Well, the word had never before sounded as heavy, as real, as it sounded that afternoon in Sonny's mouth. I just looked at him and I was probably frowning a real frown by this time. I simply couldn't see why on earth he'd want to spend his time hanging around nightclubs, clowning around on bandstands, while people pushed each other around a dance floor. It seemed—beneath him, somehow. I had never thought about it before, had never been forced to, but I suppose I had always put jazz musicians in a class with what Daddy called "good-time people."

"Are you *serious?*"

"Hell, *yes*, I'm serious."

He looked more helpless than ever, and annoyed, and deeply hurt.

I suggested, helpfully: "You mean—like Louis Armstrong?"

His face closed as though I'd struck him. "No. I'm not talking about none of that old-time, down home crap."

"Well, look, Sonny, I'm sorry, don't get mad. I just don't altogether get it, that's all. Name somebody—you know, a jazz musician you admire."

"Bird."

"Who?"

"Bird! Charlie Parker! Don't they teach you nothing in the goddamn army?"

I lit a cigarette. I was surprised and then a little amused to discover that I was trembling. "I've been out of touch," I said. "You'll have to be patient with me. Now. Who's this Parker character?"

"He's just one of the greatest jazz musicians alive," said Sonny, sullenly, his hands in his pockets, his back to me. "Maybe *the* greatest," he added, bitterly, "that's probably why *you* never heard of him."

"All right," I said, "I'm ignorant. I'm sorry. I'll go out and buy all the cat's records right away, all right?"

"It don't," said Sonny, with dignity, "make any difference to me. I don't care what you listen to. Don't do me no favors."

I was beginning to realize that I'd never seen him so upset before. With another part of my mind I was thinking that this would probably turn out to be one of those things kids go through and that I shouldn't make it seem important by pushing it too hard. Still, I didn't think it would do any harm to ask: "Doesn't all this take a lot of time? Can you make a living at it?"

He turned back to me and half leaned, half sat, on the kitchen table. "Everything takes time," he said, "and—well, yes, sure, I can make a living at it. But what I don't seem to be able to make you understand is that it's the only thing I want to do."

"Well, Sonny," I said gently, "you know people can't always do exactly what they *want* to do—"

"*No,* I don't know that," said Sonny, surprising me. "I think people *ought* to do what they want to do, what else are they alive for?"

"You getting to be a big boy," I said desperately, "it's time you started thinking about your future."

"I'm thinking about my future," said Sonny, grimly. "I think about it all the time."

I gave up. I decided, if he didn't change his mind, that we could always talk about it later. "In the meantime," I said, "you got to finish school." We had already decided that he'd have to move in with Isabel and her folks. I knew this wasn't the ideal arrangement because Isabel's folks are inclined to be dicty and they hadn't especially wanted Isabel to marry me. But I didn't know what else to do. "And we have to get you fixed up at Isabel's."

There was a long silence. He moved from the kitchen table to the window. "That's a terrible idea. You know it yourself."

"Do you have a *better* idea?"

He just walked up and down the kitchen for a minute. He was as tall as I was. He had started to shave. I suddenly had the feeling that I didn't know him at all.

He stopped at the kitchen table and picked up my cigarettes. Looking at me with a kind of mocking, amused defiance, he put one between his lips. "You mind?"

"You smoking already?"

He lit the cigarette and nodded, watching me through the smoke.

"I just wanted to see if I'd have the courage to smoke in front of you." He grinned and blew a great cloud of smoke to the ceiling. "It was easy." He looked at my face. "Come on, now. I bet you was smoking at my age, tell the truth."

I didn't say anything but the truth was on my face, and he laughed. But now there was something very strained in his laugh. "Sure. And I bet that ain't all you was doing."

He was frightening me a little. "Cut the crap," I said. "We already decided that you was going to go and live at Isabel's. Now what's got into you all of a sudden?"

"*You* decided it," he pointed out. "*I* didn't decide nothing." He stopped in front of me, leaning against the stove, arms loosely folded. "Look, brother. I don't want to stay in Harlem no more, I really don't." He was very earnest. He looked at me, then over toward the kitchen window. There was something in his eyes I'd never seen before, some thoughtfulness, some worry all his own. He rubbed the muscle of one arm. "It's time I was getting out of here."

"Where do you want to *go*, Sonny?"

"I want to join the army. Or the navy, I don't care. If I say I'm old enough, they'll believe me."

Then I got mad. It was because I was so scared. "You must be crazy. You goddamn fool, what the hell do you want to go and join the *army* for?"

"I just told you. To get out of Harlem."

"Sonny, you haven't even finished *school*. And if you really want to be a musician, how do you expect to study if you're in the *army?*"

He looked at me, trapped, and in anguish. "There's ways. I might be able to work out some kind of deal. Anyway, I'll have the G.I. Bill when I come out."

"*If* you come out." We stared at each other. "Sonny, please. Be reasonable. I know the setup is far from perfect. But we got to do the best we can."

"I ain't learning nothing in school," he said. "Even when I go." He turned away from me and opened the window and threw his cigarette out into the narrow alley. I watched his back. "At least, I ain't learning nothing you'd want me to learn." He slammed the window so hard I thought the glass would fly out, and turned back to me. "And I'm sick of the stink of these garbage cans!"

"Sonny," I said, "I know how you feel. But if you don't finish school now, you're going to be sorry later that you didn't." I grabbed him by the shoulders. "And you only got another year. It ain't so bad. And I'll come back and I swear I'll help you do *whatever* you want to do. Just try to put up with it till I come back. Will you please do that? For me?"

He didn't answer and he wouldn't look at me.

"Sonny. You hear me?"

He pulled away. "I hear you. But you never hear anything *I* say."

I didn't know what to say to that. He looked out of the window and then back at me. "OK," he said, and sighed. "I'll try."

Then I said, trying to cheer him up a little, "They got a piano at Isabel's. You can practice on it."

And as a matter of fact, it did cheer him up for a minute. "That's right," he said to himself. "I forgot that." His face relaxed a little. But the worry, the thoughtfulness, played on it still, the way shadows play on a face which is staring into the fire.

But I thought I'd never hear the end of that piano. At first, Isabel would write me, saying how nice it was that Sonny was so serious about his music and how, as soon as he came in from school, or wherever he had been when he was supposed to be at school, he went straight to that piano and stayed there until suppertime. And, after supper, he went back to that piano and stayed there until everybody went to bed. He was at the piano all day Saturday and all day Sunday. Then he bought a record player and started playing records. He'd play one record over and over again, all day long sometimes, and he'd improvise along with it on the piano. Or he'd play one section of the record, one chord, one change, one progression, then he'd do it on the piano. Then back to the record. Then back to the piano.

Well, I really don't know how they stood it. Isabel finally confessed that it wasn't like living with a person at all, it was like living with sound. And the sound didn't make any sense to her, didn't make any sense to any of them—naturally. They began, in a way, to be afflicted by this presence that was living in their home. It was as though Sonny were some sort of god, or monster. He moved in an atmosphere which wasn't like theirs at all. They fed him and he ate, he washed himself, he walked in and out of their door; he certainly wasn't nasty or unpleasant or rude, Sonny isn't any of those things; but it was as though he were all wrapped up in some cloud, some fire, some vision all his own; and there wasn't any way to reach him.

At the same time, he wasn't really a man yet, he was still a child, and they had to watch out for him in all kinds of ways. They certainly couldn't throw him out. Neither did they dare to make a great scene about that piano because even they dimly sensed, as I sensed, from so many thousands of miles away, that Sonny was at that piano playing for his life.

But he hadn't been going to school. One day a letter came from the school board, and Isabel's mother got it—there had, apparently, been other letters but Sonny had torn them up. This day, when Sonny came in, Isabel's mother showed him the letter and asked where he'd been spending his time. And she finally got it out of him that he'd been down in Greenwich Village, with musicians and other characters, in a white girl's apartment. And this scared her and she started to scream at him, and what came up, once she began—though she denies it to this day—was what sacrifices they were making to give Sonny a decent home and how little he appreciated it.

Sonny didn't play the piano that day. By evening, Isabel's mother had calmed down but then there was the old man to deal with, and Isabel herself. Isabel says she did her best to be calm but she broke down and started crying. She says she just watched Sonny's face. She could tell, by watching him, what was happening with him. And what was happening was that they penetrated his cloud, they had reached him. Even if their fingers had been a thousand times more gentle than human fingers ever are, he could hardly help feeling that they had stripped him naked and were spitting on that nakedness. For he also had to see that his presence, that music, which was life or death to him, had been torture for them and that they had endured it, not at all for his sake, but only for mine. And Sonny couldn't take that. He can take it a little better today than he could then but he's still not very good at it and, frankly, I don't know anybody who is.

The silence of the next few days must have been louder than the sound of all the music ever played since time began. One morning, before she went to work, Isabel was in his room for something and she suddenly realized that all of his records were gone. And she knew for certain that he was gone. And he was. He went as far as the navy would carry him. He finally sent me a postcard from someplace in Greece and that was the first I knew that Sonny was still alive. I didn't see him any more until we were both back in New York and the war had long been over.

He was a man by then, of course, but I wasn't willing to see it. He came by the house from time to time, but we fought almost every time we met. I didn't like the way he carried himself, loose and dreamlike all the time, and I didn't like his friends, and his music seemed to be merely an excuse for the life he led. It sounded just that weird and disordered.

Then we had a fight, a pretty awful fight, and I didn't see him for months. By and by I looked him up, where he was living, in a furnished room in the Village, and I tried to make it up. But there were lots of other people in the room, and Sonny just lay on his bed, and he wouldn't come downstairs with me, and he treated these other people as though they were his family and I weren't. So I got mad and then he got mad, and then I told him that he might just as well be dead as live the way he was living. Then he stood up and he told me not to worry about him any more in life, that he *was* dead as far as I was concerned. Then he pushed me to the door, and the other people looked on as though nothing were happening, and he slammed the door behind me. I stood in the hallway, staring at the door. I heard somebody laugh in the room and then the tears came to my eyes. I started down the steps, whistling to keep from crying, I kept whistling to myself, *You going to need me, baby, one of these cold, rainy days.*

I read about Sonny's trouble in the spring. Little Grace died in the fall. She was a beautiful little girl. But she only lived a little over two years. She died of polio and she suffered. She had a slight fever for a couple of days, but it didn't seem like anything and we just kept her in bed. And we would certainly have called the doctor, but the fever dropped, she seemed to be all right. So we thought it had just been a cold. Then, one day, she was up, playing, Isabel was in the kitchen fixing lunch for the two boys when they'd come in from school, and she heard Grace fall down in the living room. When you have a lot of children you don't always start running when one of them falls, unless they start screaming or something.

And, this time, Gracie was quiet. Yet, Isabel says that when she heard that *thump* and then that silence, something happened to her to make her afraid. And she ran to the living room and there was little Grace on the floor, all twisted up, and the reason she hadn't screamed was that she couldn't get her breath. And when she did scream, it was the worst sound, Isabel says, that she's ever heard in all her life, and she still hears it sometimes in her dreams. Isabel will sometimes wake me up with a low, moaning, strangling sound, and I have to be quick to awaken her and hold her to me and where Isabel is weeping against me seems a mortal wound.

I think I may have written Sonny the very day that little Grace was buried. I was sitting in the living room in the dark, by myself, and I suddenly thought of Sonny. My trouble made his real.

One Saturday afternoon, when Sonny had been living with us, or, anyway, been in our house, for nearly two weeks, I found myself wandering aimlessly about the living room, drinking from a can of beer, and trying to work up the courage to search Sonny's room. He was out, he was usually out whenever I was home, and Isabel had taken the children to see their grandparents. Suddenly I was standing still in front of the living room window, watching Seventh Avenue. The idea of searching Sonny's room made me still. I scarcely dared to admit to myself what I'd be searching for. I didn't know what I'd do if I found it. Or if I didn't.

On the sidewalk across from me, near the entrance to a barbecue joint, some people were holding an old-fashioned revival meeting. The barbecue cook, wearing a dirty white apron, his conked hair reddish and metallic in the pale sun, and a cigarette between his lips, stood in the doorway, watching them. Kids and older people paused in their errands and stood there, along with some older men and a couple of very tough-looking women who watched everything that happened on the avenue, as though they owned it, or were maybe owned by it. Well, they were watching this, too. The revival was being carried on by three sisters in black, and a brother. All they had were their voices and their Bibles and a tambourine. The brother was testifying and while he testified two of the sisters stood together, seeming to say, amen, and the third sister walked around with the tambourine outstretched and a couple of people dropped coins into it. Then the brother's testimony ended, and the sister who had been taking up the collection dumped the coins into her palm and transferred them to the pocket of her long black robe. Then she raised both hands, striking the tambourine against the air, and then against one hand, and she started to sing. And the two other sisters and the brother joined in.

It was strange, suddenly, to watch, though I had been seeing these street meetings all my life. So, of course, had everybody else down there. Yet, they paused and watched and listened and I stood still at the window. " *'Tis the old ship of Zion*," they sang, and the sister with the tambourine kept a steady, jangling beat, "*it has rescued many a thousand!*" Not a soul under the sound of their voices was hearing this song for the first time, not one of them had been rescued. Nor had they seen much in the way of rescue work being done around them. Neither did they especially believe in the holiness of the three sisters and the brother, they knew too much about them, knew where they lived, and how. The woman with the tambourine, whose voice dominated the air, whose face was bright with joy, was divided by very little from the woman who stood watching her, a cigarette between her heavy, chapped lips, her hair a cuckoo's nest, her face scarred and swollen from many beatings, and her black eyes glittering like coal. Perhaps they both knew this, which was why, when, as rarely, they addressed each other, they addressed each other as Sister. As the singing filled the air, the watching, listening faces underwent a change, the eyes focusing on something within; the music seemed to soothe a poison out of them; and time seemed, nearly, to fall away from the sullen, belligerent, battered faces, as though they were fleeing back to their first condition, while dreaming of their last. The barbecue cook half shook his head and smiled, and dropped his cigarette and disappeared into his joint. A man fumbled in his pockets for change and stood holding it in his hand impatiently, as though he had just remembered a pressing appointment further up the avenue. He looked furious. Then I saw Sonny, standing on the edge of the crowd. He was carrying a wide, flat notebook with a green cover, and it made him look, from where I was standing, almost like a schoolboy. The coppery sun brought out the copper in his skin, he was very faintly smiling, standing very still. Then the singing stopped, the tambourine turned into a collection plate again. The furious man dropped in his coins and vanished, so did a couple of the women, and Sonny dropped some change in the plate, looking directly at the woman with a little smile. He started across the avenue, toward the house. He has a slow, loping walk, something like the way Harlem hipsters walk, only he's imposed on this his own half-beat. I had never really noticed it before.

I stayed at the window, both relieved and apprehensive. As Sonny disappeared from my sight, they began singing again. And they were still singing when his key turned in the lock.

"Hey," he said.

"Hey, yourself. You want some beer?"

"No. Well, maybe." But he came up to the window and stood beside me, looking out. "What a warm voice," he said.

They were singing *If I could only hear my mother pray again!*

"Yes," I said, "and she can sure beat that tambourine."

"But what a terrible song," he said, and laughed. He dropped his notebook on the sofa and disappeared into the kitchen. "Where's Isabel and the kids?"

"I think they went to see their grandparents. You hungry?"

"No." He came back into the living room with his can of beer. "You want to come someplace with me tonight?"

I sensed, I don't know how, that I couldn't possibly say no. "Sure. Where?"

He sat down on the sofa and picked up his notebook and started leafing through it. "I'm going to sit in with some fellows in a joint in the Village."

"You mean, you're going to play, tonight?"

"That's right." He took a swallow of his beer and moved back to the window. He gave me a sidelong look. "If you can stand it."

"I'll try," I said.

He smiled to himself, and we both watched as the meeting across the way broke up. The three sisters and the brother, heads bowed, were singing *God be with you till we meet again.* The faces around them were very quiet. Then the song ended. The small crowd dispersed. We watched the three women and the one man walk slowly up the avenue.

"When she was singing before," said Sonny, abruptly, "her voice reminded me for a minute of what heroin feels like sometimes— when it's in your veins. It makes you feel sort of warm and cool at the same time. And distant. And—and sure." He sipped his beer, very deliberately not looking at me. I watched his face. "It makes you feel—in control. Sometimes you've got to have that feeling."

"Do you?" I sat down slowly in the easy chair.

"Sometimes." He went to the sofa and picked up his notebook again. "Some people do."

"In order," I asked, "to play?" And my voice was very ugly, full of contempt and anger.

"Well"—he looked at me with great, troubled eyes, as though, in fact, he hoped his eyes would tell me things he could never otherwise say—"they *think* so. And *if* they think so—!"

"And what do *you* think?" I asked.

He sat on the sofa and put his can of beer on the floor. "I don't know," he said, and I couldn't be sure if he were answering my question or pursuing his thoughts. His face didn't tell me. "It's not so much to *play*. It's to *stand* it, to be able to make it at all. On any level." He frowned and smiled: "In order to keep from shaking to pieces."

"But these friends of yours," I said, "they seem to shake themselves to pieces pretty goddamn fast."

"Maybe." He played with the notebook. And something told me that I should curb my tongue, that Sonny was doing his best to talk, that I should listen. "But of course you only know the ones that've gone to pieces. Some don't—or at least they haven't *yet* and that's just about all *any* of us can say." He paused. "And then there are some who just live, really, in hell, and they know it and they see what's happening and they go right on. I don't know." He sighed, dropped the notebook, folded his arms. "Some guys, you can tell from the way they play, they on something *all* the time. And you can see that, well, it makes something real for them. But of course," he picked up his beer from the floor and sipped it and put the can down again, "they *want* to, too, you've got to see that. Even some of them that say they don't—*some*, not all."

"And what about you?" I asked—I couldn't help it. "What about you? Do *you* want to?"

He stood up and walked to the window and remained silent for a long time. Then he sighed. "Me," he said. Then: "While I was downstairs before, on my way here, listening to that woman sing, it struck me all of a sudden how much suffering she must have had to go through—to sing like that. It's *repulsive* to think you have to suffer that much."

I said: "But there's no way not to suffer—is there, Sonny?"

"I believe not," he said, and smiled, "but that's never stopped anyone from trying." He looked at me. "Has it?" I realized, with this mocking look, that there stood between us, forever, beyond the power of time or forgiveness, the fact that I had held silence—so long!—when he had needed human speech to help him. He turned back to the window. "No, there's no way not to suffer. But you try all kinds of ways to keep from drowning in it, to keep on top of it, and to make it seem—well, like *you*. Like you did something, all right, and now you're suffering for it. You know?" I said nothing. "Well you know," he said, impatiently, "why *do* people suffer? Maybe it's better to do something to give it a reason, *any* reason."

"But we just agreed," I said, "that there's no way not to suffer. Isn't it better, then, just to—take it?"

"But nobody just takes it," Sonny cried, "that's what I'm telling you! *Everybody* tries not to. You're just hung up on the *way* some people try—it's not *your* way!"

The hair on my face began to itch, my face felt wet. "That's not true," I said, "that's not true. I don't give a damn what other people do, I don't even care how they suffer. I just care how *you* suffer." And he looked at me. "Please believe me," I said, "I don't want to see you—die—trying not to suffer."

"I won't," he said, flatly, "die trying not to suffer. At least, not any faster than anybody else."

"But there's no need," I said, trying to laugh, "is there? in killing yourself."

I wanted to say more, but I couldn't. I wanted to talk about will power and how life could be—well, beautiful. I wanted to say that it was all within; but was it? or, rather, wasn't that exactly the trouble? And I wanted to promise that I would never fail him again. But it would all have sounded—empty words and lies.

So I made the promise to myself and prayed that I would keep it.

"It's terrible sometimes, inside," he said, "that's what's the trouble. You walk these streets, black and funky and cold, and there's not really a living ass to talk to, and there's nothing shaking, and there's no way of getting it out—that storm inside. You can't talk it and you can't make love with it, and when you finally try to get with it and play it, you realize *nobody's* listening. So *you've* got to listen. You got to find a way to listen."

And then he walked away from the window and sat on the sofa again, as though all the wind had suddenly been knocked out of him. "Sometimes you'll do *anything* to play, even cut your mother's throat." He laughed and looked at me. "Or your brother's." Then he sobered. "Or your own." Then: "Don't worry. I'm all right now and I think I'll *be* all right. But I can't forget—where I've been. I don't mean just the physical place I've been, I mean where I've *been*. And *what* I've been."

"What have you been, Sonny?" I asked.

He smiled—but sat sideways on the sofa, his elbow resting on the back, his fingers playing with his mouth and chin, not looking at me. "I've been something I didn't recognize, didn't know I could be. Didn't know anybody could be." He stopped, looking inward, looking helplessly young, looking old. "I'm not talking about it now because I feel *guilty* or anything like that—maybe it would be better if I did, I don't know. Anyway, I can't really talk about it. Not to you, not to anybody," and now he turned and faced me. "Sometimes, you know, and it was actually when I was most *out* of the world, I felt that I was in it, that I was *with* it, really, and I could play or I didn't really have to *play*, it just came out of me, it was there. And I don't know how I played, thinking about it now, but I know I did awful things, those times, sometimes, to people. Or it wasn't that I *did* anything to them—it was that they weren't real." He picked up the beer can; it was empty; he rolled it between his palms: "And other times—well, I needed a fix, I needed to find a place to lean, I needed to clear a space to *listen*—and I couldn't find it, and I—went crazy, I did terrible things to *me*, I was terrible *for* me." He began pressing the beer can between his hands, I watched the metal begin to give. It glittered, as he played with it like a knife, and I was afraid he would cut himself, but I said nothing. "Oh well. I can never tell you. I was all by myself at the bottom of something, stinking and sweating and crying and shaking, and I smelled it, you know? *my* stink, and I thought I'd die if I couldn't get away from it and yet, all the same, I knew that everything I was doing was just locking me in with it. And I didn't know," he paused, still flattening the beer can, "I didn't know, I still *don't* know, something kept telling me that maybe it was good to smell your own stink, but I didn't think that *that* was what I'd been trying to do—and—who can stand it?" And he abruptly dropped the ruined beer can, looking at me with a small, still smile, and then rose, walking to the window as though it were the lodestone rock. I watched his face, he watched the avenue. "I couldn't tell you when Mama died—but the reason I wanted to leave Harlem so bad was to get away from drugs. And then, when I ran away, that's what I was running from—really. When I came back, nothing had changed, *I* hadn't changed, I was just—older." And he stopped, drumming with his fingers on the windowpane. The sun had vanished, soon darkness would fall. I watched his face. "It can come again," he said, almost as though speaking to himself. Then he turned to me. "It can come again," he repeated. "I just want you to know that."

"All right," I said, at last. "So it can come again. All right."

He smiled, but the smile was sorrowful. "I had to try to tell you," he said.

"Yes," I said. "I understand that."

"You're my brother," he said, looking straight at me, and not smiling at all.

"Yes," I repeated, "yes. I understand that."

He turned back to the window, looking out. "All that hatred down there," he said, "all that hatred and misery and love. It's a wonder it doesn't blow the avenue apart."

We went to the only nightclub on a short, dark street, downtown. We squeezed through the narrow, chattering, jam-packed bar to the entrance of the big room, where the bandstand was. And we stood there for a moment, for the lights were very dim in this room and we couldn't see. Then, "Hello, boy," said a voice, and an enormous black man, much older than Sonny or myself, erupted out of all that atmospheric lighting and put an arm around Sonny's shoulder. "I been sitting right here," he said, "waiting for you."

He had a big voice, too, and heads in the darkness turned toward us.

Sonny grinned and pulled a little away, and said, "Creole, this is my brother. I told you about him."

Creole shook my hand. "I'm glad to meet you, son," he said, and it was clear that he was glad to meet me *there*, for Sonny's sake. And he smiled. "You got a real musician in *your* family," and he took his arm from Sonny's shoulder and slapped him, lightly, affectionately, with the back of his hand.

"Well. Now I've heard it all," said a voice behind us. This was another musician, and a friend of Sonny's, a coal-black, cheerful-looking man, built close to the ground. He immediately began confiding to me, at the top of his lungs, the most terrible things about Sonny, his teeth gleaming like a lighthouse and his laugh coming up out of him like the beginning of an earthquake. And it turned out that everyone at the bar knew Sonny, or almost everyone; some were musicians, working there, or nearby, or not working, some were simply hangers-on, and some were there to hear Sonny play. I was introduced to all of them and they were all very polite to me. Yet, it was clear that, for them, I was only Sonny's brother. Here, I was in Sonny's world. Or, rather: his kingdom. Here, it was not even a question that his veins bore royal blood.

They were going to play soon, and Creole installed me, by myself, at a table in a dark corner. Then I watched them, Creole, and the little black man, and Sonny, and the others, while they horsed around, standing just below the bandstand. The light from the bandstand spilled just a little short of them and, watching them laughing and gesturing and moving about, I had the feeling that they, nevertheless, were being most careful not to step into that circle of light too suddenly: that if they moved into the light too suddenly, without thinking, they would perish in flame. Then, while I watched, one of them, the small black man, moved into the light and crossed the bandstand and started fooling around with his drums. Then—being funny and being, also, extremely ceremonious—Creole took Sonny by the arm and led him to the piano. A woman's voice called Sonny's name, and a few hands started clapping. And Sonny, also being funny and being ceremonious, and so touched, I think, that he could have cried, but neither hiding it nor showing it, riding it like a man, grinned, and put both hands to his heart and bowed from the waist.

Creole then went to the bass fiddle and a lean, very bright-skinned brown man jumped up on the bandstand and picked up his horn. So there they were, and the atmosphere on the bandstand and in the room began to change and tighten. Someone stepped up to the microphone and announced them. Then there were all kinds of murmurs. Some people at the bar shushed others. The waitress ran around, frantically getting in the last orders, guys and chicks got closer to each other, and the lights on the bandstand, on the quartet, turned to a kind of indigo. Then they all looked different there. Creole looked about him for the last time, as though he were making certain that all his chickens were in the coop, and then he—jumped and struck the fiddle. And there they were.

All I know about music is that not many people ever really hear it. And even then, on the rare occasions when something opens within, and the music enters, what we mainly hear, or hear corroborated, are personal, private, vanishing evocations. But the man who creates the music is hearing something else, is dealing with the roar rising from the void and imposing order on it as it hits the air. What is evoked in him, then, is of another order, more terrible because it has no words, and triumphant, too, for that same reason. And his triumph, when he triumphs, is ours. I just watched Sonny's face. His face was troubled, he was working hard, but he wasn't with it. And I had the feeling that, in a way, everyone on the bandstand was waiting for him, both waiting for him and pushing him along. But as I began to watch Creole, I realized that it was Creole who held them all back. He had them on a short rein. Up there, keeping the beat with his whole body, wailing on the fiddle, with his eyes half closed, he was listening to everything, but he was listening to Sonny. He was having a dialogue with Sonny. He wanted Sonny to leave the shoreline and strike out for the deep water. He was Sonny's witness that deep water and drowning were not the same thing—he had been there, and he knew. And he wanted Sonny to know. He was waiting for Sonny to do the things on the keys which would let Creole know that Sonny was in the water.

And, while Creole listened, Sonny moved, deep within, exactly like someone in torment. I had never before thought of how awful the relationship must be between the musician and his instrument. He has to fill it, this instrument, with the breath of life, his own. He has to make it do what he wants it to do. And a piano is just a piano. It's made out of so much wood and wires and little hammers and big ones, and ivory. While there's only so much you can do with it, the only way to find this out is to try; to try and make it do everything.

And Sonny hadn't been near a piano for over a year. And he wasn't on much better terms with his life, not the life that stretched before him now. He and the piano stammered, started one way, got scared, stopped; started another way, panicked, marked time, started again; then seemed to have found a direction, panicked again, got stuck. And the face I saw on Sonny I'd never seen before. Everything had been burned out of it, and, at the same time, things usually hidden were being burned in, by the fire and fury of the battle which was occurring in him up there.

Yet, watching Creole's face as they neared the end of the first set, I had the feeling that something had happened, something I hadn't heard. Then they finished, there was scattered applause, and then, without an instant's warning, Creole started into something else, it was almost sardonic, it was *Am I Blue*. And, as though he commanded, Sonny began to play. Something began to happen. And Creole let out the reins. The dry, low, black man said something awful on the drums, Creole answered, and the drums talked back. Then the horn insisted, sweet and high, slightly detached perhaps, and Creole listened, commenting now and then, dry, and driving, beautiful and calm and old. Then they all came together again, and Sonny was part of the family again. I could tell this from his face. He seemed to have found, right there beneath his fingers, a damn brand-new piano. It seemed that he couldn't get over it. Then, for a while, just being happy with Sonny, they seemed to be agreeing with him that brand-new pianos certainly were a gas.

Then Creole stepped forward to remind them that what they were playing was the blues. He hit something in all of them, he hit something in me, myself, and the music tightened and deepened, apprehension began to beat the air. Creole began to tell us what the blues were all about. They were not about anything very new. He and his boys up there were keeping it new, at the risk of ruin, destruction, madness, and death, in order to find new ways to make us listen. For, while the tale of how we suffer, and how we are delighted, and how we may triumph is never new, it always must be heard. There isn't any other tale to tell, it's the only light we've got in all this darkness.

And this tale, according to that face, that body, those strong hands on those strings, has another aspect in every country, and a new depth in every generation. Listen, Creole seemed to be saying, listen. Now these are Sonny's blues. He made the little black man on the drums know it and the bright, brown man on the horn. Creole wasn't trying any longer to get Sonny in the water. He was wishing him Godspeed. Then he stepped back, very slowly, filling the air with immense suggestion that Sonny speak for himself.

Then they all gathered around Sonny and Sonny played. Every now and again one of them seemed to say, amen. Sonny's fingers filled the air with life, his life. But that life contained so many others. And Sonny went all the way back, he really began with the spare, flat statement of the opening phrase of the song. Then he began to make it his. It was very beautiful because it wasn't hurried and it was no longer a lament. I seemed to hear with what burning he had made it his, with what burning we had yet to make it ours, how we could cease lamenting. Freedom lurked around us and I understood, at last, that he could help us to be free if we would listen, that he would never be free until we did. Yet, there was no battle in his face now, I heard what he had gone through, and would continue to go through until he came to rest in earth. He had made it his: that long line, of which we knew only Mama and Daddy. And he was giving it back, as everything must be given back, so that, passing through death, it can live forever. I saw my mother's face again, and felt, for the first time, how the stones of the road she had walked on must have bruised her feet. I saw the moonlit road where my father's brother died. And it brought something else back to me, and carried me past it, I saw my little girl again and felt Isabel's tears again, and I felt my own tears begin to rise. And I was yet aware that this was only a moment, that the world waited outside, as hungry as a tiger, and that trouble stretched above us, longer than the sky.

Then it was over. Creole and Sonny let out their breath, both soaking wet, and grinning. There was a lot of applause and some of it was real. In the dark, the girl came by and I asked her to take drinks to the bandstand. There was a long pause, while they talked up there in the indigo light and after a while I saw the girl put a Scotch and milk on top of the piano for Sonny. He didn't seem to notice it, but just before they started playing again, he sipped from it and looked toward me, and nodded. Then he put it back on top of the piano. For me, then, as they began to play again, it glowed and shook above my brother's head like the very cup of trembling.

Themes in Literature

Themes—central and controlling ideas—exist in all good art. The famous statue of a discus thrower sculpted in ancient times portrays an athlete, but its *theme* is the grace and power represented in athletics. Some modern sculptures, on first glance, may seem like nothing more than pieces of copper, aluminum, or steel welded together. Yet if you look at them carefully and think about them, you can understand that they express feelings of speed, freedom, rising hope, or other ideas. These ideas that you perceive are probably the themes that the sculptor wants to communicate to you through the work.

Music expresses themes related to the full range of human emotions—love, happiness, suffering, death, hope, longing, freedom, patriotism—whatever the composer has in mind to communicate through his or her art. Themes also emerge in painting, architecture, pottery, needlework, and every other art and craft originating in the human mind—including writing.

Themes are easy to identify in nonfiction writing where they are stated for you in titles and headlines or are clearly defined in the body of the article: "Smoking Is Responsible for Billions of Dollars Spent on Health Care"; "Candidates Compete for the Farm Vote"; "Good Brawls Sell More Tickets Than Good Hockey."

Themes in fiction, however, require closer reading and a little more thought. To discover the theme of a story, you must examine the story elements: the characters and their thoughts, their conflicts, their actions, and the world which the author has created for them.

Does "digging" for themes ruin a story, as some students of literature complain? It should not, because a story without ideas to communicate is really no story at all. It may be fun to read a book where the hero and heroine have adventure after adventure without reason or sense, but when you are through reading you will have to admit you have done nothing but pass time. Such stories quickly die out because they have nothing to say. Well-told stories, on the other hand, with important themes, live forever and are rediscovered by each new generation of readers. The theme of escape to freedom has kept the novel *Huckleberry Finn* alive for more than a hundred years. The story of *Romeo and Juliet* has delighted audiences for more than three hundred years not because it is just a love story, but because it points out how petty family quarrels can lead to the tragic end of love.

You will examine the themes in "Sonny's Blues" as they are expressed in these story elements:

1. conflicts
2. action and dialogue
3. characters
4. Baldwin's imagery and descriptions

· I ·
Themes and Conflict

A war is certainly one kind of conflict; and it is inconceivable that the people of any country would go to war without some compelling force—a theme. For the Allies the theme of World War I was to make the world safe for democracy. That was the controlling theme, even though the reasons and causes for the war may be found elsewhere. For the United States World War II was fought to stop German and Japanese expansionism.

Stories also have themes related to their conflicts. In "A Rose for Emily" the conflict between old and new generations helped to point out the theme of change with passing time. In "The Guest" Daru's inner conflicts emphasized his lack of control over events, a major theme in the story.

In "Sonny's Blues" the older brother, the unnamed narrator of the story, begins by describing his inner conflict over his feelings for his brother Sonny. What important idea or theme, one that appears several times during the story, can you find expressed in the following conflict?

Sonny has just been arrested for peddling and using heroin:

> I couldn't believe it: but what I mean by that is that I couldn't find any room for it anywhere inside me. I had kept it outside me for a long time. I hadn't wanted to know. I had had suspicions, but I didn't name them, I kept putting them away. I told myself that Sonny was wild, but he wasn't crazy. And he'd always been a good boy, he hadn't ever turned hard or evil or disrespectful, the way kids can, so quick, especially in Harlem. I didn't want to believe that I'd ever see my brother going down, coming to nothing, all that light in his face gone out, in the condition I'd already seen so many others. Yet it had happened and here I was, talking about algebra to a lot of boys who might, every one of them for all I knew, be popping off needles every time they went to the head. Maybe it did more for them than algebra could.

The narrator is an algebra teacher living in his straight, conventional world. His brother is very much outside the mainstream and now has been arrested on drug charges. The narrator has desperately wanted to keep those two worlds separated. He had grown up in the shadowy world around him, but to this point believed he had escaped it, or at least had escaped its worst effects. "I had kept it outside me for a long time. I hadn't wanted to know," he says.

In those two lines the narrator's conflict is revealed. He has grown up and is teaching in a place where drug use seems to be a reality of life. And then he brings up a major question to be answered in the story—"Maybe it [drugs] did more for them than algebra could." That theme runs throughout the story. When a person is raised in the ambience that Harlem provides its youth, can that person escape by the conventional route—school, represented by the math class—or is it better to take what seems an easier escape route—the temporary release from suffering that drugs provide?

EXERCISE A

Read the following passage from the story and answer the questions that follow using the information you have learned in this part of the lesson.

> Dear brother,
>
> You don't know how much I needed to hear from you. I wanted to write you many a time but I dug how much I must have hurt you and so I didn't write. But now I feel like a man who's been trying to climb up out of some deep, real deep and funky hole and just saw the sun up there, outside. I got to get outside.
>
> I can't tell you much about how I got here. I mean I don't know how to tell you. I guess I was afraid of something or I was trying to escape from something. . . . I'm glad Mama and Daddy are dead and can't see what's happened to their son and I swear if I had known what I was doing I would never have hurt you so, you and a lot of other fine people who were nice to me and who believed in me.

1. Sonny tells of a need he feels. This need is a conflict that is repeated in the story so often that you soon realize it is an important theme. Which one of the following describes the theme?
   ☐ a. a need to be closer to his mother and father
   ☐ b. feeling trapped and needing to escape
   ☐ c. a need to find a way to write
   ☐ d. a need to be conventional

2. Another theme in the story points to the effects deviant behavior produces on friends and family. Copy a phrase or sentence from the story that tells about one effect.

   _____

   _____

   _____

   _____

   _____

Now check your answers using the Answer Key at the back of the book. Correct any wrong answers and review this part of the lesson if you do not understand why an answer is wrong.

· 2 ·
Themes: Action and Dialogue

The important actions and events of any good story are skillfully employed by authors to express the important ideas or themes in their work. Some events or actions are so appropriate for expressing themes that you come across them again and again in literature.

Wars and revolutions are frequently used to emphasize the idea of social change. You saw that theme in "A Rose for Emily" where the Civil War was used to mark the end of an era in the old South. The uprising in Algeria was the moving force, the controlling idea, that took events out of the hands of Daru the schoolmaster in "The Guest."

A journey is another common method authors use to develop themes. Herman Melville's *Moby-Dick* uses the voyage of a ship, the *Pequod,* in pursuit of the great white whale, to suggest a pilgrimage through life and a maniacal pursuit of a singular goal. Mark Twain used a journey on a raft down the Mississippi in *Huckleberry Finn* to depict both an escape to freedom and a journey through life. Phoenix Jackson's journey in "A Worn Path" symbolized dedication to a purpose.

Themes are also expressed in conversations, or dialogue, between characters. Notice the dialogue in "Sonny's Blues" when the brothers discuss suffering in an extended conversation. Here are excerpts from that conversation:

> [Sonny says] "While I was downstairs before, on my way here, listening to that woman sing, it struck me all of a sudden how much suffering she must have had to go through—to sing like that. It's *repulsive* to think you have to suffer that much."
>
> I said: "But there's no way not to suffer—is there, Sonny?"
>
> "I believe not," he said, and smiled, "but that's never stopped anyone from trying. . . . No, there's no way not to suffer. But you try all kinds of ways to keep from drowning in it. . . .
>
> "It's terrible sometimes, inside," he said, "that's what's the trouble. You walk these streets, black and funky and cold, and there's not really a living ass to talk to . . . and there's no way of getting it out—that storm inside. You can't talk it and you can't

make love with it, and when you finally try to get with it and play it, you realize *nobody's* listening. So *you've* got to listen. You got to find a way to listen."

Throughout the story James Baldwin suggests that the experience of growing up and living in Harlem involves suffering. It's not physical pain but inner suffering, and "you try all kinds of ways to keep from drowning in it," Sonny says. What is worse is that you are alone with your suffering. No one will share it with you, and no one will listen to you. Sonny is trying two ways to deal with his suffering—one way is through drugs, and the other way is his music.

The climactic action of the story comes when Sonny is playing his blues with Creole and his band in a Greenwich Village nightclub. At that point Sonny finally purges his suffering through his music. The blues represent not only Sonny's suffering, but the suffering of a whole people.

EXERCISE B

Read the following passage from the story and answer the questions that follow using the information you have learned in this part of the lesson.

The narrator recalls sitting in the living room as a child with family relatives and friends after Sunday dinner:

> There they sit, in chairs all around the living room, and the night is creeping up outside. . . . You can see the darkness growing against the windowpanes and you hear the street noises every now and again . . . but it's real quiet in the room. For a moment nobody's talking, but every face looks darkening, like the sky outside. . . . Everyone is looking at something a child can't see. . . . The silence, the darkness coming, and the darkness in the faces frighten the child obscurely. He hopes that the hand which strokes his forehead will never stop—will never die. . . .
>
> But something deep and watchful in the child knows that this is bound to end, is already ending. In a moment someone will get up and turn on the light. . . . And when light fills the room, the child is filled with darkness. He knows that every time this happens he's moved just a little closer to that darkness outside. The darkness outside is what the old folks have been talking about. It's what they've come from. It's what they endure.

1. A "theme word" appears repeatedly in this passage as it does throughout the story. It is closely related to the theme of suffering. Which one of the following is the theme word?

   ☐ a. quiet

   ☐ b. child

   ☐ c. outside

   ☐ d. darkness

2. What is the sentence near the end of the passage that suggests that as a child grows he moves from the safety of his family to the suffering of the world around him?

   _____

   _____

   _____

   _____

Now check your answers using the Answer Key at the back of the book. Correct any wrong answers and review this part of the lesson if you do not understand why an answer is wrong.

· 3 ·
Themes and Characters

The main character in a short story and in most novels is often used to develop and project the story's main themes. Therefore, a good way to identify themes in a story is to analyze the main character, or protagonist. Ask yourself, Has this character learned something new in the course of the story or come to some realization of truth? What has happened to the character, and why has it happened? If you can answer questions like these, you'll probably discover the major themes of the story.

Secondary and even minor characters in a story are also frequently used to point out or to illustrate themes. Colonel Sartoris, for example, is used in "A Rose for Emily" to illustrate the idea of changing attitudes from one generation to the next. The relatives in "A Christmas Memory" make very brief appearances, but they show how a crabbed outlook on life can destroy people's simple joys.

In "Sonny's Blues" Sonny is obviously the protagonist, and if you think about what he goes through and what happens to him in the story, you will soon discover a main theme: Suffering must find a release or it will destroy you. Sonny finds release from his suffering in his music, and the implication is that he has finally chosen music over drugs. Early in the story, James Baldwin uses a minor character to show the other side of the coin—an addict who has chosen drugs.

> I saw this boy standing in the shadow of a doorway, looking just like Sonny. . . . Then I saw that it wasn't Sonny, but somebody we used to know, a boy from around our block. He'd been Sonny's friend. . . . And now, even though he was a grown-up man, he still hung around that block, still spent hours on the street corners, was always high and raggy.

The narrator and the addict discuss Sonny's recent arrest for using and selling drugs, and then the conversation takes a new turn. The addict says:

> "I'm surprised at Sonny, though . . . I thought Sonny was a smart boy, I thought he was too smart to get hung."
>
> "I guess he thought so, too," I said sharply, "and that's how he got hung. And how about you? You're pretty goddamn smart, I bet."
>
> Then he looked directly at me, just for a minute. "I ain't smart," he said. "If I was smart, I'd have reached for a pistol a long time ago."
>
> "Look. Don't tell *me* your sad story, if it was up to me, I'd give you one." Then I felt guilty—guilty, probably, for never having supposed that the poor bastard *had* a story of his own, much less a sad one. . . .

The addict, a minor character in the story, is used to show what Sonny is in danger of becoming. The narrator hates him because of that resemblance, not wanting to face the awful truth that in a short time his brother could be like the addict. (You probably noticed that the narrator says that seen in the shadows the boy looked just like Sonny.) The conversation illustrates a common attitude that society has toward drug addicts—"You think you're pretty goddamn smart." Then the author brings you back to the major theme of the story.

The addict says if he were "smart" he would have committed suicide— "reached for a pistol." The narrator feels guilty about his comment. The addict was probably experiencing the same suffering that the author refers to throughout the story. The addict found his way to relieve his suffering in drugs. His other choice was death. Sonny will face the same choices, but he has one more choice than the addict—he has his music, the blues.

EXERCISE C

Read the following passage from the story and answer the questions that follow using the information you have learned in this part of the lesson.

> It was strange, suddenly, to watch, though I had been seeing these street meetings all my life. So, of course, had everybody else down there. Yet, they paused and watched and listened and I stood still at the window. " 'Tis the old ship of Zion," they sang . . . "it has rescued many a thousand!" Not a soul under the sound of their voices was hearing this song for the first time, not one of them had been rescued. . . . As the singing filled the air, the watching, listening faces underwent a change, the eyes focusing on something within; the music seemed to soothe a poison out of them; and time seemed, nearly, to fall away from the sullen, belligerent, battered faces, as though they were fleeing back to their first condition, while dreaming of their last.

1. The singers and their audience are very minor characters in the story. But they are tied into a major theme. What is that theme?
   - ☐ a. The old song they sing is a forerunner of blues music and like the blues represents suffering.
   - ☐ b. They are street gospel singers, which relates to the fact that the author was himself a preacher in his youth.
   - ☐ c. Everybody in Harlem knows and loves the old spirituals.
   - ☐ d. The singers see the darkness that exists outside their world.

2. By the end of the story you see that Sonny's inner conflict can be released when it is expressed through his music. What phrase near the end of the passage suggests that the street music is having a similar effect on the audience?

_____

_____

_____

Now check your answers using the Answer Key at the back of the book. Correct any wrong answers and review this part of the lesson if you do not understand why an answer is wrong.

· 4 ·

Themes and Imagery

The term *imagery* refers to the language that an author uses to appeal to readers' senses of sight, sound, taste, smell, or touch. A writer uses imagery to convey feelings, attitudes, and ideas to readers. The author's thoughts, feelings, and ideas become themes in the story, so the imagery must necessarily be related to the themes.

James Baldwin talks about several ideas in the story: suffering, living with suffering, feeling trapped and wanting to escape to freedom, suffering versus self-destruction, and expressing inner conflict through music. You will recognize some of these themes as they are expressed in the following quotations from the story. The images the author uses to express themes are in italics.

> I stared at it [the news of Sonny's arrest] in the swinging lights of the subway car, and in the faces and bodies of the people, and in my own face, *trapped in the darkness which roared outside.*

> They [the algebra students] were filled with rage. All they really knew were *two darknesses, the darkness of their lives, which was now closing in on them, and the darkness of the movies, which had blinded them to that other darkness. . . .*

> [From Sonny's letter] But now I feel like a man who's been trying to climb up *out of some deep, real deep and funky hole and just saw the sun up there, outside.* I got to get *outside.*

You find those references throughout the story, so you know darkness is something the author considers important. When an author considers an image important enough to repeat over and over again, you can be certain that it relates to a theme. Darkness in the context of "Sonny's Blues" embodies fear, rage, and hopelessness, both in the people and in the world outside them. There is also the "darkness of the movies." How can the bright screen be dark? It is the false optimism depicted in movies, the author says, that creates an illusion of a bright world. The illusion is actually a blinding darkness that disguises the darkness of the students' real world.

The other image in the quotations deals with the feeling of being trapped and desperately wanting to escape. Sonny is trying to climb out of the darkness of a deep and funky (foul) hole into the light. "I got to get outside," he says, which is the whole sense of the story. Sonny is searching for a way out of the fear and darkness—first through drugs, and then through his music.

EXERCISE D

Read the following passage from the story and answer the questions that follow using the information you have learned in this part of the lesson.

> So we drove along, between the green of the park and the stony, lifeless elegance of hotels and apartment buildings, toward the vivid, killing streets of our childhood. These streets hadn't changed, though housing projects jutted up out of them now like rocks in the middle of a boiling sea. Most of the houses in which we had grown up had vanished. . . . But houses exactly like the houses of our past yet dominated the landscape, boys exactly like the boys we once had been found themselves smothering in these houses, came down into the streets for light and air and found themselves encircled by disaster. Some escaped the trap, most didn't. Those who got out always left something of themselves behind, as some animals amputate a leg and leave it in the trap.

1. "The boys . . . came down into the streets for light and air and found themselves encircled by disaster." What is the idea expressed by the image in that sentence?
   - ☐ a. The boys really don't know which they prefer, being at home or feeling free to roam the streets.
   - ☐ b. When they play in the streets the boys are sure to be surrounded by rival gangs.
   - ☐ c. Escaping the confinement of their homes, the boys are lured into an even more dangerous trap.
   - ☐ d. The boys themselves are the "disaster" and their lives consist of running in circles.

2. There are many thought-provoking images in that passage. Copy at least two of those images, other than those in question 1.

_____

_____

_____

_____

_____

_____

_____

Now check your answers using the Answer Key at the back of the book. Correct any wrong answers and review this part of the lesson if you do not understand why an answer is wrong.

Comprehension Questions

For each of the following statements or questions, select the option that best completes a statement or is the most accurate response to a question.

Recalling Specific Facts
1. The first-person narrator of the story is a
   ☐ a. police officer.
   ☐ b. lawyer.
   ☐ c. businessman.
   ☐ d. teacher.

Recalling Specific Facts
2. What happened to the narrator's daughter, Grace?
   ☐ a. She died of polio.
   ☐ b. She was arrested.
   ☐ c. She became addicted to drugs.
   ☐ d. She left home.

Recalling Specific Facts
3. Who was Creole?
   ☐ a. He was a street minister.
   ☐ b. He was a jazz musician.
   ☐ c. He was a local junkie.
   ☐ d. He was Sonny's father.

Organizing Facts
4. The narrator said he hated the drug addict who discussed Sonny's arrest. What did the narrator do just before he went into the subway station?
   ☐ a. Feeling exasperated, he hit the man.
   ☐ b. He gave the man five dollars.
   ☐ c. He turned and left the man standing there.
   ☐ d. He shoved the man out of the way.

Organizing Facts
5. When Sonny was in school he lived for a while with the narrator's wife and her parents. Where did he go from there?
   ☐ a. He joined the navy.
   ☐ b. He was arrested and went to jail.
   ☐ c. He returned to live with his brother in a housing project.
   ☐ d. He just roamed the streets.

Organizing Facts

6. The narrator's mother tells him about his father's brother who was killed by an automobile. When did that happen?
   - ☐ a. long before the beginning of this story
   - ☐ b. while the narrator was in the army
   - ☐ c. long after the beginning of the story
   - ☐ d. just after Sonny moved away

Knowledge of Word Meanings

7. Sonny looked at his brother with *"mocking,* amused defiance." What does *mocking* mean as it is used here?
   - ☐ a. expressing scorn or contempt
   - ☐ b. imitating or mimicking
   - ☐ c. showing feigned anger
   - ☐ d. a kind of snarling challenge

Knowledge of Word Meanings

8. "On the sidewalk . . . some people were holding an old-fashioned *revival meeting."* A *revival meeting* is a
   - ☐ a. pep rally.
   - ☐ b. protest meeting.
   - ☐ c. religious meeting.
   - ☐ d. gang meeting.

Knowledge of Word Meanings

9. The narrator was *apprehensive* as he watched his brother. *Apprehensive* means that he felt
   - ☐ a. proud.
   - ☐ b. a bit angry.
   - ☐ c. fatherly.
   - ☐ d. uneasy.

Drawing a Conclusion

10. Sonny played the piano constantly while living with relatives. You have to conclude that the relatives were
    - ☐ a. music lovers.
    - ☐ b. making Sonny take lessons.
    - ☐ c. very patient people.
    - ☐ d. under some obligation to him.

Drawing a Conclusion

11. From the way the narrator describes Harlem, it would seem that he feels that most people living there are
    ☐ a. neighborly.
    ☐ b. useless.
    ☐ c. trapped.
    ☐ d. deserted.

Drawing a Conclusion

12. Sonny took his brother to a nightclub. From the way they were received there you have to conclude that
    ☐ a. the people were suspicious of them.
    ☐ b. Sonny was known and liked there.
    ☐ c. no one either noticed or cared about them.
    ☐ d. they were in a hostile environment.

Making a Judgment

13. When the narrator was in the army, Sonny was a teenager. You can conclude that
    ☐ a. they didn't understand each other very well.
    ☐ b. they were close during this time.
    ☐ c. they were enemies.
    ☐ d. there was an unspoken bond between them.

Making a Judgment

14. It is obvious that when Sonny was in school he
    ☐ a. stayed and studied for his brother's sake.
    ☐ b. would have been a good student except for the environment.
    ☐ c. wasn't making an effort to learn.
    ☐ d. was a violent kid even then.

Making an Inference

15. The street singer sang, " 'Tis the old ship of Zion, it has rescued many a thousand!" The narrator suggests that
    ☐ a. no one in the audience had been rescued.
    ☐ b. the song was the release the people needed.
    ☐ c. the whole thing was like a circus sideshow.
    ☐ d. no one listened and no one cared.

Making an Inference

16. Near the end of the story, while Sonny is playing the piano, the narrator says, "Now these are Sonny's blues." He is implying that
    ☐ a. the music represented Sonny's suffering.
    ☐ b. Sonny had written this music and it was rightfully his.
    ☐ c. no one was listening to what Sonny had to say.
    ☐ d. it was Sonny's turn and he was playing alone.

Understanding Characters

17. The narrator and his brother, Sonny, represent two different life-styles. Which one of the following pairs is the best comparison of their differences?
    ☐ a. law-abiding vs. criminal
    ☐ b. moral vs. immoral
    ☐ c. conventional vs. unconventional
    ☐ d. satisfied vs. unsatisfied

Understanding Characters

18. The narrator finally understood what Sonny wanted from people. What was it?
    ☐ a. He wanted everyone to leave him alone to live his life as he pleased.
    ☐ b. He wanted people to listen to him and understand how he felt.
    ☐ c. He wanted to be a great jazz musician, just like Charlie Parker.
    ☐ d. He wanted to be sure that drugs would never dominate his life again.

Understanding Main Ideas

19. Which one of the following quotations from the story embodies a main idea?
    ☐ a. They were singing *If I could only hear my mother pray again!*
    ☐ b. It was not to be believed, and I kept telling myself that. . . .
    ☐ c. It's *repulsive* to think you have to suffer that much.
    ☐ d. . . . I saw this boy standing in the shadow of a doorway, looking just like Sonny.

Understanding Main Ideas

20. Listening to Sonny play the blues, the narrator says, "He had made it his: that long line, of which we knew only Mama and Daddy." If you had to base a title for the story on this quotation, which one of the following would be the best?
    ☐ a. "A Legacy of Pain"
    ☐ b. "Up from Slavery"
    ☐ c. "A History of Jazz"
    ☐ d. "Out of Harlem"

Understanding Main Ideas

21. After Sonny had played in the nightclub, his brother sent drinks to the bandstand. Sonny took a sip and nodded to his brother. What might be the significance of that action?
    - ☐ a. It was a way for the narrator to show that he liked the music.
    - ☐ b. The author is saying that an alcoholic drink is far better than heroin.
    - ☐ c. After all their fighting, it was a way for the brothers to make up.
    - ☐ d. Sonny knew that his brother had listened and had understood him.

Recognizing Tone

22. "A great block of ice got settled in my belly and kept melting there. . . ." What feeling does that quotation convey?
    - ☐ a. heady exhilaration
    - ☐ b. icy determination
    - ☐ c. cool strength
    - ☐ d. cold fear

Recognizing Tone

23. "I ain't smart," he [the addict] said. "If I was smart, I'd have reached for a pistol a long time ago." That quotation reflects a feeling of
    - ☐ a. despair.
    - ☐ b. longing.
    - ☐ c. anger.
    - ☐ d. intrigue.

Appreciation of Literary Forms

24. "All they really knew were two darknesses, the darkness of their lives, which was now closing in on them, and the darkness of the movies, which had blinded them to that other darkness. . . ." Darkness is used here as a metaphor in two different ways. Which ways?
    - ☐ a. darkness as skin color, and darkness as trickery
    - ☐ b. darkness as the devil or hell, and darkness as disbelief
    - ☐ c. darkness as fear, unhappiness, and despair, and darkness as falsehood
    - ☐ d. darkness as racism, and darkness as white supremacy

Appreciation of Literary Forms

25. In many places the Bible instructs readers that there is eternal life beyond earthly suffering. Which one of the following images from the story reflects that idea?

    ☐ a. Freedom lurked around us and I understood, at last, that he could help us to be free if we would listen. . . .

    ☐ b. And he was giving it back, as everything must be given back, so that, passing through death, it can live forever.

    ☐ c. Sonny's fingers filled the air with life, his life.

    ☐ d. . . . the world waited outside, as hungry as a tiger, and that trouble stretched above us, longer than the sky.

Now check your answers using the Answer Key at the back of the book. Make no mark for right answers. Correct any wrong answers you may have by putting a check mark (✓) in the box next to the right answer. Count the number of questions you answered correctly and plot the total on the Comprehension Scores Graph at the back of the book.

Next, look at the questions you answered incorrectly. What types of questions were they? Count the number you got wrong of each type and enter the numbers in the spaces below.

Recalling Specific Facts	_____
Organizing Facts	_____
Knowledge of Word Meanings	_____
Drawing a Conclusion	_____
Making a Judgment	_____
Making an Inference	_____
Understanding Characters	_____
Understanding Main Ideas	_____
Recognizing Tone	_____
Appreciation of Literary Forms	_____

Now use these numbers to fill in the Comprehension Skills Profile at the end of the book.

Extension Activities

Discussion Guide

Discussing Themes

1. There are a number of themes in the story including: suffering, darkness, feeling trapped, and wanting to escape. How can you tie all of these into one dominant theme that is suggested in the title "Sonny's Blues"?
2. Themes in stories challenge you to think about what the author is saying to you. What sorts of thoughts have you had as a result of reading this story?
3. The story develops its themes around the relationship between two brothers. But there is a flashback in the middle of the story that tells of the narrator's last conversation with his mother. How does that part of the story contribute to the dominant theme?

Discussing the Story

4. What do you think of Sonny's decision to leave school to play the piano? What alternatives could he have chosen that may have served him better?
5. Everyone experiences some kind of inner conflict or suffering in life. How severe do you think your suffering is, and how do you deal with it? If you think your life is comfortable and without any significant suffering, explain why.
6. Pursuit of freedom is an important theme in the story. What does freedom mean to you? What does it mean to you to "be free"?

Discussing the Author's Work

7. Go through the table of contents to recall the stories you have read so far. Some stories may be characterized as dark and brooding; others are more optimistic in their approach to life. Some are in between. Compare James Baldwin with the other authors. How would you characterize his writing?
8. This is the longest story you have read in this book. Did you find it difficult reading or did Baldwin keep your attention all the way through? Explain your opinion and your reasons for feeling the way you do.
9. Baldwin was a preacher in a Harlem church as a youth. Why does his writing make you feel he is still a preacher? Try to find specific passages that relate to church services and congregations, and to ideas found in the Bible.

Writing Exercise

Complete two or more of the following writing projects that are related to expressing themes. If you wish, you may combine your choices into one larger project.

1. Tell about a conflict or problem in your life or one that you have read about. Show how that problem is common enough in the world to be called a theme.

2. Describe an action—something that has happened to you—or a conversation you have had, and show how this expresses an important idea.

3. Tell about someone you know, or about a character you know from fiction or nonfiction reading, who represents an important idea to you.

4. Write a short poem that contains descriptive images. After you have written the poem, explain how your images reflect ideas you are trying to communicate to your readers.

UNIT
Twelve

Unit Twelve

Introduction

What the Story Is About

Mrs. Turpin and her husband Claud are southern middle-class country people of about a generation ago, before the civil rights movement. They own a small farm with cows and pigs, and they raise a little cotton. Mrs. Turpin is a *good* woman, as she will be the first to tell you. She has a good disposition, she says, she "does for the church," and she keeps her farm and the hogs clean and neat. She is pleased with herself and grateful that God had made her what she is:

> Her heart rose. He had not made her a nigger or white-trash or
> ugly! He had made her herself and given her a little of everything.
> Jesus, thank you! she said. Thank you thank you thank you!

It's obvious to readers that in spite of her pleasure with herself and her position in life, Mrs. Turpin has a fatal flaw. She is bigoted, prejudiced, and lacks compassion.

The first part of the story takes place in a doctor's office where there is a cross section of Mrs. Turpin's world—a well-dressed, pleasant lady, a "white-trash" family, and, briefly, a black delivery boy. That setting offers an opportunity to hear her views and thoughts on class and racial differences. There is one person in the room, however, who hates Mrs. Turpin and her views intensely. That person is a fat, unattractive, emotionally disturbed girl whose face is badly scarred with acne. Her name is Mary Grace, a name that may have been given to her by the author to remind readers of the important prayer in Roman Catholic ritual that begins, "Hail Mary full of Grace. . . ." In a sudden and seemingly unprovoked attack, Mary Grace shocks Mrs. Turpin with the revelation that perhaps she is not as good a woman as she thinks she is.

The title of the story, "Revelation," refers to the revelation in the doctor's office, and it has a parallel in the last book of the New Testament Bible—"The Revelation of St. John the Divine"—popularly referred to by the short name "Revelation." You might want to read this book of the Bible either before or after reading Flannery O'Connor's "Revelation" in order to understand how the judgment on Mrs. Turpin by Mary Grace compares to the biblical account of the last judgment of the world.

Mary Flannery O'Connor was born in Savannah, Georgia, in 1925. She died only 39 years later (1964) at her mother's farm in Milledgeville, not far from where Alice Walker ("Everyday Use") was born.

O'Connor's use of vivid descriptions, dialect, humor, and irony combine to create powerful and disturbing characters, as you will see in "Revelation." She was a devout Roman Catholic and also a keen observer of the religious beliefs of people. Religion and expressions of religious faith—both real and feigned—are important elements in her stories.

If you would like to read more of Flannery O'Connor's work, her novels include *Wise Blood* and *The Violent Bear It Away*. Her short-story collections are *A Good Man Is Hard to Find* and *Everything That Rises Must Converge*.

What the Lesson Is About

In this lesson you will use many of the elements of fiction that you have studied—setting, character, plot, conflict—and apply those elements to a discussion of literature.

Actually, you already have had considerable experience discussing literature after reading each story in this collection and as you worked your way through the lessons. Your most intense look at the meaning of a story was undertaken in the previous unit, "Sonny's Blues," which dealt with theme, the central idea and the reason behind an author's writing. You are well prepared, therefore, to take a close look at "Revelation," analyze it, and discuss it.

Analysis originates in imagining and self-questioning—imagining yourself in the story's situation and asking how and why events occur, and why you feel the way you do. Imagining and self-questioning is the approach you will take in this unit to learn how to analyze and discuss literature. Keep the following questions in mind as you read Flannery O'Connor's "Revelation." They will help you with the discussion of the story that follows.

1. Imagine yourself in the doctor's office at the beginning of the story. What is your reaction to the setting and the people?

2. Why does Mary Grace attack Mrs. Turpin?

3. Pay close attention to the climax and conclusion of the story. What do they signify? Are there *two* climaxes in the story? If so, how does each create questions for you to discuss?

4. What thoughts or ideas occur to you as you learn the outcome of the story?

Revelation

by Flannery O'Connor

*T*he doctor's waiting room, which was very small, was almost full when the Turpins entered and Mrs. Turpin, who was very large, made it look even smaller by her presence. She stood looming at the head of the magazine table set in the center of it, a living demonstration that the room was inadequate and ridiculous. Her little bright black eyes took in all the patients as she sized up the seating situation. There was one vacant chair and a place on the sofa occupied by a blond child in a dirty blue romper who should have been told to move over and make room for the lady. He was five or six, but Mrs. Turpin saw at once that no one was going to tell him to move over. He was slumped down in the seat, his arms idle at his sides and his eyes idle in his head; his nose ran unchecked.

Mrs. Turpin put a firm hand on Claud's shoulder and said in a voice that included anyone that wanted to listen, "Claud, you sit in that chair there," and gave him a push down into the vacant one. Claud was florid and bald and sturdy, somewhat shorter than Mrs. Turpin, but he sat down as if he were accustomed to doing what she told him to.

Mrs. Turpin remained standing. The only man in the room besides Claud was a lean stringy old fellow with a rusty hand spread out on each knee, whose eyes were closed as if he were asleep or dead or pretending to be so as not to get up and offer her his seat. Her gaze settled agreeably on a well-dressed gray-haired lady whose eyes met hers and whose expression said: If that child belonged to me, he would have some manners and move over—there's plenty of room there for you and him too.

Claud looked up with a sigh and made as if to rise.

"Sit down," Mrs. Turpin said. "You know you're not supposed to stand on that leg. He has an ulcer on his leg," she explained.

Claud lifted his foot onto the magazine table and rolled his trouser leg up to reveal a purple swelling on a plump marble-white calf.

"My!" the pleasant lady said. "How did you do that?"

"A cow kicked him," Mrs. Turpin said.

"Goodness!" said the lady.

Claud rolled his trouser leg down.

"Maybe the little boy would move over," the lady suggested, but the child did not stir.

"Somebody will be leaving in a minute," Mrs. Turpin said. She could not understand why a doctor—with as much money as they made charging five dollars a day just to stick their head in the hospital door and look at you—couldn't afford a decent-sized waiting room. This one was hardly bigger than a garage. The table was cluttered with limp-looking magazines and at one end of it there was a big green glass ash tray full of cigarette butts and cotton wads with little blood spots on them. If she had had anything to do with the running of the place, that would have been emptied every so often. There were no chairs against the wall at the head of the room. It had a rectangular-shaped panel in it that permitted a view of the office where the nurse came and went and the secretary listened to the radio. A plastic fern in a gold pot sat in the opening and trailed its fronds down almost to the floor. The radio was softly playing gospel music.

Just then the inner door opened and a nurse with the highest stack of yellow hair Mrs. Turpin had ever seen put her face in the crack and called for the next patient. The woman sitting beside Claud grasped the two arms of her chair and hoisted herself up; she pulled her dress free from her legs and lumbered through the door where the nurse had disappeared.

"Oh, *you* aren't fat," the stylish lady said.

"Ooooo I am too," Mrs. Turpin said, "Claud he eats all he wants to and never weighs over one hundred and seventy-five pounds, but me I just look at something good to eat and I gain some weight," and her stomach and shoulders shook with laughter. "You can eat all you want to, can't you, Claud? she asked turning to him.

Claud only grinned.

"Well, as long as you have such a good disposition," the stylish lady said, "I don't think it makes a bit of difference what size you are. You just can't beat a good disposition."

Next to her was a fat girl of eighteen or nineteen, scowling into a thick blue book which Mrs. Turpin saw was entitled *Human Development*. The girl raised her head and directed her scowl at Mrs. Turpin as if she did not like her looks. She appeared annoyed that anyone should speak while she tried to read. The poor girl's face was blue with acne and Mrs. Turpin thought how pitiful it was to have a face like that at that age. She gave the girl a friendly smile but the girl only scowled the harder. Mrs. Turpin herself was fat but she had always had good skin, and, though she was forty-seven years old, there was not a wrinkle in her face except around her eyes from laughing too much.

Next to the ugly girl was the child, still in exactly the same position, and next to him was a thin leathery old woman in a cotton print dress. She and Claud had three sacks of chicken feed in their pump house that was in the same print. She had seen from the first that the child belonged with the old woman. She could tell by the way they sat—kind of vacant and white-trashy, as if they would sit there until Doomsday if nobody called and told them to get up. And at right angles but next to the well-dressed pleasant lady was a lank-faced woman who was certainly the child's mother. She had on a yellow sweat shirt and wine-colored slacks, both gritty-looking and the rims of her lips were stained with snuff. Her dirty yellow hair was tied behind with a little piece of red paper ribbon. Worse than niggers any day, Mrs. Turpin thought.

The gospel hymn playing was, "When I looked up and He looked down," and Mrs. Turpin, who knew it, supplied the last line mentally. "And wona these days I know I'll we-eara crown."

Without appearing to, Mrs. Turpin always noticed people's feet. The well-dressed lady had on red and grey suede shoes to match her dress. Mrs. Turpin had on her good black patent leather pumps. The ugly girl had on Girl Scout shoes and heavy socks. The old woman had on tennis shoes and the white-trashy mother had on what appeared to be bedroom slippers, black straw with gold braid threaded through them—exactly what you would have expected her to have on.

Sometimes at night when she couldn't go to sleep, Mrs. Turpin would occupy herself with the question of who she would have chosen to be if she couldn't have been herself. If Jesus had said to her before he made her, "There's only two places available for you.

You can either be a nigger or white-trash," what would she have said? "Please Jesus, please," she would have said, "just let me wait until there's another place available," and he would have said, "No, you have to go right now and I have only those two places so make up your mind." She would have wiggled and squirmed and begged and pleaded but it would have been no use and finally she would have said, "All right, make me a nigger then—but that don't mean a trashy one." And he would have made her a neat clean respectable Negro woman, herself but black.

Next to the child's mother was a red-headed youngish woman, reading one of the magazines and working a piece of chewing gum, hell for leather, as Claud would say. Mrs. Turpin could not see the woman's feet. She was not white-trash, just common. Sometimes Mrs. Turpin occupied herself at night naming the classes of people. On the bottom of the heap were most colored people, not the kind she would have been if she had been one, but most of them; then next to them—not above, just away from—were the white-trash; then above them were the home-owners, and above them the home-and-land owners, to which she and Claud belonged. Above she and Claud were people with a lot of money and much bigger houses and much more land. But here the complexity of it would begin to bear in on her, for some of the people with a lot of money were common and ought to be below she and Claud and some of the people who had good blood had lost their money and had to rent and then there were colored people who owned their homes and land as well. There was a colored dentist in town who had two red Lincolns and a swimming pool and a farm with registered white-face cattle on it. Usually by the time she had fallen asleep all the classes of people were moiling and roiling around in her head, and she would dream they were all crammed in together in a boxcar, being ridden off to be put in a gas oven.

"That's a beautiful clock," she said and nodded to her right. It was a big wall clock, the face encased in a brass sunburst.

"Yes, it's very pretty," the stylish lady said agreeably. "And right on the dot too," she added, glancing at her watch.

The ugly girl beside her cast an eye upward at the clock, smirked, then looked directly at Mrs. Turpin and smirked again. Then she returned her eyes to her book. She was obviously the lady's daughter because, although they didn't look anything alike as to disposition, they both had the same shape of face and the same blue eyes. On the lady they sparkled pleasantly but in the girl's seared face they appeared alternately to smolder and to blaze.

What if Jesus had said, "All right, you can be white-trash or a nigger or ugly"!

Mrs. Turpin felt an awful pity for the girl, though she thought it was one thing to be ugly and another to act ugly.

The woman with the snuff-stained lips turned around in her chair and looked up at the clock. Then she turned back and appeared to look a little to the side of Mrs. Turpin. There was a cast in one of her eyes. "You want to know wher you can get one of themther clocks?" she asked in a loud voice.

"No, I already have a nice clock," Mrs. Turpin said. Once somebody like her got a leg in the conversation, she would be all over it.

"You can get you one with green stamps," the woman said. "That's most likely wher he got hisn. Save you up enough, you can get you most anythang. I got me some joo'ry."

Ought to have got you a wash rag and some soap, Mrs. Turpin thought.

"I get contour sheets with mine," the pleasant lady said.

The daughter slammed her book shut. She looked straight in front of her, directly through Mrs. Turpin and on through the yellow curtain and the plate glass window which made the wall behind her. The girl's eyes seemed lit all of a sudden with a peculiar light, an unnatural light like night road signs give. Mrs. Turpin turned her head to see if there was anything going on outside that she should see, but she could not see anything. Figures passing cast only a pale shadow through the curtain. There was no reason the girl should single her out for her ugly looks.

"Miss Finley," the nurse said, cracking the door. The gum-chewing woman got up and passed in front of her and Claud and went into the office. She had on red high-heeled shoes.

Directly across the table, the ugly girl's eyes were fixed on Mrs. Turpin as if she had some very special reason for disliking her.

"This is wonderful weather, isn't it?" the girl's mother said.

"It's good weather for cotton if you can get the niggers to pick it," Mrs. Turpin said, "but niggers don't want to pick cotton any more. You can't get the white folks to pick it and now you can't get the niggers—because they got to be right up there with the white folks."

"They gonna *try* anyways," the white-trash woman said, leaning forward.

"Do you have one of those cotton-picking machines?" the pleasant lady asked.

"No," Mrs. Turpin said, "they leave half the cotton in the field. We don't have much cotton anyway. If you want to make it farming now, you have to have a little of everything. We got a couple of acres of cotton and a few hogs and chickens and just enough white-face that Claud can look after them himself."

"One thang I don't want," the white-trash woman said, wiping her mouth with the back of her hand. "Hogs. Nasty stinking things, a-grunting and a-rootin all over the place,"

Mrs. Turpin gave her the merest edge of her attention. "Our hogs are not dirty and they don't stink," she said. "They're cleaner than some children I've seen. Their feet never touch the ground. We have a pig-parlor—that's where you raise them on concrete," she explained to the pleasant lady, "and Claud scoots them down with the hose every afternoon and washes off the floor." Cleaner by far than that child right there, she thought. Poor nasty little thing. He had not moved except to put the thumb of his dirty hand into his mouth.

The woman turned her face away from Mrs. Turpin. "I know I wouldn't scoot down no hog with no hose," she said to the wall.

You wouldn't have no hog to scoot down, Mrs. Turpin said to herself.

"A-grunting and a-rootin and a-groanin," the woman muttered.

"We got a little of everything," Mrs. Turpin said to the pleasant lady. "It's no use in having more than you can handle yourself with help like it is. We found enough niggers to pick our cotton this year but Claud he has to go after them and take them home again in the evening. They can't walk that half a mile. No they can't. I tell you," she said and laughed merrily, "I sure am tired of buttering up niggers, but you got to love em if you want em to work for you. When they come in the morning, I run out and I say, 'Hi yawl this morning?' and when Claud drives them off to the field I just wave to beat the band and they just wave back." And she waved her hand rapidly to illustrate.

"Like you read out of the same book," the lady said, showing she understood perfectly.

"Child, yes," Mrs. Turpin said. "And when they come in from the field, I run out with a bucket of icewater. That's the way it's going to be from now on," she said. "You may as well face it."

"One thang I know," the white-trash woman said. "Two thangs I ain't going to do: love no nigger or scoot down no hog with no hose." And she let out a bark of contempt.

The look that Mrs. Turpin and the pleasant lady exchanged indicated they both understood that you had to *have* certain things before you could *know* certain things. But every time Mrs. Turpin exchanged a look with the lady, she was aware that the ugly girl's peculiar eyes were still on her, and she had trouble bringing her attention back to the conversation.

"When you got something," she said, "you got to look after it." And when you ain't got a thing but breath and britches, she added to herself, you can afford to come to town every morning and just sit on the Court House coping and spit.

A grotesque revolving shadow passed across the curtain behind her and was thrown palely on the opposite wall. Then a bicycle clattered down against the outside of the building. The door opened and a colored boy glided in with a tray from the drugstore. It had two large red and white paper cups on it with tops on them. He was a tall, very black boy in discolored white pants and a green nylon shirt. He was chewing gum slowly, as if to music. He set the tray down in the office opening next to the fern and stuck his head through to look for the secretary. She was not in there. He rested his arms on the ledge and waited, his narrow bottom stuck out, swaying slowly to the left and right. He raised a hand over his head and scratched the base of his skull.

"You see that button there, boy?" Mrs. Turpin said. "You can punch that and she'll come. She's probably in the back somewhere."

"Is thas right?" the boy said agreeably, as if he had never seen the button before. He leaned to the right and put his finger on it. "She sometime out," he said and twisted around to face his audience, his elbows behind him on the counter. The nurse appeared and he twisted back again. She handed him a dollar and he rooted in his pocket and made the change and counted it out to her. She gave him fifteen cents for a tip and he went out with the empty tray. The heavy door swung too slowly and closed at length with the sound of suction. For a moment no one spoke.

"They ought to send all them niggers back to Africa," the white-trash woman said. "That's wher they come from in the first place."

"Oh, I couldn't do without my good colored friends," the pleasant lady said.

"There's a heap of things worse than a nigger," Mrs. Turpin agreed. "It's all kinds of them just like it's all kinds of us."

"Yes, and it takes all kinds to make the world go round," the lady said in her musical voice.

As she said it, the raw-complexioned girl snapped her teeth together. Her lower lip turned downwards and inside out, revealing the pale pink inside of her mouth. After a second it rolled back up. It was the ugliest face Mrs. Turpin had ever seen anyone make and for a moment she was certain that the girl had made it at her. She was looking at her as if she had known and disliked her all her life—all of Mrs. Turpin's life, it seemed too, not just all the girl's life. Why, girl, I don't even know you, Mrs. Turpin said silently.

She forced her attention back to the discussion. "It wouldn't be practical to send them back to Africa," she said. "They wouldn't want to go. They got it too good here."

"Wouldn't be what they wanted—if I had anythang to do with it," the woman said.

"It wouldn't be a way in the world you could get all the niggers back over there," Mrs. Turpin said. "They'd be hiding out and lying down and turning sick on you and wailing and hollering and raring and pitching. It wouldn't be a way in the world to get them over there."

"They got over here," the trashy woman said. "Get back like they got over."

"It wasn't so many of them then," Mrs Turpin explained.

The woman looked at Mrs. Turpin as if here was an idiot indeed but Mrs. Turpin was not bothered by the look, considering where it came from.

"Nooo," she said, "they're going to stay here where they can go to New York and marry white folks and improve their color. That's what they all want to do, every one of them, improve their color."

"You know what comes of that, don't you?" Claud asked.

"No, Claud what?" Mrs. Turpin said.

Claud's eyes twinkled. "White-face niggers," he said with never a smile.

Everybody in the office laughed except the white-trash and the ugly girl. The girl gripped the book in her lap with white fingers. The trashy woman looked around her from face to face as if she thought they were all idiots. The old woman in the feed sack dress continued to gaze expressionless across the floor at the high-top shoes of the man opposite her, the one who had been pretending to be asleep when the Turpins came in. He was laughing heartily, his hands still spread out on his knees. The child had fallen to the side and was lying now almost face down in the old woman's lap.

While they recovered from their laughter, the nasal chorus on the radio kept the room from silence.

> *"You go to blank blank*
> *And I'll go to mine*
> *But we'll all blank along*
> *To-geth-ther,*
> *And all along the blank*
> *We'll hep eachother out*
> *Smile-ling in any kind of*
> *Weath-ther!"*

Mrs. Turpin didn't catch every word but she caught enough to agree with spirit of the song and it turned her thoughts sober. To help anybody out that needed it was her philosophy of life. She never spared herself when she found somebody in need, whether they were white or black, trash or decent. And of all she had to be thankful for, she was most thankful that this was so. If Jesus had said, "You can be high society and have all the money you want and be thin and svelte-like, but you can't be a good woman with it," she would have had to say, "Well don't make me that then. Make me a good woman and it don't matter what else, how fat or how ugly or how poor!" Her heart rose. He had not made her a nigger or white-trash or ugly! He had made her herself and given her a little of everything. Jesus, thank you! she said. Thank you thank you thank you! Whenever she counted her blessings she felt as buoyant as if she weighed one hundred and twenty-five pounds instead of one hundred and eighty.

"What's wrong with your little boy?" the pleasant lady asked the white-trashy woman.

"He has a ulcer," the woman said proudly. "He ain't give me a minute's peace since he was born. Him and her are just alike," she said, nodding at the old woman, who was running her leathery fingers through the child's pale hair. "Look like I can't get nothing down them two but Co' Cola and candy."

That's all you try to get down em, Mrs. Turpin said to herself. Too lazy to light the fire. There was nothing you could tell her about people like them that she didn't know already. And it was not just that they didn't have anything. Because if you gave them everything, in two weeks it would all be broken or filthy or they would have chopped it up for lightwood. She knew all this from her own experience. Help them you must, but help them you couldn't.

All at once the ugly girl turned her lips inside out again. Her eyes fixed like two drills on Mrs. Turpin. This time there was no mistaking that there was something urgent behind them.

Girl, Mrs. Turpin exclaimed silently, I haven't done a thing to you! The girl might be confusing her with somebody else. There was no need to sit by and let herself be intimidated. "You must be in college," she said boldly, looking directly at the girl. "I see you reading a book there."

The girl continued to stare and pointedly did not answer.

Her mother blushed at this rudeness. "The lady asked you a question, Mary Grace," she said under her breath.

"I have ears," Mary Grace said.

The poor mother blushed again. "Mary Grace goes to Wellesley College," she explained. She twisted one of the buttons on her dress. "In Massachusetts," she added with a grimace. "And in the summer she just keeps right on studying. Just reads all the time, a real book worm. She's done real well at Wellesley; she's taking English and Math and History and Psychology and Social Studies," she rattled on, "and I think it's too much. I think she ought to get out and have fun."

The girl looked as if she would like to hurl them all through the plate glass window.

"Way up north," Mrs. Turpin murmured and thought, well, it hasn't done much for her manners.

"I'd almost rather to have him sick," the white-trash woman said, wrenching the attention back to herself. "He's so mean when he ain't. Look like some children just take natural to meanness. It's some gets bad when they get sick but he was the opposite. Took sick and turned good. He don't give me no trouble now. It's me waitin to see the doctor," she said.

If I was going to send anybody back to Africa, Mrs. Turpin thought, it would be your kind, woman. "Yes, indeed," she said aloud, but looking up at the ceiling, "it's a heap of things worse than a nigger." And dirtier than a hog, she added to herself.

"I think people with bad dispositions are more to be pitied than anyone on earth," the pleasant lady said in a voice that was decidedly thin.

"I thank the Lord he has blessed me with a good one," Mrs. Turpin said. "The day has never dawned that I couldn't find something to laugh at."

"Not since she married me anyways," Claud said with a comical straight face.

Everybody laughed except the girl and the white-trash.

Mrs Turpin's stomach shook. "He's such a caution," she said, "that I can't help but laugh at him."

The girl made a loud ugly noise through her teeth.

Her mother's mouth grew thin and tight. "I think the worst thing in the world," she said, "is an ungrateful person. To have everything and not appreciate it. I know a girl," she said "who has parents who would give her anything, a little brother who loves her dearly, who is getting a good education, who wears the best clothes, but who can never say a kind word to anyone, who never smiles, who just criticizes and complains all day long."

"Is she too old to paddle?" Claud asked.

The girl's face was almost purple.

"Yes," the lady said, "I'm afraid there's nothing to do but leave her to her folly. Some day she'll wake up and it'll be too late."

"It never hurt anyone to smile," Mrs. Turpin said. "It just makes you feel better all over."

"Of course," the lady said sadly, "but there are just some people you can't tell anything to. They can't take criticism."

"If it's one thing I am," Mrs. Turpin said with feeling, "it's grateful. When I think who all I could have been besides myself and what all I got, a little of everything, and a good disposition besides, I just feel like shouting, 'Thank you, Jesus, for making everything the way it is!' It could have been different!" For one thing, somebody else could have got Claud. At the thought of this, she was flooded with gratitude and a terrible pang of joy ran through her. "Oh thank you, Jesus, Jesus, thank you!" she cried aloud.

The book struck her directly over her left eye. It struck almost at the same instant that she realized the girl was about to hurl it. Before she could utter a sound, the raw face came crashing across the table toward her, howling. The girl's fingers sank like clamps into the soft flesh of her neck. She heard the mother cry out and Claud shout, "Whoa!" There was an instant when she was certain that she was about to be in an earthquake.

All at once her vision narrowed and she saw everything as if it were happening in a small room far away, or as if she were looking at it through the wrong end of a telescope. Claud's face crumpled and fell out of sight. The nurse ran in, then out, then in again. Then the gangling figure of the doctor rushed out of the inner door. Magazines flew this way and that as the table turned over. The girl fell with a thud and Mrs. Turpin's vision suddenly reversed itself and she saw everything large instead of small. The eyes of the white-trashy woman were staring hugely at the floor. There the girl, held down on one side by the nurse and on the other by her mother, was wrenching and turning in their grasp. The doctor was kneeling astride her, trying to hold her arm down. He managed after a second to sink a long needle into it.

Mrs. Turpin felt entirely hollow except for her heart which swung from side to side as if it were agitated in a great empty drum of flesh.

"Somebody that's not busy call for the ambulance," the doctor said in the off-hand voice young doctors adopt for terrible occasions.

Mrs. Turpin could not have moved a finger. The old man who had been sitting next to her skipped nimbly into the office and made the call, for the secretary still seemed to be gone.

"Claud!" Mrs. Turpin called.

He was not in his chair. She knew she must jump up and find him but she felt like some one trying to catch a train in a dream, when everything moves in slow motion and the faster you try to run the slower you go.

"Here I am," a suffocated voice, very unlike Claud's, said.

He was doubled up in the corner on the floor, pale as paper, holding his leg. She wanted to get up and go to him but she could not move. Instead, her gaze was drawn slowly downward to the churning face on the floor, which she could see over the doctor's shoulder.

The girl's eyes stopped rolling and focused on her. They seemed a much lighter blue than before, as if a door that had been tightly closed behind them was now open to admit light and air.

Mrs. Turpin's head cleared and her power of motion returned. She leaned forward until she was looking directly into the fierce brilliant eyes. There was no doubt in her mind that the girl did know her, knew her in some intense and personal way, beyond time and place and condition. "What you got to say to me?" she asked hoarsely and held her breath, waiting, as for a revelation.

The girl raised her head. Her gaze locked with Mrs. Turpin's. "Go back to hell where you came from, you old wart hog," she whispered. Her voice was low but clear. Her eyes burned for a moment as if she saw with pleasure that her message had struck its target.

Mrs. Turpin sank back in her chair.

After a moment the girl's eyes closed and she turned her head wearily to the side.

The doctor rose and handed the nurse the empty syringe. He leaned over and put both hands for a moment on the mother's shoulders, which were shaking. She was sitting on the floor, her lips pressed together, holding Mary Grace's hand in her lap. The girl's fingers were gripped like a baby's around her thumb. "Go on to the hospital," he said. "I'll call and make the arrangements."

"Now let's see that neck," he said in a jovial voice to Mrs. Turpin. He began to inspect her neck with his first two fingers. Two little moon-shaped lines like pink fish bones were indented over her windpipe. There was the beginning of an angry red swelling above her eye. His fingers passed over this also.

"Lea' me be," she said thickly and shook him off. "See about Claud. She kicked him."

"I'll see about him in a minute," he said and felt her pulse. He was a thin gray-haired man, given to pleasantries. "Go home and have yourself a vacation the rest of the day," he said and patted her on the shoulder.

Quit your pattin me, Mrs. Turpin growled to herself.

"And put an ice pack over that eye," he said. Then he went and squatted down beside Claud and looked at his leg. After a moment he pulled him up and Claud limped after him into the office.

Until the ambulance came, the only sounds in the room were the tremulous moans of the girl's mother, who continued to sit on the floor. The white-trash woman did not take her eyes off the girl. Mrs. Turpin looked straight ahead at nothing. Presently the ambulance drew up, a long dark shadow, behind the curtain. The attendants came in and set the stretcher down beside the girl, and lifted her expertly onto it and carried her out. The nurse helped the mother gather up her things. The shadow of the ambulance moved silently away and the nurse came back in the office.

"That ther girl is going to be a lunatic, ain't she?" the white-trash woman asked the nurse, but the nurse kept on to the back and never answered her.

"Yes, she's going to be a lunatic," the white-trash woman said to the rest of them.

"Po' critter," the old woman murmured. The child's face was still in her lap. His eyes looked idly out over her knees. He had not moved during the disturbance except to draw one leg up under him.

"I thank Gawd," the white-trash woman said fervently, "I ain't a lunatic."

Claud came limping out and the Turpins went home.

As their pick-up truck turned into their own dirt road and made the crest of the hill, Mrs. Turpin gripped the window ledge and looked out suspiciously. The land sloped gracefully down through a field dotted with lavender weeds and at the start of the rise their small yellow frame house, with its little flower beds spread out around it like a fancy apron, sat primly in its accustomed place between two giant hickory trees. She would not have been startled to see a burnt wound between two blackened chimneys.

Neither of them felt like eating so they put on their house clothes and lowered the shade in the bedroom and lay down, Claud with his leg on a pillow and herself with a damp washcloth over her eye. The instant she was flat on her back, the image of a razor-backed hog with warts on its face and horns coming out behind its ears snorted into her head. She moaned, a low quiet moan.

"I am not," she said tearfully, "a wart hog. From hell." But the denial had no force. The girl's eyes and her words, even the tone of her voice, low but clear, directed only to her, brooked no repudiation. She had been singled out for the message, though there was trash in the room to whom it might justly have been applied. The full force of this fact struck her only now. There was a woman there who was neglecting her own child but she had been overlooked. The message had been given to Ruby Turpin, a respectable, hard-working, church-going woman. The tears dried. Her eyes began to burn instead with wrath.

She rose on her elbow and the washcloth fell into her hand. Claud was lying on his back, snoring. She wanted to tell him what the girl had said. At the same time, she did not wish to put the image of herself as a wart hog from hell into his mind.

"Hey, Claud," she muttered and pushed his shoulder.

Claud opened one pale baby blue eye.

She looked into it warily. He did not think about anything. He just went his way.

"Wha, whasit?" he said and closed the eye again.

"Nothing," she said. "Does you leg pain you?"

"Hurts like hell," Claud said.

"It'll quit terreckly," she said and lay back down. In a moment Claud was snoring again. For the rest of the afternoon they lay there. Claud slept. She scowled at the ceiling. Occasionally she raised her fist and made a small stabbing motion over her chest as if she was defending her innocence to invisible guests who were like the comforters of Job, reasonable-seeming but wrong.

About five-thirty Claud stirred. "Got to go after those niggers," he sighed, not moving.

She was looking straight up as if there were unintelligible handwriting on the ceiling. The protuberance over her eye had turned a greenish-blue. "Listen here," she said.

"What?"

"Kiss me."

Claud leaned over and kissed her loudly on the mouth. He pinched her side and their hands interlocked. Her expression of ferocious concentration did not change. Claud got up, groaning and growling, and limped off. She continued to study the ceiling.

She did not get up until she heard the pick-up truck coming back with the Negroes. Then she rose and thrust her feet in her brown oxfords, which she did not bother to lace, and stumped out onto the back porch and got her red plastic bucket. She emptied a tray of ice cubes into it and filled it half full of water and went out into the back yard. Every afternoon after Claud brought the hands in, one of the boys helped him put out hay and the rest waited in the back of the truck until he was ready to take them home. The truck was parked in the shade under one of the hickory trees.

"Hi yawl this evening?" Mrs. Turpin asked grimly, appearing with the bucket and the dipper. There were three women and a boy in the truck.

"Us doin nicely," the oldest woman said. "Hi you doin?" and her gaze stuck immediately on the dark lump on Mrs. Turpin's forehead. "You done fell down, ain't you?" she asked in a solicitous voice. The old woman was dark and almost toothless. She had on an old felt hat of Claud's set back on her head. The other two women were younger and lighter and they both had new bright green sunhats. One of them had hers on her head; the other had taken hers off and the boy was grinning beneath it.

Mrs. Turpin set the bucket down on the floor of the truck. "Yawl hep yourselves," she said. She looked around to make sure Claud had gone. "No. I didn't fall down," she said, folding her arms. "It was something worse than that."

"Ain't nothing bad happen to you!" the old woman said. She said it as if they all knew that Mrs. Turpin was protected in some special way by Divine Providence. "You just had you a little fall."

"We were in town at the doctor's office for where the cow kicked Mr. Turpin," Mrs. Turpin said in a flat tone that indicated they could leave off their foolishness. "And there was this girl there. A big fat girl with her face all broke out. I could look at that girl and tell she was peculiar but I couldn't tell how. And me and her mama was just talking and going along and all of a sudden WHAM! She throws this big book she was reading at me and . . ."

"Naw!" the old woman cried out.

"And then she jumps over the table and commences to choke me."

"Naw!" they all exclaimed, "naw!"

"Hi come she do that?" the old woman asked. "What ail her?"

Mrs. Turpin only glared in front of her.

"Somethin ail her," the old woman said.

"They carried her off in an ambulance," Mrs. Turpin continued, "but before she went she was rolling on the floor and they were trying to hold her down to give her a shot and she said something to me." She paused. "You know what she said to me?"

"What she say?" they asked.

"She said," Mrs. Turpin began, and stopped, her face very dark and heavy. The sun was getting whiter and whiter, blanching the sky overhead so that the leaves of the hickory tree were black in the face of it. She could not bring forth the words. "Something real ugly," she muttered.

"She sho shouldn't said nothing ugly to you," the old woman said. "You so sweet. You the sweetest lady I know."

"She pretty too," the one with the hat on said.

"And stout," the other one said. "I never knowed no sweeter white lady."

"That's the truth befo' Jesus," the old woman said. "Amen! You des as sweet and pretty as you can be."

Mrs. Turpin knew exactly how much Negro flattery was worth and it added to her rage. "She said," she began again and finished this time with a fierce rush of breath, "that I was an old wart hog from hell."

There was an astounded silence.

"Where she at?" the youngest woman cried in a piercing voice.

"Lemme see her. I'll kill her!"

"I'll kill her with you!" the other one cried.

"She b'long in the sylum," the old woman said emphatically. "You the sweetest white lady I know."

"She pretty too," the other two said. "Stout as she can be and sweet. Jesus satisfied with her!"

"Deed he is," the old woman declared.

Idiots! Mrs. Turpin growled to herself. You could never say anything intelligent to a nigger. You could talk at them but not with them. "Yawl ain't drunk your water," she said shortly. "Leave the bucket in the truck when you're finished with it. I got more to do than just stand around and pass the time of day," and she moved off and into the house.

She stood for a moment in the middle of the kitchen. The dark protuberance over her eye looked like a miniature tornado cloud which might any moment sweep across the horizon of her brow. Her lower lip protruded dangerously. She squared her massive shoulders. Then she marched into the front of the house and out the side door and started down the road to the pig parlor. She had the look of a woman going single-handed, weaponless, into battle.

The sun was a deep yellow now like a harvest moon and was riding westward very fast over the far tree line as if it meant to reach the hogs before she did. The road was rutted and she kicked several good-sized stones out of her path as she strode along. The pig parlor was on a little knoll at the end of a lane that ran off from the side of the barn. It was a square of concrete as large as a small room, with a board fence about four feet high around it. The concrete floor sloped slightly so that the hog wash could drain off into a trench where it was carried to the field for fertilizer. Claud was standing on the outside, on the edge of the concrete, hanging onto the top board, hosing down the floor inside. The hose was connected to the faucet of a water trough nearby.

Mrs. Turpin climbed up beside him and glowered down at the hogs inside. There were seven long-snouted bristly shoats in it—tan with liver-colored spots—and an old sow a few weeks off from farrowing. She was lying on her side grunting. The shoats were running about shaking themselves like idiot children, their little slit pig eyes searching the floor for anything left. She had read that pigs were the most intelligent animal. She doubted it. They were supposed to be smarter than dogs. There had even been a pig astronaut. He had performed his assignment perfectly but died of a heart attack afterwards because they left him in his electric suit, sitting upright throughout his examination when naturally a hog should be on all fours.

A-gruntin and a-rootin and a-groanin.

"Gimme that hose," she said, yanking it away from Claud. "Go on and carry them niggers home and then get off that leg."

"You look like you might have swallowed a mad dog," Claud observed, but he got down and limped off. He paid no attention to her humors.

Until he was out of earshot, Mrs. Turpin stood on the side of the pen, holding the hose and pointing the stream of water at the hind quarters of any shoat that looked as if it might try to lie down. When he had had time to get over the hill, she turned her head slightly and her wrathful eyes scanned the path. He was nowhere in sight. She turned back again and seemed to gather herself up. Her shoulders rose and she drew in her breath.

"What do you send me a message like that for?" she said in a low fierce voice, barely above a whisper but with the force of a shout in its concentrated fury. "How am I a hog and me both? How am I saved and from hell too?" Her free fist was knotted and with the other she gripped the hose, blindly pointing the stream of water in and out of the eye of the old sow whose outraged squeal she did not hear.

The pig parlor commanded a view of the back pasture where their twenty beef cows were gathered around the hay-bales Claud and the boy had put out. The freshly cut pasture sloped down to the highway. Across it was their cotton field and beyond that a dark green dusty wood, which they owned as well. The sun was behind the wood, very red, looking over the paling of trees like a farmer inspecting his own hogs.

"Why me?" she rumbled. "It's no trash around here, black or white, that I haven't given to. And break my back to the bone every day working. And do for the church."

She appeared to be the right size woman to command the arena before her. "How am I a hog?" she demanded. "Exactly how am I like them?" and she jabbed the stream of water at the shoats. "There was plenty of trash there. It didn't have to be me.

"If you like trash better, go get yourself some trash then," she railed. "You could have made me trash. Or a nigger. If trash is what you wanted why didn't you make me trash?" She shook her fist with the hose in it and a watery snake appeared momentarily in the air. "I could quit working and take it easy and be filthy," she growled. "Lounge about the sidewalks all day drinking root beer. Dip snuff and spit in every puddle and have it all over my face. I could be nasty.

"Or you could have made me a nigger. It's too late for me to be a nigger," she said with deep sarcasm, "but I could act like one. Lay down in the middle of the road and stop traffic. Roll on the ground."

In the deepening light everything was taking on a mysterious hue. The pasture was growing a peculiar glassy green and the streak of highway had turned lavender. She braced herself for a final assault and this time her voice rolled out over the pasture. "Go on," she yelled, "call me a hog! Call me a hog again. From hell. Call me a wart hog from hell. Put that bottom rail on top. There'll still be a top and bottom!"

A garbled echo returned to her.

A final surge of fury shook her and she roared, "Who do you think you are?"

The color of everything, field and crimson sky, burned for a moment with a transparent intensity. The question carried over the pasture and across the highway and the cotton field and returned to her clearly like an answer from beyond the wood.

She opened her mouth but no sound came out of it.

A tiny truck, Claud's, appeared on the highway, heading rapidly out of sight. Its gears scraped thinly. It looked like a child's toy. At any moment a bigger truck might smash into it and scatter Claud's and the niggers' brains all over the road.

Mrs. Turpin stood there, her gaze fixed on the highway, all her muscles rigid, until in five or six minutes the truck reappeared, returning. She waited until it had had time to turn into their own road. Then like a monumental statue coming to life, she bent her head slowly and gazed, as if through the very heart of the mystery, down into the pig parlor at the hogs. They had settled all in one corner around the old sow who was grunting softly. A red glow suffused them. They appeared to pant with a secret life.

Until the sun slipped finally behind the tree line, Mrs. Turpin remained there with her gaze bent to them as if she were absorbing some abysmal life-giving knowledge. At last she lifted her head. There was only a purple streak in the sky, cutting through a field of crimson and leading, like an extension of the highway, into the descending dusk. She raised her hands from the side of the pen in a gesture hieratic and profound. A visionary light settled in her eyes. She saw the streak as a vast swinging bridge extending upward from the earth through a field of living fire. Upon it a vast horde of souls were rumbling toward heaven. There were whole companies of white-trash, clean for the first time in their lives, and bands of black niggers in white robes, and battalions of freaks and lunatics shouting and clapping and leaping like frogs. And bringing up the end of the procession was tribe of people whom she recognized at once as those who, like herself and Claud, had always had a little of everything and the God-given wit to use it right. She leaned forward to observe them closer. They were marching behind the others with great dignity, accountable as they had always been for good order and common sense and respectable behavior. They alone were on key. Yet she could see by their shocked and altered faces that even their virtues were being burned away. She lowered her hands and gripped the rail of the hog pen, her eyes small but fixed unblinkingly on what lay ahead. In a moment the vision faded but she remained where she was, immobile.

At length she got down and turned off the faucet and made her slow way on the darkening path to the house. In the woods around her the invisible cricket choruses had struck up, but what she heard were the voices of the souls climbing upward into the starry field and shouting hallelujah.

Discussing Literature

The best stories provide enjoyment in two ways: they excite your emotions, and they stimulate your thinking. Ultimately, the extent to which a story provides this dual experience determines the extent to which a story is successful. Good writers know this, and they work very hard to create stories that read well—that arouse your feelings and that provide ideas worth thinking about.

You, on the other hand, need to approach a story with a disposition to be entertained and a mind ready to think about the ideas the author is presenting. For a story to have both meaning and entertainment value, there must be an active partnership between the author and you, as the reader. The author must do a good job of creating and organizing the story elements, and you must approach the work with curiosity.

Meanings are derived from stories using the same feelings and thought processes you use to deal with real-life situations. First, you observe what is evident or obvious in the situation. Next, you notice as many facts and details as you can. You listen to what people are saying and you watch what they are doing. Finally, you give special attention to how all of these factors come together to create an outcome or conclusion to the situation.

One of the pleasures of reading is discussing with friends what you think and how you feel about a story, just as you would discuss a movie you have seen. In the course of a discussion, you instinctively draw on all of your observations—of situation, characters, details, outcomes—and tell your listeners what you think about your observations and how you feel. Your thoughts and feelings result, for the most part, from a process of imagining and self-questioning. That is basically how you will approach analyzing and discussing "Revelation." In this lesson you will discuss "Revelation" using the following elements:

1. the story situation, including the setting and the characters
2. the action of the story
3. the climax of the story
4. the outcome of the story and your conclusions

· I ·

Discussing the Story Situation

A story is an experience that happens in your mind through your reading. Just like a real-life experience, the story experience is filled with people, places, and actions. So there is no reason why you cannot analyze and discuss a story experience just as you are able to analyze and discuss what happened to you in school today.

You might object, though, that "Revelation" took place years ago, among types of people you have never encountered, and in a place you have never been. How can you "experience" something that is totally beyond any *real* experience you have ever had? The way you experience a story, of course, is through your imagination. Using your imagination is the largest part of the enjoyment of reading.

Once you have projected yourself into the story you will find it easy to become curious about the people and the events. There are all kinds of questions to ask. What kinds of people are these? (Analyze the story characters.) What is it like to be in this place? (Analyze the setting.) What is the importance of the actions and events? (Analyze the story situation.) How do all of these elements relate to the ideas the author is trying to present to you? (Analyze the story.) The answers that you find to your questions provide the substance for discussion. A good place to begin is with the opening paragraph of "Revelation."

> The doctor's waiting room, which was very small, was almost full when the Turpins entered and Mrs. Turpin, who was very large, made it look even smaller by her presence. She stood looming at the head of the magazine table set in the center of it, a living demonstration that the room was inadequate and ridiculous. Her little bright black eyes took in all the patients as she sized up the seating situation.

Imagine yourself in the doctor's office when Mrs. Turpin arrives. The first thing you notice is how she dominates the room. You try to imagine what she is like. The author helps you by saying, "she stood *looming* at the head of the magazine table." She not only dominates a situation but she is also domineering—especially with her husband, as you will read in the following passage.

> Mrs. Turpin put a firm hand on Claud's shoulder and said in a voice that included anyone that wanted to listen, "Claud, you sit in that chair there," and gave him a push down into the vacant one. Claud was florid and bald and sturdy, somewhat shorter than Mrs. Turpin, but he sat down as if he were accustomed to doing what she told him to.

Given just these two views of Claud and Mrs. Turpin you begin to form an opinion of the characters. You can at least discuss your first impressions. You can also react to the setting. As you realized when studying "Sonny's Blues" and other stories, the setting is chosen or designed for a story because it is an appropriate place for the action of the story. The author also uses the setting to help develop important ideas. The Harlem setting of "Sonny's Blues," for example, was appropriate for a story dealing with the inner conflicts of urban blacks. As you analyze "Revelation," a good question to ask is what part the doctor's waiting room plays in developing Flannery O'Connor's message.

The small waiting room is dominated by a large woman with very definite opinions about the structure of society and her place in it. Crowded together in the small space are all the people of the various classes she is so concerned with: the well-dressed lady, the "white-trash" family, a black, and herself and Claud representing "nice average people" who have a little of everything according to her way of thinking.

Mary Grace does not fit into any of Mrs. Turpin's well-defined social classes. Mary Grace is intelligent, perceptive, ugly, and emotionally disturbed. She becomes the one who delivers the "revelation" that shocks Mrs. Turpin into realizing that she is no more blessed in God's eyes than any of the people she feels superior to.

As a story progresses, you discover a more complex picture of the main character. As you read, there are more questions to ask and more for you to talk about. The setting may also change, as it does very dramatically at the end of "Revelation," and when that happens you will ask new questions and discuss the significance of the new situation and setting.

EXERCISE A

Read the following passage from the story and answer the questions that follow using the information you have learned in this part of the lesson.

> Next to the ugly girl was the child, still in exactly the same position, and next to him was a thin leathery old woman in a cotton print dress. She and Claud had three sacks of chicken feed in their pump house that was in the same print. . . . She could tell by the way they sat—kind of vacant and white-trashy, as if they would sit there until Doomsday if nobody called and told them to get up. And at right angles but next to the well-dressed pleasant lady was a lank-faced woman who was certainly the child's mother. She had on a yellow sweat shirt and wine-colored slacks, both gritty-looking, and the rims of her lips were stained with snuff. Her dirty yellow hair was tied behind with a little piece of red paper ribbon. Worse than niggers any day, Mrs. Turpin thought.
>
> The gospel hymn playing was, "When I looked up and He looked down," and Mrs. Turpin, who knew it, supplied the last line mentally, "And wona these days I know I'll we-eara crown."

1. Mrs. Turpin looks at these people as
   ☐ a. poor and deserving of God's mercy.
   ☐ b. typical country people.
   ☐ c. unfashionable but steady.
   ☐ d. ignorant, dirty, and low-class.

2. What are the lines that the author uses to suggest that Mrs. Turpin thinks she will surely go to heaven, but "white-trashy people and niggers" probably won't?

_____

_____

_____

_____

Now check your answers using the Answer Key at the back of the book. Correct any wrong answers and review this part of the lesson if you do not understand why an answer is wrong.

· 2 ·
Discussing the Action

After you have oriented yourself to the story situation and become familiar with the characters, the next thing you turn your attention to is the action. What are the characters saying and doing? In real-life situations it is not unusual to ask yourself *why* a person said what they did, or *why* they have acted in a certain way. Asking questions is a natural part of experiencing the world as a curious and cautious person. You judge people by what they say and do—which is exactly what you do when you analyze and discuss a story.

In a story you usually have the additional advantage of knowing what a character is thinking, as well as what he or she is saying and doing, to help you with your analysis. In "Revelation" some of the most important action is going on in Mrs. Turpin's mind. Her thoughts in the passage you just analyzed in Exercise A reveal that she is a bigot, but she is also confused by the structure in society, as she perceives that structure.

> Sometimes Mrs. Turpin occupied herself at night naming the classes of people. On the bottom of the heap were most colored

people . . . then next to them—not above, just away from—were the white-trash; then above them were the home-owners, and above them the home-and-land owners, to which she and Claud belonged. Above she and Claud were people with a lot of money and much bigger houses and much more land. But here the complexity of it would begin to bear in on her, for some of the people with a lot money were common . . . and some of the people who had good blood had lost their money . . . and then there were colored people who owned their homes and land as well. . . . Usually by the time she had fallen asleep all the classes of people were moiling and roiling around her head, and she would dream they were all crammed together in a boxcar, being ridden off to be put in a gas oven.

Now you can ask yourself what the story is about and answer with some conviction that it is about bigotry and the effort of a very self-assured woman to sort out all the class distinctions she sees and to make sense of them. They do not make sense, of course, and so her thoughts wind up "moiling and roiling around in her head." You will probably ask yourself why the author designed the awful dream for Mrs. Turpin. Is there some real-life parallel for the crammed boxcar on its way to the gas oven?

As you recall from reading the lesson about plot, the action of a story becomes more complicated as it moves along. As the action becomes more complicated, more questions are raised, and the more there is to analyze and discuss. The insignificant and bigoted conversation continues in the doctor's waiting room and Mary Grace becomes more and more agitated. Her fury is directed at the person who has the highest opinion of herself, the prideful Mrs. Turpin. Finally, you are faced with discovering the meaning of the girl's vicious attack on Mrs. Turpin and the one thing that Mary Grace has to say:

> "What you got to say to me?" she [Mrs. Turpin] asked hoarsely and held her breath, waiting, as for a revelation.
>   The girl raised her head. Her gaze locked with Mrs. Turpin's. "Go back to hell where you came from, you old wart hog," she whispered. Her voice was low but clear. Her eyes burned for a moment as if she saw with pleasure that her message had struck its target.

You have to ask, "What is that event all about?" The answer is not easy, but if you think about it and read the passage closely, you see that the author has given you an important clue. Flannery O'Connor says that Mrs. Turpin "held her breath, waiting, as for a revelation." The girl delivers a scathing accusation much like an Old Testament prophet may have done. The message strikes its target, the author says, and later in the story you see a very different Mrs. Turpin.

EXERCISE B

Read the following passage from the story and answer the questions that follow using the information you have learned in this part of the lesson.

Mr. and Mrs. Turpin are home and are resting:

> The instant she was flat on her back, the image of a razor-backed hog with warts on its face and horns coming out behind its ears snorted into her head. She moaned, a low quiet moan.
>
> "I am not," she said tearfully, "a wart hog. From hell." But the denial had no force. The girl's eyes and her words, even the tone of her voice, low but clear, directed only to her, brooked no repudiation. She had been singled out for the message, though there was trash in the room to whom it might justly have been applied. The full force of this fact struck her only now.

1. It is clear that Mary Grace's words have had a profound effect on Mrs. Turpin. The most important effect is that she
   □ a. is no longer convinced that she is in a class above others.
   □ b. has lost forever what she liked to call her "good disposition."
   □ c. is so furious that she fears she now has the temperament of a wart hog.
   □ d. will look more kindly on people who are mentally disturbed.

2. What are the sentences that tell you Mrs. Turpin is unable to deny Mary Grace's accusation?

   _____

   _____

   _____

   _____

   _____

Now check your answers using the Answer Key at the back of the book. Correct any wrong answers and review this part of the lesson if you do not understand why an answer is wrong.

· 3 ·
Discussing the Climax of the Story

Authors usually use a story's climax and its conclusion to bring together the various ideas of the plot. In the story's climax and conclusion, you will find clues to a story's meaning. There are actually two climaxes in "Revelation." One high point in the action comes with Mary Grace's attack on Mrs. Turpin, which produces a crisis—a change, or turning point—in the story. After the attack you see a new Mrs. Turpin, and in discussing the story you have to ask why or how her change has come about. She is angry and indignant that she was attacked. Yet the attack also worries and confuses her.

> The message had been given to Ruby Turpin, a respectable, hard-working, church-going woman. The tears dried. Her eyes began to burn instead with wrath. . . .
>
> Claud slept. She scowled at the ceiling. Occasionally she raised her fist and made a small stabbing motion over her chest as if she was defending her innocence to invisible guests who were like the comforters of Job, reasonable-seeming but wrong.

In the Old Testament of the Bible, Job was a good man who was afflicted, or tried, by God in all sorts of terrible ways to test his faith. Not knowing why he was being afflicted, Job searched for answers. Various people came to Job to try to comfort him and provide reasons for his suffering. They were all well-meaning people, but they were all wrong in the advice they gave Job. Mrs. Turpin is in a similar position. She is a good woman by her standards, so why was she singled out for so vicious an attack and accusation?

There is another question you might ask: Why is she so disturbed by the accusation of a girl who is obviously demented? The answer emerges as the story moves along toward its second climax and its conclusion.

EXERCISE C

Read the following passage from the story and answer the questions that follow using the information you have learned in this part of the lesson.

Mrs. Turpin is at the pig parlor and begins a long, questioning tirade:

> "What do you send me a message like that for?" she said in a low fierce voice. . . . "How am I a hog and me both? How am I saved and from hell too?"

She goes on in this way, then says:

> "You could have made me trash. Or a nigger. If trash is what you wanted why didn't you make me trash?"

Finally she says:

> "Go on," she yelled, "call me a hog! Call me a hog again. From hell. Call me a wart hog from hell. Put that bottom rail on top. There'll still be a top and bottom!"

1. As you read Mrs. Turpin's long tirade, you have to ask the question, "Who is she talking to?" Who *is* she talking to?
   - ☐ a. Mary Grace
   - ☐ b. no one
   - ☐ c. God
   - ☐ d. herself

2. Mrs. Turpin has always considered herself a good, Christian woman. She wants to know how she can be good and bad at the same time. What are the sentences that ask that question?

   _____

   _____

   _____

Now check your answers using the Answer Key at the back of the book. Correct any wrong answers and review this part of the lesson if you do not understand why an answer is wrong.

· 4 ·

Discussing the Outcome of the Story and the Reader's Conclusions

In the comprehension exercises following each lesson there are three types of questions that deal directly with your ability to analyze and discuss stories. The questions require you to make inferences, judgments, and conclusions. All three are made by putting together pieces of information and by relating the pieces of information to each other and to the story situation. You synthesize all the information and emerge with the ideas the author is trying to communicate to you. Finally, you add your own thoughts and feelings to the author's—based on your personal experiences and background—and you are prepared to discuss each part of the story as you see it.

That process continues throughout the story as you pick up more information and more ideas. The information and ideas are contained in all the story elements that have been discussed at length in previous lessons—settings, the characters, their conflicts, the action, the way the author expresses himself or herself, the tone, the symbols, and the imagery. By the time you reach the conclusion of the story you will have reached some definite conclusions of your own that you can talk about in an informed and intelligent way.

You are approaching the end of "Revelation." You have seen Mrs. Turpin expressing her self-assurance and her bigotry, and you have seen Mary Grace in the symbolic role of an accusatory prophet. Now Mrs. Turpin is angry and confused. Her comfortable ideas about herself and her place in what she imagines to be God's scheme of things has been shattered. What happens now?

> A final surge of fury shook her and she roared, "Who do you think you are?"
>
> The color of everything, field and crimson sky, burned for a moment with a transparent intensity. The question carried over the pasture and across the highway and the cotton field and returned to her clearly like an answer from beyond the wood. . . .
>
> Then like a monumental statue coming to life, she bent her head slowly and gazed, as if through the very heart of mystery, down into the pig parlor at the hogs. . . . A red glow suffused them. They appeared to pant with a secret life. . . .
>
> Mrs. Turpin remained there with her gaze bent to them as if she were absorbing some abysmal life-giving knowledge.

That passage is the beginning of Mrs. Turpin's vision in which she receives the answer to her questions. To understand the story, you must interpret the symbolism. You can start, once again, by asking questions. How does the rest of the story relate to the moment when Mrs. Turpin stands gazing at the hogs? What does the author mean when she says the hogs "appeared to pant with a secret life"? What does it mean when Mrs. Turpin stares at the hogs "as if she were absorbing some abysmal (profound) life-giving knowledge"?

After setting up her smug hierarchy of classes where she is somewhere near the top and white trash and blacks are at the bottom, things have been turned upside down for her. She has been placed with what she considers the lowest order of creatures—the hogs. As Ruby Turpin stares at the pigs, her answer comes, because here lies the unfathomable, life-giving knowledge. What is that knowledge?"

The answer comes in the vision which is quoted in Exercise D. In this exercise you are asked to answer some questions, but you will also be helped a little with the interpretation of the story.

EXERCISE D
Read the following passage from the story and answer the questions that follow using the information you have learned in this part of the lesson.

At last she lifted her head. There was only a purple streak in the sky, cutting through a field of crimson and leading, like an extension of the highway, into the descending dusk. She raised her hands from the side of the pen in a gesture hieratic and profound [sacred and deeply felt]. A visionary light settled in her eyes. She saw the streak as a vast swinging bridge extending upward from the earth through a field of living fire. Upon it a vast horde of souls were rumbling toward heaven. There were whole companies of white-trash, clean for the first time in their lives, and bands of black niggers in white robes, and battalions of freaks and lunatics shouting and clapping and leaping like frogs.

The author is making a comparison between Mrs. Turpin's vision and the revelation of how the world will end as represented in the biblical Book of Revelations.

1. What is the meaning of Mrs. Turpin's vision so far?
   - ☐ a. Her old ideas about the order of people in the world is being confirmed by God.
   - ☐ b. She sees that all the people that God has created are on their way to heaven; there are no high and low orders of people in God's eyes.
   - ☐ c. Her vision is simply a religious ecstasy that will probably have no effect on Mrs. Turpin when it is over.
   - ☐ d. Mrs. Turpin is so convinced that she is really a hog that she sees everyone on their way to heaven except herself.

And bringing up the end of the procession was a tribe of people whom she recognized at once as those who, like herself and Claud, had always had a little of everything and the God-given wit to use it right. She leaned forward to observe them closer. They were marching behind the others with great dignity, accountable as they had always been for good order and common sense and respectable behavior. They alone were on key. Yet she could see by their shocked and altered faces that even their virtues were being burned away.

In the Bible, when Jesus is talking about those who will be saved in the last days of the world, He says, "Many that are first shall be last; and the last shall be first." The author seems to be alluding to that when she puts people like Mrs. Turpin and Claud at the end of the line of souls that are going to heaven.

2. What is the sentence that suggests that just as people's poor qualities are stripped away from them as they approach God, so are the good points of more fortunate people stripped away from them. That is, all souls come to God in their original state. Copy the sentence here.

_____

_____

_____

Now check your answers using the Answer Key at the back of the book. Correct any wrong answers and review this part of the lesson if you do not understand why an answer is wrong.

Comprehension Questions

For each of the following statements or questions, select the option that best completes a statement or is the most accurate response to a question.

Recalling Specific Facts

1. Why had the Turpins gone to the doctor's office?
   - ☐ a. Mrs. Turpin had an injury over her eye.
   - ☐ b. Neither Claud nor Mrs. Turpin felt well.
   - ☐ c. Claud had been kicked by a cow.
   - ☐ d. It was for Mrs. Turpin's weight problem.

Recalling Specific Facts

2. What did the black workers do on the Turpins' farm?
   - ☐ a. They cared for the hogs.
   - ☐ b. They picked cotton.
   - ☐ c. They did odd jobs.
   - ☐ d. They were year-round servants.

Organizing Facts

3. What did Mrs. Turpin do when she returned home?
   - ☐ a. She went directly to the pig parlor.
   - ☐ b. She had a chat with the black workers.
   - ☐ c. She saw a vision.
   - ☐ d. She tried to nap.

Organizing Facts

4. What was one of the things that confused Mrs. Turpin when she thought about the class order of people in the world?
   - ☐ a. seeing white trash families that are neat and clean
   - ☐ b. her jealousy of people with a lot of money
   - ☐ c. the fact that there are black people with land and money
   - ☐ d. the fact that she had to be nice to black people at times

Knowledge of Word Meanings

5. "I thank Gawd," the white-trash woman said *fervently,* "I ain't a lunatic." What does *fervently* mean?
   - ☐ a. with feeling
   - ☐ b. with disgust
   - ☐ c. with venom
   - ☐ d. with sympathy

Knowledge of Word Meanings

6. The girl's eyes and her words . . . *brooked no repudiation.* You can conclude that what the girl said
   - ☐ a. should not be given any credibility.
   - ☐ b. could not be dismissed as untrue.
   - ☐ c. would mean nothing in the long run.
   - ☐ d. provided food for thought.

Drawing A Conclusion

7. Mrs. Turpin classified three people in the doctor's office as "white trash" because they
   - ☐ a. were of a different national origin.
   - ☐ b. were racially mixed.
   - ☐ c. were dirty and poorly dressed.
   - ☐ d. spoke with an accent.

Drawing a Conclusion

8. Which one of the following is a fair statement about the people in the doctor's waiting room, with possible exception of Mary Grace?
   - ☐ a. They are all ignorant and narrow-minded.
   - ☐ b. They have keen insight into human nature.
   - ☐ c. They are knowledgeable and up-to-date on farming methods.
   - ☐ d. They all hate one another.

Making a Judgment

9. Why was Mrs. Turpin pleasant to her black workers?
   - ☐ a. It was part of her good disposition.
   - ☐ b. She was behaving as her class is supposed to.
   - ☐ c. She was afraid they wouldn't work otherwise.
   - ☐ d. It was just common humanity.

Making a Judgment

10. Mrs. Turpin showed the black delivery boy how to call the nurse by pushing a button. " 'Is thas right?' the boy said agreeably, as if he had never seen the button before." Which option best expresses the interaction between the two characters?
    - ☐ a. She was being helpful; he appreciated it.
    - ☐ b. She was being hateful; he was disrespectful.
    - ☐ c. She was condescending; he was artificially polite.
    - ☐ d. She was superior; he was inferior.

Making a Judgment

11. Mary Grace's mother
    - ☐ a. was proud of her daughter's intelligence.
    - ☐ b. was embarrassed by her daughter's behavior.
    - ☐ c. understood her daughter's condition.
    - ☐ d. felt she wasn't doing enough for her daughter.

Making an Inference

12. The expression "vacant and white-trashy" suggests that Mrs. Turpin considered these people
    - ☐ a. stupid as well as dirty.
    - ☐ b. without feelings.
    - ☐ c. homeless as well as foolish.
    - ☐ d. godless.

Making an Inference

13. " 'I think the worst thing in the world,' she [the pleasant lady] said, 'is an ungrateful person.' " Whom is she talking about?
    - ☐ a. blacks
    - ☐ b. the blond child
    - ☐ c. "white-trash"
    - ☐ d. her daughter

Making an Inference

14. When Mrs. Turpin fell asleep thinking about the classes of people "she would dream they were all crammed in together in a boxcar, being ridden off to be put in a gas oven." The author is alluding to
    - ☐ a. the argument that blacks should be shipped back to Africa.
    - ☐ b. the Nazi persecution of Jews in World War II.
    - ☐ c. the fact that Mrs. Turpin will sort out her problems in a dream.
    - ☐ d. the relocation of native Americans onto reservations in the 1880s.

Understanding Characters

15. It is Mrs. Turpin's opinion that Claud
    - ☐ a. is a deep thinker.
    - ☐ b. doesn't have a good disposition like her.
    - ☐ c. doesn't think much about anything.
    - ☐ d. is not in her class.

Understanding Characters

16. Mrs. Turpin classifies the white trash woman as ignorant and dirty. In fact, the woman is
    ☐ a. exactly that.
    ☐ b. rather likable.
    ☐ c. smarter than she seems.
    ☐ d. just the opposite.

Understanding Characters

17. Mary Grace is used in the story as a kind of
    ☐ a. leveling influence in the waiting room.
    ☐ b. symbol of what Mrs. Turpin might become.
    ☐ c. reflection of her mother's true nature.
    ☐ d. messenger from God.

Understanding Main Ideas

18. Mr. and Mrs. Turpin truly consider themselves good, kind, and religious people. Still, the worst bigotry and racial slurs pour out of them. What is a possible explanation for that behavior?
    ☐ a. They feel that their behavior is normal and acceptable and doesn't hurt anyone.
    ☐ b. They are uneducated people totally isolated from others who are not like themselves.
    ☐ c. They consider everyone but themselves trash and refuse to listen to other opinions.
    ☐ d. They feel that they are so much better than other people that they can say whatever they please.

Understanding Main Ideas

19. What is the lesson of Mrs. Turpin's vision?
    ☐ a. Blacks and white trash are really superior to Mrs. Turpin.
    ☐ b. She will be punished by God for her ignorance.
    ☐ c. All people are equal when they come before God.
    ☐ d. She was not a truly religious person after all.

Recognizing Tone

20. Tone reflects an author's attitude. What is Flannery O'Connor trying to do by including the terrible old clichés of bigotry such as "send the niggers back to Africa," and "they can go to New York and marry white folks and improve their color"?

  ☐ a. The author wants you to hate Mrs. Turpin.

  ☐ b. The author is emphasizing the absurdity of these remarks.

  ☐ c. The author secretly sympathizes with that attitude.

  ☐ d. The author is showing that those types of people are basically evil.

Recognizing Tone

21. "She [Mrs. Turpin] stood looming at the head of the magazine table" . . . "She appeared to be the right size woman to command the arena before her." Expressions like those in the story create the impression that Mrs. Turpin is

  ☐ a. an old battle-ax.

  ☐ b. like a lady wrestler.

  ☐ c. like a wart hog.

  ☐ d. large and self-assured.

Recognizing Tone

22. The author shows you one Mrs. Turpin at the beginning of her tirade, and another following her vision. How would you describe the two moods?

  ☐ a. furious at first, and then subdued

  ☐ b. self-assured at first, and then doubtful

  ☐ c. antagonistic at first, and then conciliatory

  ☐ d. confused at first, and then furious

Appreciation of Literary Forms

23. " 'One thang I know,' the white-trash woman said. 'Two thangs I ain't going to do . . .' " With that dialogue the author is

  ☐ a. suggesting a comparison.

  ☐ b. beginning a metaphor.

  ☐ c. imitating dialect.

  ☐ d. using exaggeration.

Appreciation of Literary Forms

24. "The shoats were running about shaking themselves like idiot children." That sentence is an example of

    ☐ a. a metaphor.
    ☐ b. an alteration.
    ☐ c. alliteration.
    ☐ d. a simile.

Appreciation of Literary Forms

25. "The sun was behind the wood, very red, looking over the paling [fence] of trees like a farmer inspecting his own hogs." The author does a great deal in that sentence. Which one of the following best describes what she is doing?

    ☐ a. She uses simile and personification to draw a comparison between the setting sun and Mrs. Turpin at the pig parlor.
    ☐ b. She uses alliteration to create an ironic tone for the story.
    ☐ c. She creates an atmosphere of beauty and serenity in preparation for Mrs. Turpin's vision.
    ☐ d. The sun is used as a metaphor to compare nature with the follies of humankind.

Now check your answers using the Answer Key at the back of the book. Make no mark for right answers. Correct any wrong answers you may have by putting a check mark (✓) in the box next to the right answer. Count the number of questions you answered correctly and plot the total on the Comprehension Scores Graph at the back of the book.

Next, look at the questions you answered incorrectly. What types of questions were they? Count the number you got wrong of each type and enter the numbers in the spaces on the next page.

Recalling Specific Facts   _____

Organizing Facts   _____

Knowledge of Word Meanings   _____

Drawing a Conclusion   _____

Making a Judgment   _____

Making an Inference   _____

Understanding Characters   _____

Understanding Main Ideas   _____

Recognizing Tone   _____

Appreciation of Literary Forms   _____

Now use these numbers to fill in the Comprehension Skills Profile at the end of the book.

Extension Activities

Discussion Guide

Discussing Literature

1. **The story situation.** Describe how you feel when sitting in a doctor's waiting room. How do you size up the people there?
2. **The action.** Why do you think the author felt it necessary to make Mary Grace's attack on Mrs. Turpin so violent? How would the story be different if the author had Mary Grace just stand up, shout at Mrs. Turpin, and leave?
3. **The climax and conclusion of the story.** The great seventeenth-century author John Milton wrote a long poem titled *Samson Agonistes.* It is the story of Samson of the Bible. Samson, who was famous for his great strength, sinned against God and was captured by the Philistines. Later he destroyed his captors, giving up his life in the process. The poem is filled with intense emotion. It ends with these lines:

> Of true experience from this great event
> With peace and consolation hath dismissed,
> And calm of mind, all passion spent.

How does the ending of "Revelation" resemble the ending of Milton's poem?

Discussing the Story

4. What is your opinion of the racial slurs and insults in the story? Why do you think O'Connor uses racist characters?
5. What is your opinion of Mary Grace? What is her purpose in the story?
6. Do you think Mrs. Turpin will be a different woman as a result of her experience? Explain your opinion. If you think she will be different, tell *how* you think she will be different.

Discussing the Author's Work

7. Both James Baldwin and Flannery O'Connor were raised in religious environments. That is reflected in both "Sonny's Blues" and "Revelation." In what ways are the stories similar? How are they different?
8. Flannery O'Connor uses grotesque or deformed people in a number of her stories. Who are the grotesque characters in this story? Why do you think she uses such characters?
9. In studying literature, what advantage would you gain from a knowledge of both the Old and New Testaments of the Bible?

Writing Exercise

Write a critical review of "Revelation." The words *criticism* or *critical* in talking about literature mean a discussion not just what you like or dislike about the story.

Your discussion should present thoughts and ideas you have about characters or events in the story or about the author's writing. To make your critical review better and easier to write, focus on one element of the story that you found especially interesting—a character, an event, a theme.

Answer Key

Unit One: The Garden Party

The Short Story

EXERCISE A

1. b 2. And it seemed to her that kisses, voices, tinkling spoons, laughter, the smell of crushed grass were somehow inside of her.

EXERCISE B

1. d 2. Laura gave a loud childish sob. "Forgive my hat," she said.

EXERCISE C

1. b 2. True, they were far too near. They were the greatest possible eyesore, and they had no right to be in that neighborhood at all.

EXERCISE D

1. a 2. Laura will bring the leftover sandwiches and cream puffs to the cottage where she sees the dead man.

Comprehension Questions

1. d	2. b	3. a	4. b	5. c	6. b	7. d	8. c	9. d
10. a	11. c	12. d	13. a	14. a	15. a	16. c	17. b	18. b
19. d	20. d	21. b	22. c	23. c	24. b	25. c		

Unit Two: A Worn Path

Setting

EXERCISE A

1. c 2. She paused quietly on the sidewalk where people were passing by.

EXERCISE B

1. b 2. the field; the wagon track; a ravine with a spring; a swamp; the road

EXERCISE C

1. d 2. There sat a buzzard. It [the scarecrow] was silent as a ghost.

EXERCISE D

1. b 2. She entered a door, and there she saw nailed up on the wall the document that had been stamped with the gold seal and framed in the gold frame, which matched the dream that was hung up in her head.

Comprehension Questions

1. b	2. d	3. b	4. a	5. b	6. a	7. d	8. b	9. a
10. c	11. c	12. a	13. d	14. b	15. a	16. b	17. a	18. d
19. c	20. a	21. d	22. b	23. a	24. c	25. a		

Unit Three: A Summer's Reading/My Oedipus Complex

Point of View

EXERCISE A

1. c   2. the "I" character, or Larry

        a narrator who is outside the story; an unseen observer; an omniscient narrator

EXERCISE B

1. d   2. ". . . I'm reading a lot to pick up my education." "I got a list of books in the library once, now I'm gonna read them this summer."

EXERCISE C

1. b   2. Mrs. Left and Mrs. Right: I put my feet out from under the clothes—I called them Mrs. Left and Mrs. Right.

EXERCISE D

1. a   2. Really, it was like going for a walk with a mountain! He either ignored the wrenching and pummeling entirely, or else glanced down with a grin of amusement from his peak.

Comprehension Questions

1. b	2. a	3. b	4. d	5. c	6. a	7. d	8. b	9. c
10. a	11. d	12. c	13. b	14. b	15. d	16. a	17. d	18. c
19. b	20. a	21. c	22. d	23. b	24. d	25. c		

Unit Four: Everyday Use

Character

EXERCISE A

1. c   2. . . . a lame animal, perhaps a dog run over by some careless person. . . .

EXERCISE B

1. a   2. He just stood there grinning, looking down on me like somebody inspecting a Model A car. Every once in a while he and Wangero sent eye signals over my head.

EXERCISE C

1. c   2. Why don't you do a dance around the ashes? I'd wanted to ask her.

EXERCISE D

1. b   2. When I looked at her like that something hit me in the top of my head. . . .

Comprehension Questions

1. d	2. b	3. c	4. a	5. c	6. b	7. d	8. a	9. b
10. a	11. c	12. d	13. b	14. c	15. b	16. d	17. c	18. b
19. d	20. a	21. c	22. d	23. b	24. d	25. a		

Unit Five: The Lagoon

Conflict

EXERCISE A

1. c   2. White men care not for such things, being unbelievers and in league with the Father of Evil. . . .

EXERCISE B

1. a   2. "What did I care who died?"

EXERCISE C

1. a   2. ". . . I began to think of killing and of a fierce death. . . ." (Anything following this phrase in the passage may also be considered a correct answer.)

EXERCISE D

1. b   2. "Now I can see nothing—see nothing!"

Comprehension Questions

1. a	2. d	3. c	4. b	5. b	6. d	7. a	8. c	9. a
10. b	11. d	12. c	13. b	14. a	15. c	16. a	17. d	18. c
19. b	20. a	21. a	22. d	23. c	24. a	25. b		

Unit Six: The Guest

Plot

EXERCISE A

1. c   2. . . . the little room was cluttered with bags of wheat that the administration left as a stock to distribute. . . . Now shiploads of wheat were arriving from France and the worst was over.

EXERCISE B

1. b   2. . . . he felt strangely empty and vulnerable.

EXERCISE C

1. a   2. The Arab had now turned toward Daru and a sort of panic was visible in his expression.

EXERCISE D

1. d   2. . . . he was alone.

Comprehension Questions

1. c	2. a	3. d	4. c	5. b	6. b	7. b	8. d	9. b
10. a	11. b	12. d	13. c	14. a	15. c	16. d	17. a	18. b
19. c	20. b	21. a	22. b	23. a	24. c	25. b		

Unit Seven: A Christmas Memory

Use of Language

EXERCISE A

1. b   2. Lugging it like a kill, we commence the long trek out.

EXERCISE B

1. c   2. The buggy is empty, the bowl is brimful.

EXERCISE C

1. a   2. "What you want with Haha?"
        "Mrs. Haha, ma'am? Anyone to home?"

EXERCISE D

1. d   2. Sample answers: somber, lovely, liveliest, hateful, bitter-odored

   green as May buds; smooth as creek pebbles

   wallowing in the pleasures of conspiracy; tabulating dead flies

   the carnage of August

Comprehension Questions

1. d	2. c	3. b	4. c	5. c	6. a	7. b	8. d	9. b
10. d	11. a	12. b	13. a	14. a	15. d	16. a	17. c	18. d
19. b	20. a	21. a	22. c	23. c	24. b	25. d		

Unit Eight: The Black Cat

Tone and Mood

EXERCISE A

1. c   2. (In the *rabid* desire to say something easily, I scarcely knew what I uttered at all.)

EXERCISE B

1. a   2. Sample answers: I continued my caresses; I soon found a dislike to it arising; disgust and annoyance; sense of shame; unutterable loathing

EXERCISE C

1. d   2. the cellar

EXERCISE D

1. c   2. Sample answers: fangs of the Arch-Fiend; anomalous and inhuman; out of hell; throats of the damned; demons that exult in the damnation

Comprehension Questions

1. c	2. c	3. a	4. b	5. d	6. b	7. a	8. d	9. c
10. c	11. a	12. a	13. d	14. a	15. c	16. d	17. b	18. d
19. c	20. a	21. d	22. b	23. a	24. c	25. c		

Unit Nine: A Rose for Emily

Symbolism

EXERCISE A

1. c   2. . . . a crayon portrait of Miss Emily's father.

EXERCISE B

1. a   2. She looked bloated, like a body long submerged in motionless water, and of that pallid hue.

EXERCISE C

1. d   2. . . . and in a way, people were glad. At last they could pity Miss Emily. Being left alone, and a pauper, she had become humanized. Now she too would know the old thrill and the old despair of a penny more or less.

EXERCISE D

1. b   2. . . . dear, inescapable, impervious, tranquil, and perverse.

Comprehension Questions

1. a	2. c	3. d	4. c	5. c	6. d	7. c	8. c	9. a
10. d	11. a	12. b	13. b	14. c	15. a	16. b	17. d	18. a
19. c	20. b	21. b	22. a	23. d	24. b	25. d		

Unit Ten: The Kugelmass Episode

Humor and Satire

EXERCISE A

1. d   2. What he didn't realize was that at this very moment students in various classrooms across the country were saying to their teachers, "Who is this character on page 100? A bald Jew is kissing Madame Bovary?"

EXERCISE B

1. a   2. At the same moment, he appeared in the bedroom of Charles and Emma Bovary's house at Yonville. Before him was a beautiful woman, standing alone with her back turned to him as she folded some linen.

EXERCISE C

1. a   2. "Sex and romance," Kugelmass said from inside the box. "What we go through for a pretty face."

EXERCISE D

1. c   2. "He's a lacklustre little paramedic who's thrown in his lot with a jitterbug."

Comprehension Questions

1. c	2. a	3. d	4. b	5. b	6. d	7. a	8. b	9. d
10. a	11. a	12. b	13. a	14. a	15. c	16. c	17. d	18. c
19. a	20. b	21. c	22. c	23. a	24. b	25. a		

Unit Eleven: Sonny's Blues

Themes in Literature

EXERCISE A

1. b   2. Sample answers: I dug how much I must have hurt you; I swear if I'd known what I was doing I wouldn't have hurt you so, you and a lot of other people who were nice to me and who believed in me.

EXERCISE B

1. d   2. He knows that every time this happens he's moved just a little closer to that darkness outside.

EXERCISE C

1. a   2. . . . the music seemed to soothe a poison out of them. . . .

EXERCISE D

1. c   2. Sample answers: the stony, lifeless elegance of the hotels; the vivid, killing streets of our childhood; like rocks in the middle of a boiling sea; found themselves smothering in these houses; Some escaped the trap. . . . as some animals amputate a leg and leave it in the trap.

Comprehension Questions

1. d	2. a	3. b	4. b	5. a	6. a	7. a	8. c	9. d
10. c	11. c	12. b	13. a	14. c	15. a	16. a	17. c	18. b
19. c	20. a	21. d	22. d	23. a	24. c	25. b		

Unit Twelve: Revelation

Discussing Literature

EXERCISE A

1. d   2. "When I looked up and He looked down . . . And wona these days I know I'll we-eara crown."

EXERCISE B

1. a   2. But the denial had no force. The girl's eyes and her words, even the tone of her voice, low but clear, directed only to her, brooked no repudiation.

EXERCISE C

1. c   2. "How am I a hog and me both? How am I saved and from hell too?"

EXERCISE D

1. b   2. Yet she could see by their shocked and altered faces that even their virtues were being burned away.

Comprehension Questions

1. c	2. b	3. d	4. c	5. a	6. b	7. c	8. a	9. c
10. c	11. b	12. a	13. d	14. b	15. c	16. a	17. d	18. a
19. c	20. b	21. d	22. a	23. c	24. d	25. a		

Comprehension Scores Graph

Use this graph to plot your comprehension scores. At the top of the graph are the names of the stories in the book. To mark your score for a unit, find the name of the story you just read and follow the line beneath it down until it crosses the line for the number of questions you got right. Put an *x* where the lines meet. As you mark your score for each unit, graph your progress by drawing a line to connect the *x*'s. The numbers on the right show your comprehension percentage score.

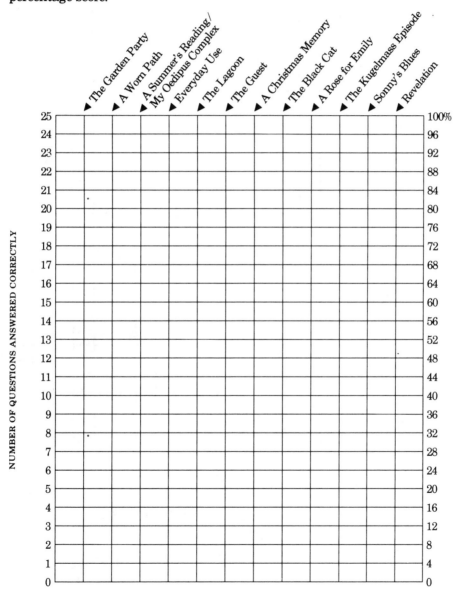

NUMBER OF QUESTIONS ANSWERED CORRECTLY

COMPREHENSION PERCENTAGE SCORE

Stories (top of graph): The Garden Party · A Worn Path · A Summer's Reading / My Oedipus Complex · Everyday Use · The Lagoon · The Guest · A Christmas Memory · The Black Cat · A Rose for Emily · The Kugelmass Episode · Sonny's Blues · Revelation

Questions	Percentage
25	100%
24	96
23	92
22	88
21	84
20	80
19	76
18	72
17	68
16	64
15	60
14	56
13	52
12	48
11	44
10	40
9	36
8	32
7	28
6	24
5	20
4	16
3	12
2	8
1	4
0	0

Comprehension Skills Profile

Use this profile to see which comprehension skills you need to work on. Fill in the number of incorrect answers for each skill every time you complete a unit. For example, if you have two incorrect answers for Recognizing Tone, you will blacken two spaces above that skill label. The numbers on the left side show your total number of wrong answers for each comprehension skill. The profile will show you which kinds of questions you consistently get wrong. Your instructor may want to give you extra help with these skills.

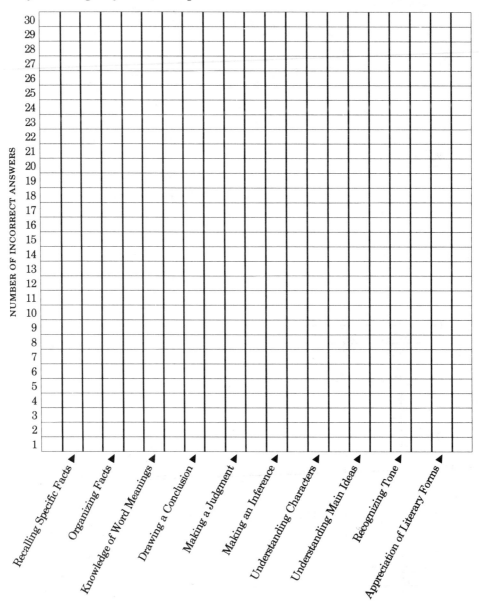